Finiteness Matters

Linguistik Aktuell/Linguistics Today (LA)

ISSN 0166-0829

Linguistik Aktuell/Linguistics Today (LA) provides a platform for original monograph studies into synchronic and diachronic linguistics. Studies in LA confront empirical and theoretical problems as these are currently discussed in syntax, semantics, morphology, phonology, and systematic pragmatics with the aim to establish robust empirical generalizations within a universalistic perspective.

For an overview of all books published in this series, please see
http://benjamins.com/catalog/la

Volume 231

Finiteness Matters. On finiteness-related phenomena in natural languages
Edited by Kristin Melum Eide

Finiteness Matters

On finiteness-related phenomena in natural languages

Edited by

Kristin Melum Eide
Norwegian University of Science and Technology

John Benjamins Publishing Company
Amsterdam / Philadelphia

The paper used in this publication meets the minimum requirements of the American National Standard for Information Sciences – Permanence of Paper for Printed Library Materials, ANSI z39.48-1984.

DOI 10.1075/la.231

Cataloging-in-Publication Data available from Library of Congress:
LCCN 2016011007 (PRINT) / 2016024259 (E-BOOK)

ISBN 978 90 272 5714 7 (HB)
ISBN 978 90 272 6697 2 (E-BOOK)

John Benjamins Publishing Company · https://benjamins.com

Table of contents

Introduction

Kristin Melum Eide
Norwegian University of Science and Technology

No single introductory chapter, be it ever so thorough, could in and by itself realistically aim at doing justice to the vast literature existing on the topic of finiteness; to the range of empirical descriptions over how this linguistic phenomenon is realized morphologically and syntactically in individual natural languages, and how its semantic underpinnings are described and discussed within a plethora of different approaches and frameworks. In this introduction I will hence limit myself to the notions and theoretical developments that seem most relevant to serve as a useful backdrop for the ten following chapters of this volume.

Discussions of finiteness features in natural languages usually start out with the observation that the term *finiteness* is used to cover many different (albeit partly overlapping) concepts. Many authors have put forth that "the traditional notion of finiteness is ill-defined" and questioned "whether it is altogether a universally valid concept" (Nikolaeva 2007b: 3). Other authors have straightforwardly suggested that it is not; "the term [finiteness] is not amenable to a theory-proof definition" (Koptjevskaja-Tamm 1994). Cowper (this volume) states that "The term 'finite' has been used in the grammatical literature for centuries, but its meaning is difficult to pin down", and Ledgeway (2007: 335) repeats his conclusion from Ledgeway (2000: 187–9) that "although standardly recognized by linguists of many diverse theoretical persuasions, finiteness continues to figure among [...] the most poorly understood concepts of linguistic theory". This point is reiterated in even more recent works such as McFadden & Sundaresan (2014: 1).[1] They suggest that "given the increasing amount of empirical evidence challenging conventional definitions of finiteness" one might expect that we would have, by now, a better handle on what finiteness in natural languages consists in. Instead, these authors also adhere to Ledgeway's claim quoted above that finiteness even today "remains one of the least understood concepts in linguistic theory". Or, in Klein's (2006: 245) words, "the notion of finiteness is used by everybody and understood by

1. This is the introductory chapter to a volume of eleven papers presenting new evidence on the nature of finiteness from Indo-Aryan and Dravidian languages; five "original" papers and five commentary papers, plus one free-standing paper (by Amritavalli).

DOI 10.1075/la.231.01eid

nobody". All in all, this is not very uplifting reading to an author or editor optimistically aiming at a working definition for the notion of finiteness. Nevertheless, we will home in on such a working definition in this introductory chapter; drawing on morphological, syntactic and semantic factors evoked in the very rich theoretical discourse on this topic.

For now, a quite simple example will illustrate our starting point. Whichever use of the term finiteness one adheres to, most readers would agree that the two occurrences of *be* in (1) are non-finite, and *is* is finite. In what follows, we investigate the linguistic constructs trying to capture such intuitions, with a view to determine their usefulness to the purposes of the proposals put forth in this volume.

(1) To be finite or not to be finite – that is the finiteness question.

Nikolaeva (2007b: 1 ff) offers an informative overview of the origins of finiteness as a linguistic notion. She explains that the term *finite* in European linguistics goes back to the Latin *finitus* in the sense of 'referring to a particular person'. The term was first applied to personal pronouns and later to "verbs expressing person and number." Priscianus Caesariensis (c. 500 AD) and his influential *Institutiones grammaticae* are often quoted as the source of the view that the agreement features of the verb (i.e. person and number) are what determines the finiteness of a clause; a view that became standard for grammars in the Western tradition (cf. e.g. Maas 2004: 362; Klein 2006: 270; Nikolaeva 2007b: 1). As pointed out by Mc Fadden and Sundaresan (2014: 2):

> This did indeed describe a sensible and real split within the verb forms in Latin and the other classical European languages. The forms bearing person and number agreement are distinctive, being also the only forms with full tense and mood marking, and have a special syntactic distribution. The forms of verbs that did not bear this marking were quite different morphologically, generally behaving more like nouns or adjectives and inflecting for categories like case and gender which never appeared on the finite forms.

The split between the non-finite and finite verb forms in the classical European languages is thus a split between verb forms with a more "nouny" or "adjectival" behaviour and verb forms that display typically verbal features like mood and especially tense. The latter feature also came to carry a special significance in much of the linguistic literature; according to Maas (2004: 363) tense is the category most often correlated with finiteness. Tense however typically pairs up with agreement in many well-studied languages, and to date the most widespread diagnostic for finiteness (especially within formal approaches) is the presence of morphologically expressed tense and agreement features on the verb. Most of the papers in the present volume take their point of departure from this more traditional view on finiteness, before elaborating on, modifying and diverging from this tradition in novel and interesting ways.

Grammarians working within more typological frameworks observed early on that these inflectional diagnostics for finiteness fail to have a universal application. Firstly, not all languages employ overtly expressed agreement or tense features or express any type of finiteness marker obligatorily (creoles being a case in point, cf. van de Vate & Veenstra this volume; Romaine 1993; Muysken & Law 2001); a range of languages clearly depend on other overt grammatical features for expressing finiteness, e.g. mood (Holmberg et al. 1993), but also negation markers (Amritavalli 2014) or even spatial markers or participant markers (Ritter & Wiltschko 2005, 2009, 2014)). Distributional criteria of finiteness seem to have a wider application, since cross-linguistically certain verb forms predominantly or exclusively occur in independent, root, or "finite" clauses and contexts whereas other verb forms predominantly or exclusively occur in dependent, embedded, or "non-finite" clauses and contexts. For this view, cf. e.g. Trask (1993: 103–4); where *finite* denotes "a form of a verb or auxiliary which can in principle serve as the only verb form in a sentence",[2] or Matthews' (1997) definition "…any verb whose form is such that it can stand in a simple declarative sentence". Formalist approaches like Hornstein (1990: 146) also claim that infinitives cannot head independent clauses: "[I]t holds across all natural languages. Matrix clauses must be finite."

Within the Principles and Parameters framework, the main topic by far has been the effects of finiteness, in particular in the form of attempts at understanding the relation between the morphological exponents of finiteness and the syntactic operations seemingly depending on these exponents. To some extent, the debate also revolved around the semantic interpretations of referential elements (subject, tense marking) these morphological exponents relate to or allow for, especially in an embedded clause. Already in the earliest days of generative grammar, the focus shifted from analysing finiteness as an inflectional feature of the verb to viewing it as a more abstract category belonging to the clause as a whole; a category occupying a specific position in a clausal structure originally dubbed AUX and later renamed I(NFL). Capturing the insight that this clausal head in important respects defines the nature and distribution of the clause as a syntactic element, INFL came to be seen as the head of the clause hosting the tense and agreement features of the verb; features that, in some languages, could be realized as null phonologically. Firstly, there are observable differences between finite

2. But note that Trask uses morphological criteria as well, as a finite verb "typically carries the maximum in morphological marking for such categories as tense and agreement permitted in a language" (Trask 1993: 103–4).

sentences and non-finite sentences with respect to a range of syntactic processes such as the ability to act as "barriers" to the creation of syntactic dependencies e.g. between an anaphor *herself* and its syntactic antecedent *Mary* (2ab), or a moved constituent and its trace (3ab). Chomsky (1973: 238) stated the "Tensed-S Condition" (4) to account for such facts.

(2) a. Mary expected [herself to be the winner].
b. *Mary expected [that herself would be the winner].

(3) a. Mary seems [to t_{mary} be absent].
b. *Mary seems [that t_{mary} is absent].

(4) The Tensed-S Condition: No rule can involve X, Y in the structure … X … [α… Y …] … where α is a tensed sentence.

Moreover, the finiteness feature make-up of a clause seemed to be involved in the licensing of an overtly realized subject, and in languages exhibiting case features on noun phrases, a visible subject occurring as the subject of a finite clause typically surfaced with a nominative case marking.[3] This encouraged authors to search for the hidden relation between the finiteness inflection on the verb and the nominative case on its subject, e.g. as two different manifestations of one and the same underlying syntactic relation (cf. seminal works like Chomsky 1995, 2000, 2001; Pesetsky & Torrego 2001, 2004, among many others).[4] With respect to the reference of this subject a finite clause evidently allowed its subject to have independent reference, unlike non-finite clauses that usually require silent subjects ("PRO") obligatorily controlled by a noun phrase in the matrix clause. A range of objections and refinements to Chomsky's initial observations have been offered over the years, including a quest for the recalcitrant universal feature acting as the trigger for finiteness-related phenomena (cf. the next subsection). However, the most widespread view in Principles and Parameters Theory, even in the most recent approaches, maintains that finiteness is a binary category which, in addition to controlling the realization of the subject argument and creating domains opaque to certain syntactic processes, regulates the tense and agreement

3. That is, in case systems prevailingly employing a nominative-accusative case system.

4. But cf. also e.g. Sigurđsson (2012) for the view that there has been a (tacit) meaning shift involved in the seminal literature discussing this conjecture (p. 221): "As a matter of fact, though, the term abstract Case or just Case has undergone a meaning shift, from suggesting a link between morphology and NP-licensing in morphological case languages (Chomsky 1980: 24, 1981), to referring exclusively to NP-licensing (Chomsky 2001: 6ff.). That is, without changing the terminology, Chomsky has in effect abandoned Vergnaud's Conjecture, contending that "structural Case is demoted in significance" (2000: 127) and that "Case assignment is divorced from movement" (2001: 17).

features on the verb (Nikolaeva 2007b: 6). McFadden and Sundaresan (2014: 7) add that a clause's ability to function as an independent assertion is also widely held to be a side effect of its finiteness feature within the Principles and Parameters framework.[5]

In the formally inclined language acquisition literature, the relation between acquiring the morphology of finiteness and verb movement (in particular to the second position in Germanic languages) has been a hot topic for decades. Westergaard's contribution to the present volume offers a thorough guided tour through this literature (cf. also Jin & Eide, this volume). The relation between finiteness morphology and verb movement has clearly always evoked a lot of interest in the linguistic community at large, ever since the seminal analysis of den Besten (1977/1983). Here verb second in Germanic was analysed as movement of the finite verb into C; cf. for instance Weerman (1989: 14), "The second position is only available for *finite* verbs and not for *non-finite* verbs."[6,7] The observation by den Besten that the finite verb in declarative main clauses occurs in the same position as the complementizer in embedded clauses gave rise to many theories on possible relations between finiteness, the V2 position and complementizers. Holmberg and Platzack (1988, 1995) and Platzack (1995, 2010) have been main proponents of the idea that the abstract finiteness feature of the clause actually resides in this V2 position in V2 languages[8] and that it must be checked either by moving a verb with the right specifications (i.e. carrying overtly realized finiteness

5. Lohnstein (2000, 2001) develops a compositional theory of sentence moods making use of Frege's (1892) three acts linked to form an assertion: thinking (forming the thought), judging (determining the truth of the proposition), and claiming (providing the illucutionary force of claiming). Different speech acts (such as yes-no questions, *wh*-questions, exclamations and directives) address only a subset of these three; e.g. yes-no questions address the "thinking" part of the assertion process. Lohnstein and Bredel (2004) elaborate on the relation between inflectional morphology and sentence mood (in German), and put forth that only a subset of finite markers (i.e. indicative present and preterit and the subjunctive preterit) may perform the role usually attributed to finiteness markers; i.e. in serving as morphological ques to the act of asserting. Finite markers such as imperative and subjunctive present do not lead to assertions and cannot be used as ordinary declaratives.

6. Holmberg (2015: 368 ff.) quotes Truckenbrodt (2006) (who in turn builds on Lohnstein (2000) a.o.) for the insight that in V2 languages V2 has a special semantic role to play in creating assertions, as finite morphology without V2 may create exclamations and directives but not assertions (cp. *Dass du das Fenster öffnest*! lit. 'that you the window open' and *Du öffnest das Fenster* 'you open the window'.

7. Cf. Lohnstein (2000, 2001) and Lohnstein & Bredel (2004) that not all finite markers have the same effect when appearing in this position and hence differ in the sentence mood they give rise to.

8. Cf. Holmberg (2015) for a discussion on whether the term "V2 language" is a meaningful, well-defined notion. "The answer is that it is" (op.cit. p. 342).

features) or otherwise lexicalized by an overtly realized complementizer. In the relevant languages, one task of the complementizer in embedded clauses is hence the same as that of a finite verb in main clauses, to license the finiteness features of the clause. In turn, this licensing has other syntactic effects, such as allowing for the assignment of nominative case to the subject, and semantic effects, such as anchoring the utterance to the situational context and to the time of utterance.[9] In this connection it is interesting to note that many (Germanic) languages and dialects have inflected complementizers showing agreement with the subject of the clause resembling (but also often slightly differing from) subject-verb agreement in the same languages. Within the generative approaches this phenomenon has received considerable attention since Bayer's (1984) seminal paper on Bavarian (cf. e.g. Haegeman (1992), Zwart (1993), Weiss (2005) and many others).

Unlike early formal theories, that were mostly preoccupied with the syntactic and partially also the morphological aspects of finiteness but said little or nothing about the *content* of the finiteness category, approaches from the functionalism camp always sought to provide finiteness with a semantic underpinning, addressing the conceptual concept that lies behind finiteness (cf. Nikolaeva 2007b: 7). A much-quoted approach with an affinity to the functionalist camp is Klein (1994 and subseq.), who sees as one main contribution of finiteness to provide the utterance with an *assertion* feature, thus linking finiteness to illocution (more on Klein's approach below). However, functional and formalist frameworks alike have brought forth a number of proposals relating the semantic and pragmatic function of finiteness to *anchoring*; that is "the act of appropriately embedding an utterance in the context" (Gretsch & Perdue 2007: 437). Finiteness in these approaches is most often seen as the anchoring of the event, or the situation described by the clause, to the utterance context, cf. Amritavalli (2014: 284).

> Event anchoring is what is identified as "finiteness," or the ability of a clause to "stand alone." It is usual to assume that the anchoring in question is temporal anchoring (of the event time to speech time, via a reference time); and that its syntactic reflex is tense. In the generative tradition, this assumption is attributed to Stowell (1995), but it is in fact a traditional assumption, as the discussion in Comrie (1976: 1–2) shows. Finite clauses are described as carrying "independent tense" or "absolute tense," which is "deictic," because it locates "the time of a situation relative to the situation of the utterance" (loc. cit.).

9. Note however that the semantic contribution of finiteness is crucially assumed by these authors to be different from that of a tense marker; instead "finiteness is a prerequisite for tense and mood" (Holmberg and Platzack 1995: 23), and "a finite verb is not identical with a tensed verb; finite verb forms may have tense or lack it" (ibid.); the authors mention imperatives as a case in point.

To sum up this initial introduction, the typical hallmarks of finiteness of the most well-studied languages discussed in the literature have been *morphological* markers, since finiteness typically is reflected as visible tense and agreement features on the verb. Furthermore, finiteness has been shown to have *syntactic* effects in regulating the realization of the subject argument (case, visibility) and creating domains opaque to certain syntactic processes (binding, extraction). Finiteness is clearly involved in verb movement operations such as the verb-second rule of Germanic languages (since there exists a morphosyntactic restriction on the V2 position that only finite verbs appear here), and aspects related to embeddability versus independence of clauses headed by certain verb forms.[10] Finally, finiteness has *semantic*, *conceptual* and *pragmatic* aspects in being linked to deixis. Firstly in playing a part in anchoring of the described event and the utterance as a whole to the overall context, moreover to speech act phenomena such as illocution and assertion, and finally in restricting the interpretation of referential expressions, for instance in ascribing either independent or dependent interpretations to the subject argument and the tense marker of an embedded clause.

1. A quest for universal morphological reflexes of finiteness

Already in the eighties cross-linguistic data emerged that showed how morphological markers of tense and agreement are sometimes not very reliable diagnostics for finiteness effects in other domains, such as syntactic opacity, embeddability, or the realization and independent reference of the subject argument (cf. Cowper, this volume, for a thorough discussion). Even if finiteness equalled tense in most approaches, many investigations showed that clauses might very well show finiteness effects without overt tense markings. George and Kornfilt (1981) demonstrated that both tensed

10. Lohnstein (2000, 2001) and Lohnstein and Bredel (2004) develop a theory where movement to the V2 postion (identified in Lohnstein & Bredel as the position M^0) "seems to be the position relevant for marking the place of the modal anchoring of the respective proposition. This can be either the context of discourse or the grammatical context. Take modal anchoring to be a two-place relation between a proposition and some kind of context. For every proposition the relevant context has to be specified by some regular grammatical means. Since propositions expressed by unembedded clauses are anchored in the context of discourse, and propositions expressed by embedded clauses are anchored in the grammatical context, it appears that the position of the finite verb marks the anchoring place of the respective proposition. Let us take that to be the case. Then we can assume that the finite verb occupying the M^0 position indicates that the modal anchoring of the proposition takes place in the context of discourse, otherwise (i.e. if the finite verb remains in its final position) the proposition is anchored in the grammatical context" (Lohnstein & Bredel 2004: 256 ff).

and gerundive (i.e. tenseless) constructions seemed to be opaque to certain syntactic operations, as long as they exhibited agreement markings. They suggested that finiteness in natural languages was defined by person agreement instead of tense.[11] However, Raposo's (1987) study of agreeing infinitives in European Portuguese showed that even verb forms that were clearly non-finite, occurring only in dependent contexts, could carry overt agreement markers. Hence, agreement at least cannot be a sufficient trigger for finiteness effects; cf. (5ab) from Rouveret (1980: 76) and (5c) from Raposo (1987: 86):

(5) a. O João lamenta [eles terem gastado esse
the John regret.PRES.3SG they have.INF.3PL. spent that
dinhero para nada]
money for nothing
'John regrets their having spent that money for nothing.'

b. É dificil [os meninos trabalharem].
be-PRES-3SG difficult the children work.INF.3PL
'It is difficult for the children to work.'

c. Será dificil [eles aprovarem á proposta].
be.FUT difficult they approve.INF. 3PL. the proposal
'It will be difficult for them to approve the proposal.'

Neither could it be a necessary condition for finiteness that agreement is overtly expressed; cf. e.g. standard Mainland Scandinavian languages where finite verbs never carry agreement marking (cf. also Åfarli, this volume). Moreover, just as George and Kornfilt (1981) observed that constructions may show finiteness effects without tense (e.g. Turkish gerundives), tense distinctions also show up in constructions that are clearly non-finite by other diagnostics; cf. the Latin tensed infinitives in indirect speech (note that these constructions are Exceptional Case marking constructions, i.e. *Accusativus cum Infinitivo*); cf. (6ab).[12]

11. Note that these authors later observe that agreement cannot be a necessary ingredient of finiteness, since there are languages where there is no overtly realized agreement that still exhibit finiteness effects.

12. Cf. also Sigurðsson (this volume) advocating that infinitives are capable of "shifted tense". Furthermore, Heageman (1985) is a seminal paper demonstrating that West Flemish "personal infinitives" exhibit tense distinctions, i.e. temporally independent readings as present, past or future, even though they are not visibly inflected for tense. Haegeman accounts for these constructions by assuming that the INFL of these infinitives are specified as [+Tense, −AGR]. Cf. Cowper (this volume) for more details.

(6) a. Dicit se venire/se venisse/se venturum esse
says.3.SG. self come/self have.come/self will.come be
'He says he is coming/has come/will come.'
(literally: he says himself come/have come/will be come)

b. Dixit se venire/se venisse/se venturum esse
said.3.SG self come/self have.come/self will.come be
'He said he is/was coming; has/had come; would/will come.'
(literally: he said himself come/have come/will be come)

That is, neither tense nor agreement are by themselves sufficient indicators of finiteness. On the other hand, in Balkan languages like Greek and Albanian (certain) subjunctives employed in clausal complementation show signs of being non-finite as regards syntactic transparency in allowing for control into these embedded clauses although the embedded verb is arguably finite (i.e., carrying agreement and otherwise indistinguishable from the corresponding indicative form); cf. the Greek example in (7a) from Roussou (2009:1812) and the Albanian example in (7b) from Dobrovie-Sorin (2001:47).

(7) a. O Kostas matheni na odhiji.
the Kostas learn.3SG. PRT drive.3.SG.
'Kostas is learning (how) to drive.'

b. I kërkova të recitojë një poezi.
him asked.1.SG. PRT recite.3-SG a poem
'I asked him to recite a poem.'

The only marker of non-finiteness in these cases is the particle preceding the finite verb, *na* in Greek and *të* in Albanian. That is, the occurrence of a finite verb form, or at least a verb form indistinguishable from a finite form, is clearly not sufficient to create a finite domain. Creole languages, as briefly mentioned above, offer the other side of the coin. In most Creole languages we find a comparable situation to that in Balkan languages in the lack of a formal finiteness distinction expressed on the verb. Whereas we find a lack of a non-finite form (e.g. an infinitive) in the Balkan languages alluded to above, Creoles typically lack verb forms specializing as either finite or non-finite; cf. Romaine (1993:62). Instead, Creoles too employ the same form in finite and non-finite functions, but without any agreement markings. Muysken and Law (2001:51):

> Similarly, the verb not only has the same form for subjects of different person and number in finite clauses, [...] it also has the same form as in nonfinite clauses, as shown in [(8)]. Nevertheless, the same form of the verb does not necessarily have the same grammatical property. In particular, an overt subject is possible in [...] [[8a)], but not in [(8b)], even though the form of the verb is superficially the same:

(8) a. Li plante mayi li.
3SG plant corn SG
'He plants his corn.'

b. Jan te seye (*li) plante mayi li.
Jan ANTERIOR try 3SG plant corn 3SG
'Jan tried to plant his corn.'

Whereas Balkan languages, somewhat unexpectedly, exhibit non-finiteness effects like syntactic transparency and control in the presence of finite markers, Creoles exhibit finiteness effects, like the licensing of a visible subject, in the presence of a non-finite form; at least a form not licensing such a subject in an embedded context, like (8b).

Moreover, even in languages where the finiteness distinction is assumed to be very much in place, like English or Norwegian, we clearly find exclamations and utterances often referred to as *Mad Magazine Sentences,* cf. Akmajian (1984); Siegel (1987); Grohmann (2000), where seemingly non-finite verbs are the only verbs in independent utterances. Cf. (9a) from Siegel (1987) and (9b) from Eide (2005), and of course even in the most well-studied languages we find examples of finite embedded clauses.

(9) a. John eat caviar? (I thought he hated the stuff.)
b. Jeg ikke drikke øl på en fredag? (Særlig.) Norwegian
I-NOM not drink-INF beer on a Friday? As-if
'Me not drink beer on a Friday? As if.'

Thus, the simple correlations of overt finiteness markers and the finite behavior of the clause simply could not be upheld as more empirical data emerged. However, as the data got more complex, so did the theory; and the once monolithic INFL was split into several categories like AGR and T (Pollock 1989). McFadden and Sundaresan (2014: 6).

> This opened up the possibility, at least in theory, to extend the finiteness dialogue to clauses where the tense and agreement-marking seemed to make different predictions, such as "agreeing infintives" in Portuguese (Raposo 1987) or non-agreeing tensed participles in Lezgian (Nikolaeva 2007[c]); one could, for instance, claim that it is tense rather than agreement that defines finiteness in European Portuguese, whereas in Lezgian and Lezgian-like languages, it is the other way around, with agreement rather than tense instantiating clausal finiteness.

Landau (2004) is reluctant to give up on the importance of AGR and T-features to the semantic and syntactic effects of finiteness, but claims that the relationship is less direct than hitherto assumed. He proposes a "scale of finiteness" and a "calculus of control" to derive the degree of syntactic opacity and possibility for control into non-finite and seemingly finite embedded clausal complements. His proposal puts forth a quite complex combination matrix of AGR and T features realized on both

C and INFL, together with a feature realized on the subject, an *R-feature* dependent on T and AGR features on INFL in determining the independent reference of the subject, to account for the full set of possibilities found in the relevant languages. Sundaresan and McFadden (2009) demonstrate that even this complex machinery is not sufficient to account for the facts cross-linguistically, since in an array of languages (e.g. Tamil, Irish, Middle English) clauses that are demonstrably non-finite in every sense of the word will allow for overt, referentially independent subjects. Example (10) is quoted from McFadden and Sundaresan (2014: 9), but with some minor spelling differences.[13]

(10) That were shame vnto the sayd syre launcelot,
'That were shame unto you,' said sir Launcelot'

[thou an armed knyghte to slee a naked man by treson].
'You.NOM an armed knight to slay a naked man by treason'

"That would be a disgrace on you," said sir Lancelot, "for you, an armed knight, to slay a naked man by treason."

McFadden and Sundaresan (2014: 10) conclude that such data seriously undermine a simple correlation between subject reference and clausal finiteness, in the manner assumed in standard GB and Minimalist theories, but also in more sophisticated proposals such as Landau (2004) and Szabolcsi (2009). To the extent that such a relationship exists, it "must be potentially mediated by other factors" (loc. cit).

As the recalcitrant data emerged from a typologically wider set of languages, the abstract finiteness features were assumed to only sometimes trigger morphological reflexes resembling tense and agreement features. However, even if it is quite plausible that a clausal syntactic category may exist that only sometimes has a phonetically visible exponent; the opposite situation, that tense and agreement markers occur where they are not expected, is in many respects worse to explain, since they must be made to not count as finite in exactly these contexts. Postulating underlying relations between morphology and syntax that seem to run counter to observable facts puts a strain on explanatory questions like learnability. Such facts have led many authors to give up on isolating the specific contributions of finiteness. Adger (2007: 58), for instance, states that since the canonical markers of finiteness, T and AGR, are not confined to the topmost layers of the clause, but may appear "very low down" (i.e. in the VP), we may conclude that "there is no clear mapping from the traditional notion of finiteness to the categories of formal grammar."

13. As pointed out to me by series editor Elly van Gelderen, this is how the quote appears in the MED version of Malory: ⟨http://quod.lib.umich.edu/c/cme/MaloryWks2?rgn=main;view=fulltext⟩, p. 209.

In the same vein, regarding the quest for a universal morphosyntactic trigger for finiteness or its counterpart, non-finiteness, Nikolaeva (2007c: 178 ff) concludes that

> [R]elating the cluster of finiteness properties in independent clauses to the presence of one syntactic element is a purely theory-internal device not supported by empirical evidence if a broader cross-linguistic picture is taken into account. Some types of non-assertive independent clause show reduction of finiteness as far as tense/agreement inflection and subject licensing are concerned, but languages show different patterns of combinations of these properties, which suggests that they do not have a common source. Reduction of finiteness in independent clauses is better viewed as a cross-linguistic tendency than a universal syntactic generalization.

2. Binarity versus graduality – and a way to reconcile the two in recent approaches

Within formalist approaches the quest for a universal trigger for finiteness effects used to be a search either for a morphological trigger, or for a more abstract clausal syntactic trigger observable only through its syntactic and semantic effects, or a combination of binary features that were either present or absent [± Tense, ± AGR]. Even if more features are considered, such as *dependent v. independent,* within the generative literature there has certainly been a preference for binary features. In contrast, functionalist frameworks have often seen finiteness as a scalar phenomenon signalled by visible features that combine to yield a specific degree of finiteness.[14] These features are tense, modality, and aspect markers, agreement, case markings on the subject and object, articles, determiners, and topic markers (cf. Givón 1990: 853;[15] Bisang 2001: 1401–1402). The more visible features of this sort, the "more finite" the clause. This view is rooted in large typological investigations comparing finiteness markers in geographically and

14. In a sense, this is also what Landau (2004) does, only with T and AGR features present in the C-domain and the T-domain within a minimalist framework and still with an apparatus of binary feature values that are either present or absent.

15. Givón (1990) claims, more specifically, that the degree of conceptual integration of a dependent event into an embedding event is reflected by the degree of syntactic dependence of a dependent clause relative to a prototypical main clause. That is, the more integrated or dependent a clause is, the less properties it has of a prototypical main clause. Hence (op. cit.: 853) finiteness is "the systematic grammatical means used to express the degree of integration of a clause into its immediate clausal environment", and conversely the degree of independence increases with the number of overt expression of verbal properties such as tense and agreement, mood and aspect.

genetically diverse languages less shaped by the "Eurocentrism" in more formalistically inclined linguistics. It remains a fact that the most well-studied languages in linguistics to date are of European origin, and the (early) linguistic models built, although aiming to have universal validity across all languages, tend to take the historically most robust and well-known generalizations from the most familiar languages as their fundament. Nikolaeva (2007b: 8) states that finiteness seems to be both gradual and binary in nature and that both sides of this coin must be acknowledged, if the notion of finiteness is going to continue to have some validity in our theorizing:

> [I]f the notion of finiteness has a cross-linguistic applicability, its nature must be viewed as somewhat more complex. Both the gradual and binary nature of finiteness can be captured by making a principled distinction between an abstract binary category that regulates certain syntactic processes, on the one hand, and its individual morphological manifestations, on the other.

The history of the finiteness notion in modern linguistics has been a trajectory from viewing finiteness as a morphological category to seeing it as a more abstract clausal category with various morphological and syntactic reflexes (although typically AGR and tense). Currently we are observing the tendency within formalist frameworks to take this to an even higher level of abstraction. This kind of theoretical refinement is facilitated by certain recent developments in linguistic theory, and we will discuss three such strains of research here. Firstly, finiteness is reanalysed from being viewed as a syntactic category residing in the I-domain with a specific feature make-up (e.g. AGR, T) to being viewed instead as an even more abstract conceptual category. While presumably still residing in a specific projection or domain of the clause (e.g. FinP) this projection is currently most often seen as more naturally belonging to the C-domain of the clause, interfacing with the context, rather than the inflectional I-domain.[16] Secondly, the gradual nature of finiteness advocated in typological approaches may be captured in a formalist model by means of a more fine-grained approach to clausal selection (cf. Speas & Tenny 2003; McFadden & Sundaresan 2014). Thirdly, there is renewed focus on the conceptual content of the finiteness category as expressing contextual anchoring and thus belonging with deixis.[17] This conceptual category of finiteness may obviously

16. But cf. Ritter and Wiltschko (2014: 1334), who state that they see anchoring as belonging to the I-domain and not to the C-domain; the C-domain expresses linking to the larger structure whereas the I-domain locates the event in time or space.

17. I would like to point out that what may be seen as a renewed interest in the collaboration of finiteness markers with V2 and the attempts by Lohnstein (2000, 2001), Truckenbrodt (2006) and others to give a compositional analysis of how certain finiteness markers interact with verb movement (V2) to encode specific semantic effects pertaining to sentence mood and anchoring can easily be seen as aspects of the same development.

trigger overt realizations of morphological markers that are widely different from anything that used to be considered linguistic markers of finiteness, not only mood markings (Holmberg et al. 1993), but also categories only loosely related to mood, such as (finite) negation in the Dravidian language Kannada (Amritavalli 2014). Recently careful scrutiny of hitherto less studied languages like *Halkomelem* and *Blackfoot* reveals that languages may also employ other types of markers to signal event anchoring, like location markers or specific person/utterance participant features (Ritter & Wiltschko 2005, 2009, 2014; cf. also Sigurðsson 2004, 2010 for an approach to participant features as means of anchoring even in Germanic languages).

Just as the I-domain was once split into several subcategories each heading projections with their own specifications (cf. e.g. Pollock 1989), Rizzi (1997) advocated that the C-domain should be split into a hierarchy of (mostly) discourse-related projections (op.cit: 297), where ForceP hosts (roughly) the illocutionary force of the clause, TopP and FocP host topic- and focus-related phrases, and FinP "expresses a distinction related to tense but more rudimentary than tense and other inflectional specifications on the verbal system: finiteness [...]; which in turn selects an IP system with the familiar characteristics of finiteness: mood distinctions, subject agreement licensing nominative case, overt tense distinctions (these specifications being subjected to some cross-linguistic variation [...])." (op. cit: 284); cf. (11):

(11) **C-domain:** [ForceP > TopP > FocP > FinP [**I-domain:** [TP...]]]][18]

This "split-CP" hypothesis is mostly taken as implicit in recent approaches to finiteness, although authors may still chose to refer instead to "the C-domain" and remain "agnostic as to whether we are dealing with single head or a series of heads in the left periphery of the clause, as in Rizzi (1997)" cf. for instance Ritter and Wiltschko (2014: 1367).

Cinque (1999) took the cartographic approach one step further and proposed a *universal functional sequence* of functional heads for the entire clause. The clausal spine previously analysed in a quite simple structure consisting in the categories CP, IP and VP (and later vP), understood as either simplex heads or as domains, was now decomposed into some sixty syntactic heads, with a much more specialized semantic contribution and overtly realized as morphosyntactic elements like inflections, auxiliaries, free-standing particles or verbs. Cinque's study demonstrated that ordering

18. Note that Rizzi distinguishes two TOP-positions; in addition to the one referred here, there is another TopP just below the FocP position. In addition, series editor Werner Abraham (p.c.) adds that: "To all appearances, two FOC positions and scopes have to be distinguished: contrastive FOC and Verum FOC [...]. Also there are claims to the extent that German (and other languages) have no Infl position up in the vicinity of what used to be Comp." I am grateful to Werner Abraham for pointing this out.

restrictions between types of syntactic elements reflected in natural languages could be given a principled account by assuming such a universal hierarchy. Although no language in and by itself employs all morphosyntactic elements instantiating the heads along the entire functional sequence, partial sequences of rather rigid ordering were attested across languages, and via combining these partial sequences, Cinque arrived at his proposed hierarchy. Likewise, adverbs were taken to be realized as phrases in the specifier positions of these heads, restricted via semantic harmony and obviously subject to the same universal hierarchy such that e.g. evidential adverbs were realised as the specifier of the head hosting evidential modals or particles (cf. Cinque 1999: 106).

(12) [frankly $Mood_{speech\ act}$ [fortunately $Mood_{evaluative}$ [allegedly $Mood_{evidential}$
[probably $Mod_{epistemic}$ [once T(Past) [then T(Future) [perhaps $Mood_{irrealis}$
[necessarily $Mod_{necessity}$ [possibly $Mod_{possibility}$ [usually $Asp_{habitual}$
[again$Asp_{repetitive(I)}$ [often $Asp_{frequentative(I)}$ [intentionally $Mod_{volitional}$
[quickly $Asp_{celerative(I)}$ [already T(Anterior) [no longer $Asp_{terminative}$
[still $Asp_{continuative}$ [always $Asp_{perfect(?)}$ [just $Asp_{retrospective}$
[soon $Asp_{proximative}$ [briefly $Asp_{durative}$
[characteristically(?) $Asp_{generic/progressive}$ [almost $Asp_{prospective}$
[completely $Asp_{SgCompletive(I)}$ [tutto $Asp_{PlCompletive}$
[well Voice [fast/early $Asp_{celerative(II)}$ [again $Asp_{repetative(II)}$
[often $Asp_{frequentative(II)}$ [completely $Asp_{SgCompletive(II)}$

McFadden and Sundaresan (2014: 14 ff) present the analysis of Speas and Tenny (2003) as a promising approach to capturing the more gradual sides of finiteness. In Speas and Tenny's analysis, the Cinque hierarchy is put to use to account for clausal selection, assuming that different predicates select for different portions of the functional sequence in (12). McFadden and Sundaresan (2014: 15) elaborate on this:

> Thus, a speech predicate, like 'say' would select a clause of the largest size, one that specifically included a SpeechActP and all the other phrases below it in the Cinque hierarchy. On the other hand, a clause selected by a direct perception predicate like 'hear' would be the smallest, containing at its root the Epistemological phrase. This model seamlessly extends into lower portions of the clausal hierarchy involving the inflectional domain, where we might expect to find heads like Rizzi's Fin, as well as those responsible for tense, mood, agreement, and aspect. This gives us a natural way to reconfigure finiteness, not as a binary property, but as something that is scaled or graded. At its simplest, this means that a clause with more structure is more finite than one with less.

The third direction of recent finiteness research rather relevant to a number of chapters in this volume is the renewed interest in "finiteness as anchoring". This seems to have two sources in particular. Firstly, there are a number of recent proposals aiming at describing exactly how "event anchoring" can be made explicit in a formalist notation (semantic and syntactic), approaching the notion of anchoring with tools such as viewpoint or logophoricity (Bianchi 2003; Sigurðsson 2004). Secondly, the proposals by Ritter and Wiltschko (2005, 2009, 2014) that finiteness can be expressed in certain languages by anchoring systems making reference to categories quite different from tense or even mood seem to require an even higher level of abstraction, where tense and agreement features become arbitrary or at least language-specific, or perhaps even quite irrelevant.

Nevertheless, these approaches to anchoring typically take their point of departure from analyses of tense as the deictic anchoring category *par excellence*. The classical analysis of tense as a deictic category anchoring the clause to the utterance context is Reichenbach (1947), where three relevant time points were proposed: Time of event E, time of speech S, and a "mediating" reference time R. Reichenbach believed that all tenses expressed by natural language could be stated as a relative ordering of these three time points. A much-quoted approach with some affinity to the functionalist camp is Klein's (1994, 1998, 2006, 2009).[19] In contrast to the role ascribed to tense in Reichenbachian proposals, Klein advocates instead the role of finiteness in anchoring. In this theory, finiteness is thus not merely a morphological category, but a host for the crucial elements *Assertion* and *Topic Time*. Assertion determines the illocutionary force of a sentence, and Topic Time amounts to one of the three time spans distinguished, Time of Utterance (TU), Topic Time (TT) and Time of Situation (TSit). Topic Time refers to the time for which a particular utterance makes an assertion, referring to a time span to which the assertion made is constrained. In Klein's view, tense expresses a temporal ordering between Time of Utterance and Topic Time, whereas Aspect expresses a temporal ordering relation between Topic Time and Time of Situation. Although Klein hence clearly builds on the insights from Reichenbach, there are some important differences between Klein's notion of Topic Time and Reichenbach's reference Time R. Crucially, R is a mediator of a viewpoint, a relative time point serving as an anchor for the event time. Klein's Topic Time is a time for which the truth of the assertion is evaluated. In the present volume, both Klein's and Reichenbach's approaches are discussed and used. Sigurðsson's analysis takes the classical Reichenbachian approach as fundamental to his theory, whereas van de Vate and Veenstra build on Klein's approach.

Bianchi (2003) develops an analysis of finiteness as anchoring where both semantic and syntactic features of the category are discussed. Taking as her point of departure

19. Klein's theories are also advocated in several formalist approaches, e.g. Demirdache and Uribe-Extebarria (2000, 2004).

Holmberg and Platzack's (1995) view that the function of finiteness is to relate the predication to the time of the utterance, she proposes that (p. 245)

> [T]he syntactic feature of finiteness encodes the logophoric anchoring of the clause […]. [Finite clauses] are anchored directly to the Speech event, which constitutes the external "centre of deixis".

Noting that most syntactic approaches to temporal structure assume that the Reichenbachian time points and their relations are encoded in designated functional projections of the clausal structure (p. 221), Bianchi presents the hypothesis that "The Speech time S is syntactically represented in [+finite] Fin^0, the lowest head of the Complementizer system interfacing with the inflectional structure (Rizzi 1997)".

Ritter and Wiltschko (2014) build on their own work from 2009 and assume that the anchoring attributed to Fin^0 by Bianchi (2003) and many other authors is in fact hosted by INFL, analysed here as a monolithic, "pre-Pollockian", unsplit category. They present the *Parametric Substantiation Hypothesis* (p. 1335) investigating the claims that (a) Universal Grammar makes available a set of hierarchically organized functional categories: the universal spine, and (b) Languages vary in the substantive content associated with functional categories. Thus, whereas INFL serves as a universal anchoring category (following Ritter & Wiltschko 2009), it is not intrinsically associated with substantive content, the possible content of this anchoring category is instead subject to cross-linguistic variation. Thus, in Halkomelem Salish this category is instantiated by means of locative auxiliaries, contrasting along a spatial dimension, and in the Algonquian language Blackfoot, a third core deictic category is involved, namely person. Specific "order" suffixes signal the identity versus non-identity of event participants and specific utterance participants. Ritter and Wiltschko (2009) assume that the functional equivalence of contrastive tense in English with location marking in Halkomelem and person marking in Blackfoot is a result of their categorial equivalence, whereas these markings still constitute different categories. Ritter and Wiltschko (2014) take this assumption a step further and argue instead that the three categories instantiate the same abstract anchoring category, namely INFL (op. cit. p. 1344).

The working definition of finiteness that we were trying to home in on during this introduction should incorporate the most promising recent strands of research, and it seems clear from what is observed thus far that cross-linguistically, finiteness serves as an anchoring category for the clause, via creating a "logophoric center" serving to anchor the predication event. Following the lead of Ritter and Wiltschko (2014), we see this category as a universal category that hosts language-specific substantive content. Morphologically this anchoring can be signaled in different languages via location markers, person features or agreement, tense, mood, or other related categories such as (finite) negation. Obviously, this anchoring must also be allowed to exist and encoded without any such explicit morphological markers, since in Creole languages and many other languages like e.g. Chinese there are no obligatory morphological exponents of finiteness whatsoever, and a finite domain evidently may be signaled solely via the occurrence of an overt subject, or otherwise must be licensed only by pragmatic-contextual means. The syntactic projection hosting the (overt or covert) anchoring category must be an obligatory category of the syntactic spine, but whether it is located in the I-domain, as in Ritter and Wiltschko (2014) or in the C-domain (specifically Fin^0), as in Rizzi (1997) and Bianchi (2003) is open to debate. The approach in McFadden and Sundaresan (2014) exploiting an analysis inspired by Speas and Tenny's (2003) analysis of clausal selection allows us to capture the gradual nature of finiteness particularly in embedded clauses.[20]

As mentioned above, most of the papers in this volume take their point of departure from the more traditional views on finiteness and elaborate on these approaches in innovative ways. We thus hope that the preceding discussion and the tour through some of the most relevant proposals in the literature on finiteness serves as a useful backdrop against which to read the remaining ten chapters of this book.

3. The individual papers of this volume

We have grouped the individual papers of this volume into three sections. The first section *Finiteness: underlying relations* primarily deals with syntactic and semantic relations at work underlying finite constructions, but also addresses the relations between finiteness proper and some of its close relatives and co-travelers like "pseudo-finiteness", (Cowper), tense (Sigurðsson) binding (Reuland) and verb second (Eide). *Morphosyntactic exponents of (non-)finiteness* is the main topic of the second section where the discussions revolve more around the possible expression of finiteness in individual languages like Norwegian and English (Åfarli), West Flemish (Haegeman and Weir) and the Creole language Saamáka (van de Vate and Veenstra). Thirdly, we include a section dealing with *Finiteness in language acquisition* where finiteness markers and their relation to verb movement is one important topic (Westergaard); the relation between syntax and phonology another (Blom and Vasić); and finiteness in

20. Another promising strain of research is the one discussed in several notes throughout this introductory chapter, studies by e.g. Lohnstein (2001) and Truckenbrodt (2006) investigating the explicit and observable connections between subsets of finite markers and verb order phenomena (especially V2 in V2 languages) pertaining to sentence mood and assertion. The present format unfortunately does not permit the discussion of these theories in detail, neither how they may relate in potentially fruitful ways to the other strains of recent research put forth in this subsection.

bilingual acquisition a third (Jin and Eide). Needless to say, many of the discussions in the individual contributions to this volume in reality crosscut these three major topics and could quite easily be included in a different section.

Elizabeth Cowper's contribution *Finiteness and Pseudofiniteness* revisits some intriguing data sets from the classical literature on finiteness, including personal infinitives in West Flemish (Haegeman 1985) and Romanian (Alboiu & Motapanyane 2000), inflected and prepositional infinitives in Portuguese (Raposo 1987a), subjunctives in Greek (Alexiadou & Anagnostopoulou 1998, 2002), the *modo* construction in Southern Calabrian (Ledgeway 1998), and gerunds in Turkish (George and Kornfilt 1981). These constructions and data sets have often been put forth to illustrate that the two-way distinction between "finite" and "non-finite" employed in traditional and also within early Generative grammar is much to coarse grained, and that we need to appeal to notions that take an intermediate position between the two. Cowper's objective is to show that even these intermediate notions can be given principled and consistent analyses, armed with tools from the Minimalist program and the currently developing feature geometry theory (e.g. Harley & Ritter 2002; Cowper 2005). The latter is a theory of a network of dependency relations where FINITENESS occupies a particular position relative to other features such as PROPOSITION and DEIXIS within the INFL system, hence FINITENESS carries with it implication of these other categories.

At the outset, Cowper notes that the term "finite" is difficult to pin down, and that even in recent generativist literature, the term is used inconsistently. She adopts the traditional view that finiteness *per se* is a purely syntactic property, consisting of the ability to license structural case in subject position and the possible presence of agreement marking on the verb. Finiteness has no semantic correspondent to the extent that there is no particular semantic content that can be associated with the feature FINITENESS itself. However, because FINITENESS implies the presence of the interpretable feature PROPOSITION (and for some languages: DEIXIS),[21] it is very tempting, but unfortunate, to ascribe to FINITENESS certain characteristics that are in fact parasitic on other, interpretable features. Cowper's definition of finiteness thus contains no such semantic connotations, but reserves the term finiteness as a purely syntactic notion.

Cowper (2005, this volume) distinguishes between clauses denoting cognitively represented propositions (carrying the feature PROPOSITION) and clauses denoting bare events (carrying the feature EVENT). A bare event must be sensorily perceived (We saw [the car hit the lamppost]), unlike a propositional clause, which can be cognitively evaluated as true or false (We know [the car to have hit the lamppost]). FINITE

21. The inventory and specific bundling of the features are subject to parametrizion.

in general is a dependent of PROPOSITION, and armed with these assumptions, Cowper turns to the two main classes of apparent counterexamples to the nominative Case assignment-subject-verb-agreement association normally signaling finiteness. Firstly, infinitives in which nominative case and φ-feature checking seem to be present, but on what is otherwise to be diagnosed as a non-finite form, and secondly, Greek verb forms that appear to be fully finite but still seem to denote bare events rather than propositions. "This pattern calls into question whether nominative case and φ-feature checking with Infl are indeed two sides of the same coin".

Cowper's proposal consists in exploring the idea that the Case and φ-feature checking properties of Infl, normally determined by the presence or absence of FINITE, can be activated in the absence of FINITE. This seems to happen when (a) Infl itself Agrees with a case-checking head, and (b) null subjects are possible in the language. Essentially, a non-finite Infl acquires the properties associated with the FINITE feature during the course of the syntactic computation. This is what Cowper refers to as *Pseudofiniteness.* Utilizing different tests such as the possibility of a "bare event" reading, Cowper reaches at an analysis of various constructions that have more or less of the traditional markings of finiteness, and advocates that some of these constructions are finite despite appearances, some are non-finite despite appearances, whereas others are pseudofinite constructions; constructions that acquire finiteness valuation in the course of a syntactic derivation.

Halldór Ármann Sigurðsson's paper continues the discussion on the observable discrepancy between morphologically expressed finiteness-related markers, i.e. the PF-related aspects of finiteness, and their semantic and functional tasks in a clause. The chapter likewise has bearing on the question of embeddability of clauses marked as finite, i.e. their possible syntactic integration into an overarching clause. The case study is an investigation into finite markers in subordinate clauses, in the so-called Sequence-of-Tense contexts, and presents a radically new analysis for the recalcitrant problem of *Double Access Readings* (DAR). The English embedded clause in (13) below exhibits a past finite marking expressing a temporal relation of simultaneity to the embedding predicate also marked with finite past. That is, this PAST-PAST construction expresses the same temporal relation as the Russian PAST-PRESENT marking in Example (14). Icelandic may express the same relation with a past subjunctive inflection on the embedding predicate (likewise most often perceived as a finite tense marker); cf. (15).

(13) I **realized** that it *was* Mary (when I said hello). English

(14) Tanja **skazala** [čto ona **tancuet**]. Russian
Tanja said that she dances (Comrie 1986: 275)
'Tanja said that she was dancing
(at the moment of Tanja's saying so).'

(15) María **sagði** [að Ólafur **væri** veikur
Mary said that Olaf were.PST.SBJ sick
(*í gær)]. Icelandic
(*in yesterday)
'Mary said that Olaf was sick (*yesterday).'
(= sick at the moment of Mary's saying so).'

Sigurðsson seeks to give a unified account of these three different ways of finite-marking the embedded predicate, where the syntactic and semantic aspects of the constructions remain constant (temporal simultaneity of the finite embedded predicate with the finite past of the embedding clause). He takes as his point of departure the Reichenbachian (1947) tense system of the universal temporal relations S (speech time), R (reference time) and E (event time) and makes the claim that any finite clause contains three syntactically active Tense heads roughly corresponding to S, R and E (understood as relations between time points rather than points in time). These three T-heads are correspondingly subscripted T_S (residing in the C-domain of the clause), T_R (residing in the referential T-domain) and T_E (residing in the V-domain) and together these three heads constitute the temporal part of the clausal spine. Tense systems typically involve a non-finite and a finite part, and whereas the non-finite part expresses a computational relation between E and R, simply noted as (E $\leftrightarrow$ R), the task of the finite part of a tense is to express a computational relation between S and (E $\leftrightarrow$ R).

Since all finite clauses contain exactly these three T-heads, it follows that the finite tense of the embedded clause also signals the presence of a T_S. To keep these two apart, let us the subscript the T_S of the embedding clause is as T_{S1} and that of the subordinate clause T_{S2}. In the unmarked case, T_{S1} and T_{S2} are both deictic and acquire their temporal reading in relation to the NOW of the speech event (e.g. Mary ***works*** tonight because Susan ***left*** in the afternoon). However, in Sequence-of-Tense contexts, the embedded T_{S2} becomes anaphoric in relation a matrix T controller (typically a verb of saying, reporting, believing, or predicates of "cognitive altered states" such as *realizing*). Sigurðsson refers to the relevant Sequence-of-Tense contexts as "shifted T" or "T_s Shift", which is "really a perceived secondary Speech Tense" where its anaphoricity is parasitic on a relevant speech-like event of the matrix clause. T_s is always silent ("by necessity") but is commonly accompanied by finite morphological marking of the subordinate clause; "a fact that has caused much confusion in the literature".

Sigurðsson argues that overt Sequence of Tense marking (like in the English example in (13) or the Icelandic example in (15)) is a type of semantically vacuous Tense agreement. Overt agreement processes in general are PF processes taking place in the post-syntactic externalization component of language. Accordingly, "overt agreement reflects syntax but has no syntactic or semantic import". In Sigurðsson's view, the mapping from abstract internal language (computation) to perceptible external language (e.g. morphological units) is fundamentally non-isomorphic, implying that the degree of finiteness morphologically expressed by an embedded clause or the actual finiteness marker chosen (e.g. finite past, finite present, past subjunctive) by no means gives us direct access to the underlying degree of integration and embeddability.

Anaphors and pronominals are widely discussed as elements that rely on some notion of finiteness for their distribution, at least in the most well-studied Indo-European languages. As quoted above, finiteness is prone to create domains opaque to certain syntactic operations, anaphoric binding typically mentioned as a case in point (cf. e.g. Nikolaeva 2007b: 6; MacFadden & Sundaresan 2014: 7). Eric Reuland's paper on universals and variation in encoding anaphoric dependencies takes as its starting point the Canonical Binding Theory (CBT) in Chomsky (1981):

1. A. An anaphor is bound in its local domain (governing category)
   B. A pronominal is free in its local domain (governing category)
2. A binds b iff a and b are co-indexed and a c-commands b.
3. γ is a governing category for α if and only if γ is the minimal category containing α, a governor of α, and a SUBJECT.

A subject in this context is to be understood as "the most prominent nominal category accessible to α, either the specifier of TP, or the finite agreement". From the perspective of finiteness, Reuland says, the core opacity factor in the CBT is the subject. Finiteness plays a role only indirectly in the CBT, in the fact that it makes available one particular flavor of a SUBJECT, namely finite AGR, which suffices to serve as a SUBJECT in certain clausal structures of certain languages. But in fact, finiteness is indeed an important component of explanatory binding theory as a significant factor in its own right, playing a role in "defining opacity for binding domains and providing the means to escape from them" (cf. also Reuland 2011: Chapter 8).

As has become clear since the eighties, natural languages utilize systems with more distinctions than just the difference between anaphor and pronominal; for instance, Dutch has a 3-way system with pronominals, simple anaphors (SE-anaphors) and complex anaphors (SELF-anaphors), and Icelandic, Norwegian and the other Mainland Scandinavian languages have a 4-way system: pronominals, simple anaphors, complex anaphors both of the form SE-SELF (e.g. Norwegian *seg selv*) and the form Pronominal-SELF (e.g. Norwegian *han selv*; cf. Hellan 1988). Likewise, there is significant cross-linguistic variation in binding domains, especially of SE-anaphors. Whereas in Dutch and German binding of SE-anaphors is rather local, in the Mainland Scandinavian languages the antecedent may be far beyond the local subject, as long as no finite clause boundary intervenes (cf. (17) below from Hellan 1988), whereas in Icelandic and Faroese (and certain Mainland Scandinavian dialects) an anaphoric dependency can be established even beyond this domain (see e.g. Sigurðsson 1990 and Lødrup 2009). Allowing parametrization of binding domains is not enough to save CBT, says Reuland. Reuland and Sigurjónsdóttir (1997) show for instance that there is a significant contrast between the infinitival and subjunctive domains. Simplex anaphors can be syntactically bound within the infinitival domain, but require other mechanisms when their dependency crosses a subjunctive ("finite") clause boundary.

Binding of simplex anaphors (like Dutch *zich*) can be syntactically encoded by Agree, where Agree involves exchanging/copying of φ-feature bundles between the dependent element and its antecedent. These φ-feature bundles are interpreted as variables in the interpretive procedure. Feature sharing creates identity of variables, and crucially takes place via the heads on the path between these elements.

(16) DP T V zich

R1 R2 R3

These dependencies are syntactic dependencies, where R1 is the canonical agreement relation between subject and finite Tense, R2 reflects the relation between the verbal projection and the Tense system, R3 is the Case dependency between V and its object. Structural Case is assumed to be uninterpretable Tense (Pesetsky & Torrego 2007), and plays a crucial role in Reuland's account of binding (this is a morphosyntactic parameter responsible for the distribution of simplex anaphors versus pronominals). The composition of the chain R1, R2, and R3 links *zich* to its subject DP. This yields a syntactic encoding of the binding relation.

In principle, this process of Agree-chain-formation with SE-anaphors can cross clause boundaries, giving rise to long-distance binding. Consider (17); from Hellan (1988):

(17) Jon$_i$ bad oss [PRO$_1$ forsøke [å PRO$_2$ få deg [til PRO$_3$ å snakke pent om seg$_i$]]]
Jon asked us (to) try to get you to talk nicely about SE
'John asked us to try to get you to talk nicely about him.'

The crucial difference between infinitival clauses and finite clauses as regards binding is that infinitival clauses contain a head FIN encoding logophoricty (cf. Rizzi 1997; Bianchi 2003) and merged as unvalued, whereas in finite clauses FIN already has an intrinsic value. Thus, infinitival clauses are underspecified in two respects, Tense and Finiteness. The most deeply embedded CP may link up the SE-anaphor to the highest subject, skipping the intermediate PRO subjects as antecedents because the intermediate C-domains each contain unvalued FIN, allowing for the formation of a chain all the way from the anaphor to the topmost C. When an intermediate C contains an intrinsically valued FIN head, economy requires that SE is valued as soon as possible, and forces the T-SE chain to link to the most local valued FIN.

Indices are not allowable morphosyntactic objects within the minimalist version of the Principles and Parameters theory, hence cannot enter into grammatical operations. This means that the definition of binding itself must be given without recourse to indices. Reuland adopts the cross-linguistically invariant definition of binding in Reinhart (2006: 171), a logical notion of binding:

(18) **A-binding** (logical syntax binding)
α A-binds β iff α is the sister of a λ-predicate whose operator binds β.

Moreover, Reuland substitutes principle B of the classical binding theory with Reinhart and Reuland's (1993) condition B (*A reflexive predicate is reflexive-marked*). Examining new data from a range of languages, Reuland furthermore argues that the purpose of reflexive marking in all its different disguises is to avoid creating uninterpretable identity relations that would be unintelligible to the interpretive component of language.

The paper by Kristin Melum Eide *Finiteness, inflection, and the syntax your morphology can afford* is a contribution to the debate on the potential relation between morphological markings of finiteness and the syntax that "tends to go hand in hand with a visible finiteness distinction" (cf. e.g. Weerman 1989; Gretsch & Perdue 2007; Lasser 1997 and many others). Two Germanic languages, Modern English and Modern Norwegian, are compared with respect to a range of syntactic constructions, where it is argued that in both languages these constructions syntactically require an explicitly encoded finiteness feature, or, for the second set of constructions, the explicitly encoded absence of such a feature. In many approaches to the English verbal system, the distinction between auxiliaries and main verbs amounts to a sort of diacritic where the two types of verbal elements are simply stipulated to belong to two different verbal categories. The two types of verbal categories, auxiliaries and main verbs, differ in their respective feature specifications, and hence, main verbs are banned from many of the positions where auxiliaries appear, and vice versa. The main tenet of Eide's proposal is the objective to replace these diacritics with some content and to shed some much needed light onto the question of what exactly the differing feature specifications between main verbs and auxiliaries consist in (except from simply a purported feature ±AUX or ±V). A comparison between English and Norwegian is specifically useful to this end, since the finiteness markings on the verb seemingly are expressed to a quite comparable degree in English and Norwegian. Neither of the languages expresses subject-verb agreement in the preterit, and whereas English distinguishes the 3rd PSG in the present tense with the inflection (-s), other present tense forms show no person agreement. Norwegian displays no subject-verb agreement in in any of its finite forms.

However, even without any explicit person marking, Norwegian clearly has a full verbal paradigm of finite and non-finite forms for all types of verb, where any verb form carries two pieces of information: [±Past] and [±Finite], cf. (19a). One main claim of the paper is that Modern English no longer exhibits a comparable morphological finiteness distinction in the productive verbal paradigms of main verbs (the 3rd PSG -s is counted as an agreement marker not relevant for finiteness *per se*), and that only a past/non-past distinction is productive in new Modern English main verbs. This makes the feature make-up of the main verbs quite different in the two languages.

(19)

a	+Finite	–Finite
+Past	**Preterit**	**Participle**
–Past	**Present**	**Infinitive**

b

+Past	**Preterit/Participle**
–Past	**Present/Infinitive**

Old English had a morphologically expressed finite distinction in main verbs, like its West and North Germanic siblings and hence also like modern Norwegian, but English lost this trait sometime on its road from Old English to Middle English. An important claim of this paper (cf. also Eide 2009a, b) is that this observation allows us to get a different take on The Rich Agreement Hypothesis (RAH; e.g. Rohrbacher 1999), where the existence of a "rich enough" morphology in a language is linked to its use of generalized verb movement up the clausal spine. As noted by McWhorter (2005: 287), this hypothesis has been put forth by many authors, but "overall, the explanations… lack explanatory power or falsifiability". Eide's claim is that the reason for the lack of explanatory power is due to the previous accounts failing to find the *right* morphological distinction missing from English but present in its Germanic siblings, and she advocates that this "right morphological distinction" is in fact the privative finiteness distinction, expressed in verbal paradigms rather independently of tense and agreement markers; Norwegian being a case in point. That said, agreement often shows up on finite forms, but this is due to non-finite forms behaving like anaphora and hence falling under Rizzi's (1990: 26) *Anaphor agreement effect* ("Anaphors do not occur in syntactic positions construed with agreement").

Although English main verbs are bereft of a productive morphologically expressed finiteness distinction (except for in a few, but frequent irregular main verbs distinguishing preterits from participles), obviously finiteness exists in modern English as well. Firstly, it exists as a semantic anchoring requirement (cf. finiteness-as-anchoring or S-finiteness discussed above), and secondly, it clearly exists in auxiliaries. Auxiliaries *have* and *be* exhibit full paradigms of finite and non-finite forms, albeit to a very differing degree.[22] The modals and auxiliary *do,* on the other hand, exist only as finite forms and are hence banned from positions where non-finiteness is explicitly required by a given syntactic operation or construction.

22. Whereas *be* has different forms for different persons especially in the singular, *have* patterns with main verbs as regards inventory of forms, but behaves like an auxiliary syntactically.

(20)

+Past	**Preterit/Participle**
–Past	**Present/Infinitive**

a. English main verbs

[+Past,+Finite]	**Preterit**
[–Past, +Finite]	**Present**

b. English modals, auxiliary *do*

	+Finite	–Finite
+Past	**Preterit**	**Participle**
–Past	**Present**	**Infinitive**

c. English *have/be*, Norwegian main verbs, modals and auxiliaries.

Hence, the finiteness feature is unevenly distributed across verbs and auxiliaries in English, but evenly distributed in all verbal categories in the rest of the Germanic languages. Again, using Norwegian as the example, all main verbs, modals and auxiliaries have a full paradigm of finite and non-finite forms in Norwegian.

What is gained by this approach is not only trying to provide the differences regarding feature make-up of verbal categories with something more than diacritics, i.e. a finiteness feature which is (mostly) morphologically encoded and hence ought to be readily detectable and thus learnable by children. In comparing English to Norwegian specifically we find a pattern in which the constructions and operations that ask for or reject, respectively, a finiteness feature in Norwegian are the same ones that ask for wiz. reject an auxiliary in English. In Eide's proposal, this is the observation serving as the primary building block for an approach claiming the importance of morphologically expressed finiteness to syntactic operations.

In many seminal works within the Principles and Parameters framework, the status and behavior of expletives have been given great significance, and impersonal constructions, like existential constructions and passives, have been utilized to shed light on the make-up of the finite T in natural languages. It is within this tradition that Tor Åfarli addresses the status of agreement features in finiteness-related phenomena in his paper. Specifically, he claims that agreement cannot be a universal ingredient of finite T universally, an assumption otherwise often entertained within many analyses in the Principles and Parameters framework especially of the English expletive constructions. Instead, he argues that unvalued agreement features (i.e. agreement probes) in finite T exist only if there is a visible subject-verb agreement in the language. Åfarli reaches at this conclusion via a comparison of the familiar English expletive constructions with impersonal constructions in several Norwegian dialects.

The impersonal constructions in many Norwegian dialects exhibit a pattern that on the surface resembles, but also differs from, the familiar facts in English. Just like there is an interaction between the type of expletive and the type of associate licensed or required in an English expletive construction as regards agreement matching (cf. (21)), there is an interesting interaction in these aforementioned dialects between the agreement properties of the passive participle and the particular type of expletive that occurs in the sentence (cf. (22)). Note that although there is no visible agreement between the finite verb and subject in Norwegian (including these dialects), there is visible agreement between the passive participle and the postverbal DP, provided the expletive is *der* (the cognate of English *there*), cf. ((22bc)). Expletive *det* (corresponding to English *it*) does not trigger agreement between the passive participle and the postverbal DP; cf. (22b). Instead the expletive (*det*) seems to be valuating the agreement features of the participle in such instances, cf. (22 a).

(21) a. It/*There is raining outside.
c. There is/*are rain outside.
d. There *is/are raindrops outside.

(22) a. Det vart **skote** eit dyr. (subject & participle are n, SG)
it was shot an animal
'An animal was shot.'

b. Det vart **skote** fleire elgar/dyr. (subject & participle are n, SG)
it was shot many elks/animals
'Many elks/animals were shot.'

c. Der vart **skotne** fleire
there was shot many
elgar/dyr. (participle & postverbal DP are m/n, PL)
elks/animals
'Many elks/animals were shot.'

Åfarli compares the valuation procedures of passive participles in the Norwegian dialects with the valuation procedure of finite T in languages like English, which exhibit this type of finite T agreement. He assumes that English *there* and Norwegian *der* are similar not only in being adverb-based and cognates, but also that they are both bereft of agreement features and hence unable to value the unvalued agreement features of a verbal probe, whether this probe is finite T (as in English) or the passive participle (as in the relevant Norwegian dialects). The postverbal DP in the various construction types is likewise subject to close scrutiny, and exhibits parallels, but also some interesting differences as regards valuation and licensing. After considering the cross-linguistic similarities and differences between the relevant impersonal constructions Åfarli reaches at the following conclusions.

a. Finite T (like a passive participle) in a given language/dialect may or may not contain (unvalued) verbal agreement features.
b. Finite T (like a passive participle) contains verbal agreement features only if such features are morphologically visible in the language/dialect (as a type).
c. Unvalued verbal agreement features in finite T (like a passive participle) must be valued by the agreement features of a DP.
d. The agreement features of DPs are inherently valued.

These investigations show that agreement cannot be an essential ingredient in finite T, and has potentially far-reaching theoretical ramifications regarding questions about the relation between agreement and case licensing. It also links up to Cowper's paper (this volume), as she too reaches the conclusion that agreement cannot be a obligatory ingredient of (syntactic) finiteness.

Finiteness and response particles in West Flemish is the title of the contribution by Liliane Haegeman and Andrew Weir. This paper provides evidence that even clausal proforms may contain reflexes of finiteness, specifically, the spell-out of φ-features (agreement markings). In this case, the agreement markings seem to be an instantiation of finite agreement specific to these particular particles. The authors provide data from the West Flemish Lapscheure dialect, where response particles (a strict root phenomenon) *yes* and *no* come in two variants,[23] one bare variant (*ja* 'yes' and *nee* 'no') and one agreeing variant (e.g. *ja-g* 'yes-you' and *nee-g* 'no-you'). The latter group includes specialized reversal particles serving to deny or reverse a declarative statement, seemingly composed of the agreeing particles *ja* 'yes' and *nee* 'no' augmented with additional morphology, a 'reversal schwa' (*ja-g-e* 'oh yes, you do', *nee-g-e* 'oh no, you don't'). Haegeman and Weir consider some earlier analyses of this phenomenon, in particular the analysis by Van Craenenbroeck (2010) of the corresponding particles in the Wambeek dialect, and conclude that a different analysis is needed to account for the Lapscheure data, especially since the type of agreement displayed by these particles is not the type of "postverbal" agreement visible on the V2 finite verb and the complementizer in finite embedded clauses, but is in fact more similar to the subject pronoun in preverbal position. A PF-deletion type of analysis (where the clausal complement of the response particle is assumed to be elided whereas only the subject clitic remains overt, attached to the response particle) is also not so straight-forwardly implemented, since whereas PF-deletion in general is optional, a clausal complement of an agreeing response particle where the clausal complement supplies everything but the subject cannot be overtly realized as an alternative to "PF-deletion": An overtly realized clause after a response particle needs to contain its own subject.

Haegeman and Weir take their lead from Van Craenenbroeck (2010) that a TP proform is involved in these structures, and from Krifka (2013) they adopt the idea that the particles *ja/nee* are on fact themselves the TP proforms. This explains why these particles cannot co-occur with clausal remnants (i.e. the purported "complement" of the subject clitic) since *ja/nee* are in fact clauses themselves, or more accurately, they are clausal proforms. These particular clausal preforms are drawn from the lexicon with phi-features that are spelled out as agreement. Agreeing *ja/nee* interact with clausal syntax but the subject marking is not itself derived in the

23. A similar situation exists in other, neighboring dialects.

narrow syntax. The authors now use phonological criteria to demonstrate that the schwa marking the reversal particles must be inflections rather than anything else. And if this schwa is a type of inflection, this implies that the agreement marking infixed between the response particle and the schwa must also be a type of inflection, it could not be a clitic (or else it would display a behavior with no precedent elsewhere in West Flemish morphology).

The TP proform, according to the analysis, moves to the left periphery in order to satisfy the V2 requirement, which (following Haegeman 1996) is a movement to the left peripheral Fin head. Since V2 is a root phenomenon in this dialect, this explains the strict root property of these agreeing response particles. SubjP, a specialized functional projection for subjects (Rizzi 2006; Rizzi & Schlonsky 2006, 2007) is another ingredient of the analysis. SubjP hosts the subject criterion, serving the discourse function of encoding the "subject of predication" of a clause. In Rizzi and Schlonsky's system the head Fin can sometimes be enriched with nominal features (φ-features) and satisfy the subject criterion, as long as this Fin+phi head is independently checked by the presence of a constituent with matching φ-features in Spec-FinP. The agreement markings of the response particles allow these elements to satisfy the Subject Criterion, since the Fin+phi head essentially has the semantics of a pronoun.

In the remainder of their paper, Haegeman and Weir demonstrate how co-occurrence restrictions of various discourse particles (*ba*) and light-verbs (*doen*) can be derived within their analysis, implying for instance that the reversal morphology displayed in the reversal response particles drives movement to a high PolFocP (Holmberg 2001, 2007, 2013) scoping over FinP, SubjP and the TP where the response particles are base generated.

Whereas e.g. Cowper (this volume) relies on a purely syntactic definition of finiteness, Marleen van de Vate and Tonjes Veenstra opt for a semantically based definition of finiteness in their paper. In order to answer the question whether the English/Portuguese-based creole language Saamáka (or Saramaccan) distinguishes between finite and non-finite clauses, they firstly carefully examine the previous proposals on this subject, including a thorough survey of the literature on the purported finite v. non-finite distinction in the relevant creole language Papiamentu. Secondly they present an analysis of embedded clauses in Saamáka headed by the particle *fu*, which they analyze as a subjunctive/irrealis complementizer (following e.g. Damonte 2002 and Aboh 2006). Since there is a general consensus that there do exist finite clauses in Saamáka (in fact Bickerton 1981, 1984 and Byrne 1987 claim that all clauses are finite in Saamáka), if van de Vate and Veenstra succeed in finding evidence that there exist non-finite clauses, one might assume that the finite vs. non-finite distinction has been established for this language.

Drawing on the discussion surrounding the finiteness distinction in Papiamientu, indeed a topic of many debates, van de Vate and Veenstra state the following:

"Whether the language has this distinction has not been settled yet. A reason for this is that the authors have different ideas regarding the definition of the category of finiteness, and this makes it rather difficult to compare their findings". Mufwene and Dijkhoff (1989), for instance, argue that finiteness is a morphological distinction, and that it is a prototypical inflectional category. Since there is no cross-linguistic pattern of semantic and syntactic characteristics, it is rather difficult to define it in another way. Creole languages are morphologically poor and thus Mufwene and Dijkhoff claim that these languages do not exhibit the finite v. non-finite distinction. Kouwenberg (1990) on the other hand argues that Papiamientu does distinguish between finite and infinitival clauses on the basis of the possibility of overt realization of tense. She notes that certain embedded clauses without overt morphology are bereft of TAM markings, and these clauses must hence be non-finite. The corresponding clauses with overt subjects accept TAM markings and hence count as finite.

Van de Vate and Veenstra as mentioned above base their notion of finiteness on the semantic aspects of finiteness, and to this end they utilize the finiteness theory of Klein (1992, 1998, 2006, 2009). In this theory the semantic contribution of finiteness is to function as a carrier of the features *Assertion* and *Topic Time.* Three time spans are distinguished, Time of Utterance (TU), Topic Time (TT) ad Time of Situation (TSit). Topic Time refers to the time for which a particular utterance makes an assertion, referring to a time span to which the assertion made is constrained. Tense expresses a temporal ordering between Time of Utterance and Topic Time, whereas Aspect expresses a temporal ordering relation between Topic Time and Time of Situation. To Klein, finiteness is not merely a morphological category, but a host for the crucial elements Topic Time and Assertion. Assertion determines the illocutionary force of a sentence. Applying Klein's theory to Saamáka, van de Vate & Veenstra investigate whether the chosen embedded clause types headed by *fu* are in fact capable of expressing either of the features assertion or topic time.

The outcome of their investigation is that *fu*-headed clauses are not capable of expressing Assertion, since the eventuality embedded under *fu* is always interpreted as not realized, not having obtained, and hence not asserted at the Time of Utterance. Moreover, after demonstrating that although *fu* may embed the particle *bi* which is sometimes analyzed as a tense head, the authors argue that *bi* is in fact something else, namely an anchor time (which is different form a tense head). Again, since the eventuality in question is irrealis and there is no claim that it has ontological existence, there is no need to place this eventuality on a time line. Hence such clauses do not have a Topic Time in the relevant sense. Therefore, they see their hypothesis as proven, that Saamáka indeed employs infinitival, non-finite clauses incapable of any of the semantic characteristic features of finite clauses, i.e. Topic Time and Assertion.

Finally the authors sketch a syntactic analysis of the particle *fu* within a cartographic approach (Rizzi 1997, Cinque 1999), where *fu* is assumed to occupy a higher Fin-related head, in a split-FinP analysis where Fin^0 is split into two distinct heads with different properties.

Turning now to the acquisition papers of this volume, Marit Westergaard's paper deals with the much-discussed purported causal relation between verb movement, specifically verb second in Germanic languages, and the presence of finite morphology on the verb in first language acquisition. Children tend to go through a stage in which they use uninflected forms, typically infinitives (often referred to as Optional Infinives, OIs), in contexts where an adult speaker of the same language would use an inflected, finite form. The occurrence of OIs is often said to correlate with word order phenomena such that only finite forms surface in the verb second position, whereas the uninflected OI shows up in a non-V2 position (e.g. the clause-final position in the acquisition of German and Dutch). An extensive literature on this topic is reviewed and discussed as a backdrop to the author's own investigation into word order and finiteness morphology in the first language acquisition of root *wh*-questions by Norwegian and English-speaking children. What is usually meant by "finite morphology" in this literature is the presence of agreement markers. This is the case for instance in variants of what is known as the Rich Agreement Hypothesis (cf. e.g. Rohrbacher 1999),[24] where rich person and number agreement is seen as a prerequisite to the existence of verb movement in a language and correspondingly in the acquisition of that language. Sometimes, a particular exponent of agreement is given a distinguished role as a trigger for the acquisition of verb movement, e.g. 2Psg (as in Clahsen & Penke 1992), or in the requirement that the distinction between 1st and 2nd person be visible on regular verbs in at least some tenses (Rohrbacher 1999: 116). Some authors argue instead that it is finiteness itself that is of primary importance in the link between morphology and verb movement, independently of agreement morphology (cf. e.g. Verrips & Weissenborn 1992). Westergaard also reviews the literature advocating that there is no such causal relation between morphological tense/agreement markers and word order. Several of these approaches (e.g. Plunkett & Strömquist 1990; Boser et al. 1992; Josefsson 1999) propose instead that what is really at stake here is the omission of auxiliaries, where the "OI" verb form and the corresponding lack of finite inflection are

24. In fact this is a bit inaccurate, since the Rich Agreement Hypothesis usually deals with the movement from V-to-I and not the movement from I-to-C; the latter usually thought to be the relevant movement for verb second. However, there is a general consensus that the former is a prerequisite for the latter in that there is no I-to-C movement without a preceding movement of V-to-I.

in fact target-like. The finite part of the complex verb construction, which is supposed to appear in the V2 position,[25] is simply missing from the utterance. Mostly, the omitted auxiliary is a modal, as can be evidenced from the modal reading of the relevant expressions, and also by the fact that the OI is a target-like infinitival form.

Westergaard joins forces with the latter camp and shows that in a thorough investigation of two corpora containing the production data of English and Norwegian children the vacillation between V2 and non-V2 word order in root *wh*-questions is by no means regulated by the presence or absence of finiteness markers in the clause. Instead, this variation in child Norwegian can be explained on the basis of a range of "micro-cues", e.g. the complexity of the *wh*-phrase (disyllabic versus monosyllabic), the complexity of the subject (as phrasal or pronominal), and the type of verb (especially the copula versus lexical verb), and information structure (especially known versus new referent). The literature on these constructions has observed that there is a difference in frequency between English children and children acquiring other Germanic languages with respect to the occurrence and interpretation of OIs versus finite verb forms, and with respect to lack of subject-aux inversion in *wh*-questions (cf. e.g. Klima & Bellugi 1966); a difference which has been attributed to presence versus absence of a positive value of the V2 parameter (e.g. Wexler 1999). V2 movement affects only finite verbs; hence children learning a language such as German or Dutch will only provide finite structures in *wh*-questions. Westergaard argues instead that the difference is due to the fact that English children require the use of auxiliaries to a much greater extent than do Norwegian children, since in Norwegian all verbs can take part in the subject-verb inversion (or V2), whereas English children require an auxiliary to fulfill the "residual V2" requirement in English root wh-clauses (since this movement is limited to auxiliaries in English). Also English children have to face the challenge of acquiring the progressive employing *be* as a functional element, a construction absent from Norwegian. Since auxiliaries are acquired late in all clause types, this gives the Norwegian children an advantage. They usually do not need an auxiliary for a target-like root *wh*-question, as any verb can move to second position in Norwegian wh-questions. Westergaard shows that the auxiliaries *do* and *be* pose the biggest challenge for English-speaking children, accounting for approximately 90% of the non-finite wh-questions produced. These auxiliaries are not relevant for Norwegian children, and Norwegian-speaking children are thus faced with problematic auxiliary contexts in wh-questions much less frequently

25. Note that Westergaard follows Rizzi (1996) in assuming that the subject-auxiliary inversion English displays e.g. in root WH-clauses belongs to the same cluster of phenomena as Germanic V2; what he dubs "residual V2" in English.

than English-speaking children. In conclusion, Westergaard argues that the alleged causal correlation between finiteness morphology and syntactic movement does not hold with respect to the acquisition of V2 word order.

The chapter authored by Elma Blom and Nada Vasić deals with finiteness in first and second language acquisition of Dutch. Three groups of informants were tested; two different L1 groups (mean age 7 and mean age 5) and one L2 group (mean age 7; L1 Turkish) where the age and proficiency levels of each group implied that the morphological and syntactic features of finiteness would be in place, and all groups show high accuracy rates as regards obligatory finiteness markers in obligatory contexts. However, the focus of the investigation was what the authors dub *residual errors,* types of errors that tend to linger on even after the stage where morphosyntactic properties of finiteness markings are acquired. These residual errors typically consist in the occasional drop of the finiteness marker suffix, with the most vulnerable inflectional ending seemingly being -t. Recent studies have shown that -t drop is attested at least up until the age of five in certain 2SG and 3SG contexts, where it is obligatory in the target language (cf. Blom 2007; Polišenská 2010). Blom and Vasić wanted to test the hypothesis that phonological properties of the verb form may be at the heart of these residual errors, in particular the aspects pertaining to *phonological complexity* and *sonority* of the consonants in the coda cluster hosting the inflection. Inflecting a verb results in increased complexity of the coda cluster on the suffixation of -t, giving rise to CC or CCC clusters, which may create difficulties in articulatory planning when other words follow the verb (cf. e.g. Blom & Baayen 2013). *The Sonority Sequencing Principle* (Clements 1990), on the other hand, predicts that children may experience particular difficulties with using the *-t* suffix after a plosive sound. The authors pose the following two research questions:

1. Does sonority of the stem-final phoneme affect children's accuracy with the non-syllabic -t inflection?
2. Do L2 children outperform younger Dutch L1 children with matching Dutch proficiency regarding verb inflection use, and is their performance similar to age-matched Dutch L1 peers?

The experiment was set up as part of a larger battery of tests comprising the production and processing of definite articles (Blom & Vasić 2011; Vasić & Blom 2011) and subject-verb agreement. The two most relevant experiments to this investigation were one elicitation task and a repetition task. The elicitation task was an experimental task eliciting 3SG inflection, where the children had to describe pictures by completing a lead-in by the experimenter. The second task was administered to assess whether the children were able to produce the required clusters, a non-word repetition task in which the children repeated words with the same sequence of sounds as in the coda of the 3SG verbs in the inflection test.

The results of the study show that the answer to research question 2 is yes, since the age-matched L1 and L2 groups (mean age 7) did indeed outperform the younger L1 children (mean age 5). This outcome suggests that L2 children can benefit from their L1 in the domain of verb inflection, paralleling findings in other studies on child L2 Dutch e.g. Blom & Baayen 2013) as well as child L2 English (Blom et al. 2012). Regarding research question 1, the outcome of the study suggests that both sonority and complexity are relevant properties affecting children's production of residual finiteness errors. The combination of a stem-final plosive and 3SG -t yields the most marked cluster (plosive-plosive), and children used the 3SG -t inflection more often when the verb stem ended with a sonorant or fricative compared to a plosive. This outcome supports findings in other studies that indicated phonological effects on the use of English verb inflection (e.g. Blom et al. 2012; Blom & Paradis 2013). Cluster complexity seems also to be relevant to inflection production because the verb *drinkt* caused more residual errors than the other two verb forms where the stem ended in a plosive (koopt 'buys' and knipt 'cuts'). Also, the group of L1 children who failed to produce *drinkt* in the inflection task overlapped with the group that failed to produce *binkt* in the non-word task.

Interestingly, the children also showed asymmetries between the inflection task and the non-word repetition task, e.g. when failing to produce the right verb cluster -nkt (as in *drinkt*) in the inflection task they left out the inflection -t (drink), while in the non-word repetition task they left out -k (bint). This suggests that there exist differences related to retrieving and producing an inflected verb versus repeating and producing a non-word.

Blom and Vasić mention that their results may be relevant to and compatible with a Missing Surface Inflection Hypothesis (MSIH) approach (Haznedar & Schwartz 1997; Prévost 2003). Here L2 children's errors with finiteness markings result from insertion of a morphological default (e.g. a zero suffix) in a functional position that is fully specified for Tense and Agreement. Ionin and Wexler (2002: 118) state that zero-marked forms are "finite forms that have simply not received morphological agreement marking and that can be used across all tense/agreement contexts". Prévost (2003: 88) assumes that in child L2 German such verb forms "are unspecified for person features but specified as [+finite]". If retrieval of the correct form fails, the default rule applies, resulting in omission of finiteness markings on verbs that are syntactically finite. Blom and Vasić's results do not completely adhere to the predictions of this hypothesis, since a default zero-suffix as in the MSIH would predict consistency in errors, whereas the present study also reveals that children not only produced errors taking the form of bare forms, but also substituted verb forms (e.g. use of *-en* inflection).

The paper concludes that there is evidence for the hypothesis that phonological factors impact on Dutch L1 and L2 children's residual errors with finiteness, and asymmetries between the outcomes of the two tasks described above point to an interplay between phonological and morphological factors. The paper thus sheds new light on the relation between the morphosyntax of finiteness and the overt realization of finiteness markers, which are clearly subject to phonological constraints.

Fufen Jin and Kristin Melum Eide investigate the acquisition of finiteness-related phenomena in Norwegian by a bilingual Norwegian-Mandarin child in their paper *Contradictory parameter settings in one mind (...)*. The child is born into a Chinese immigrant family in Trondheim, Norway, and whereas the language spoken in the home is definitely Mandarin, he is exposed to Norwegian on a daily basis in the day care center (8 hours a day, five days a week from the age of 15 months old). The child has to face all the finiteness-related macro-parametric differences between Norwegian and Mandarin listed and discussed in the paper; e.g. the presence v. absence of finiteness markings, the presence v. absence of V2 in main clause declaratives, the presence v. absence of V1 in imperatives and yes/no-questions, the presence v. absence of verb movement and *wh*-movement in root wh-clauses, the different word order of main clause declaratives and embedded declaratives in Norwegian and the absence of such an asymmetry in Mandarin (these differences are likely to be susceptible to cross-linguistic influence and are hence discussed at some length in the paper). In addition, the child also has to cope with a range of micro-parametric differences between the two variants of Norwegian he is exposed to on a daily basis in the day-care center, e.g. regarding the presence v. absence of verb movement in certain *wh*-clauses and the actual morphological exponents in the inflectional paradigm encoding finiteness. The two variants in question are *Østnorsk* and *Trønder*, where the first variant corresponds to a spoken version of the written standard *bokmål*, typically found in the area around the capital of Oslo. The *Trønder* variant is spoken in the middle of Norway in the areas surrounding the regional capital Trondheim. Whereas the child is exposed to the *Østnorsk* variant mainly through children's books in the daily one-hour reading time in the day-care center and cartoons through his TV time in the afternoons, the three main care-givers in the day-care center were all native speakers of the local variant *Trønder* and thus contributed the child with a robust exposure to this variant.

The recordings were collected during a period of one year, from the boy was 5.11 years until he was 6.11. That is, he is about the same age as the informants of the study reported in Blom and Vasić's paper, this volume. As mentioned in their paper, the morphosyntactic features of finiteness in Germanic languages are often observed to be largely in place at this age, even for bilingual children. However, since this is to a certain extent a trilingual child exposed to three different languages, and since there exist in fact almost no investigations of bilingual and trilingual Norwegian children of this age, the authors anticipate that there are potentially interesting features to be found regarding language acquisition of finiteness-related phenomena even in a small-scale study such as this, in the production of one child recorded over the period of one year.

What has been the topic of some controversy is whether the course and developmental patterns of bilingual acquisition is comparable to that of monolingual acquisition. Whereas researchers in the "autonomous" camp (e.g. De Houwer 1990; Meisel 2001; Hinzelin 2003) have advocated the view that in bilingual acquisition, the two grammatical systems develop independently of each other, those who adhere to the "interdependence hypothesis" (e.g. Hulk & Müller 2000; Yip & Matthews 2007) predict that there is a systematic influence of the grammar of one language on the grammar of the other language during acquisition. Accordingly, they argue that the course and developmental patterns of bilingual acquisition can be quite different from those of monolingual acquisition. On this background, Jin and Eide find it interesting to investigate whether this Mandarin boy (named Lele) has the same linguistic competence as his monolingual peers regarding the selected finiteness-related phenomena.

The outcome of the investigation is that the bilingual informant Lele performs at an attainment level at least comparable to his monolingual Norwegian peers regarding finiteness-related phenomena. His production data in Norwegian indicates little difficulty in setting the contradictory parameters to their proper values. He is also sensitive to micro-cues e.g. placement of verbs occurring with simplex *wh*-words, presence and absence of adverbs that trigger non-V2 word order in root declaratives, as well as the presence of connectives, coordinators, and left dislocation constructions. On the morphological level, his results were compared to the results of acquisition of tense inflection reported for monolingual Norwegian children at ages 4, 6 and 8 (Simonsen & Bjerkan 1998). There is a tendency among his monolingual peers to overgeneralize the paradigm of the large weak class WL into the small weak class WS and the strong verb class, and Lele exhibits the same tendency. In the choice of exponent for a certain inflected form there is some cross-linguistic influence from one Norwegian variety to another, that is, on the micro-level.

On the macro-level, the authors find little evidence of cross-linguistic influence from Mandarin into Lele's spoken Norwegian. The only clear verb placement errors observed possibly resulting from transfer of Mandarin features are uttered under circumstances quite challenging communicatively and emotionally. There are certain utterances where the finiteness distinction is not observed as required, e.g. one example where Lele seems to be transferring the construction *Topic chain* from his Mandarin first language. However, the rate at which errors are made regarding both verb placement and inflectional paradigms is no higher than monolingual Norwegian children at a comparable age. Thus the tentative results of this study indicate that at least for this bilingual informant at this specific age, no developmental delay or differing developmental path can be observed as compared to that of monolingual Norwegian-speaking children. The authors thus conclude that their findings are more consistent with the autonomous hypothesis.

References

Aboh, Enoch Oladé. 2006. Complementation in Saramaccan and Gungbe: The case of C-type particles. *Natural language and Linguistic Theory* 24: 1–55. doi:10.1007/s11049-005-1815-4

Adger, David. 2007. Three domains of finiteness: A minimalist perspective. In Irina Nikolaeva (ed.), 23–58.

Akmajian, Adrian. 1984. Sentence types and form-function fit. *Natural Language and Linguistic Theory* 2: 1–23. doi:10.1007/BF00233711

Alboiu, Gabriela & Motapanyane, Virginia. 2000. The generative approach to Romanian grammar: An overview. In *Comparative Studies in Romanian Syntax*, Virginia Motapayane (ed.), 1–48. Oxford: Elsevier.

Alexiadou, Artemis & Anagnostopoulou, Elena. 1999. EPP without Spec, IP. In *Specifiers: Minimalist Approaches*. David Adger, Susan Pintzuk, Bernadette Plunkett & George Tsoulas (eds.), 93–109. Oxford: OUP.

Amritavalli, Raghavachari. 2014. Separating tense and finiteness: Anchoring in Dravidian. *Natural Language and Linguistic Theory* 32: 283–306. doi:10.1007/s11049-013-9219-3

Bayer, Josef. 1984. Comp in Bavarian syntax. *The Linguistic Review* 3: 209–274. doi:10.1515/tlir.1984.3.3.209

Bianchi, Valentina. 2003. On finiteness as logophoric anchoring. In *Temps et points de vue/ Tense and Point of View*, Jacqueline Guéron & Liliane Tasmovski (eds.), 213–246. Nanterre: Université Paris X.

Bickerton, Derek. 1981. *Roots of Language*. Ann Arbor MI: Karoma.

Bickerton, Derek. 1984. The Language Bioprogram Hypothesis. *The Behavioral and Brain Sciences* 7: 173–188. doi:10.1017/S0140525X00044149

Bisang, Walter. 2001. Finite vs. non finite languages. In *Language Typology and Language Universals*, Vol. 2, Martin Haspelmath, Ekkehard König, Wulf Oesterreicher & Wolfgang Raible (eds.), 1400–1413. Berlin: Mouton de Gruyter.

Blom, Elma. 2007. Modality, infinitives and finite bare verbs in Dutch and English child language. *Language Acquisition* 14(1): 75–113. doi:10.1080/10489220701331821

Blom, Elma & Baayen, Harald. 2013. The impact of verb form, sentence position, home language and L2 proficiency on subject-verb agreement in child L2 Dutch. *Applied Psycholinguistics* 34(4): 777–811. doi:10.1017/S0142716412000021

Blom, Elma, Paradis, Johanne & Sorenson-Duncan, Tamara. 2012. Effects of input properties, vocabulary size and L1 on the development of third person singular *-s* in child L2 English. *Language Learning* 62(3): 965–994. doi:10.1111/j.1467-9922.2012.00715.x

Blom, Elma & Vasić, Nada. 2011. The production and processing of determiner-noun agreement in child L2 Dutch. *Linguistic Approaches to Bilingualism* 1–3: 265–290. doi:10.1075/lab.1.3.03blo

Blom, Elma & Paradis, Johanne. 2013. Past tense production by English second language learners with and without language impairment. *Journal of Speech, Language and Hearing Research* 56: 281–294. doi:10.1044/1092-4388(2012/11-0112)

Boser, Katharina, Lust, Barbara, Santelmann, Lynn & Whitman, John. 1992. The syntax of V2 in early child German grammar: The Strong Continuity Hypothesis. *Proceedings of the North-eastern Linguistic Society* 22: 51–66.

Byrne, Francis. 1987. *Grammatical Relations in a Radical Creole. Verb Complementation in Saramaccan* [Creole Language Library 3]. Amsterdam: John Benjamins. doi:10.1075/cll.3

Chomsky, Noam. 1973. Conditions on transformations. In *A Festschrift for Morris Halle*, Stephen R. Anderson & Paul Kiparsky (eds.), 232–285. New York NY: Holt, Rinehart and Winston.

Chomsky, Noam. 1980. On binding. *Linguistic Inquiry* 11: 1–46.

Chomsky, Noam. 1981. *Lectures on Government and Binding*. Dordrecht: Foris.

Chomsky, Noam. 1995. *The Minimalist Program*. Cambridge MA: The MIT Press.

Chomsky, Noam. 2000. Minimalist inquiries: The framework. In *Step by Step: Essays on Minimalist Syntax in Honor of Howard Lasnik*, Roger Martin, David Michaels & Juan Uriagereka (eds.), 89–115. Cambridge MA: The MIT Press.

Chomsky, Noam. 2001. Derivation by phase. In *Ken Hale. A Life in Language*, Michael Kenstowicz (ed.), 1–52. Cambridge MA: The MIT Press.

Cinque, Guglielmo. 1999. Adverbs and Functional Heads: A Cross-linguistic Perspective. Oxford: OUP.

Clahsen, Harald & Penke, Martina. 1992. The acquisition of agreement morphology and its syntactic consequences: New evidence on German child language from the Simone-corpus. In *The Acquisition of Verb Placement: Functional Categories and V2 Phenomena in Language Acquisition*, Jürgen Meisel (ed.), 181–223. Dordrecht: Kluwer.

Clements, George Nick. 1990. The role of the sonority cycle in core syllabification. In *Papers in Laboratory Phonology* I, John Kingston & Mary Beckman (eds.), 283–333. Cambridge: CUP. doi:10.1017/CBO9780511627736.017

Comrie, Bernard. 1976. Aspect. Cambridge: CUP.

Comrie, Bernard. 1986. Tense in indirect speech, *Folia Linguistica* 20: 265–296. doi:10.1515/flin.1986.20.3-4.265

Cowper, Elizabeth. 2005. The geometry of interpretable features: Infl in English and Spanish. *Language* 81(1): 10–46.

van Craenenbroeck, Jeroen. 2010. *Ellipsis in Dutch Dialects*. Oxford: OUP.

Damonte, Federico. 2002. The complementizer layer in Saramaccan. In *Current Issues in Generative Grammar. 10th Colloquium on Generative Grammar, Selected Papers*, Manuel Leonetti, Olga Fernandez Soriano & Victoria Escandell Vidal (eds.), 31–50. Alcalá de Henares: University of Alcalá de Henares.

Demirdache, Hamida & Uribe-Etxebarria, Myriam. 2000. The primitives of temporal relations. In *Step by Step: Essays on Minimalist Syntax in Honor of Howard Lasnik*, Roger Martin, David Michaels & Juan Uriagereka (eds.), 157–186. Cambridge MA: The MIT Press.

Demirdache, Hamida & Uribe-Etxebarria, Myriam. 2004. The syntax of time adverbs. In *The Syntax of Time* [Current Studies in Linguistics 37], Jacqueline Guéron & Jacqueline Lecarme (eds.), 143–179. Cambridge MA: The MIT Press.

De Houwer, Annick. 1990. *The Acquisition of Two Languages from Birth: A case Study*. Cambridge: CUP. doi:10.1017/CBO9780511519789

den Besten, Hans. 1977/1983. On the interaction of root transformations and lexical deletive rules. Ms, University of Amsterdam. Published 1981 in *Groninger Arbeiten zur Germanischen Linguistik* 20, 1–78; republished in Werner Abraham (ed.). 1983. *On the Formal Syntax of Westgermania* [Linguistik Aktuell/Linguistics Today 3], 47–131. Amsterdam: John Benjamins. doi:10.1075/la.3.03bes

Dobrovie-Sorin, Carmen. 2001. Head-to-Head Merge in Balkan subjunctives and locality. In *Comparative Syntax of Balkan Languages*, María Luisa Rivero & Angela Ralli (eds.). Oxford: OUP.

Eide, Kristin Melum. 2005. *Norwegian Modals* [Studies in Generative Grammar 74]. Berlin: Mouton De Gruyter.

Eide, Kristin Melum. 2009a. Tense, finiteness and the survive principle: Temporal chains in a crash-proof grammar. In *Towards a Derivational Syntax: Survive-minimalism* [Linguistik Aktuell/Linguistics Today 144], Michael T. Putnam (ed.) 91–132. Amsterdam: John Benjamins. doi:10.1075/la.144.05eid

Eide, Kristin Melum. 2009b. Finiteness: The haves and the have-nots. In *Advances in Comparative Germanic Syntax* [Linguistik Aktuell/Linguistics Today 141], Artemis Alexiadou, Jorge Hankamer, Thomas McFadden, Justin Nuger & Florian Schäfer (eds.), 357–390. Amsterdam: John Benjamins. doi:10.1075/la.141.15fin

Frege, Gottlob. 1892. Der Gedanke. *Logische Untersuchungen*, Günther Patzig (ed.). 1986(3), 30–53. Göttingen: Vandenhoeck & Ruprecht.

George, Leland M. & Cornfilt, Jaklin. 1981. Finiteness and boundedness in Turkish. In *Binding and Filtering,* Frank Heny (ed.), 105–127. London: Croom Helm.

Givón, Talmy. 1990. *Syntax. A Functional-typological Introduction,* Vol. II. Amsterdam: John Benjamins. doi: 10.1075/z.50

Gretsch, Petra & Perdue, Clive. 2007. Finiteness in first and second language acquisition. In Irina Nikolaeva (ed.), 432–484.

Grohmann, Kleanthes. 2000. Null modals in Germanic (and Romance): Infinitival exclamatives. *Belgian Journal of Linguistics* 14: 43–61. doi:10.1075/bjl.14.04gro

Haegeman, Liliane. 1985. INFL, COMP and nominative case assignment in Flemish infinitivals. In *Features and Projections,* Pieter Muysken & Henk van Riemsdijk (eds.), 123–137. Dordrecht: Foris.

Haegeman, Liliane. 1992. *Theory and Description in Generative Syntax. A Case Study in West Flemish.* Cambridge: CUP.

Haegeman, Liliane. 1996. Verb second, the split CP and null subjects in early Dutch finite clauses. *GenGenP.* ⟨http://ling.auf.net/lingBuzz/001059⟩

Harley, Heidi & Ritter, Elizabeth. 2002. Person and number in pronouns: A feature-geometric analysis. *Language* 78(3): 482–526. doi:10.1353/lan.2002.0158

Haznedar, Belma & Schwartz, Bonnie D. 1997. Are there optional infinitives in child L2 acquisition? In *Proceedings of the 21st Annual Boston University Conference on Language Development.* Elizabeth Hughes, Mary Hughes & Annabel Greenhill (eds.), 257–268. Somerville MA: Cascadilla Press.

Hellan, Lars.1988. *Anaphora in Norwegian and the Theory of Grammar.* Dordrecht: Foris.

Hinzelin, Marc-Olivier. 2003. The acquisition of subjects in Bilingual children: Pronoun use in Portuguese-German children. In *(In)Vulnerable Domains in Multilingualism* [Hamburg Studies on Multilingualism 1], Natascha Müller (ed.), 107–137. Amsterdam: John Benjamins. doi:10.1075/hsm.1.05hin

Holmberg, Anders. 2001. The syntax of yes and no in Finnish. *Studia Linguistica* 55(2): 141–175. doi:10.1111/1467-9582.00077

Holmberg, Anders. 2007. Null subjects and polarity focus. *Studia Linguistica* 61(3): 212–236. doi:10.1111/j.1467-9582.2007.00135.x

Holmberg, Anders. 2013. The syntax of answers to polar questions in English and Swedish. *Lingua* 128: 31–50. doi:10.1016/j.lingua.2012.10.018

Holmberg, Anders. 2015. Verb second. In *Syntax -Theory and Analysis: An International Handbook,* Tibor Kiss & Artemis Alexiadou (eds.), 342–382. Berlin: Walter de Gruyter.

Holmberg, Anders, Nikanne, Urpo, Oraviita, Irmeli, Reime, Hannu & Trosterud, Trond. 1993. The structure of INFL and the finite clause in Finnish. In *Case and Other Functional Categories in Finnish Syntax*, Anders Holmberg & Urpo Nikanne (eds.), 177–206. Berlin: Mouton de Gruyter.
Holmberg, Anders & Platzack, Christer. 1988. On the role of inflection in Scandinavian Syntax. *Working Papers in Scandinavian Syntax* 42: 25–42.
Holmberg, Anders & Platzack, Christer. 1995. *The Role of Inflection in Scandinavian Syntax.* Oxford: OUP.
Hornstein, Norbert. 1990. *As Time Goes By – Tense and Universal Grammar.* Cambridge MA: The MIT Press.
Hulk, Aafke & Müller, Natascha. 2000. Bilingual first language acquisition at the interface between syntax and pragmatics. *Bilingualism: Language and Cognition* 3: 227–244. doi:10.1017/S1366728900000353
Ionin, Tania & Wexler, Ken. 2002. Why is 'is' easier than 's'? Acquisition of tense/agreement morphology by child L2-English learners. *Second Language Research* 18(2): 95–136. doi:10.1191/0267658302sr195oa
Josefsson, Gunlög. 1999. Non-finite root clauses in Swedish child language. *Working Papers in Scandinavian Syntax* 63: 105–150.
Klein, Wolfgang. 1992. The present perfect puzzle. *Language* 68: 525–552. doi:10.2307/415793
Klein, Wolfgang. 1994. *Time in Language.* London: Routledge.
Klein, Wolfgang. 1998. Assertion and finiteness. In *Issues in the Theory of Language Acquisition: Essays in Honor of Jürgen Weissenborn*, Norbert Dittmar & Zvi Penner (eds.), 225–245. Bern: Peter Lang.
Klein, Wolfgang. 2006. On finiteness. In *Semantics in Acquisition,* Veerle van Geenhoven (ed.), 245–272. Heidelberg: Springer. doi:10.1007/1-4020-4485-2_10
Klein, Wolfgang. 2009. Finiteness, Universal Grammar and the language faculty. In *Crosslinguistic Approaches to the Psychology of Language: Research in the Tradition of Dan Isaac Slobin,* Jiansheng Guo, Elena Lieven, Nancy Budwig, Susan Ervin-Tripp, Keiko Nakamura & Seyda Ozcaliskan (eds.), 333–344. New York NY: Psychology Press.
Klima, Edward S. & Bellugi [-Klima], Ursula. 1966. Syntactic regularities in the speech of children. In *Psycholinguistic Papers,* John Lyons & Roger J. Wales (eds.), 183–208. Edinburgh: EUP. Also published in Barbara Lust & Claire Foley (eds.). 2004. *First Language Acquisition: The Essential Readings,* 344–366. Oxford: Blackwell.
Koptjevskaja-Tamm, Maria. 1994. Finiteness. In *The Encyclopedia of Language and Linguistics,* Ronald E. Asher (ed.), 1245–1248. Oxford: Pergamon.
Kouwenberg, Silvia. 1990. Complementizer 'pa'. *Journal of Pidgin and Creole Languages* 5: 39–52. doi:10.1075/jpcl.5.1.03kou
Krifka, Manfred. 2013. Response particles as propositional anaphors. In *Proceedings of SALT 23,* Todd Snider (ed.), 1–18. Ithaca NY: CLC Publications.
Landau, Idan. 2004. The scale of finiteness and the calculus of control. *Natural Language and Linguistic Theory* 22: 811–877. doi:10.1007/s11049-004-4265-5
Lasser, Ingeborg. 1997. *Finiteness in Adult and Child German* [MPI Series in Psycholinguistics 8]. Wageningen: Ponsen and Looijen.
Ledgeway, Adam. 1998. Variation in the Romance infinitive: The case of southern Calabrian inflected infinitive. *Transactions of the Philological Society* 96(1): 1–61. doi:10.1111/1467-968X.00023

Ledgeway, Adam. 2000. *A Comparative Syntax of the Dialects of Southern Italy: A Minimalist Approach*. Oxford: Blackwell.

Ledgeway, Adam. 2007. Diachrony and finiteness: Subordination in the dialects of southern Italy. In *Finiteness. Theoretical and Empirical Foundations*, Irina Nikolaeva (ed.), 335–431. Oxford: OUP.

Lødrup, Helge. 2009. Animacy and long distance binding in Norwegian. *Nordic Journal of Linguistics* 32: 111–136. doi:10.1017/S0332586509002054

Lohnstein, Horst. 2000. *Satzmodus – kompositionell. Zur Parametrizierung der Modus-phrase im Deutshen*. Berlin: Akademie-Verlag.

Lohnstein, Horst. 2001. Sentence mood constitution and indefinite noun phrases. *Theoretical Linguistics* 27(2–3): 187–214. Special issue *NP Interpretation and Information Structure*, Klaus von Heusinger & Kerstin Schwabe (eds.). doi:10.1515/thli.2001.27.2-3.187

Lohnstein, Horst & Bredel, Ursula. 2004. Inflectional morphology and sentence mood in German. In Horst Lohstein & Susanne Trissler (eds.), *Syntax and Semantics of the Left Periphery*, 235–264. Berlin: Mouton de Gruyter. doi:10.1515/9783110912111

Maas, Utz. 2004. 'Finite' and 'nonfinite' from a typological perspective. *Linguistics* 42(2): 359–385. doi:10.1515/ling.2004.012

Matthews, Peter H. 1997. *The Concise Oxford Dictionary of Linguistics*. Oxford: OUP.

McFadden, Thomas & Sundaresan, Sandhya. 2014. Finiteness in South Asian languages: An introduction. *Natural language and Linguistic Theory* 32: 1–27. doi:10.1007/s11049-013-9215-7

McWhorter, John. 2005. *Defining Creole*. Oxford: OUP.

Meisel, Jürgen. 2001. The simultaneous acquisition of two first languages: Early differentiation and subsequent development of grammars. In *Trends in Bilingual Acquisition* [Trends in Language Acquisition Research 1], Jasone Cenoz & Fred Genesee (eds.), 11–41. Amsterdam: John Benjamins. doi:10.1075/tilar.1.03mei

Mufwene, Salikoko & Dijkhoff, Marta. 1989. On the so-called 'infinitive' in Atlantic Creoles. *Lingua* 77: 297–330. doi:10.1016/0024-3841(89)90043-0

Muysken, Pieter & Law, Paul. 2001. Creole studies: A theoretical linguist's field guide. *Glot International* 5 (2): 47–57.

Nikolaeva, Irina (ed.). 2007. *Finiteness. Theoretical and Empirical Foundations*. Oxford: OUP.

Nikolaeva, Irina. 2007b. Introduction. In Irina Nikolaeva (ed.), 1–19.

Nikolaeva, Irina. 2007c. Constructional economy and nonfinite independent clauses. In Irina Nikolaeva (ed.), 138–180.

Pesetsky, David & Torrego, Esther. 2001. T-to-C movement: Causes and consequences. In *Ken Hale: A Life in Language*, Michael Kenstowicz (ed.), 355–426. Cambridge MA: The MIT Press.

Pesetsky, David & Torrego, Esther. 2004. Tense, case, and syntactic categories. In *The Syntax of Time*, Jacqueline Guéron & Jacqueline Lecarme (eds.), 495–537. Cambridge MA: The MIT Press.

Pesetsky, David & Torrego, Esther. 2007. The syntax of valuation and the interpretability of features. In *Phrasal and Clausal Architecture: Syntactic Derivation and Interpretation* [Linguistik Aktuell/Linguistics Today 101], Simin Karimi, Vida Samiian & Wendy Wilkins (eds.), 262–294. Amsterdam: John Benjamins. doi:10.1075/la.101.14pes

Platzack, Christer. 1995. The loss of verb second in English and French. In *Clause Structure and Language Change*, Adrian Battye & Ian Roberts (eds.), 200–226. Oxford: OUP.

Platzack, Christer. 2010. *Den fantastiska grammatiken: En minimalistisk beskrivning av Svenskan.* Stockholm: Norstedts.
Plunkett, Kim & Strömqvist, Sven. 1990. The acquisition of Scandinavian languages. *Gothenburg Papers in Theoretical Linguistics* 59.
Polišenská, Daniela. 2010. Dutch children's acquisition of verbal and adjectival inflection. Ph.D. dissertation, University of Amsterdam. ⟨http://www.lotpublications.nl/publish/issues/Polisenska/index.html⟩
Pollock, Jean-Yves. 1989. Verb movement, UG and the structure of IP. *Linguistic Inquiry* 20: 365–424.
Prévost, Philippe. 2003. Truncation and missing surface inflection in initial L2 German. *Studies in Second Language Acquisition* 25: 65–97. doi:10.1017/S0272263103000032
Raposo, Eduardo P. 1987. Case theory and Infl-to-Comp: The inflected infinitive in European Portuguese. *Linguistic Inquiry* 14: 101–136.
Reichenbach, Hans. 1947. *Elements of Symbolic Logic.* New York NY: Macmillan.
Reinhart, Tanya. 2006. *Interface Strategies: Optimal and Costly Computations.* Cambridge MA: The MIT Press.
Reinhart, Tanya & Reuland, Eric. 1993. Reflexivity. *Linguistic Inquiry* 24(4): 657–720.
Reuland, Eric. 2011. *Anaphora and Language Design.* Cambridge MA: The MIT Press.
Reuland, Eric & Sigurjónsdóttir, Sigríður. 1997. Long distance binding in Icelandic: Syntax or discourse? In *Atomism in Binding,* Hans Bennis, Pierre Pica & Johan Rooryck (eds.), 323–334. Dordrecht: Foris.
Ritter, Elizabeth & Wiltschko, Martina. 2005. Anchoring utterances without tense. In *West Coast Conference on Formal Linguistics (WCCFL)* 24, John Alderete, Chung-hye Han & Alexei Kochetov (eds.), 345–351. Somerville MA: Cascadilla Proceedings Project.
Ritter, Elizabeth & Wiltschko, Martina. 2009. Varieties of INFL: TENSE, LOCATION and PERSON. In *Alternatives to Cartography,* Jeroen van Craenenbroeck (ed.), 153–201. Berlin: De Gruyter. doi:10.1515/9783110217124.153
Ritter, Elizabeth & Wiltschko, Martina. 2014. The composition of INFL. An exploration of tense, tenseless languages, and tenseless constructions. *Natural Language and Linguistic Theory* 32: 1331–1386. doi:10.1007/s11049-014-9248-6
Rizzi, Luigi. 1990. On the anaphor agreement effect. *Rivista di Linguistica* 2: 27–42.
Rizzi, Luigi. 1996. Residual verb second and the *wh*-criterion. In *Parameters and Functional Heads,* Adriana Belletti & Luigi Rizzi (eds.), 63–90. Oxford: OUP.
Rizzi, Luigi. 1997. The fine structure of the left periphery. In *Elements of Grammar: Handbook in Generative Syntax,* Liliane Haegeman (ed.), 281–337. Dordrecht: Kluwer.
Rizzi, Luigi. 2006. On the form of chains: Criterial positions and ECP effects. In *Wh-movement: Moving on,* Lisa Lai-shen Cheng & Norbert Corver (eds.), 97–133. Cambridg, MA: The MIT Press.
Rizzi, Luigi & Shlonsky, Ur. 2006. Satisfying the subject criterion by a non-subject: English locative inversion and heavy NP shift. In *Phases of Interpretation,* Mara Frascarelli (ed.), 341–361. Berlin: Mouton de Gruyter. doi:10.1515/9783110197723.5.341
Rizzi, Luigi & Shlonsky, Ur. 2007. Strategies of subject extraction. In *Interfaces + Recursion = Language? Chomsky's Minimalism and the View from Syntax-semantics,* Hans-Martin Gärtner & Uli Sauerland (eds.), 115–160. Berlin: Mouton de Gruyter.
Rohrbacher, Bernhard Wolfgang. 1999. *Morphology-Driven Syntax: A Theory of V to I Raising and Pro-drop* [Linguistik Aktuell/Linguistics Today 15]. Amsterdam: John Benjamins. doi:10.1075/la.15

Romaine, Suzanne. 1993. *Pidgin and Creole Languages.* London: Longman.

Rouveret, Alain. 1980. Sur la notion de proposition finie: Gouvernement et inversion. *Recherches Linguistiques* 9: 76–140.

Roussou, Anna. 2009. In the mood for control. *Lingua* 119(12): 1811–1836. doi:10.1016/j.lingua.2008.11.010

Trask, Robert Lawrence. 1993. *A Dictionary of Grammatical Terms in Linguistics.* London: Routledge.

Siegel, Muffy. 1987. Compositionality, case, and the scope of auxiliaries. *Linguistics and Philosophy* 10: 53–75. doi:10.1007/BF00603392

Sigurðsson, Halldór Ármann. 1990. Long distance reflexives and moods in Icelandic. In *Modern Icelandic Syntax,* Joan Maling & Annie Zaenen (eds.), 309–346. New York NY: Academic Press.

Sigurðsson, Halldór. 2004. The syntax of person, tense, and speech features. *Italian Journal of Linguistics* 16: 219–251.

Sigurðsson, Halldór. 2010. On EPP effects. *Studia Linguistica* 64: 159–189.

Sigurðsson, Halldór. 2012. Minimalist C/case. *Linguistic Inquiry* 43: 191–227. doi:10.1162/LING_a_00083

Simonsen, Hanne G. & Bjerkan, Kirsten M. 1998. Testing past tense inflection in Norwegian: A diagnostic tool for identifying SLI children? *International Journal of Applied Linguistics* 8(2): 251–270. doi:10.1111/j.1473-4192.1998.tb00132.x

Speas, Peggy & Tenny, Carol. 2003. Configurational properties and point-of-view roles. In *Asymmetry in Grammar,* Vol. I: *Syntax and Semantics* [Linguistik Aktuell/Linguistics Today 57], Anna Maria Di Scullio (ed.), 315–144. Amsterdam: John Benjamins. doi:10.1075/la.57.15spe

Stowell, Tim. 1995. What do the present and past tenses mean? In *Temporal Reference, Aspect and Actionality,* Vol.1: *Semantic and Syntactic Perspectives,* Pier Marco Bertinetto, Valentina Bianchi, James Higginbotham & Mario Squartini (eds.), 381–396. Torino: Rosenberg and Sellier.

Sundaresan, Sandhya & McFadden, Thomas. 2009. DP distribution and finiteness in Tamil and other languages: Selection vs case. *Journal of South Asian Linguistics* 2: 5–34.

Szabolcsi, Anna. 2009. Overt nominative subjects in infinitival complements in Hungarian. In *Approaches to Hungarian* 11: *Papers from the 2007 NYU Conference,* Marcel den Dikken & Robert M. Vago (eds.), 251–276. Amsterdam: John Benjamins. doi:10.1075/atoh.11.11sza

Truckenbrodt, Hubert. 2006. On the semantic motivation of syntactic verb movement to C in German. *Theoretical Linguistics* 32(3): 257–306.

Vasić, Nada & Blom, Elma. 2011. Production and processing of determiners in Turkish-Dutch L2 children. In *BUCLD 35: Proceedings of the 35th annual Conference on Language Acquisition and Development,* Nick Danis, Kate Mesh & Hyunsuk Sung (eds.), 616–627. Somerville: Cascadilla Press.

Verrips, Maaike & Weissenborn, Jürgen. 1992. Routes to verb placement in early German and French: The independence of finiteness and agreement. In *The Acquisition of Verb Placement: Functional Categories and V2 Phenomena in Language Acquisition,* Jürgen Meisel (ed.), 283–331. Dordrecht: Kluwer.

Weerman, Fred. 1989. *The V2 Conspiracy. A Synchronic and a Diachronic Analysis of Verbal Positions in Germanic Languages.* Dordrecht: Foris.

Weiss, Helmut. 2005. Inflected complementizers in continental West Germanic dialects. *Zeitschrift für Dialektologie und Linguistik* 72(2): 148–166.

Wexler, Kenneth. 1999. Very early parameter setting and the unique checking constraint: A new explanation of the optional infinitive stage. In *Language Acquisition: Knowledge Representation and Processing,* Antonella Sorace, Caroline Heycock & Richard Shillock (eds.), special issue of *Lingua,* 23–79. Amsterdam: Elsevier.

Yip, Virginia & Matthews, Stephen. 2007. *The Bilingual Child: Early Development and Language Contact.* Cambridge: CUP. doi:10.1017/CBO9780511620744

Zwart, Jan-Wouter. 1993. Dutch Syntax: A Minimalist Approach. Ph.D. dissertation, University of Groningen [Groningen Dissertations in Linguistics 10].

PART I

Finiteness: Underlying relations

Finiteness and Pseudofiniteness*

Elizabeth Cowper
University of Toronto

I argue that finiteness is a purely syntactic property, licensing case on the subject and agreement on the verb. Semantic properties associated with finiteness follow from the position of Finite in the geometry of clausal interpretable features. Considering possible counterexamples from Romance languages as well as West Flemish, modern Greek, and Turkish, I show that Romance personal and inflected infinitives are characterized by a *pseudofinite* Infl, available only in null-subject languages, which lacks Finite, but bears an unvalued case feature. Pseudofinite clauses, including the Southern Calabrian *modo* construction, must be assigned case externally. West Flemish personal infinitives are finite, headed by a hybrid Comp/Infl head. Turkish agreeing gerunds have nominal syntax, and Greek subjunctive clauses are either finite or nonfinite, depending on their case-assigning properties.

Keywords: finiteness; feature geometry; case; agreement; clause structure

1. Introduction

The term "finite" has been used in grammatical literature for centuries, but its meaning is difficult to pin down. Even in recent generative linguistic literature, the term is used inconsistently. This paper adopts the traditional view that finiteness *per se* is a purely syntactic property, consisting of the ability to license structural case in subject position and the possible presence of agreement marking on the verb. The semantic properties that finiteness seems to bring with it arise from the fact that the feature Finite occupies a particular position in a network of dependency relations sometimes called a feature geometry (Sagey 1986, Avery 1996, Béjar & Hall 2000, Harley & Ritter 2002,

* I am very grateful to Maria Kyriakaki, Gabriela Alboiu, and Hitay Yükseker for their help with the Greek, Romanian, and Turkish data discussed here, and to colleagues and students at the University of Toronto for many helpful discussions. The paper is much better than it would have been without their help and the insightful comments of an anonymous reviewer; all errors are mine alone.

doi 10.1075/la.231.02cow

Cowper 2005), in which the other features have semantic content. The implicational relations among the features give rise to the illusion that finiteness itself has semantic content. The empirical picture is further muddied by the existence of constructions that I characterize as pseudofinite. In a pseudofinite clause the verb licenses structural case on its subject, and may also bear agreement morphology, but the clause lacks the semantic properties implied by true finiteness.

2. Historical and Theoretical Context

2.1 Finiteness in traditional grammar

Traditional grammarians divided verb forms into two major classes: the so-called finite forms, including indicative, subjunctive, optative and imperative, and non-finite forms, including infinitives and participles. There were two main criteria underlying this distinction, neither of which can be characterized as semantic. These are, first, the verb's ability to appear as the main verb of a full, independent clause, and second, its ability to take personal endings (Binnick 1991:69). According to Jespersen (1924), the first criterion is of paramount importance, although his discussion is undermined by the fact that he includes in the category of "independent sentence" elliptical utterances such as exclamations and answers to questions, some of which lack verbs altogether. As for personal endings, though Jespersen does not directly state that they are criterial in determining that a verb is finite, it is clear from his discussion of the English imperative that he regards the possibility of agreement marking as relevant to the finiteness of a verb form (Jespersen 1924:314). He rejects the idea that English imperatives might be analyzed as infinitival, on the grounds that imperative verbs in Danish, German, French, Latin and Greek have personal endings. He concludes from this that imperatives are finite, and that the imperative is thus properly characterized as a mood. Similar connections between agreement marking and finiteness are found in Subirats-Rüggeberg's 1990 discussion of Thiébault (1802), and in Dyscolus (1981), a second-century Greek grammar.

2.2 Finiteness in Generative Grammar

In the early years of generative grammar, mood was not much discussed; however, a standard view of infinitival clauses (Soames & Perlmutter 1979) was that an underlyingly finite clause took on infinitival form if the subject was removed, either by subject raising or by Equi-NP deletion. Implicit in this treatment is the assumption that a finite verb requires an overt subject, and that an overt subject requires a finite verb. While many authors in the past few decades have implicitly equated *finite* with *tensed*, George & Kornfilt (1981) show that in Turkish, both tensed and gerundive constructions exhibiting person agreement with their subjects constitute opaque domains. They argue that gerunds are nominal, and that the finiteness distinction is manifest both in nominals and in clauses. They entertain the hypothesis that finiteness can be equated with the presence of person agreement, but reject it on the grounds that languages with no morphological agreement can also exhibit a finiteness distinction.

More recent approaches that take nominative case and subject-verb agreement to be two manifestations of a single AGREE relation (e.g., Chomsky 1995, 2000, 2001; Schütze 1997; Pesetsky & Torrego 2001, 2004, 2007) can in principle equate finiteness with nominative case and subject agreement, even in languages that lack overt agreement marking. The connection between finiteness on the one hand, and case and agreement on the other, was also made explicit in the theory of Government and Binding, where nominative case is assigned to subject position by a [+TENSE] Infl. Only in finite clauses is Infl [+TENSE], and such an Infl contains a nominal element, AGR, which carries person and number features corresponding to those of the subject. Hornstein (1990: 146) notes that "matrix clauses must be finite," and in later work (Hornstein 1995: 68) states that "nominative case is solely a function of whether Tns is finite."

The linking of finiteness with the presence of Case and Agreement is undermined by the existence of so-called personal or inflected infinitives (Haegeman 1985; Raposo 1987a,b, 1989; Pountain 1995; Quicoli 1996), on the one hand, and apparently finite forms which bear agreement but fail to assign nominative case (Alexiadou & Anagnostopoulou 1999a,b, 2002), on the other. The challenge taken up in the present paper is to provide an account of these apparent counterexamples while nonetheless retaining the fundamental insight that the essence of finiteness is the ability to assign nominative case to a subject and to agree in person and number with that subject. To the extent that the term *tense* has to do with the semantic relation between the time associated with a clause and some other time such as the moment of speech, finiteness and tense should not be equated.

2.3 Assumptions and Background

Leaving the difficult cases aside for the moment, let us consider what features are found in Infl and how finiteness fits into the overall picture. I assume that functional categories are the projections of privative features that are grammatically active in a given language, and that these features are chosen from a set made available by Universal Grammar (Chomsky 2000), and intrinsically organized into semantically determined dependency relations. These dependencies can be expressed in terms of a feature geometry, such as those proposed for pronouns by Harley & Ritter (2002) and for Infl in English and Spanish by Cowper (2005). Harbour & Elsholtz (2012) argue that feature geometries *per se* have no status in the grammar. To the extent that dependencies exist, they are due to semantic selection of one feature by another, and are thus intrinsic to the features themselves. I find their arguments generally persuasive, but there is one feature – Finite – that appears to lack semantic content altogether, but nonetheless behaves as though it participates in dependency relations with other features of the Infl system, suggesting that the dependency structure may not be entirely redundant. The features and dependency relations of the English and Spanish Infl systems are shown in (1), adapted from Cowper (2005) following proposals by Cowper & Hall (2007) and Clarke (2013).[1]

(1) a. English:

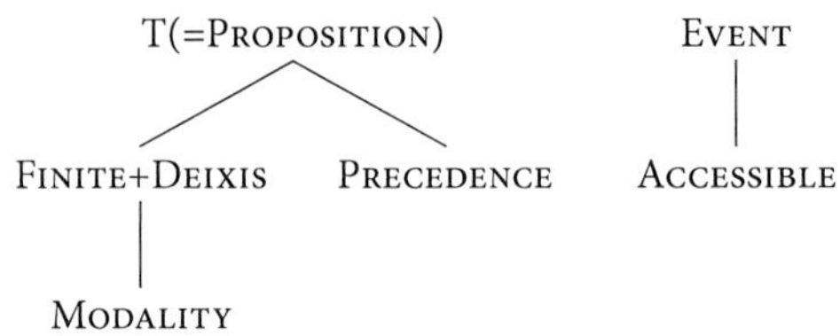

b. Spanish:

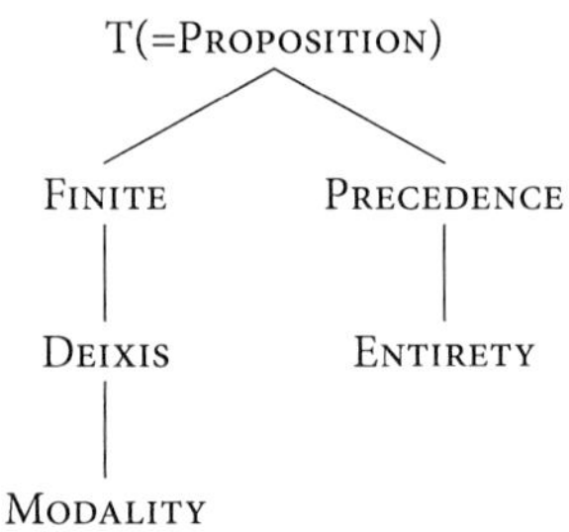

The tree structures in (1) represent the dependency relations among the features, with a dominated feature dependent upon the feature that dominates it. All of the features dominated by T are dependent on the feature Proposition, which distinguishes clauses denoting cognitively represented propositions from what Cowper (2005) calls bare events. A bare event, like the subordinate clauses in (2), must be sensorily perceived, while a propositional clause, like the ones in (3), can be cognitively evaluated as true or false.

(2) a. We saw the [car hit the lamppost].
    b. We heard [the children playing next door].
    c. *We saw [two plus two equal four].

1. Modality corresponds to Cowper's (2005) Irrealis, which characterizes English modal verbs and Spanish future and conditional tenses. Accessible is Clarke's (2013) refinement of Cowper's (2005) Interval, which characterizes imperfective viewpoint aspect, and is spelled out in English by the participial suffix *-ing*.

(3) a. We know [the car to have hit the lamppost].
b. We believe [the children to be playing next door].
c. We proved [two plus two to equal four].

The features dependent upon PROPOSITION thus appear only in clauses denoting propositions in the sense just described. The feature ACCESSIBLE in (1a) is a dependent of EVENT. In other words, the presence of ACCESSIBLE in Infl entails the presence of EVENT. A clause with EVENT in Infl is interpreted as eventive; in the absence of EVENT the clause receives a stative interpretation. If ACCESSIBLE is present, the internal structure of the event denoted by the clause is visible; this characterizes what is traditionally called imperfective viewpoint aspect (Comrie 1976). In the absence of ACCESSIBLE, the event denoted by the clause is an unanalysed whole, with no linguistically accessible internal structure, giving perfective viewpoint aspect. The semantic representation of a dependent feature is thus stated in terms of the semantic representation of its dominating feature, making the dependent feature uninterpretable in the absence of the dominating feature. For example, PRECEDENCE specifies that a moment associated with the event or state denoted by the clause must precede the temporal anchor of the clause. The definition of PRECEDENCE thus involves existential quantification over moments. The dependent feature ENTIRETY replaces this existential quantifier with a universal quantifier, with the effect of requiring all the moments associated with the event or state to precede the temporal anchor of the clause. Without PRECEDENCE, ENTIRETY cannot compose semantically with the rest of the sentence. Similar intrinsic dependencies hold from ACCESSIBLE to EVENT, from MODALITY to DEIXIS, and from DEIXIS to PROPOSITION. These features are discussed in some detail in Cowper (2005).

The only feature whose position in the dependency structure is not determined by intrinsic entailment relations is FINITE. Kyriakaki (2006) argues that whereas in English, all finite clauses are semantically propositional, in modern Greek, not only propositional clauses, but also clauses denoting bare events, are finite. She claims that while in English, FINITE is a dependent of PROPOSITION, in modern Greek, PROPOSITION is a dependent of FINITE. I return to the position of FINITE in Greek in Section 4.

The illusion that finiteness *per se* has semantic content thus arises from its position in the network of dependency relations among interpretable features. In at least English, French, and Spanish, a finite clause is necessarily a proposition, rather than a bare event or state, and a deictic clause is necessarily finite. However, there is no particular semantic content that can be associated with the feature FINITE itself. This can be seen in the sentences in (4), which illustrate what is often called the obviation effect in Romance languages (Luján 1999, Roussou 2001, Bélanger 2002). The sentence in (4a), with an infinitival complement clause, expresses exactly the same meaning as the ungrammatical (4b), which has a finite complement. When the subjects of the two clauses differ, as in (4c), the lower subject must check case, and the finite construction is required for purely syntactic reasons. There is no semantic difference in the content of Infl between (4a) and (4c).

(4) a. Marie veut partir maintenant.
Marie want.PRS.3SG leave.INF now
'Marie wants to leave now.'

b. *Marie$_i$ veut qu' elle$_i$ parte maintenant.
Marie want.PRS.3SG that she leave.SBJV.3SG now
'Marie wants to leave now.'

c. Marie veut que Paul parte maintenant.
Marie want.PRS.3SG that Paul leave.SBJV.3S now
'Marie wants Paul to leave now.'

As stated above, the featural analysis of Infl is set within the theory of Distributed Morphology (Halle & Marantz 1993), and more generally within the Minimalist Program (Chomsky 2000). We therefore distinguish the formal features themselves from the Lexical Items (LIs) that participate in the narrow syntactic computation, and from the Vocabulary Items (VIs) that are inserted postsyntactically to spell out the features of each syntactic head. The dependency structures in (1) represent the features of Infl in English and Spanish, and the entailment relations among them. Languages vary in which features they make use of, whether or not features are bundled together into LIs, which features can project as syntactic heads, and how the various heads are ultimately spelled out by VIs. For example, as argued in Cowper (2005), Spanish but not English uses ENTIRETY, while English but not Spanish uses ACCESSIBLE. The two languages also differ in how the features are bundled into LIs. In Present-Day English, FINITE is grouped into a single LI with DEIXIS, essentially eliminating any systematic distinction between indicative and subjunctive clauses,[2] while in Spanish (and also in French), FINITE may appear without DEIXIS.

As for VIs, forms traditionally called indicative typically spell out DEIXIS, with indicative past tenses also spelling out PRECEDENCE, and in some languages ENTIRETY as well. MODALITY is spelled out by English modals and by future tense forms in languages that have a morphological future, with the conditional in such languages spelling out both MODALITY and PRECEDENCE. The fact that MODALITY entails DEIXIS, and thus by implication FINITE, accounts for the fact that English modals are always finite, and that there seem to be no future or conditional infinitives crosslinguistically.

2. For some speakers, there is a vestigial subjunctive in English; this will be set aside for the purposes of this paper.

Clauses with Proposition but without Finite typically take infinitival form, as do many non-propositional clauses. Finite clauses without Deixis are generally called subjunctive: they internally license nominative subjects, and exhibit agreement marking. This view of finiteness and the subjunctive is consistent with observations made by many authors. The lack of Deixis captures the observation that the subjunctive may lack independent time reference (Farkas 1982), or may express a point of view other than that of the speaker (Jespersen 1924: 319). The claim that the subjunctive differs from non-finite propositional clauses only in the syntactic properties of case and agreement can be taken as the basis of the frequent observation (Poplack 1991; Mailhac 2000 and references cited there) that the subjunctive sometimes carries no meaning.

3. Personal and inflected infinitives: Case and agreement without finiteness?

If we take as a working assumption that the core properties of Finite are nominative Case checking and φ-feature agreement between Infl and the argument that checks nominative Case, and further assume that Finite is in general a dependent of Proposition, there are two main classes of possible counterexamples that must be dealt with. In this section, I discuss personal and inflected infinitives, in which nominative case and φ-feature checking seem to be present, but on a verb form that would otherwise be treated as infinitival and which can describe a bare event rather than a proposition. In the next section, I turn to the case of Greek, where verb forms that appear to be fully finite can sometime head clauses that denote bare events, and where nominative case checking is sometimes absent.

Personal and inflected infinitives occur in various languages, as discussed by Haegeman (1985), Raposo (1987a), Raposo (1989), Pountain (1995), Ledgeway (1998), and Sitaridou (2009). Ledgeway, among others, makes a distinction between the personal infinitive, which has no overt agreement marking but takes an overt nominative subject, and the inflected infinitive, which both has morphological agreement and takes an overt nominative subject. For the purposes of this discussion, we adopt these terms.

3.1 Personal Infinitives

Haegeman (1985) discusses personal infinitives in West Flemish. These constructions, like the one shown in (5) below, appear only in adjuncts with a preposition such as *mee* 'with,' *voor* 'for,' or *deur* 'by.'

(5) West Flemish (Haegeman 1985: 125)

a. Mee ik da te zeggen hee-se dat hus gekocht.
with I that to say has-she that house bought
'Because of my saying that she has bought that house.'

b. Voor gie da te grygen go-je vele moeten veranderen.
for you that to get go-you much must change
'In order to get that you'll have to change a lot.'

Haegeman assumes that Infl is specified for the features [±TENSE, ±AGR]. Ordinary finite clauses are [+TENSE, +AGR], and ordinary infinitives [−TENSE, −AGR]. She assumes that Portuguese inflected infinitives, to be discussed below, are [−Tense, +AGR], and claims that the West Flemish personal infinitives are [+TENSE, −AGR]. As expected from a clause with a [+TENSE] Infl, these clauses can have independent temporal reference, as shown in (6).

(6) West Flemish (Haegeman 1985: 131–132)

a. Mee ik da gisteren te zeggen hee-se dat hus gekocht.
with I that yesterday to say has-she that house bought
'Because of my saying that yesterday she has bought that house.'

b. mee ik da gisteren te zeggen goa-se dat hus kopen.
with I that yesterday to say goes-she that house buy
'Because of my saying that yesterday, she will buy that house.'

c. Mee ik tnoaste joar weg te goan heen-k dat hus verkocht.
with I next year away to go have-I that house sold
'Because of my going away next year, I have sold that house.'

For Haegeman, the ability of this [+TENSE, −AGR] Infl to assign nominative case comes from the fact that it is a constituent of Comp, and a Comp containing such an Infl is "in some sense finite" (Haegeman 1985: 129). She proposes that the prepositions *mee, voor*, and *deur* select this type of Comp, and being case-assigners themselves, transmit their case-assigning property to Infl in Comp. She notes that it is Infl, and not the governing preposition, that assigns case to the subject of the infinitive; the prepositions in question normally govern accusative case, and these subjects are uniformly nominative. Essentially, her idea amounts to saying that the relation between the embedded Infl and the case-assigning preposition activates the case-assigning properties of Infl, despite the fact that Infl does not bear the feature [+AGR].

Personal infinitives are also found in Romanian, as shown in (7). Like the personal infinitive in West Flemish, the Romanian personal infinitive appears in adjuncts governed by a preposition, and takes a nominative subject. The Romanian construction differs from the one found in West Flemish in that in Romanian, as in personal infinitives in Romance languages generally, the subject must follow the verb.

(7) Romanian (Alboiu & Motapanyane 2000: 39)

a. Am plecat [înainte de [(*pe-Ion Maria) a-l săruta
have.1SG left before of PE-Ion Maria to-him kiss.INF

(Maria pe Ion)]]
Maria PE Ion

'I left before Mary kissed John.'

b. Îi ţinea la uşă [pentru a avea tu/*tine timp să
them kept.3SG at door for to have you.NOM/*ACC time SA

strângi vasele].
pick dishes.the

'He was keeping them at the door [for you to have time to pick up the dishes].'

3.2 Inflected Infinitives

Raposo's (1987a) analysis of the Portuguese inflected infinitive, illustrated in (8), is very similar to Haegeman's (1985) treatment of the West Flemish personal infinitive.

(8) a. Despois de eles chegarem viram as ruínas.
after of they.NOM arrive.INF.3PL see.PST.3PL the ruins
'After they arrived, they saw the ruins.' (Ledgeway 1998: 7)

b. Eu lamento os deputados terem trabalhado pouco.
I regret.PRS.1SG the deputies have.INF.3PL work.PTCP little
'I regret (that) the deputies have worked little.' (Raposo 1987a: 87)

Raposo assumes that the feature [+AGR] alone is insufficient for Infl to assign nominative case to its subject, and concludes, based on a detailed discussion of the various contexts in which the inflected infinitive appears, that "a tenseless Infl positively specified for AGR can assign nominative Case to a lexical subject only if it is itself specified for Case" (Raposo 1987a: 107). In addition, Raposo correlates the possibility of personal and inflected infinitives with the fact that Portuguese is a null-subject language. Following Chomsky (1982), he assumes that only in null-subject languages can Infl be specified for Case.

3.3 Prepositional infinitives

Raposo (1989) analyzes a different sort of inflected infinitive in Portuguese, which he calls the Prepositional Infinitive Construction. This construction differs from the one illustrated in (8) in several ways. First, it has a preposition between what looks like the subject and the verb, as shown in (9).

(9) Eu vi os meninos **a** lerem esse livro.
I saw the children **to** read.INF.3PL that book
'I saw the children reading that book.' (Raposo 1989: 277)

Second, the preposition in some cases makes a clearly aspectual contribution, as shown by the difference in meaning between (9) above and (10) below.

(10) Eu vi os meninos lerem o livro.
I saw the children read.INF.3PL the book
'I saw the children read the book.' (Raposo 1989: 279)

Third, the subject cannot be nominative if the infinitival clause is governed by a case-assigner, as shown in (11).

(11) *Eu vi [eles a trabalharem].
I saw they to work.INF.3PL
'I saw they working.' (Raposo 1989: 288)

In fact, in (12a) the subject is cliticized to, and thus arguably checks case with, the matrix verb. In (12b), the subject is oblique, suggesting that its case is valued by the preposition *con*.

(12) a. Os actores$_i$ viram-nos$_{j/*i}$ [ec$_j$ a representarem a cena]
the actors saw-them EC to represent.3PL the scene
'The actors saw them representing the scene.' (Raposo 1989: 290)

b. Eu sonhei con [tigo a entrares na minha casa].
I dreamed with you.OBL to enter.INF.2SG in.the my house
'I dreamed about you entering my house.' (Raposo 1989: 290)

Fourth, the construction can appear on its own in sentences like (13). Under these circumstances the subject is, surprisingly, nominative.

(13) Eles a fumarem marijuana! Que horror!
they to smoke.INF.3PL marijuana what horror
'They smoking marijuana! How awful!' (Raposo 1989: 289)

Raposo notes, however, that Portuguese has small clauses similar to (13), such as (14), in which the subject also bears nominative case, and suggests that in these instances nominative case is assigned by default.

(14) [Ele um imbecil]? Não acho!
he an idiot? not think.PRS.1SG
'Him an idiot? I don't think so!' (Raposo 1989: 290)

Raposo argues that prepositional infinitives have a small clause structure, headed by the preposition *a*, whose predicate is a plain infinitival. The overt subject appears in the small clause subject position, and the infinitival subject is an empty category. The preposition is responsible for the agreement on the infinitival and for the case-licensing of the phonologically null infinitival subject, while the overt nominal preceding *a* either receives its case from an external case-licenser, or surfaces as nominative by default.

If Raposo is correct, then the inner layer of the prepositional infinitive can, at least partly, be assimilated to the inflected infinitive construction, in that Infl is in the domain of a case-assigning preposition, and thus acquires the ability to agree with its subject.

Ledgeway (1998) gives an overview of personal and inflected infinitives in various Romance languages, including several spoken in southern Italy, Sicily and Sardinia, as well as Spanish, Portuguese and Romanian. His main goal is to argue that a particular construction in Southern Calabrian, superficially almost identical to the present indicative, is actually an inflected infinitive. We will turn to this construction later, but for the moment simply note that all the other examples cited by Ledgeway are amenable to analysis in terms similar to those proposed by Raposo and Haegeman, namely that personal and inflected infinitives arise only when Infl is specified for case. Ledgeway claims that the subject of a personal infinitive is always postverbal, whereas an inflected infinitive can normally have its subject either before or after the verb. While this is essentially true for the Romance cases, the West Flemish personal infinitive always takes a preverbal subject, as seen above. This difference in word order will be set aside; I assume that it can be derived from independent differences between Germanic and Romance clause structure.

4. Greek Subjunctives: ϕ-Agreement without nominative case?

Like other languages of the Balkan *Sprachbund,* Greek makes very little use of truly infinitival verb forms. The so-called subjunctive tense form in Greek, as discussed by Alexiadou & Anagnostopoulou (1999b) and Alexiadou & Anagnostopoulou (2002), appears in a wide range of constructions with diverse syntactic properties. Sometimes, a subjunctive clause is clearly finite, denoting a proposition and checking both φ-features and nominative case, as shown in (15).

(15) Elpizo i Maria na aporripsi tin prosfora.
hope.1SG.PRS the.NOM Maria NA reject.PFV.3SG the.ACC offer
'I hope Maria will reject the offer.' (Kyriakaki 2006: 55)

Sometimes, as discussed by Kyriakaki (2006), the same subjunctive form, with full φ agreement, is used in clauses that denote not propositions, but bare events. When that happens, however, the subject, if overt, does not bear nominative case. In (16), the contrast between propositional and bare eventive subjunctives is particularly salient.

(16) Greek (Kyriakaki 2006: 53)
a. Perimene o ðimitris na erɵi
wait.PAST.3SG the.NOM Dimitris.NOM NA come.PFV. 3SG
(alla ekane laɵos).
but made mistake
'She expected that Dimitris would arrive, but she was wrong.'

b. Perimene to ðimitri na erθi
wait.PST.3SG the.ACC Dimitris.ACC NA come.PFV.3SG
(#alla ekane laθos).
but made mistake
'She was waiting for Dimitris to arrive, but she was wrong.'

The two sentences have the same matrix verb *perimene,* which is interpreted as *expect* when its complement is propositional (16a), but as *wait for* when its complement denotes a bare event (16b). Interestingly, in the latter case, the subject of the subjunctive clause is not nominative, but accusative; in fact this is the only morphological difference between the two sentences.

Alexiadou & Anagnostopoulou (1999b: 16,17) argue that the *na*-subjunctive construction is also used in control constructions, as shown in (17), and in raising constructions, as in (18).

(17) Control:
a. O Petros kseri na kolibai.
The Peter know.3SG NA swim.3SG
'Peter knows how to swim.'

b. Ego ksero na kolibo.
I know.1SG NA swim.1SG
'I know how to swim.'

(18) Raising:
Ta peðia arxisan na trexoun.
the.PL children.NOM start.PST.3PL NA run.3PL
'The children started to run.'

It seems that in Greek subjunctive clauses marked by *na,* nominative subjects appear only when the clause is clearly finite; i.e., when it denotes a proposition, but that φ-feature agreement is consistently present, whether the clause denotes a proposition or a bare event. This pattern calls into question whether nominative case and φ-feature checking with Infl are indeed two sides of the same coin.

5. A proposal: Pseudofiniteness

In this section, I explore the idea that the Case and φ-feature checking properties of Infl, normally determined by the presence or absence of FINITE, can be activated in the absence of FINITE. This seems to happen when (a) Infl itself Agrees with a case-checking head, and (b) null subjects are possible in the language. Essentially, a non-finite Infl acquires the properties associated with the FINITE feature during the course of the syntactic computation. I will refer to this situation as *Pseudofiniteness.*

5.1 The source of pseudofiniteness in Romance languages

Personal and inflected infinitives in Romance languages exhibit Case and Agreement properties by virtue of (a) a relation they bear to a higher case-checking element and (b) some property that characterizes Infl only in null-subject languages. The higher case-checking element can be a verb, as in (19a), a preposition, as in (19b), or a matrix Infl, as in (19c).

(19) a. Portuguese: (Ledgeway 1998: 10)
O João lamenta [eles terem gastado esse
the John regret.PRS.3SG they have.INF.3PL spend.PTCP that
dinheiro para nada].
money for nothing
'John regrets their having spent that money for nothing.'

b. Old Italian: (Ledgeway 1998: 3)
Una giovane, senza [vederla egli], passò.
a youth.F without see.INF.her he pass.PST.3SG
'A young lady went by without his seeing her.'

c. Portuguese: (Raposo 1989: 283)
É dificil [os meninos trabalharem].
be.PRS.3SG difficult the children work.INF.3PL
'It is difficult for the children to work.'

Following Raposo, I assume that what makes Infl accessible to the higher case-marking element is that either it heads a projection in the search space of the case-checker, or it has moved to the head of such a projection.[3]

In (19a), then, the embedded Infl heads an IP in direct object position. In (19b), it has moved to the head of the CP complement of the preposition, and in (19c) it heads the associate of a null expletive in subject position. The question that arises, under minimalist assumptions, is how an Agree relation can be established between the case-checking head (henceforth the probe) and the constituent headed by Infl. On standard assumptions, the case-checker bears uninterpretable φ-features, and will match an active goal that also bears φ-features. Normally, what makes the goal active is an uninterpretable unvalued Case feature. Recall Raposo's observation that personal/inflected infinitives are restricted to null-subject languages, and his assumption that only in these languages can Infl be specified for Case. Under the minimalist program, this amounts to saying that in null-subject languages, Infl can bear the sort

3. Kornfilt (2001a) argues, on the basis of Turkish, that the case-assigning ability of Agr in non-finite constructions can be activated (her term is "unlocked") if Agr is indexed in one of several ways: by φ-marking, by θ-marking, or by being coindexed with an operator.

of uninterpretable case feature normally borne by nominals. Suppose that this feature is optionally added to Infl in the numeration, independently of the feature FINITE. If Infl is finite, then the feature will be valued and deleted by FINITE. If Infl is non-finite, then the derivation will crash unless the case feature enters into an Agree relation with a probe. Once the Agree relation is established, two things happen. First, the uninterpretable case feature is deleted, and second, Infl acquires the ability to check nominative case on a subject (always), and to spell out φ-feature agreement on the infinitival verb (depending on the morphological resources of the language).

5.2 Apparent pseudofiniteness in West Flemish

I have proposed that in Romance languages, both the null-subject property and the possibility of pseudofiniteness arise from the fact that Infl can bear an uninterpretable case feature. This correlation does not hold in West Flemish, and a different account is thus required.

In fact, there are systematic differences between the West Flemish personal infinitives described by Haegeman and those found in Romance languages. While there is no evidence that, apart from their ability to license nominative case and bear agreement, personal and inflected infinitives in Romance have any more structure than do plain infinitives, the West Flemish personal infinitives seem to have a projection that plain infinitives lack. Haegeman (1985: 125–129) discusses the focus marker *tet*, which may appear in finite clauses and in personal infinitives, but which cannot appear in plain infinitives, as shown in (20)–(22).

(20) Plain infinitive with PRO subject:
a. dan-k proberen voor PRO weg te goan
   that-I try for PRO away to go
   'that I try to go away'
b. *dan-k proberen vor-tet PRO weg te goan
   that-I try for-FOC PRO away to go

(21) Plain ECM infinitive:
a. dan-k gisteren Valère zagen weggoan
   that-I yesterday Valère saw away-go
   'That I saw Valère leave yesterday'
b. *dan-k gisteren tet Valère zagen weggoan
   that-I yesterday FOC Valère saw away-go

(22) Personal infinitive with *mee:*
a. mee Valère weg te goan
   with Valère away to go
   'with Valère going away'

b. mee tet Valère weg te goan
with FOC Valère away to go
'with Valère going away'

Haegeman places *tet* in Comp, and following Koopman (1984) and Platzack (1983), assumes that Comp may also itself contain Infl. For her, Comp in a personal infinitive is, in fact, finite. In addition to the possible presence of *tet,* personal infinitives are semantically different from plain infinitives, in that personal infinitives always denote propositions. Plain infinitives can denote bare events, as seen in (21a). In addition, as we saw in (5), personal infinitives are always able to take their own temporal modifiers, and are thus temporally independent of the matrix clause containing them. The possibility arises, then, that personal infinitives in West Flemish are properly finite, rather than pseudofinite; i.e., that they are headed by an Infl bearing the feature FINITE.

5.3 Pseudofiniteness and Finiteness: A comparison

Given the dependency structure in (1), we must now ask what it means for a non-finite Infl to acquire case-assigning and agreement properties. Is the FINITE feature activated in such a way as to bring with it the feature(s) that dominate it in the dependency structure, or are the case and agreement properties added in such a way as not to alter the feature structure of Infl?

The only feature whose presence is entailed by the presence of FINITE is PROPOSITION. Truly finite clauses always denote propositions, as opposed to bare events, as shown in (23) below. In (23a), the verb *saw* refers to a direct, visual perception of an event, while in (23b) it refers to a cognitive realization of a proposition.

(23) a. We saw [the children eat(ing) the cookies].
b. We saw [(that) the children were eating the cookies].

The question, then, is whether personal/inflected infinitives can ever denote bare events. If they can, then the superficial properties of finiteness are present, but Infl has not thereby become fully finite.

The Portuguese examples in (24) contain inflected infinitives denoting bare events.

(24) a. eu vi os meninos lerem o livro.
I saw the children read.INF.3PL the book
'I saw the children read the book.' (Raposo 1989: 279)

b. Eu vi [eles trabalharem].
I saw they.NOM work.INF.3PL
'I saw them work.' (ibid: 288)

c. Os actores$_i$ viram [eles$_{*i/j}$ representarem
The actors saw they (≠ the actors) represent.INF.3PL

a cena].
the scene

'The actors saw them represent the scene.' (ibid: 302)

d. [os meninos a dormirem] é/*são um
the children to sleep.INF.3PL be.PRES.3SG/*3PL a

espectaculo lindissimo.
spectacle beautiful.SUPERL

'The children sleeping is/*are a beautiful sight.' (ibid: 282)

I therefore conclude that true finiteness and pseudofiniteness differ, not only in their provenance, but also in their representations. A truly finite clause is headed by Infl containing the feature FINITE, the presence of which entails the presence of the feature PROPOSITION, while a pseudofinite clause is headed by an Infl which has acquired the Case- and φ-checking properties of FINITE, without the feature itself.

Following this line of thought, we are led to conclude that the West Flemish personal infinitive is a truly finite, rather than a pseudofinite, construction. While this resolves the difficulty caused by the fact that West Flemish is not a null-subject language, it raises another question. Why, if these personal infinitives are truly finite, are they restricted, like the pseudofinite constructions in Portuguese, to case-marked contexts? A truly finite Infl should inherently have the ability to license nominative case on its subject. In addition, it should not appear with the infinitival marker *te* 'to'.

Haegeman (1985) adopts a version of the idea of Platzack (1983) that Comp and Infl may form a single projection, and suggests that in personal infinitives, Infl appears in Comp, rather than heading a separate projection below Comp. This approach provides another means by which the inflectional head of the clause might come to bear an uninterpretable case feature, assuming that Comp, but not Infl alone, can be argumental and thus potentially case-marked. Just as Infl in a null-subject language has nominal properties that make it able to carry an uninterpretable case feature, an Infl in Comp in West Flemish can do the same thing. Under the current approach, then, West Flemish would have a hybrid Comp/Infl head, bearing both the feature FINITE and an uninterpretable Case feature. Assuming that this close connection between Infl and Comp characterizes V2 languages, we would not expect to find the West Flemish sort of personal infinitives in English.

5.4 Pseudofiniteness and syntactic operations

Quicoli (1996) discusses inflected infinitives in Portuguese, and shows that they differ systematically from non-inflected infinitives with respect to various types of movement from the embedded subject position. Whereas A-movement (including ECM) is generally possible with plain infinitives and impossible with inflected infinitives and finite clauses, A′-movement is impossible with plain infinitives and possible with inflected infinitives and finite clauses. These phenomena are illustrated in (25)–(29).

A-movement from embedded subject position:

(25) Subject raising

a. Plain infinitive:

Os embaixadores parecem ter chegado a
the ambassadors seem.prs.3pl have.inf reach.ptcp to

um acordo.
an agreement

'The ambassadors seem to have reached an agreement.' (Quicoli 1996: 57)

b. Inflected infinitive:

*Os embaixadores parecem terem chegado a
the ambassadors seem.prs.3pl have.inf.3pl reach.ptcp to

um acordo.
an agreement

'The ambassadors seem to have reached an agreement.' (ibid.)

c. Finite clause:

*Os embaixadores parecem que chegarem a
the ambassadors seem.prs.3pl that reach.pst.3pl to

um acordo.
an agreement

'The ambassadors seem that [they] reached an agreement.' (ibid)

(26) ECM/Object clitic placement

a. Plain infinitive:

José nos viu sair da casa.
José us see.pst.3sg leave.inf of.the house

'José saw us leave the house.' (Quicoli 1996: 68)

b. Inflected infinitive:

*José nos viu sairmos da casa.
José us see.pst.3sg leave.inf.1pl of.the house

'José saw us leave the house.' (ibid.)

(27) Passive

a. Plain infinitive:

Os soldados foram vistos cair.
the soldiers be.pst.3pl see.ptcp.pl fall.inf

'The soldiers were seen to fall.' (Quicoli 1996: 69)

b. Inflected infinitive:
*Os soldados foram vistos cairem.
the soldiers be.PST.3PL see.PTCP.PL fall.INF.3PL
'The soldiers were seen to fall.' (ibid.)

A′ movement from embedded subject position:

(28) Wh-Movement
a. Plain infinitive:
*Que jogadores você lamenta ter abandonado
which players you regret have.INF abandon.PTCP
a equipe?
the team
'Which players do you regret to have abandoned the team?'
(Quicoli 1996: 56)

b. Inflected infinitive:
Que jogadores você lamenta terem abandonado
which players you regret have.INF.3PL abandon.PTCP
a equipe?
the team
'Which players do you regret to have abandoned the team?' (ibid.)

c. Finite clause:
Que jogadores você lamenta que tenham abandonado
which players you regret that have.PRS.3PL abandon.PTCP
a equipe?
the team
'Which players do you regret that [they] have abandoned the team?'
(ibid.)

(29) Topicalization
a. Plain infinitive:
*As estrelas parecia sorrir.
the stars seem.PST.3SG smile.INF
'The stars, it seemed to smile.' (Quicoli 1996: 62)

b. inflected infinitive:
As estrelas parecia sorrirem
the stars seem.PST.3SG smile.INF.3PL
'The stars, it seemed to smile.' (ibid.)

c. Finite clause:
As estrelas parecia que sorriam.
the stars seem.PST.3SG that smile.PST.3PL
'The stars, it seemed that [they] smiled.' (ibid.)

Quicoli's analysis of the phenomena exemplified above is based on the assumption that, in inflected infinitives, Infl contains AGR. Following Chomsky (1981), AGR is an accessible SUBJECT for the purposes of the Binding Theory. When the movement leaves an NP-trace, as in (25)–(27), the presence of AGR in Infl makes the lower clause the binding domain for the trace, and the sentence is ruled out by Condition A. When the movement is to an A′-position, as in (28) and (29), the inflected infinitive is well-formed due to the fact that the trace is case-marked. The plain infinitive in such cases is ruled out by the Case Filter.

These examples are straighforwardly accounted for under the current approach as well. Let us consider (28) and (29) first. In the (b) and (c) examples, the uninterpretable case feature on the embedded subject is valued and deleted by the embedded Infl. In the truly finite (c) examples this is routine; in the pseudofinite (b) examples the valuing/deletion happens as a consequence of the fact that the embedded Infl bears an uninterpretable case feature of its own. This case feature enters into an Agree relation with a higher case-assigner and, on being checked, gives Infl the ability to value and delete the case feature on its subject. In the (a) examples, however, the uninterpretable case feature on the embedded subject cannot be deleted, because the embedded Infl has no case feature and thus does not acquire the ability to check case on its subject. The subject then undergoes A′-movement to the matrix spec/CP, and ultimately its unchecked uninterpretable case feature causes the derivation to crash.

Exactly the opposite situation holds in (25)–(27). Here, the higher clause contains a case-assigning probe that requires an active DP with which to Agree. In the plain infinitive (a) examples, the embedded subject has an uninterpretable case feature and is thus visible to the probe from the higher clause. In the (b) and (c) examples, however, the uninterpretable case feature is deleted within the lower clause, and thus the embedded subject is not visible to the probe. When the embedded clause is finite, as in (25c), the embedded subject has its case valued by the FINITE feature on the embedded Infl. When the embedded clause is pseudofinite, as in the (b) examples, the embedded Infl itself has an uninterpretable case feature that satisfies the probe. The embedded subject then has its case valued by the embedded Infl, and no Agree relation can arise between the higher probe and the embedded subject. Thus the higher probe cannot exhibit φ-feature agreement with the embedded subject, and the embedded subject can neither bear the case assigned by the higher probe, nor move to the specifier position associated with it. If, on the other hand, the probe were to bypass the embedded Infl and target the embedded subject, then the uninterpretable case feature on the embedded Infl would not be deleted and the derivation would crash.

6. Pseudofiniteness in Southern Calabrian

Let us now turn to the intriguing case of the Southern Calabrian *modo* construction. Ledgeway (1998) argues, at length and in considerable detail, that the distribution of this construction is identical to that of the personal/inflected infinitives in other Italian dialects, most particularly Old Neapolitan.

What makes this construction unusual, for an inflected infinitive, is that the verb forms are identical to those of the present indicative. The differences between the *modo* construction and the present indicative are as follows. First, the *modo* construction has a special particle, historically derived from the Latin word *modo*. Ledgeway shows that this morpheme is not a complementizer – it can co-occur with *wh*-phrases, unlike the ordinary complementizer, as in (30), and it appears to the right of the subject and the negative marker, as shown in (31).

(30) a. Si sapiti chi (*ca) mi fici a mia
if know.PRS.2SG what (*that) me.ACC do.PST.3SG to me
'If you knew what (*that) he did to me' (Ledgeway 1998: 28)

b. E' 'na città, comu ma vi dicu,
be.PRS.3SG a.F city how MODO you.PL say.PRES.1S
antica e…moderna.
old.F and…modern.F
'It's a city, how can I put it, old and …modern.' (ibid.: 29)

c. Non avia chimmu mangia.
not have.IPFV.3SG what.MODO eat.PRS.3SG
'He had nothing to eat.' (ibid.: 29)

d. Dumandaru si mmi ponnu aiutari a nui.
ask.PST.3PL if MODO can.PRS.3PL help.INF to us
'They asked if they could help us.' (ibid.: 30)

(31) a. Ma jeu nommu mi tradu rispundìa.
but I not.MODO REFL.1 betray.PRS.1SG answer.PST.1SG
'But so that I would not betray myself, I replied.' (ibid.: 24)

b. Vogghiu lu diavulu mu ti mangia!
want.PRS.1SG the devil MODO you.ACC eat.PRS.3SG
'I wish that the devil [should] eat you up!' (ibid.: 24)

Second, the present indicative proper is temporally deictic, and alternates with other tenses like past and future. The *modo* construction is temporally transparent, with its time reference entirely determined by that of the matrix clause. No tense forms other than the present can appear in a *modo* clause, regardless of the time reference of that clause, as seen in (32).

(32) a. Conditional > Present
vollarïa ['u cangiu misteri].
want.COND.1SG MODO change.PRS.1SG job
'I should like to change trade.' (Ledgeway 1998: 34)

b. Preterite > Present
Vozza [ma sapa sulu cui ci fà
want.PST.3SG MODO know.PRS.3SG only who there do.PRS.3SG
'a sfumatura a li parmari.
the trimming to the.PL palm.tree.PL
'He wanted to know who trimmed the palm trees.' (ibid.)

c. Imperfect > Present
M'havia scordatu c'havia ['u
refl.1SG.have.IPFV.1SG forget.PTCP that.have.IPFV.1SG MODO
viu a unu].
see.PRS.1SG to one
'I had forgotten that I had to see someone.' (ibid.)

Also, the *modo* construction appears with complementizers that in other Romance languages take only infinitival clauses, such as *mbeci* 'instead of' (33), and it cannot appear with complementizers that typically take only finite clauses, such as *nzina* 'until, *ntramentri* 'while' and *cu tutti* 'although' as in (34).

(33) a. E di notti vai facendu 'u spirdu casa casa,
and of night go.PRS.2SG do.GER the spirit house house
mbeci **mu** ti curchi e **mu** ti
instead MODO REFL.2 lie.PRS.2SG and MODO REFL.2
levi prestu a matina
get.up.PRS.2SG early the morning
'And at night time you go around haunting the houses, instead of going to bed and getting up early in the morning.'
cf. *E di notti vai facendu 'u spirdu casa casa, mbeci **chi** ti curchi e **chi** ti levi prestu a matina. (Ledgeway 1998: 37)

b. Imbeci **ma** jamu avanti, jamu arretu.
instead MODO go.PRS.1PL forwards go.PRS.1PL backwards
'Instead of going forwards, we're going backwards.'
cf. *Imbecia **chi** jamu avanti, jamu arretu. (ibid)

(34) a. Girdàvamu nzina **cchi** non venìa a maschera.
shout.IPFV.1PL until that not come.IPFV.3SG the usherette
'We shouted until the usherette came.'
cf. *Girdàvamu nzina non **ma** vena a maschera. (Ledgeway 1998: 36)

b. Ntramentri **chi** jeu travagghiava, iddhu si ripusava.
in.while that I work.IPFV.1SG he REFL.3 rest.PRS.3SG
'While I was working, he was resting.'
cf. *Ntramenti jeu **mi** travvagghiu, iddhu si ripusava. (ibid.)

c. Cu tuttu **chi** chiuvìa, nisciu mi
with all that rain.IPFV.3SG go.out.PST.3SG MODO

zzappa l'ortu.
dig.PRS.3SG the.garden

'Although it was raining, he went out to dig the garden.'
cf. *Cu tuttu **mi** chiuvi, nisciu mi zzappa l'ortu. (ibid.)

Ledgeway proposes that the *modo* construction is, in fact, an inflected infinitive, and that the present indicative paradigm encodes only agreement, not tense. It is of interest that Southern Calabrian makes very little use of the ordinary infinitive, reserving it for complements of modals. In fact, in contexts that trigger obviation in many Romance languages – complements to volitional verbs – these dialects use the *modo* construction even when the subjects are coreferential, as shown in (35).

(35) a. Vollarïa ['u cangiu misteri].
want.COND.1SG MODO change.PRS.1SG job
'I should like to change trade.' (Ledgeway 1998: 34)

b. Vozza [ma sapa sulu cui ci fà
want.PST.3SG MODO know.PRS.3SG only who there do.PRS.3SG

'a sfumatura a li parmari]
the trimming to the.PL palm.tree.PL

'He wanted to know who trims the palm trees.' (ibid.)

c. Eu vogghiu [mi ti pagu]
I want.PRS.1SG MODO you pay.PRS.1SG
'I want to pay you.' (ibid.: 44)

One difference between the *modo* construction and the Old Neapolitan inflected infinitive construction is that in Old Neapolitan, the inflected infinitive always appears with a case-assigning element immediately governing it, just like the personal/inflected infinitives in Portuguese and West Flemish discussed above. In contrast, the *modo* construction does not invariably have a case-assigning element governing it. However, it is entirely possible that the *modo* element itself provides a case specification for the Infl in the *modo* clause. Suppose that is the case. Then the *modo* construction is, like personal and inflected infinitives in other languages, not finite but rather pseudofinite. We thus expect that we might find *modo* clauses denoting bare events rather than propositions, and indeed we do, as shown in (36).

(36) a. 'Ncumincia ma vi sàgghia 'u sangu a
begin.PRS.3SG MODO you.PL.DAT rise.PRS.3SG the blood to

'lu cerbeddhu.
the brain

'Your blood begins to flow to your brain.' (Ledgeway 1998: 25)

b. Tu fai mi ndi mangia tri parti iddu.
you make.PRS.3SG MODO PART eat.PRS.3SG three parts he
'You make him eat three parts of it.' (ibid.: 39)

c. Li fazzu mu stannu tranquilli.
them.M.PL make.PRS.1SG MODO stay.PRS.3PL calm.M.PL
'I'll make them relax.' (ibid.: 40)

d. Ti faci mu ti passa 'u malucori.
you make.PRS.3SG MODO you.DAT go.away.PRS.3SG the sorrow.
'It will make your pain go away.' (ibid.: 40)

I thus conclude that the Southern Calabrian *modo* construction is pseudofinite, and that the fact that it has nominative subjects and φ-feature agreement is due to the fact that its Infl is specified for case, just like personal and inflected infinitives in West Flemish and Portuguese. The question, then, is why the Southern Calabrian pseudofinite forms are morphophonologically indistinguishable from finite forms, while in the other languages, there is a special inflected infinitival form. More generally, how is the derivationally created pseudofinite Infl morphologically realized? Clearly the so-called present indicative forms cannot be represented as spelling out either DEIXIS or FINITE. If we assume, with Ledgeway and many other authors, that present is not featurally marked, but is the default interpretation of an unmarked tense, then it could be that what "present tense" morphology spells out is simply φ.

7. Greek again

Let us return now to the question of the Greek subjunctive with *na*. We saw that while the verb in such a clause always exhibits φ-agreement with the subject, the subject bears nominative case only if the clause is propositional. This pattern is different both from the situation with Portuguese inflected infinitives, and from the superficially quite similar situation in Southern Calabrian just discussed. In those languages, nominative case can appear on the subjects of non-propositional clauses, and we concluded that such clauses were pseudofinite rather than truly finite.

The simplest analysis of the propositional *na-* subjunctive clauses in Greek is to say that they are both propositional and truly finite; in other words, Infl in such a clause bears both PROPOSITION and FINITE, like subjunctive clauses in French and many other languages. An overt subject in such a clause checks nominative Case, as the result of checking φ-features with a finite Infl.

This approach leaves several cases unaccounted for, examples of which are given in (37), and which could, in principle, be treated as pseudofinite.

(37) a. Bare eventive complements with accusative subjects:
Perimene to ðimitri na erθi.
wait.PST.3SG the.ACC Dimitris.ACC NA come.PFV.3SG
'She was waiting for Dimitris to arrive.' (Kyriakaki 2006: 53)

b. Obligatory control clauses:
Ego ksero na kolibo.
I know.1SG NA swim.1SG
'I know how to swim.' (Alexiadou & Anagnostopoulou 2002: 16)

c. Raising clauses:
Ta peðia arxisan na trexoun.
the.PL child.PL.NOM start.PST.3PL NA run.3PL
'The children started to run.' (ibid.: 17)

However, these clauses lack one of the two defining characteristics of pseudofiniteness: Case on the subject is not checked internally to the clause. In (37a), the accusative case on the subject of the embedded clause can be attributed to a checking relation with the higher verb, while in (37b) and (37c), the subject position of the lower clause arguably checks no case at all. Ideally, then, we should treat these clauses as straightforwardly nonfinite.

This result is entirely consonant with Alexiadou & Anagnostopoulou's (1999b) proposal that in Greek, φ-feature agreement on the verb is not necessarily the result of a Case-related probe in Infl. Rather, they claim that it also happens whenever a subject checks Infl's EPP feature. This means that in Greek – and perhaps also in other Balkan languages that putatively lack infinitives – the presence of φ-agreement on the verb is completely independent of whether that verb is finite.

8. Turkish Gerunds: Case and agreement without finiteness

Let us now return to the Turkish constructions discussed by George & Kornfilt (1981). They divide Turkish complement clauses into two types: direct complements, as in (38), and gerunds, as in (39). The (a) examples have overt, internally case-marked subjects and exhibit φ-feature agreement, while the (b) examples have neither of these properties.

(38) Direct complements:
a. Ahmet [biz viski-yi iç-ti-k] san-ɨyor.
Ahmet we whiskey-ACC drink-PST-1PL believe-PRS
'Ahmet believes (that) we drank the whiskey.'
(George & Kornfilt 1981: 118)

b. Ahmet [biz-i viski-yi iç-ti] san-ɨyor.
Ahmet we-ACC whiskey-ACC drink-PST believe-PRS
'Ahmet believes us to have drunk the whiskey.' (ibid.)

(39) Gerunds:

a. (ben) [kɨz-ɨm-ɨn viski-yi
I daughter-my-GEN whiskey-ACC
iç-me-sin]-e razɨ ol-du-m
drink-GER-3SG-DAT consent-PST-1SG
'I consented to my daughter's drinking the whiskey.' (ibid.)

b. (ben) [viski-yi iç-meg'-]e razɨ ol-du-m
I whiskey-ACC drink-GER-DAT consent-PST-1SG
'I consented to drink the whiskey.' (ibid.)

George & Kornfilt (1981) characterize the (a) examples as finite, and the (b) examples as non-finite. However, they also argue at length that gerunds are nominal, rather than purely clausal. Gerunds can themselves bear overt case, such as the dative marking on the gerunds in (39). They can appear in all positions in which ordinary nominals appear, and they are inflected with nominal morphology. Thus, the subject of a gerund is genitive, like the possessor in a nominal, and the agreement affixes are the same as those found in the possessive construction. We have provisionally defined finiteness as the ability to check nominative case and trigger φ-agreement; let us now consider where constructions like (39a) fit in.

Following George and Kornfilt, and updating their analysis where necessary, the embedded clauses/gerunds in (38) and (39) have the structures in (40) and (41). I have provisionally used the generic term FP for the projection headed by case and agreement features in finite clauses.

(40) a. [biz viski-yi iç-ti-k]
we whiskey-ACC drink-PST-1PL
'(Ahmet believes that) we drank the whiskey.'

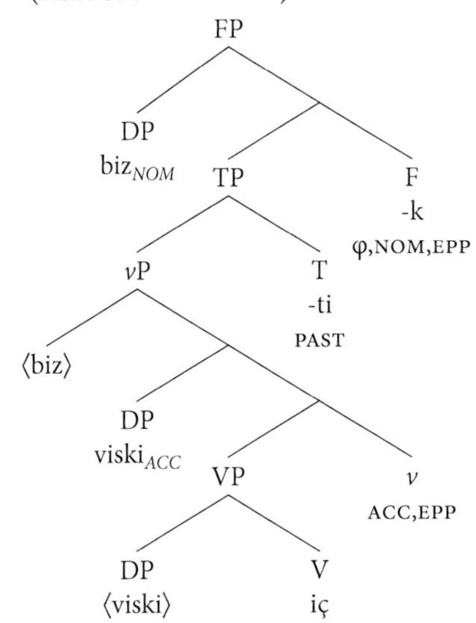

b. [biz-i viski-yi iç-ti]
we-ACC whiskey-ACC drink-PST
'(Ahmet believes) us to have drunk the whiskey.'

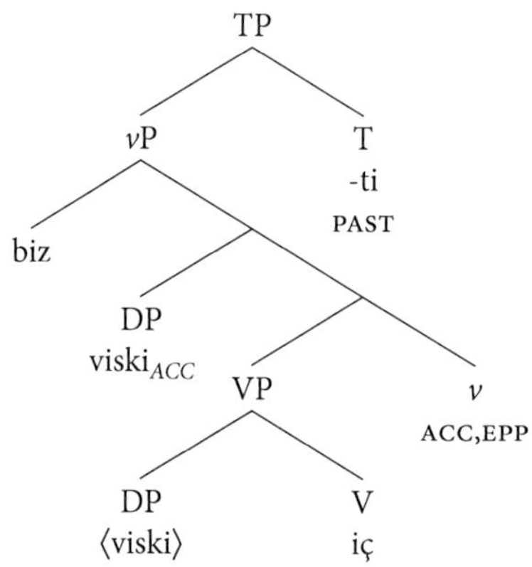

(41) a. [kɨz-ɨm-ɨn viski-yi iç-me-sin]-e
daughter-my-GEN whiskey-ACC drink-GER-3SG-DAT
'(I consented) to my daughter's drinking the whiskey.'

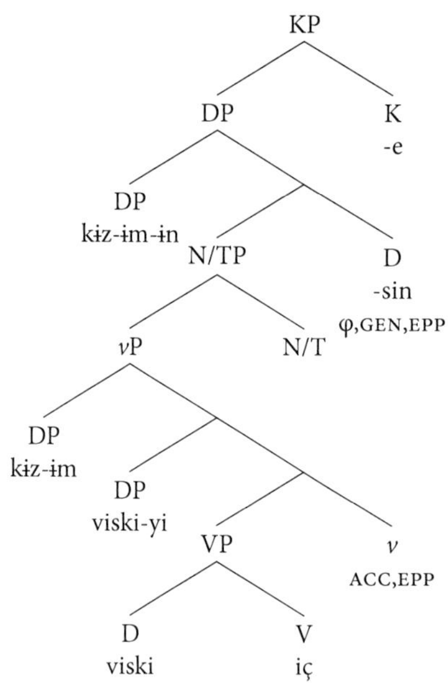

b. [viski-yi iç-meg'-]e
whiskey-ACC drink-GER-DAT
'(I consented) to drink the whiskey.'

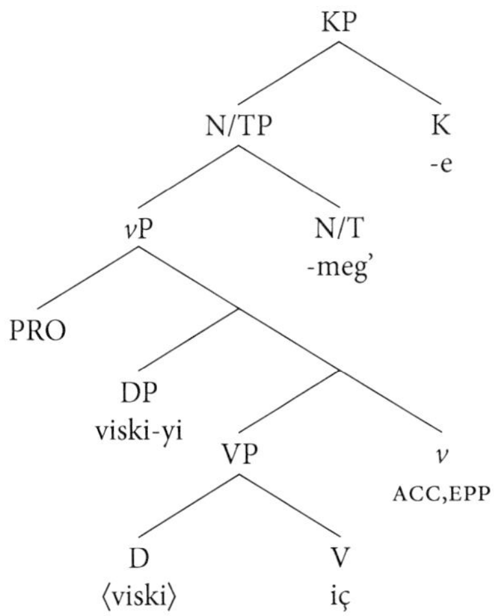

In Turkish, there are clear parallels to be drawn between the clausal projection, labelled FP in (40a), and the nominal projection, labelled DP in (41a). Both of these functional heads license φ-feature agreement on the head and structural case on the specifier. These are the properties labelled *finiteness* by George & Kornfilt (1981), and called AGR by people working on Turkish syntax since then (see also Kornfilt 2001a,b). I have labelled the gerundive projection N/T, to reflect its hybrid role as an element encoding both nominal category and, in some cases, something like tense (±FUTURE, according to George & Kornfilt). Its parallel in the clausal system is T, which would host the feature PRECEDENCE from the dependency structure in (1).

Let us assume, uncontroversially, that clauses such as the complement clause in (38a) are finite, and that the complements in (38b) and (39b) are non-finite. The question then is whether (39a) should be treated as nonfinite, finite, or possibly pseudofinite. As before, we assume that if a clause denotes a bare event, it cannot be truly finite. The sentences in (42) contain gerundive clauses with casemarked subjects and φ-feature agreement, but which denote bare events.

(42) a. Çocuk-lar-ɨn viski-yi iç-me-sin gör-ül-ecek bir
child-PL-GEN whiskey-ACC drink-GER-3PL see-PSV-GER one
manzara deg'il.
sight is-not
'The children drinking the whiskey is not a sight to be seen.'
(Hitay Yükseker, p.c.)

b. Çocuk-lar-ɨn bahçe-de oyna-ma-sɨn-ɨ duy-du-k
child-PL-GEN garden-LOC play-GER-3PL-ACC hear-PST-1PL
'We heard the children playing in the garden.' (Hitay Yükseker, p.c.)

The fact that so-called finite gerunds can refer to bare events eliminates the possibility that they are truly finite. Given our characterization of pseudofiniteness, and the idea that finiteness might cut across the nominal/sentential distinction, we might be led to look for an external case-assigner that would perhaps be activating the case-assigning ability of the D-head in (40b), (41b) and (42). However, it is important to note that the DP dominating the construction itself bears case – the case valued by whatever checks it. It is thus unlikely that an analysis along the lines proposed for pseudofinite clauses in Romance can be pursued here. In addition, as Kornfilt (2001a) notes, these clauses are not, in fact, restricted to case-marked contexts. I therefore conclude that the Turkish agreeing gerunds are neither finite nor pseudofinite. Rather, they exhibit ordinary possessive nominal behaviour: genitive case on their subjects and possessive agreement on their heads.

9. Conclusion

I have shown that the traditional understanding of finiteness, namely that it consists of the ability to assign structural (nominative) case to a subject, and the possibility of having φ-feature agreement encoded on the verb, is essentially correct. Finiteness is thus a purely syntactic property, but one which forms part of a dependency structure that encodes the syntactic and semantic properties of Infl. It thus exhibits certain partial correlations with semantic properties such as deixis and the proposition/event distinction. All truly finite clauses are propositional, though not all propositions are finite, and all temporally deictic clauses are finite, though not all finite clauses are temporally deictic.

We have also seen a set of constructions that have the superficial properties normally associated with finiteness, but which differ systematically from finite clauses. Infl in these clauses, which we call pseudofinite, acquires the ability to value nominative case and bear φ-feature agreement during the course of the syntactic computation. Pseudofiniteness is triggered by the presence of an uninterpretable case feature on a nonfinite Infl, an option available only in null-subject languages.

Not all constituents whose heads lack FINITE but nonetheless exhibit φ-agreement with their specifiers are pseudofinite, however. We saw that in Greek, non-finite Infl checks φ-features, but not nominative case, as a reflex of EPP-checking, and that Turkish gerunds that agree with a genitive specifier have the ordinary syntax of possessive nominals. It remains to be seen whether there is a property analogous to pseudofiniteness in the nominal system crosslinguistically.

We also saw that not every instance of nominative case is the result of valuation by a φ-probe in a finite or pseudofinite Infl. Sometimes, as argued by Raposo (1989), nominative case arises by default.

The main theoretical question arising from this discussion is whether FINITE, as the only purely syntactic feature in the dependency structure of Infl, forces us to conclude, contra Harbour & Elsholtz (2012), that interpretable formal features must indeed be extrinsically arranged in a feature geometry that is not simply a convenient depiction of relations that can be derived from the semantics of the various features. Ideally, it should be possible to make the position of FINITE in the dependency structure follow from something else – perhaps from some constraint on how the features must map to syntactic projections. But that answer must await further work.

References

Alboiu, Gabriela & Motapanyane, Virginia. 2000. The generative approach to Romanian grammar: An overview. In *Comparative Studies in Romanian Syntax*, Virginia Motapanyane (ed.), 1–48. Oxford: Elsevier.

Alexiadou, Artemis & Anagnostopoulou, Elena. 1999a. EPP without Spec,IP. In *Specifiers: Minimalist Approaches*, David Adger, Susan Pintzuk, Bernadette Plunkett & George Tsoulas (eds.), 93–109. Oxford: OUP.

Alexiadou, Artemis & Anagnostopoulou, Elena. 1999b. Raising without infinitives and the nature of agreement. In *WCCFL 18 Proceedings*, Sonya Bird, Andrew Carnie, Jason D. Haugen & Peter Norquest (eds.), 14–26. Somerville MA: Cascadilla Press.

Alexiadou, Artemis & Anagnostopoulou, Elena. 2002. Raising without infinitives and the role of agreement. In *Dimensions of Movement: From Features to Remnants* [Linguistik Aktuell/Linguistics Today 48], Artemis Alexiadou, Elena Anagnostopoulou, Sjef Barbiers, & Hans-Martin Gärtner (eds.), 17–30. Amsterdam: John Benjamins. doi:10.1075/la.48.02ale

Avery, J. Peter. 1996. The Representation of Voicing Contrasts. Ph.D. dissertation, University of Toronto.

Béjar, Susana & Hall, Daniel Currie. 2000. Marking markedness: The underlying order of diagonal syncretisms. In *Proceedings of ESCOL 99*, Rebecca Daly & Anastasia Riehl (eds.), 1–12. Ithaca NY: CLC Publications.

Bélanger, Suzanne. 2002. A derivational relationship: The subjunctive-infinitive alternation in French. Ms, University of Toronto.

Binnick, Robert I. 1991. *Time and the Verb*. Oxford: OUP.

Chomsky, Noam. 1981. *Lectures on Government and Binding*. Dordrecht: Foris.

Chomsky, Noam. 1982. *Some Concepts and Consequences of the Theory of Government and Binding*. Cambridge MA: The MIT Press.

Chomsky, Noam. 1995. *The Minimalist Program*. Cambridge MA: The MIT Press.

Chomsky, Noam. 2000. Minimalist inquiries: The framework. In *Step by Step*, Roger Martin, David Michaels & Juan Uriagereka (eds.), 89–155. Cambridge MA: The MIT Press.

Chomsky, Noam. 2001. Derivation by phase. In *Ken Hale: A Life in Language*, Michael Kenstowicz (ed.), 1–52. Cambridge MA: The MIT Press.

Clarke, Sarah. 2013. Aspectual Scope and Contrast in English and Japanese. Ph.D. dissertation, University of Toronto.

Comrie, Bernard. 1976. *Aspect*. Cambridge: CUP.

Cowper, Elizabeth. 2005. The geometry of interpretable features: Infl in English and Spanish. *Language* 81(1): 10–46. doi:10.1353/lan.2005.0012

Cowper, Elizabeth & Hall, Daniel Currie. 2007. The morphosyntactic manifestations of modality. In *Proceedings of the 2007 CLA*, Milica Radišić (ed.). Canadian Linguistic Association.

Dyscolus, Apollonius. 1981. *The Syntax of Apollonius Dyscolus*. Amsterdam: John Benjamins. doi:10.1075/sihols.23

Farkas, Donka F. 1982. Intensionality and Romance Subjunctive Relatives. Ph.D. dissertation, University of Chicago.

George, Leland & Kornfilt, Jaklin. 1981. Finiteness and boundedness in Turkish. In *Binding and Filtering*, Frank Heny (ed.), 105–127. London: Croom Helm.

Haegeman, Liliane. 1985. INFL, COMP and nominative case assignment in Flemish infinitivals. In *Features and Projections*, Peter Muysken & Henk van Riemsdijk (eds.), 123–137. Dordrecht: Foris.

Halle, Morris & Marantz, Alec. 1993. Distributed morphology and the pieces of inflection. In *The View from Building 20: Essays in Linguistics in Honor of Sylvain Bromberger*, Kenneth Hale & Samuel Jay Keyser (eds.), 111–176. Cambridge MA: The MIT Press.

Harbour, Daniel & Elsholtz, Christian. 2012. Feature geometry: Self-destructed. Ms, Queen Mary University of London and Technische Universität Graz.

Harley, Heidi & Ritter, Elizabeth. 2002. Person and number in pronouns: A feature-geometric analysis. *Language* 78(3): 482–526. doi:10.1353/lan.2002.0158

Hornstein, Norbert. 1990. *As Time Goes By*. Cambridge MA: The MIT Press.

Hornstein, Norbert. 1995. *Logical Form: From GB to Minimalism*. Oxford: Blackwells.

Jespersen, Otto. 1924. *The Philosophy of Grammar*. London: Allen and Unwin.

Koopman, Hilda. 1984. *The Syntax of Verbs*. Dordrecht: Foris.

Kornfilt, Jaklin. 2001a. Case and agreement: Morphology and its syntactic effects in Turkish. Paper presented at the 23rd Annual Meeting of the Linguistics Society of Germany.

Kornfilt, Jaklin. 2001b. Subjects and their case in Turkish/Turkic embeddings. Paper presented at the Workshop on Altaic Languages, MIT.

Kyriakaki, Maria. 2006. The Geometry of Tense, Mood and Aspect in Greek. MA thesis, University of Toronto.

Ledgeway, Adam. 1998. Variation in the Romance infinitive: The case of the southern Calabrian inflected infinitive. *Transactions of the Philological Society* 96(1): 1–61. doi:10.1111/1467-968X.00023

Luján, Marta. 1999. A unified approach to control and obviation. In *Grammatical Analyses in Basque and Romance Linguistics* [Current Issues in Linguistic Theory 187], Jon A. Franco, Alazne Landa & Juan Martin (eds.), 105–130. Amsterdam: John Benjamins. doi:10.1075/cilt.187.07luj

Mailhac, Jean-Pierre. 2000. Sens, choix et subjonctif. *French Language Studies* 10: 229–244. doi:10.1017/S0959269500000235

Pesetsky, David & Torrego, Esther. 2001. T-to-C movement: Causes and consequences. In *Ken Hale: A Life in Language*, Michael Kenstowicz (ed.), 355–426. Cambridge MA: The MIT Press.

Pesetsky, David & Torrego, Esther. 2004. Tense, case, and the nature of syntactic categories. In *The Syntax of Time*, Jacqueline Guéron & Jacqueline Lecarme (eds.), 495–537. Cambridge MA: The MIT Press.

Pesetsky, David & Torrego, Esther. 2007. The syntax of valuation and the interpretability of features. In *Phrasal and Clausal Architecture: Syntactic Derivation and Interpretation: In Honor of Joseph Emonds* [Linguistik Akuell/Linguistics Today 101], Simin Karimi, Vida Samiian & Wendy K. Wilkins (eds.), 262–294. Amsterdam: John Benjamins. doi:10.1075/la.101.14pes

Platzack, Christer. 1983. Germanic word order and the Comp/Infl parameter. *Working Papers in Scandinavian Syntax (Trondheim)* 2.

Poplack, Shana. 1991. The inherent variability of the French subjunctive. In *Theoretical Analyses in Romance Linguistics: Selected Papers from the Nineteenth Linguistic Symposium on Romance Languages* [Current Issues in Linguistic Theory 74], Christiane Laeufer & Terrell A. Morgan (eds.), 235–263. Amsterdam: John Benjamins. doi:10.1075/cilt.74.17pop

Pountain, Christopher J. 1995. Infinitives with overt subjects: A pragmatic approach. In *Portuguese, Brazilian and African Studies: Studies Presented to Clive Willis on his Retirement*, Tom Earle & Nigel Griffin (eds.), 11–25. Warminster: Aris and Phillips.

Quicoli, A. Carlos. 1996. Inflection and parametric variation: Portuguese vs. Spanish. In *Current Issues in Comparative Grammar*, Robert Freidin (ed.), 46–80. Dordrecht: Kluwer. doi:10.1007/978-94-009-0135-3_2

Raposo, Eduardo. 1987a. Case theory and Infl-to-Comp: The inflected infinitive in European Portuguese. *Linguistic Inquiry* 18: 85–109.

Raposo, Eduardo. 1987b. Romance infinitival clauses and case theory. In *Studies in Romance Languages*, Carol Neidle & Rafael A. Nuñez Cedeño (eds.), 237–249. Dordrecht: Foris.

Raposo, Eduardo. 1989. Prepositional infinitival constructions in European Portuguese. In *The Null Subject Parameter*, Osvaldo Jaeggli & Kenneth J. Safir (eds.), 277–305. Dordrecht: Kluwer. doi:10.1007/978-94-009-2540-3_10

Roussou, Anna. 2001. Control and raising in and out of subjunctive complements. In *Comparative Syntax of the Balkan Languages*, María Luisa Rivero & Anna Ralli (eds.), 74–104. Oxford: OUP.

Sagey, Elizabeth. 1986. The Representation of Features and Relations in Nonlinear Phonology. Ph.D. dissertation, MIT.

Schütze, Carson T. 1997. INFL in Child and Adult Language: Agreement, Case, and Licensing. Ph.D. dissertation, MIT.

Sitaridou, Ioanna. 2009. On the emergence of personal infinitives in the history of Spanish. *Diachronica* 26(1): 36–64. doi:10.1075/dia.26.1.02sit

Soames, Scott & David M. Perlmutter. 1979. *Syntactic Argumentation and the Structure of English*. Berkeley CA: University of California Press.

Subirats-Rüggeberg, Carlos. 1990. The relation between infinitival and sentential complements in traditional grammar. *Lingvisticæ Investigationes* 14(1): 81–93. doi:10.1075/li.14.1.05sub

Thiébault, Dieudonné. 1802. *Grammaire philosophique, ou la métaphysique, la logique, et la grammaire réunies en un seul corps de doctrine*. Stuttgart-Bad Cannstatt: Friedrich Frommann.

The Split T Analysis

Halldór Ármann Sigurðsson
Lund University

This essay pursues *The Split T Analysis*, claiming that finite clauses have three syntactically active T heads, roughly corresponding to the Reichenbachian S, R, E: Speech Tense, T_S, in the C-domain, Referential Tense, T_R (or simply T) in the T-domain, and Event Tense, T_E, in the v-domain. This analysis, it is argued, enables a coherent account of the relationship between Tense morphology (including Tense Agreement) and Tense syntax (including Sequence of Tenses phenomena and Double Access Readings).

Keywords: double access readings; sequence of tenses; tense; tense agreement; tense computation; the syntax-PF correlation

1. Introduction[1]

Tense more than most other categories illustrates that grammar is a computational system. This was shown to be the case already in *Elements of Symbolic Logic* by Hans Reichenbach (1947) and has since been further corroborated in the work of Chomsky (1957 onward) and in numerous individual studies (including Dahl 1985; Hornstein 1990; Giorgi & Pianesi 1997; Cinque 1999; Julien 2001; Guéron & Lecarme 2004; Sigurðsson & Maling 2012). The fundamental problem raised by Tense and the various Tense systems found in languages of the world can be stated as the simple but big question in (1).

(1) How is Tense computed and expressed in natural language(s)?

The classical Reichenbachian approach to Tense is a three-part model, based on the notions Speech Time, Event Time, and, crucially, Reference Time, abbreviated as S, E, R, respectively. Tense systems typically involve a non-finite and a finite part. The non-finite part expresses a computational relation between E and R (E "sooner than" R, etc.). I designate this relation as **E↔R**, where ↔ simply denotes "a computational

1. Many thanks to Jim Wood and two anonymous reviewers for their valuable remarks and discussions.

DOI 10.1075/la.231.03sig

relation". The finite part, in turn, expresses a computational relation between S and E↔R (and not only R itself, as in Reichenbach 1947): **S↔(E↔R)**.[2] To illustrate this I will be using the following connectives (see also Sigurðsson and Maling 2012):

(2)			
a.	=	unshifted	'simultaneously as'
b.	≥	non-future (present/past)	'no later than'
c.	>	past	'sooner than'
d.	≤	non-past (present/future)	'no sooner than'
e.	<	future	'later than'

In the simple tenses this double computational relation, S↔(E↔R), is not discernible, as R and E are simultaneous. This is illustrated in (3).

(3) *The simple tenses:*

	Non-finite	Finite	Reading	Example
a.	(E = R)	> S	past	Hans left
b.	(E = R)	≤ S	present/future	Hans leaves
c.	(E = R)	< S	future	Hans will leave

In addition to the unshifted E = R, the non-finite part of tense systems like the English one has two potentially shifted relations: towards past (≥) and towards future (≤), as illustrated in (4).

(4)	Non-finite	Reading		Example
a.	E = R	unshifted	as in (most) gerunds[3]	working
b.	E ≥ R	present/past	as in past participles	(has/had) worked
c.	E ≤ R	present/future	as in infinitives	(to) work

The clear-cut past (>) and future (<) relations between E and R are not disambiguated by grammatical or systematic means in languages of this type, instead being subsumed under the more general, ambiguous relations present/past (≥) and present/future (≤). This ambiguity of the non-finite tenses is widespread across languages, perhaps universal.

2. Some constructions involve more than one R. I set this aside here (but see, for instance, Julien 2001; Sigurðsson & Maling 2012). For a more general discussion of the R notion, see Rothstein (2008).

3. I agree with Stowell (1982:563) that "the understood tense of the gerund is completely malleable to the semantics of the governing verb," at least in unmarked cases (in contrast, Hornstein (1990:115ff), argues that gerunds have their own temporal structure). That is, the internal Event Time of gerunds (and of nominalizations, as in "They witnessed the destruction of their town") is dependent or parasitic on the Tense computation of the governing predicate.

The *past-in-the-past* reading of the regular past perfect renders the cooperation of the non-finite and the finite parts of the tense system more easily detectable. It is exemplified in (5).

(5) [Albert:] Hans had read the book (at 9 o'clock).

In (5) the time of the reading event, E, was prior to R, the reference time expressed by *had* (at 9 o' clock), $E \leftrightarrow R$ in turn being prior to the speaker's (here Albert's) saying so, S. The perfect tense system in English-type languages involves the non-finite present/past (non-future) relation, $E \geq R$, as sketched in (6).

(6) *The English perfect tense system:*

	Non-finite	**Finite**	Construction	Example
a.	$(E \geq R)$	$> S$	perfect **past**	Hans **had** read the book
b.	$(E \geq R)$	$= S$	perfect **present**	Hans **has** read the book
c.	$(E \geq R)$	$< S$	perfect **future**	Hans **will** have read the book

Conversely, a truly progressive tense system, such as the Icelandic one,[4] involves the main verb present/future (non-past) relation, $E \leq R$, plus past (>S), present (=S), or future (<S) of the finite auxiliary *vera* 'be'. This is illustrated in (7)–(8) (modeled on (13)–(14) in Sigurðsson & Maling 2012).

(7) a. *Hans var að lesa.*
Hans was to read
≈ 'Hans was reading.'

b. *Hans er að lesa.*
Hans is to read
≈ 'Hans is reading.'

c. *Hans verður að lesa.*
Hans will-be to read
≈ 'Hans will be reading.'[5]

(8)

	Non-finite	**Finite**	Construction	English glosses
a.	$(E \leq R)$	$> S$	progressive, **past**	Hans **was** to read
b.	$(E \leq R)$	$= S$	progressive, **present**	Hans **is** to read
c.	$(E \leq R)$	$< S$	progressive, **future**	Hans **will be** to read

4. "[T]here is no real *temporal* distinction between the progressive tenses and the simple tenses in English, English using the progressive to express the simple tense relations even more commonly than Icelandic does (where this is also possible, and is currently spreading, due to the ambiguity of $(E \leq R)$, which means both 'future' $(E < R)$ and 'present' $(E = R)$)" (Sigurðsson & Maling 2012: 375).

5. The sentence in (7c) may also have the modal reading 'Hans must read', but that reading is irrelevant here.

A central question linguistics needs to address is where in grammar or language this tense computation takes place–is it morphological, semantic/pragmatic (as commonly assumed), or is it syntactic? In the following I will sketch a syntactic analysis.[6]

2. Basic analysis

The central hypothesis pursued here (see also Sigurðsson & Maling 2012) is that finite clauses have three syntactically active (but often silent) T heads, roughly corresponding to Reichenbachian S, R, E, as stated in (9).

(9) a. Speech T, T_S, in the C-domain
b. Referential T, T_R (or simply T) in the T-domain
c. Event T, T_E, in the v-domain

The "T-spine" of the clause is as sketched in (10).

(10) $[_{CP} \ldots T_S \ldots [_{TP} \ldots T_R \ldots [_{vP} \ldots T_E \ldots]]]$

The *past-in-the-past* reading of the past perfect in (5) can thus be analyzed as in (11).

(11) NOW $[_{CP} \ldots T_S \ldots [_{TP} \ldots T_R \ldots [_{vP} \ldots T_E \ldots]]]$
had *read*
↑_ _ _ _ _ _ _ _ _ _ _↑ ↑______↑ ↑______↑
Contextual control *Agree* *Agree*
simultaneous *past* *past*

On this approach, Agree is a *valuing relation* (pace Chomsky 2001:5). Thus, in (5)/(11) T_E (the time of the reading event) is valued under Agree as "past" in relation to T_R, which in turn is valued as "past" in relation to T_S.[7] In contrast, control, whether full

6. For my present purposes the term "computation" is confined to the narrowly syntactic computation. Much like other grammatical categories Tense has both semantic and morphological correlates (in languages with Tense morphology), thus having "many faces". The semantic interpretation of Tense takes the syntactically computed tense values as input into semantic/pragmatic processes, and the externalization component also takes the syntactically computed values as input into interface-specific processes (such as the morphological decision of past tense forms like *sang* and *shouted*). As we will see, Tense syntax is quite distinct from Tense morphology, the former building relations, the latter interpreting these relations in terms of discrete units (morphemes, etc.). The distinction between Tense syntax and interface-specific Tense semantics/pragmatics is less clear.

7. This is a slight simplification–it is actually the relation $T_E \leftrightarrow T_R$ that is valued as "past" in relation to T_S.

or partial, syntactic or contextual, is an *identity relation* (regardless of whether it is derived by movement).[8] Thus, in (5)/(11), T_S is set under contextual control as identical or simultaneous with speaker NOW.

The interpretation of any clause is subject to matching relations between the v-domain (containing the propositional content), the "grammatical" T-domain, and the "context-sensitive" C-domain. Thus, an event participant (a vP-internal NP) is valued in relation to a Person head in the T-domain, as being either +Pn or −Pn, NP_{+Pn} in turn being positively or negatively valued in relation to abstract "speaker" and "hearer" categories in the C-domain, thereby getting their 1st, 2nd or 3rd person values.[9] The general, universal computational scheme of full clauses is sketched in (12).

(12) CONTEXT $[_{CP}$ ……… $[_{TP}$ ………. $[_{vP}$ ……]]]

↑ - - - - - - - - - - - - - - ↑ ↑________ ↑ ↑________ ↑

Contextual control (identity/reference) — *Agree* (valuing) — *Agree* (valuing)

On this approach, thus, the vP-phase relates to (or "agrees with") the CP-phase via grammatical elements in the T-domain (most centrally Tense and Person). In the next section, I demonstrate how Tense computation adheres to this general scheme.

3. Anaphoric T_S

In the unmarked case, T_S is *deictic* (much as indexical pronouns prototypically are deictic). This is for example the case for both the matrix and the subordinate clauses in (13).

(13) a. [Peter:] This morning I discovered that Mary will leave in a week.
b. [Peter:] Mary works tonight because Susan left in the afternoon.

The Tense structure of (13b) is shown in (14) ($T_R = T_E$ in both CPs). Control (identity) relations are indicated by broken lines, Agree (valuation) relations with unbroken ones.

---

8. Syntactic control is more heavily constrained than contextual control, but both are referential identity relations.

9. This is a big issue and a detailed discussion of it would take us much too far afield. I refer the reader to Sigurðsson 2004b, 2014 and the references there.

(14) NOW $[_{CP} \ldots T_{S1} \ldots \ldots$ works-$T_{E1} \ldots$ $[_{CP} \ldots T_{S2} \ldots$ … left-$T_{E2} \ldots$

↑__________↑ ↑__________↑

non-past *past*

('present')

↑- - - - - - - -↑ ↑- - - - - - - - - - - - - - - -↑

simultaneous *simultaneous*

As shown, both T_{S1} and T_{S2} are set as identical or simultaneous with NOW under control (direct contextual control in the matrix CP, indirect syntactic control in the subordinate CP). Thus, the matrix event of working and the subordinate event of leaving both acquire their temporal reading (here non-past vs. past) in relation to the speaker NOW.

However, in some widely discussed contexts, subordinate T_S is shifted. Kiparsky (2002) refers to shifted T_S as "perspective time," which is a nice pedagogical term, but, as I have argued in previous work (e.g., Sigurðsson 1990, 2004b), the shifted T is really a perceived secondary Speech Tense. In the following, I will take a closer look at T_S Shift. As we will see, it crucially involves a shift of embedded T_S under control by a matrix T head, the embedded T_S thereby becoming *anaphoric* in relation to this matrix T controller.[10] In this respect, the behavior of Tense parallels the behavior of Person in so-called indexical shift phenomena (see Sigurðsson 2014; cf. Schlenker 2003; Bianchi 2006; Anand 2006). T_S Shift is not visible on the subordinate T_S itself (T_S being invisible or silent by necessity), but it is commonly accompanied by morphological marking of the subordinate finite verb in T_R (or T_R/T_E), a fact that has caused much confusion in the literature.

3.1 Sequence of Tenses (SOT) – Tense Agreement

T_S Shift is observed in *Sequence of Tenses*, as in (15).[11]

(15) I **realized** that it **was** Mary (when I said hello). *English*

(16) %*Maria* ***krävde*** *att vi* ***läste*** *boken (nästa dag)*.[12] *Swedish*
Mary demanded that we read.PST book.the (next day)
'Mary demanded that we would read the book (next day).'

---

10. Which is usually the matrix T_E, but T_R in certain exceptional cases (discussed in Sigurðsson 1990: 329–330).

11. SOT phenomena have been so widely discussed that it is almost pointless to mention some specific references, but see, for example, Enç 1987; Hornstein 1990; Giorgi & Pianesi 1997; Schlenker 2004; Giorgi 2010.

12. The percent sign indicates variable acceptance. Some speakers strongly prefer the periphrastic *skulle läsa* 'would read.'

The matrix and the subordinate verbs form a sequence of past tense, hence the term Sequence of Tenses, SOT for short. The phenomenon is sometimes referred to as *Tense Agreement*, a slightly more pertinent term (see, e.g., Anderson 1990). Both notions are formal or morphological. Semantically, the subordinate clauses in (15) and (16) have a perceived secondary Speech Tense (T_{S2}) that has been shifted into the past (under control) such that it becomes simultaneous with the past matrix events of realizing in (15) and demanding in (16). This shift is accompanied by past morphology on the subordinate finite verbs *was* and *läste* 'read', but their reading, in turn, is *non-past* in relation to T_{S2} and the matrix events. That is, semantically and syntactically, (15)–(16) illustrate T_S Shift, with a *non-past-in-the-past* reading.[13] This reading is a regular property of subordinate past subjunctives in many languages. Example (17) is Icelandic.

(17) *María* ***sagði*** *[að Ólafur* ***væri*** *veikur*
Mary said that Olaf were.PST.SBJ sick
*(*í gær)].* *Icelandic*
(*in yesterday)
'Mary said that Olaf **was** sick (*yesterday).'[14]
'(= sick at the moment of Mary's saying so).'

The Tense structure of (17) is shown in (18) (basically the same analysis applies to (15) and (16); semantically, $T_R = T_E$ in both CPs, but *sagði* 'said' and *væri* 'were' have been raised to T_R).

(18) NOW $[_{CP}$ … T_{S1} … … said-T_{E1} … $[_{CP}$ … T_{S2} … … sick-T_{E2} …
↑ _ _ _ _ _ _ ↑ ↑ ________ ↑ ↑ _ _ _ _ _ _ _ ↑ ↑ _____________ ↑
simultaneous *past* *simultaneous* *non-past ('present')*

That is, what is "past" in the past subjunctive is not the sickness eventuality (T_{E2}), but T_{S2} (the perspective time in Kiparsky 2002). While T_{S1} is deictic, T_{S2} is *anaphoric*. The embedded verb (*væri* in (17)), in turn, gets its past tense form by uninterpretable morphological agreement, being semantically non-past with respect to the shifted T_{S2} (and the matrix T_{E1}).

This kind of uninterpretable Tense Agreement is even found in some infinitival complements. This is illustrated for Icelandic in (19) (English also shows Tense Agreement in the translations, but it does so in regular finite clauses).

13. While the copula and other stative predicates typically get a *present-in-the-past* reading in SOT, dynamic predicates like *read*, as in (16), typically get a *future-in-the-past* reading. Both readings are subsumed under a general *non-past-in-the-past* reading (parallel to the simple present).

14. I.e., the narrow scope reading of *yesterday* is out (the wide scope reading is irrelevant).

(19) a. *María* **segist** *munu* *fara.* *Icelandic*
Mary says-herself will.INF go PRES.IND – PRES.INF
≈ 'Mary says that she will go.'

b. *María* **sagðist** *mundu* *fara.* PST.IND – PST.INF
Mary said-herself will.INF go
≈ 'Mary said that she would go.'

That is, meaningless Tense Agreement can be passed down into certain complement structures, seemingly in a top > bottom externalization process. As will be briefly discussed in Section 4, case agreement sometimes behaves in a parallel manner.

3.2 Double Access Reading (DAR)

Double Access Reading (see, e.g., Schlenker 2004; Anand & Hacquard 2007; Giorgi 2010) is another relevant issue in the present context. It is demonstrated in (20) for English, in (21) for Italian, and in (22) for Icelandic.[15]

(20) [Anna:] (When I met him) John knew that Mary **is** sick. *English*

(21) [Anna:] *Gianni ha saputo che Maria* **è** *malata.* *Italian*
John has known that Mary is.IND sick
[Anna:] 'John knew that Mary is sick.'

(22) [Anna:] *Jón vissi að María* **er** *veik.* *Icelandic*
John knew that Mary is.IND sick
[Anna:] 'John knew that Mary is sick.'

The term "double access" refers to the fact that the subordinate Event Time or T_{E2} (Mary's sickness eventuality) is temporally accessible to both the matrix T_{E1} of John's knowing and the matrix T_{S1} (which is simultaneous with the speaker NOW). That is, Mary's sickness holds at both the time of John's knowing about it and Anna's time of telling somebody about this knowledge of his. Mary could for instance have been sick for the last six months when Anna tells somebody that John knew about her extended illness two months ago.

Compare (20)–(22) and the examples in (23) and (24).

(23) [Anna:] *Jón vissi að María* **var** *veik.* *Icelandic*
John knew that Mary was.**PST**.IND sick
[Anna:] 'John knew that Mary was/had been sick.'

15. DAR is more restricted in Icelandic than in English and Italian as it is excluded from the complements of verbs of saying and thinking (which take an obligatory subjunctive in Modern Icelandic, as opposed to Old Norse and, e.g., Italian; see Sigurðsson 2010).

(24) [Anna:] *Jón vissi að María **væri** veik.* *Icelandic*
John knew that Mary were.**PST**.SBJ sick
[Anna:] 'John knew that Mary was sick.'

The clause in (23) is ambiguous between a "single access" and a "no access" reading. On the single access reading the sickness is simultaneous with John's knowledge but prior to Anna's utterance (access to T_{E1}). On the no access reading the sickness is prior to both John's knowledge and Anna's utterance (as in "Yesterday John knew that Mary was sick the day before").

The example in (24), in turn, has a single access SOT reading; that is, Mary's sickness is simultaneous with John's past knowledge and prior to Anna's utterance. With dynamic predicates, though, for instance 'leave' (as in "John knew that Mary left.SBJ"), the past subjunctive normally has a future reading (≈ 'John knew that Mary would leave').[16] – A single access reading where the access is to the time of utterance (T_{S1}) but not to the matrix event time is anomalous (as in, e.g., "*Yesterday John knew that Mary is sick now").

The DAR in (20)–(22) combines two single access readings: A) simultaneity of the subordinate sickness eventuality (T_{E2}) with the matrix event of John's knowledge (T_{E1}), and B) simultaneity of the sickness (T_{E2}) with the utterance time (T_{S1}). The first reading (A) is similar to the non-past-in-the-past reading of T_{E2} in SOT (when not shifted towards future). The second reading (B) is a plain present (non-past-in-the-non-past) "indicative" reading, as in (25), where the times of Anna's saying, John's knowledge and Mary's sickness are all simultaneous.

(25) [Anna:] John knows that Mary is sick.

The Tense structure of the DAR reading of (20)–(22) is thus as illustrated in (26).

(26) NOW $[_{CP}$ … T_{S1} … … knew-T_{E1} … $[_{CP}$ … T_{S2} … … sick-T_{E2} …

↑__________↑ (*past*): T_{S1} – T_{E1}

↑__________↑ (*non-past ("present")*): T_{S2} – T_{E2}

↑- - - - - - - - - -↑ (*simultaneous*): T_{E1} – T_{E2}

↑- - - - -↑ (*simultaneous*): NOW – T_{S1}

↑- - - - - - - - - -↑ (*simultaneous*): T_{S1} – T_{S2}

16. Subordinate indicatives have a non-future (present/past) reading in relation to their matrix clause, whereas subjunctive complements have a non-past (present/future) reading. Recall, from Footnote 12, that stative predicates, including the copula (as in (24)), typically get a present-in-the-past reading in SOT while dynamic predicates normally get a future-in-the-past reading, both readings being subsumed under a general non-past-in-the-past reading.

As in the plain non-past-in-the-non-past reading in (25) both T_{S1} and T_{S2} are set simultaneous with the speaker NOW under control (contextual and syntactic). As the sickness eventuality (T_{E2}) is valued under Agree as non-past ("present") in relation to T_{S2} it is transitively identical with the utterance time T_{S1} = NOW. In addition, there is a temporal control relation between the matrix and the subordinate eventualities, T_{E2} thus having access to T_{E1} as well as to the utterance time (= double access). On the other hand, as shown, there is no computational relation between T_{E1} and T_{S2}; hence the absence of T_S Shift and also of Tense Agreement (in contrast to SOT, as in (17)/(18) and (24); see further Section 3.4).

3.3 Non-SOT (absent Tense Agreement) vs. SOT

Non-SOT languages and split SOT languages do not apply Tense Agreement in complement clauses like the ones in (15)–(17), instead using the simple present tense, as illustrated for Russian and Japanese in (27) and (28).

(27) *Tanja* ***skazala*** *[čto ona* ***tancuet****].* — *Russian*
Tanja said that she dances — (Comrie 1986: 275)
'Tanja said that she was dancing
(at the moment of Tanja's saying so).'

(28) *Taroowa [Hanakoga Siatoruni* ***iru****] to* ***itta****.* — *Japanese*
Taro Hanako Seattle-in is that said — (Ogihara 1996: 5)
'Taro said that Hanako was in Seattle
(at the moment of Taro's saying so).'

Crucially, however, the present tense subordinate clauses in (27)–(28) have the same tense interpretation as the past tense subordinate clauses in (15)–(17): 'Non-past relative to the past saying in the matrix clause' (Kondrashova 2005). Reconsider the Icelandic example in (17) and its Tense structure in (18), repeated as (29) and (30).

(29) *María* ***sagði*** *[að Ólafur* ***væri*** *veikur*
Mary said that Olaf were.PST.SBJ sick
*(*í gær)].* — *Icelandic*
(*in yesterday)
'Mary said that Olaf **was** sick (*yesterday).'
'(= sick at the moment of Mary's saying so).'

(30) NOW [$_{CP}$ … T_{S1} … … said-T_{E1} … [$_{CP}$ … T_{S2} … … sick-T_{E2} …
↑_ _ _ _ _ _ _↑ ↑__________↑ ↑_ _ _ _ _ _ _↑ ↑__________↑
simultaneous *past* *simultaneous* *non-past ('present')*

Evidently, in SOT examples of this sort in Icelandic morphology, uninterpretable morphological +PAST is silently copied onto T_{S2} under control and spelled out on the verb in T_{R2} under morphological (deep PF) agreement with T_{S2}, as sketched in (31) (the curly brackets under T_{S2} indicate that the + PAST element there is PF-silent).

(31) $[_{CP}$ … said-T_{E1} … $[_{CP}$ … T_{S2} … … T_{R2}/sick-T_{E2} …
+PAST {+ PAST} +PAST
↑_ _ _ _ _ _ _ _↑ ↑________↑
Control *agreement*

This morphological agreement process is not operative in the Russian and Japanese examples in (27) and (28). That is, Russian and Japanese are morphologically different from but syntactically similar to Icelandic, English, etc.

4. Concluding remarks on the syntax-PF correlation

Tense Agreement (overt SOT) behaves like a reflex of sorts, utilizing a syntactic control relation between T_{E1} and T_{S2} as a kind of a path or a gateway to pass down the morphological tense value from the matrix verb. Strikingly, the value in examples like (15)–(17) is *shifted* (+PAST), while the syntactic control relation between T_{E1} and T_{S2} establishes an *unshifted* identity relation (as control relations generally do; here, the identity is temporal simultaneity). Tense Agreement is thus quite distinct from the syntactic matching processes (Control/Agree) that yield tense interpretation.

- Tense Agreement operates with non-syntactic features (morphological +PAST, etc.)
- Tense Agreement evidently utilizes a Control/Agree path (already laid in the syntactic *bottom* > *top* derivation) in a directional *top* > *bottom* externalization PF process

Much the same behavior is seen in other meaningless (uninterpretable) agreement phenomena, including, for example, NP-internal concord and optional case agreement of Icelandic PRO. The latter is illustrated in (32)–(33) (see Sigurðsson 2008 and the references cited there).

(32) *Hún bað Ólaf [að PRO fara bara* ***einan*** *í veisluna].*
she.NOM asked Olaf.ACC to go just alone.ACC to party.the
'She asked Olaf to just go alone to the party.'

(33) $[_{CP}$ … Olaf.ACC … $[_{CP}$ … PRO … … alone.ACC …][17]
↑____________↑↑________________↑
Control *PF case agreement*

17. Regardless of how one analyzes control, the syntactic and the morphological derivations are quite distinct (the latter bearing only indirectly on the former).

Like overt Tense Agreement, case agreement is semantically vacuous. That is, there are no semantic differences between the Acc *einan* 'alone' in (32) and the Nom *einn* 'alone' in (34).[18]

(34) *Hún* *bað* *Ólaf* *[að PRO fara bara* ***einn*** *í veisluna].*
she.NOM asked Olaf.ACC to go just alone.NOM to party.the
'She asked Olaf to just go alone to the party.'

Overt agreement processes in general are PF processes (Sigurðsson 2004a, 2006, etc., Bobaljik 2008), taking place in the post-syntactic externalization component of language, out of sight for syntax and semantics. Accordingly, overt agreement reflects syntax but has no syntactic or semantic import. Simple data from well-documented languages further substantiate this conclusion (see the documentation of the extensive meaningless agreement variation across the Germanic languages in previous work, e.g. Sigurðsson 2004a). Thus, inasmuch as speakers of English accept clauses like *The girls* ***is*** *here* (see Henry 1995), they arguably have abstract Agree, only lacking overt PF agreement.

The mapping from abstract internal language to perceptible external language is fundamentally non-isomorphic. While syntax builds relations, for example, relations between distinct Tense heads (i.e., between phases), PF reinterprets and expresses these relations as morphological and perceptible units or items (audible, visible, tactile, or combinatory, depending on the externalization mode). Lexical approaches (including Chomskyan lexicalism or "itemism" and Distributed Morphology), make sense as partial models of externalization, but they do not make sense as theories of internal syntax–the system of linguistic thought. Internal language operates with abstract minimal roots and atomic features, such as T_S, T_R, and T_E, constructing relations between such elements, whereas external language expresses discrete items such as English *sang* and *-ed*.

References

Anand, Pranav. 2006. De de se. Ph.D. dissertation, MIT.

Anand, Pranav & Hacquard, Valentine. 2007. When the present is all in the past. In *Recent Advances in the Syntax and Semantics of Tense, Mood and Aspect*, Louis de Saussure, Jacques Moeschler & Genoveva Puskás (eds.), 209–228. Berlin: Mouton de Gruyter.

18. In general, locally licensed NOM is the unmarked option in Icelandic PRO infinitives, but object controlled ACC (as opposed to the more marked quirky subject controlled ACC, object controlled DAT, etc.) is also unmarked and widely acceptable (see Sigurðsson 2008:414).

Anderson, Stephen R. 1990. The grammar of Icelandic verbs in *-st*. In *Modern Icelandic Syntax*, Joan Maling & Annie Zaenen (eds.), 187–234. San Diego CA: Academic Press.
Bianchi, Valentina. 2006. On the syntax of personal arguments. *Lingua* 116: 2023–2067. doi:10.1016/j.lingua.2005.05.002
Bobaljik, Jonathan. 2008. Where's Phi? Agreement as a postsyntactic operation. In *Phi-Theory: Phi Features across Interfaces and Modules*, Daniel Harbour, David Adger & Susana Béjar (eds.), 295–328. Oxford: OUP.
Chomsky, Noam. 1957. *Syntactic Structures*. The Hague: Mouton.
Chomsky, Noam. 2001. Derivation by phase. In *Ken Hale: A Life in Language*, Michael Kenstowicz (ed.), 1–52. Cambridge MA: The MIT Press.
Cinque, Guglielmo. 1999. *Adverbs and Functional Heads: A Cross-Linguistic Perspective*. Oxford: OUP.
Comrie, Bernard. 1986. Tense in indirect speech. *Folia Linguistica* 20: 265–296. doi:10.1515/flin.1986.20.3-4.265
Dahl, Östen. 1985. *Tense and Aspect Systems*. Oxford: Blackwell.
Enç, Mürvet. 1987. Anchoring conditions for tense. *Linguistic Inquiry* 18: 633–657.
Giorgi, Alessandra. 2010. *About the Speaker: Towards a Syntax of Indexicality*. Oxford: OUP.
Giorgi, Alessandra & Pianesi, Fabio. 1997. *Tense and Aspect: From Semantics to Morphosyntax*. Oxford: OUP.
Guéron, Jacqueline & Lecarme, Jacqueline (eds.). 2004. *The Syntax of Time*. Cambridge MA: The MIT Press.
Henry, Alison. 1995. *Belfast English and Standard English: Dialect Variation and Parameter Setting*. Oxford: OUP.
Hornstein, Norbert. 1990. *As Time Goes By: Tense and Universal Grammar*. Cambridge MA: The MIT Press.
Julien, Marit. 2001. The syntax of complex tenses. *The Linguistic Review* 18: 125–167. doi:10.1515/tlir.18.2.125
Kiparsky, Paul. 2002. Event structure and the perfect. In *The Construction of Meaning*, David I. Beaver, Luis D. Casillas Martínez, Brady Z. Clark & Stefan Kaufmann (eds.), 113–136. Stanford CA: CSLI.
Kondrashova, Natalia. 2005. Is Russian a split SOT language? Paper presented at Formal Approaches to Slavic Linguistics 14 at Princeton University.
Ogihara, Toshiyuki. 1996. *Tense, Attitudes, and Scope*. Dordrecht: Kluwer. doi:10.1007/978-94-015-8609-2
Reichenbach, Hans. 1947. *Elements of Symbolic Logic*. New York NY: Macmillan.
Rothstein, Björn. 2008. *The Perfect Time Span* [Linguistik Aktuell/Linguistics Today 125]. Amsterdam: John Benjamins. doi:10.1075/la.125
Schlenker, Philippe. 2003. A plea for monsters. *Linguistics and Philosophy* 26: 29–120. doi:10.1023/A:1022225203544
Schlenker, Philippe. 2004. Sequence phenomena and double access readings generalized. In *The Syntax of Time*, Jacqueline Guéron & Jacqueline Lecarme (eds.), 555–595. Cambridge MA: The MIT Press.
Sigurðsson, Halldór Ármann. 1990. Long distance reflexives and moods in Icelandic. In *Modern Icelandic Syntax*, Joan Maling & Annie Zaenen (eds.), 309–346. San Diego CA: Academic Press.
Sigurðsson, Halldór Ármann. 2004a. Agree and agreement: Evidence from Germanic. In *Focus on Germanic Typology*, Werner Abraham (ed.), 61–103. Berlin: Akademie-Verlag.

Sigurðsson, Halldór Ármann. 2004b. The syntax of person, tense, and speech features. *Italian Journal of Linguistics* 16: 219–251.

Sigurðsson, Halldór Ármann. 2006. Agree in syntax, agreement in signs. In *Agreement Systems* [Linguistik Aktuell/Linguistics Today 92], Cedric Boeckx (ed.), 201–237. Amsterdam: John Benjamins. doi:10.1075/la.92.10sig

Sigurðsson, Halldór Ármann. 2008. The case of PRO. *Natural Language and Linguistic Theory* 26: 403–450. doi:10.1007/s11049-008-9040-6

Sigurðsson, Halldór Ármann. 2010. Mood in Icelandic. In *Mood Systems in the Languages of Europe* [Linguistik Aktuell/Linguistics Today 120], Björn Rothstein & Rolf Thieroff (eds.), 33–55. Amsterdam: John Benjamins. doi:10.1075/slcs.120.02arm

Sigurðsson, Halldór Ármann. 2014. Context-linked Gammar. *Language Sciences* 46(Part B): 175–188. doi:10.1016/j.langsci.2014.06.010

Sigurðsson, Halldór Ármann & Maling, Joan. 2012. Silent heads. In *Functional Heads*, Laura Brugé, Anna Cardinaletti, Giuliana Giusti, Nicola Munaro & Cecilia Poletto (eds.), 368–378. Oxford: OUP. doi:10.1093/acprof:oso/9780199746736.003.0028

Stowell, Tim. 1982. The tense of infinitives. *Linguistic Inquiry* 13: 561–570.

Universals and variation

Encoding anaphoric dependencies*

Eric Reuland
Utrecht institute of Linguistics OTS

This contribution starts with an overview of current issues in the theory of binding. It sketches a modular approach based on universal principles (entailing that reflexivity must be licensed), and that yet is able to account for the cross-linguistic variation observed. It subsequently addresses three issues as case studies: Non-local binding in Scandinavian and the role played by finiteness marking; followed by an analysis of apparently locally bound pronominals in Fijian; it concludes with a novel solution to a problem posed by the anaphoric system of Chamorro that was first described in Chung (1989).

Keywords: binding; universals; finiteness marking; Scandinavian; Fijian; Chamorro

* I would like to start thanking Kristin Melum Eide for inviting me to the Finiteness Fest (NTNU Trondheim, May 6–7 2010), which she organized. My original contribution was titled *On "anaphors" and finiteness.* Its main contribution involved an issue that is still hinted at in the present paper, namely what is the role of finiteness in defining opacity for binding domains and in providing the means to escape from them. The answer to that question as I presented it at the workshop has been fully incorporated in my 2011 book (Chapter 8). In preparing that version I benefited very much from the comments I received at the workshop, for which I would like to express my gratitude. I felt it would not make much sense to publish here, what would amount to a reprint of part of that chapter. Consequently I decided to submit an article that gives an overview of the theoretical framework, which includes a rather informal discussion of the role of finiteness, but also presents a novel analysis for a puzzle in the anaphoric system of Chamorro that was first described in Chung (1989). I am very much indebted to two anonymous reviewers, for their very helpful comments. I would also like to thank Alexis Dimitriadis, Martin Everaert, Dagmar Schadler, and Anna Volkova for great work together on our project on Universals and the typology of reflexives, supported by NWO grant 360-70-330, which is gratefully acknowledged.

DOI 10.1075/la.231.04reu

1. Introduction

Developing an explanatory theory of anaphoric dependencies faces two main challenges. The empirical challenge is to account for both the unity and the cross-linguistic diversity that is so striking in this domain. The other, which is more theory internal, is to do so with a minimum of stipulations, ideally explaining the patterns observed on the basis of independent grammatical principles.

The starting point for most current discussions is the *Canonical Binding Theory* (CBT) (Chomsky 1981), the core of which is stated as follows (leaving out condition C, which does not immediately concern us here):

(1) A. An anaphor is bound in its local domain (governing category)
B. A pronominal is free in its local domain (governing category)

(2) *a* binds *b* iff *a* and *b* are co-indexed and *a* c-commands *b*

The notion of a governing category is defined as in (3):

(3) γ is a governing category for α if and only if γ is the minimal category containing α, a governor of α, and a SUBJECT[1]

Interestingly, from the perspective of the issues discussed in this volume, the core opacity factor in the CBT is the subject. Finiteness plays a role only indirectly in the CBT, namely in the fact that it makes available one particular flavor of a SUBJECT, namely finite Agr. But in fact, as will be briefly discussed in Section 4.3, but quite extensively in Reuland (2011: Ch. 8), finiteness is indeed an important component of an explanatory binding theory, as it is a significant factor in its own right.

The empirical challenge any binding theory has to face is the wide range of variation in anaphoric systems. As we will see, the only way to accommodate this variation is to deconstruct binding theory into a number of component factors.

As has become well-known since the eighties, there are systems with more distinctions than just the distinction between anaphor and pronominal. For instance, Dutch has a 3-way system. It has pronominals such as *hem* 'him', simplex anaphors (henceforth, SE-anaphors) such as *zich*, complex anaphors (SELF-anaphors) such as *zichzelf* 'himself' (Koster 1985, Everaert 1986). Icelandic, and Norwegian (with the other mainland Scandinavian languages) have a 4-way system: Pronominals, SE-anaphors, and complex anaphors both of the form SE-SELF and Pronominal-SELF (e.g. Vikner 1984, 1985; Everaert 1986; Hellan 1988). Similarly, there is significant cross-linguistic variation in binding domains, especially of SE-anaphors. Whereas in Dutch and German

1. A SUBJECT is the most prominent nominal category accessible to α, either the specifier of TP, or the finite agreement. For the notion of accessibility, see Chomsky (1981).

binding of SE-anaphors is still relatively local, in the Mainland Scandinavian languages the antecedent may be far beyond the local subject, as long as no finite clause boundary intervenes (see, for instance, Hellan 1988), whereas in Icelandic and Faroese (and certain Mainland Scandinavian dialects) an anaphoric dependency can be established even beyond this domain (see, for instance, Thráinsson 1976a, b &1991; Sigurðsson 1990; and more recently, Lødrup 2009).

This type of variation could descriptively be accommodated by allowing parametrization of binding domains (Manzini & Wexler 1987). However such a possible parameterization is not enough to 'save' the CBT. As shown in Reuland and Koster (1991), and – in more empirical detail – Reuland and Sigurjónsdóttir (1997) there is a significant contrast between the infinitival and subjunctive domains. Reuland (2011) provides an explicit derivation showing how simplex anaphors can be syntactically bound within the infinitival domain, but require other mechanisms when their the dependency crosses a subjunctive ("finite") clause boundary (see Section 4.3. for more detail).

The following facts, furthermore, go against the core of the CBT. Firstly, under structurally defined conditions certain anaphoric forms need not be bound. This can be seen in the exempt ("logophoric") use of *himself* in English illustrated in (4a), and the logophoric use of Icelandic *sig* illustrated in the following famous example, where a linguistic antecedent is absent altogether.

(4) a. John was hoping that Mary would support *(no one but) himself.

b. María var alltaf svo andstyggileg. þegar Olafur$_j$ kæmi segði hún sér$_{i/*j}$
Mary was always so nasty. When Olaf came, said she himself
áreiðanlega að fara (Thráinsson 1991, citing Sigurðsson 1986, 1990)
certainly to leave
'Mary was always so nasty. When Olaf would come, she would certainly tell himself [the person whose thoughts are being presented – not Olaf] to leave.'

Secondly, languages such as Frisian and Old English, allow locally bound 3rd person pronominals, as in (5) (see for instance, Everaert 1986, 1991 and van Gelderen 2000 for discussion):

(5) a. Jan klaaide him oan
Jan dressed him up
'Jan dressed himself.'

b. he cladde him
he dressed him
'he dressed himself.'

Since in the CBT *having to be bound* and *having to be locally free* are defining properties of anaphors and pronominals respectively, such facts require a fundamental rethinking.

Conditions on reflexivization constitute a third additional factor. As discussed in Reinhart and Reuland (1991, 1993) (henceforth R&R), the distribution of simplex versus complex anaphors in Dutch depends on properties of the predicate the anaphor is an argument of. As a first approximation, if the predicate is lexically reflexive we find the SE-anaphor *zich* as an object; if it is not lexically reflexive the complex anaphor *zichzelf* is required. A typical contrast is given in (6):

(6) a. Alice gedraagt zich (??zelf) goed
Alice behaves SE (self) well
'Alice behaves (herself) well.'

b. Alice bewondert zich *(zelf)
Alice admires SE (self)
'Alice admires herself.'

Gedragen is lexically reflexive, hence allows *zich* (and is not felicitous with *zichzelf*), *bewonderen* is not, hence requires *zichzelf*.

As R&R show, the core principle is that reflexivity of predicates must be licensed. Licensing can happen in two ways: i. by a lexical operation; ii. by a SELF-anaphor. Hence, we find a SE-anaphor where a lexical reflexivization operation is available and where the SE-anaphor being bound by its antecedent does not make a predicate reflexive. So, we typically find a SE-anaphor also in locative and directional PP's, where the argument of the preposition is not an argument of the verb, as in (7a), and as the subject of small clauses, as in (7b), where it is not a (semantic) argument of the matrix verb.

(7) a. Alice zette het flesje naast zich
Alice put the bottle next to SE
'Alice put the bottle next to her.'

b. Alice voelde [zich wegglijden]
Alice felt [SE slip away]
'Alice felt herself slip away.'

As an argument of the verb the SE-anaphor does not only appear with verbs such as *gedragen* 'behave' that are intrinsically reflexive, in the sense that they never allow an independent object (in fact such verbs are semantically always intransitive). It also occurs with grooming verbs such as *wassen* 'wash', *scheren* 'shave', etc., but not only with these. We find SE-anaphors also with a broader class of transitive verbs, such as *verdedigen* 'defend', *ontwapenen* 'disarm', etc., but never with verbs such as *haten* 'hate', *bewonderen* 'admire', or *kennen* ' know'. Note that if we broaden our scope to reflexivity in general, even a summary analysis of English shows that properties of predicates play a role. With intrinsically reflexive verbs such as *behave*, and with grooming verbs such as *wash, dress*, etc., we generally have two options: *Alice behaved herself* and *Alice behaved, the children washed/dressed themselves* and *the children washed/dressed.* But not so with *hate* or *admire*. *Alice hated* does not mean *Alice hated herself*, *the children admired* does not mean *the children admired themselves*.

For the moment it is enough to note that these and similar facts show that such differences exist.[2]

In the following sections I will first sketch a perspective on binding that makes a principled distinction between syntactic, semantic and discourse representation of anaphoric dependencies, and then show how the interplay between language specific properties, properties of predicates, the feature specification of individual pronominals and anaphors, and general principles of grammatical computation allow us to accommodate this variation. Finally I show how this framework can account for some potentially puzzling binding facts in Fijian and Chamorro.

2. Theoretical perspectives on binding

The principles and parameters theory as it developed from the approach presented in Chomsky (1981) marks an important development in that it facilitated applying the methods of generative grammar to a growing number of languages. From a descriptive and even a heuristic perspective it was highly successful. However, from an explanatory perspective it was less so. Given the rich amount of descriptive devices it became increasingly less suited to provide a sufficiently restrictive definition of "possible grammar of a human language". The minimalist program (Chomsky 1995 and subsequent work) sets out to remedy this state of affairs. Grammatical operations are in principle restricted to what has to be there by "virtual conceptual necessity", that is, *Merge* ("put together", necessary in any combinatory system), and *Agree* ("compare and match", necessary in any combinatory system with an identity predicate).[3] Any operation beyond that can only be introduced if shown to be unavoidable. Similarly, the building blocks that grammatical operations combine are restricted to morphosyntactic objects. Crucially, for present purposes, indices are not morphosyntactic objects, hence cannot enter into grammatical operations. This requires a program to determine which anaphoric dependencies are established in syntax and which are not. Moreover those binding relations that are demonstrably established in syntax must be encoded there by strictly syntactic means, specifically, Merge and Agree. Furthermore, the definition of binding itself must be given without recourse to indices.

2. As discussed in Reuland (2008), based on facts presented in Gast and Haas (2008), also German shows such contrasts, be it more indirectly.

3. In response to a reviewer, although intuitively, Agree, as it is used, seems to do a bit more than just see whether two terms (feature bundles) match (are identical), namely 'actual valuing', its workings can be emulated – admittedly in a roundabout way – by pure checking for identity.

The general, and cross-linguistically invariant, definition of binding I adopt, is given in (8), following Reinhart (2006: 171). Reinhart argues that no specifically linguistic notion of binding is necessary. What suffices is a logical notion of binding, conceived of as the closing of a property:

(8) **A-binding** (logical syntax binding)
α A-binds β iff α is the sister of a λ-predicate whose operator binds β[4]

Variable binding is not subject to locality, as is shown in (9), where the variable bound by *no soldier* is in a syntactic island, as indicated in (9b).

(9) a. *No soldier* started shooting after the enemy had threatened *him*.
b. No soldier (λx (x started shooting $[_{\text{CP-ADJUNCT}}$ after the enemy had threatened x])

Binder and bindee must be part of one sentential structure, though, as shown in the classic example of (10):[5]

(10) *No soldier* has a gun. *Will *he* attack?

Variable binding as such is, then, not syntactically encoded. In syntax the bound and the free reading of (9a) (the free reading is the one where *him* is simply valued as one of the available individuals in the discourse) are not distinguished. The difference arises when the structure is handed over to the interpretive system. Given the conception of binding in (8) the restrictions on binding observed (and approximated by the canonical binding conditions) must follow from the interplay between interpretive processes and syntactic factors, and given the conception of the minimalist program as outlined above, none of the syntactic factors should be specific to binding. Meeting these conditions becomes the more challenging in view of our increasing knowledge of language systems throughout the world, and the scepticism voiced as regards language universals by researchers in linguistic typology and in the cognitive sciences, as for instance Evans and Levinson (2009).

---

4. As an illustration of how this works consider (i):

(i) Every linguist investigates his pet theory

'Take an arbitrary linguist x, and you will see that x investigates x's pet theory.' The λ-notation allows us to write this as in (ii), where the λ-operator just expresses that whatever value is assigned to the one occurrence of x will also be assigned to the other occurrence of x:

(ii) Every linguist (λx (x investigates x's pet theory))

This is just what the logical notion of binding expresses.

5. This is presumably why binding into appositive relative clauses is ill-formed.

3. How diverse is the diversity?

In Section 1 I already sketched a number of facts that are puzzling for a general binding theory. Frisian, and Old English show that there is no absolute obligation of freedom for "pronominals", Modern English and Icelandic show that there is no absolute binding obligation for "anaphors". In view of this, it is quite unlikely that expanding the empirical domain could still yield greater "shocks". Pursuing the case of anaphors, Jayaseelan (1997) brought to the fore the case of Malayalam, illustrated in (11). As the contrast in (11) shows, Malayalam has an environment where a special, complex, form is necessary for licit local binding, as in (11a). Prima facie, one would say that this form must be an anaphor. However, as (11b) shows, this form need not be locally bound, hence is not an anaphor in the canonical sense.[6]

(11) Malayalam

a. raaman$_i$ tan-ne$_i$ *(tanne) sneehikunnu
Raman Pron[7]-ACC Pron loves
'Raman loves himself.'

b. raaman$_i$ wicaariccu [penkuttikal tan-ne$_i$ tanne
Raman thought girls Pron-ACC Pron
sneehikkunnu ennə].
love Comp
'Raman thought that the girls love him.'

Cole, Hermon, Tjung, Sim, and Kim (2008) discuss a similar contrast in Peranakan Javanese, see (12):

(12) a. [Gurue Tono$_j$]$_i$ ketok **dheen**$_{*i/j/k}$ nggon kaca.
teacher-3 Tono see 3SG in mirror
'Tono's teacher saw him/her in the mirror.'

---

6. Note that the crucial difference beween *tanne tanne* in Malayalam and long-distance anaphors in Scandinavian is that the latter are simplex, whereas the former is complex, hence prima facie more similar to anaphors of the form X-self that have been argued to be always local (for instance, Pica 1991).

7. I gloss *tan-ne tanne* here as Pron-acc Pron. The status of *tan* does not quite match that of an English or Dutch pronominal, since it must be bound within the sentence. On the other hand it is not quite an Dutch or English type anaphor either, and the glossing of *tanne* as *self* is also problematic. To put it informally, *tan* is more deficient than a pronominal, but less deficient than a SE-anaphor. Determining its precise feature structure is a matter of further research.

b. Ali$_j$ ngomong nek aku pikir [Tono$_i$ ketok **awake dheen**$_{i/j/k}$
Ali N-say COMP 1sg think Tono see body-3 3sg
nggon kaca].
in mirror
'Ali said that I thought that Tono saw himself/him in the mirror.'

The question is, do these languages add anything substantial to what we already have to do in order to accommodate English? This question clearly cannot be answered without a particular analysis of the English facts.

A similar question arises about local binding of pronominals. Evans and Levinson mention that quite a few languages in the Australian and Austronesian language families don't distinguish between pronominals and anaphors, hence pose a profound challenge to any universal binding theory. The question is again, do these languages present any challenges in addition to the challenges posed by Frisian or Old English? Again, this question cannot be answered unless we have a principled analysis of the Frisian and Old English facts.

In the next section I will outline the ingredients of an analysis of the relevant English and Frisian facts, and indicate how they can be used to accommodate the patterns in languages that prima facie look more 'exotic'. In the final section I will present a case study of Chamorro, insightfully studied in Chung (1989), and show that the facts can in principle be understood on the basis of simple, general principles.

4. Reflexivity, reflexives, economy and chains

4.1 Licensing reflexivity.

Let's first consider why so many languages, in fact all, I would claim, do something special with reflexive predicates. Also Frisian, sometimes incorrectly cited as a language without anaphors (e.g. Schladt 2000), does something special with subject experiencer verbs. Just like Dutch requires a complex anaphor *zichzelf* with subject experiencer verbs as in (13a), Frisian requires *himsels*, as in (13b), even if with agentive verbs such as *waskje* 'wash', or *ferdigenje* 'defend', a simple pronominal suffices as we already saw.

(13) a. Alice bewondert zich*(zelf)
Alice admires SE (self)
'Alice admires herself.'

b. Alice bewûnderet har*(sels)
Alice admires pron (self)
'Alice admires herself.'

As explained in detail in Reuland (2005b, 2008, and 2011), the reason is the impossibility for the computational system of human language to handle identicals unless the environment allows them to be distinguished as different occurrences, the *Inability to*

Distinguish Indistinguishables (IDI). This requires a work space with minimally either structure or order. Neither condition is satisfied at the C-I Interface. Consider the effect of reflexivization on the two arguments of a transitive verb such as *bewonderen* 'admire' and its counterparts in other languages with the object argument a simplex anaphor (SE-anaphor) such as *zich*. If two arguments of such a verb are bound by the same λ-operator, they are identified, as in (14):

(14) a. Alice λx [$_{\text{bewondert}}$ x x] + zich

b. Alice λx [$_{\text{bewondert}}$ x] + zich

?

Role 1? Role 2?

'Alice admires herself.'

If the two internal variables are identical, they are unified, as is already implied by the standard view that reflexivization turns a relation into a property.[8] Hence, indeterminacy in assigning the two thematic roles ensues, leading to ill-formedness. This is, then, whatever is special in reflexives has to remedy, as reflected in Reinhart and Reuland (1993)'s condition B given in (15):

(15) A reflexive predicate is reflexive-marked

The *reflexive-marking* in (15), licenses the reflexive interpretation by remedying the effect of the IDI. While (15) is universal, languages may vary in the means by which they license reflexivity. Reuland (2008, 2011) argues that there are essentially two routes to achieve this. One way of licensing the reflexive is for the variable to be 'protected' by a marker such as *self*, or *head*, as illustrated in Dutch (16) or Basque (17).

(16) Alice λx [x [$_{\text{bewondert}}$ x, y] [x ZELF]]

Role 1 Role 2

(17) a. aitak [bere burua] hil du

father his head kill has

'The father killed himself.'

b. aitak λx [x [$_{\text{killed}}$ x, y] [x HEAD]]

Role 1 Role 2

Due to the presence of *self* or *head* the arguments remain formally distinct at the level of logical syntax, since binding only identifies the subject variable (=the variable interpreting the trace left by the subject after quantifier raising) with a variable properly contained in the object (*x* versus [*x's head*] or [*x self*]. Hence, the variables on the grid

8. For instance, Keenan (1988) defines *(him)self* as an operator that applies to a 2-place predicate and yields a 1-place predicate.

of the verb that are linked to these arguments are not identified by the binding process, and IDI does not come into play. In (16) and (17) the arguments are not only formally, but also semantically distinct, since *himself* or *bere burua* are interpreted as proxies of *him* and *bere* respectively, as indicated in (18), where f stands for the *self*-function or the *head*-function, as illustrated in the possibility of so-called statue readings (*Ringo washed himself* can mean that *Ringo washed his statue*, but *Ringo washed* cannot, see Jackendoff 1992; Safir 2004; Reuland & Winter 2009).

(18) $\lambda x\ (P\ (x, f(x)))$

To remedy the effect of IDI, any morpheme adding the required complexity, and whose effects are visible in the interpretation will do. The claim is, therefore, that what is universal is not the linguistic means themselves – different languages clearly select different lexical items or even strategies in a broader sense, see Schladt (2000). What is universal is the particular effect to be obtained: avoiding two identical variables on one verbal grid. A simplex anaphor such as *zich* then is limited to positions where either no reflexive predicate is formed when it is bound by its antecedent, as was illustrated in (7), or when reflexivity is licensed otherwise.

The other way to license reflexivity is by an operation on argument structure, reducing the internal argument, and effecting the bundling of the internal and external thematic roles into a composite role. If the roles are bundled, the indeterminacy is resolved as well, and the composite role can unequivocally be assigned to the one argument that is visible on the grid, the external one. This bundling operation is discussed in Reinhart and Siloni (2005). They show that reduction of an argument and bundling of roles is one of a range of operations on verbal concepts that are independently needed to account for alternations (for instance between transitive *open* in *Alice opened the door*, and its one-place alternant in *The door opened*). Bundling often goes together with a special morpheme to trigger or license it, as *zich* in Dutch *Jan wast zich*, or the clitic *se* in French *Jean se lave*, but not in English, as in *John washes* where no special element shows up. As Reinhart and Siloni argue, this reduction operation may leave a residual accusative Case, depending on the Case system of the language concerned. If present, this residual Case must be checked. This is, then, the role of the SE-anaphor *zich* and its cognates in Dutch and related languages. Facilitated by the impoverished Case system in English, reduction does not leave a residual Case there, hence nothing needs to be checked.[9]

Reduction/bundling is restricted to agent-theme verbs. Specifically, lexical reflexivization does not occur with subject experiencer verbs such as the counterparts of

9. Note, though, that an impoverished case system may well be a necessary condition, but is not sufficient, as is shown by the fact that Mainland Scandinavian languages despite having a highly impoverished case system require a simplex anaphor here just like Dutch. Thanks to an anonymous reviewer for prompting me to clarify this. How to relate this contrast to other differences between these languages is a matter for further research.

hate, *admire*, *know*, etc. In Dutch this restriction shows up in the distribution of the SE-anaphor *zich* as we saw in (6). A similar restriction has been observed in a range of languages, varying from Germanic to Modern Greek, or Russian and Sakha.

This second strategy to license reflexivity is in line with the observation in Levinson (2000) that a range of languages use detransitivized verbs form to express reflexive relations. IDI explains why this is so.

Note, that in clitic languages like French or Italian, prima facie, no such restriction on the simple anaphoric clitic *se/si* is observed. So, one finds *Jean se lave* 'John washes', alongside *Jean s'adore* 'John admires himself' or *Jean se hait* 'John hates himself'. This is due to the fact that clitics have a richer internal structure than meets the eye. For instance, clitics are able to project full arguments, since like anaphors such as *himself*, or *zichzelf*, clitics in French and Italian support proxy-readings, as in *Ringo washed himself*, where *himself* may be interpreted as Ringo's statue, a reading that is absent in the case of Dutch *Ringo waste zich*, or English *Ringo washed*. As is shown in Marelj and Reuland (2016), the syntactic properties of clitics can in fact provide the necessary protection. Due to their mixed X^0/XP status (in line with Chomsky 1995, and Bošković, 1997) the argument variable they project stays formally distinct from the variable projected by their antecedent.[10] For the details of the analysis and further references I refer to Marelj and Reuland (2016).[11]

---

10. The crucial property responsible for the fact that clitics as in (i) allow IDI to be satisfied is represented in (ii): in a clitic construction the dependency between the clitic and its antecedent does not form an A-chain. An A'-type link intervenes since the clitic has been head-moved into a position in the functional system. Consequently, there cannot be a uniform A-chain between the clitic and its antecedent. Hence, the clitic chain remains distinct from the antecedent, and no IDI violation obtains.

(i) Ringo si è ammirato
Ringo admired si

(ii) Ringo …… T si^1 v ………V (si^2)
| | |
XP/A X^0/A' XP/A

Since, prima facie clitics such as *se*, *si* are so similar to simplex anaphors such as Dutch *zich*, it is illustrative to compare (ii) to its counterpart (iii) in Dutch (and other languages with non-clitic simplex anaphors).

(iii) Ringo …… T v ………V (zich)
| |
XP/A XP/A

In the *zich*-case no A'-type link intervenes. There is a uniform chain between *zich* and its antecedent and an IDI violation ensues.

11. Reinhart and Siloni concluded that bundling can take place either in the lexicon (as in languages like English, Dutch, Russian, etc,) or in the syntax (as in French, Italian,

4.2 Licensing versus enforcing reflexivity

As we saw in the previous section, IDI requires that reflexivity be licensed. It is clear that reduction and bundling also enforce reflexivity. That is, being the result of bundling **Ik was zich* must be reflexive, and given the feature mismatch between 1st person *ik* 'I' and 3rd person *zich*, cannot be reflexive. Hence the expression is ill-formed.

The same reasoning, however, does not immediately carry over to an expression like *himself*. That is, if *himself* in *John admires himself* is needed to license reflexivity, it is not clear why **John expected Alice to admire himself* is ill-formed. In English, apparently, *himself* also enforces reflexivity even if the result is illicit. From this perspective, it is English that is puzzling, not so much Malayalam and Peranakan Javanese, where the licensing element does not enforce reflexivity. The question is how to accommodate this difference.

Reuland (2001, 2005b, 2008), and Reuland and Winter (2009) argue that English *self* reflexive-marks the verb by (covert) movement. Just like *self-admiration* denotes a reflexive admiration-relation, *self* enters into a syntactic relation with the verb in (19), imposing a reflexive interpretation (for formal details see Reuland and Winter 2009):

(19) a. *John expected [Alice to admire himself]

b. *John expected [Alice to (self)-admire him(self)]

Self, as an operator on the verb, turns the verb into a reflexive predicate. But since *Alice* and *him* don't match in gender, the result is ill-formed. Crucially, if this relation between *self* and the verb is of the syntactic movement type, it is subject to restrictions on movement. For instance, movement is generally impossible from coordinations and adjuncts, as in **What did you eat [a banana and -]* or **Who did John hope that Mary would support no one but -*. If so, we expect that reflexivization of the verb by *self* is blocked, whenever an independent syntactic principle blocks movement. This is indeed what we see in (20). In (20a) *self* cannot move onto the verb (even covertly) because of the coordinate structure constraint and in (20b) *self* cannot move onto the verb due to the fact that adjuncts are islands for movement. Hence the verb is not reflexivized, and *himself* is free to be interpreted by some other process, and can end up being bound by a higher antecedent.

Serbo-Croation, etc.). However, as shown in Marelj and Reuland (2016), bundling is in fact a lexical operation throughout. What appears to be bundling in syntax, can be shown to reflect a standard local binding of clitics, coupled with their protecting structure indicated in the previous footnote, and the global parameter they proposed can be reduced to more standard parameterization patterns, such as having or not having syntactic clitics.

(20) a. Alice was glad that the Hatter had invited [the mouse and herself] for tea.

b. John was hoping that Mary would support [no one but himself]

Let's then summarize the assumptions we need: i. *Self* in English is in the head position of its phrase. Its relation to the verb is therefore a standard head-head relation subject to general conditions on movement. ii. If *self* can move onto the verb it does so. This can be derived from a general economy principle: An interpretive dependency – here between *himself* and its antecedent – is established in syntax when possible (see Reuland 2011 for extensive discussion). There is no need to assume that *self* has to move onto the verb in order to be interpreted (Reuland and Winter 2009 show that *self* can receive an interpretation – and in fact technically the same one – whether it moves or not).

The logic of this account then requires one to look for independent properties of the structure of complex anaphors in languages such as Malayalam and Peranakan Javanese that would either block movement, or else fail to trigger economy. The core property that makes *self* into a reflexivizer is that it is an intrinsically relational noun expressing a reflexive relation (see Reuland 2008; Reuland & Winter 2009; and Reuland 2011). In Malayalam the complexity marker is a pronoun-type element. If so, it would lack the lexical property to impose reflexivity. In Peranakan Javanese the body-part noun is arguably not in the head position, as brought to my attention by Dagmar Schadler (p.c.). If so, the structural conditions for it to move are not satisfied. Hence in both cases just core mechanisms of the grammatical system are sufficient to account for the variation observed.

4.3 Encoding dependencies by feature chains

Principle (15) captures the distribution of simplex versus complex anaphors, among others, but does not say anything about the distribution of simplex anaphors versus pronominals. Any such discussion must take into account the fact that languages such as Frisian and Old English do allow 3rd person pronominals to be locally bound. That is, any account must be sensitive to a morphosyntactic parameter. As shown in Reuland and Reinhart (1995) and further discussed in Reuland (2001) this factor is structural Case.

Let's first review binding of *zich*. In Reuland (2001) and Reuland (2005a) it is shown that binding of simplex anaphors can be syntactically encoded by Agree, where Agree involves exchanging/copying of φ-feature bundles between the dependent element and its antecedent. These φ-feature bundles are subsequently interpreted as variables in the interpretive procedure. Feature sharing, then, creates identity of variables.

This exchange of φ-feature values crucially takes place via the heads on the path between these elements, as illustrated in (21) (see Chomsky 2008):

(21) DP T V zich

R1 R2 R3

These dependencies are real syntactic dependencies. R1 is the canonical agreement relation between subject and finite Tense, R2 reflects the relation between the verbal projection and the Tense system. R3 is the Case dependency between V and its object (glossing over the finer articulation of the functional system).

As in Reuland (2011), I am assuming that structural accusative Case is in fact uninterpretable Tense, and visible to the T-system (Pesetsky and Torrego 2007). The *composition* of R1, R2 and R3, then, links *zich* to the subject DP. This yields a syntactic encoding of the binding relation. An element like *zich* is feature deficient. Exchange of features between *zich* and its antecedent results in filling its feature matrix, identifying their φ-feature bundles. This identity of feature bundles is interpreted by the C-I interface as variable binding. This is illustrated in (22).

(22) a. Alice voelde [zich wegglijden]
Alice felt [SE slip away]
'Alice felt herself slip away.'

b. Alice [φ T V [φ VP]]

c. Alice (λx (x voelde [x wegglijden]))

Unlike a SE-anaphor, the feature matrix of a pronominal is not deficient. As discussed in Reuland (2001), and (2011) overwriting its matrix would result in a violation of a principle of grammar, the principle of recoverability of deletions (PRD, see Chomsky 1995). Consequently, in (23) syntactic identification of φ_1 and φ_2 is impossible:

(23) a. Alice voelde [haar wegglijden]
Alice felt her away slip

b. Alice [φ_1 T V [φ_2 VP]]

c. Alice (λx (x voelde [x wegglijden]))

Since different occurrences of a variable can be bound by the same operator irrespective of what it results from, standard interpretation procedures could still map (23b) onto (23c). This however, is blocked by economy (see Reuland 2001 for a first discussion and Reuland 2010 and Reuland 2011 for a modification). Briefly, the derivation goes as follows: i. the syntactic configuration – modulo the choice of an anaphor or pronominal – allows encoding of the dependency by φ-feature identification; ii. for the pronominal, encoding the dependency by φ-feature identification would violate the PRD; iii. this leads to a cancelled derivation in the sense of Chomsky (1995), and economy forbids bypassing this grammatical prohibition by binding the pronominal anyway (rejection by the grammatical computation is final).

This analysis predicts that in a structural configuration where the conditions for feature identification/chain formation are not met, nothing prevents the pronominal to be locally bound. Hoekstra (1994) shows that Frisian has a pronominal paradigm without structural Case. This means that its Case is not uninterpretable Tense in the sense of Pesetsky and Torrego. Rather its Case is inherent, and will not be visible to the T-system. That is, there is no φ-feature link between T and V, as indicated by the X in (24b). Consequently, the preconditions for chain formation are not met. This explains why the Frisian equivalent of (23) is fine:

(24) a. Alice fielde [har fuortglieden]
Alice felt her away slip

b. Alice [φ_1 T V [φ_2 VP]]
X

c. Alice (λx (x fielde [x fuortglieden]))

As we already saw, the fact that Frisian allows locally bound 3rd person pronominals does not mean that it has no anaphors. With respect to licensing Frisian follows the general pattern, just like Dutch. Hence, with verbs not allowing lexical bundling the self-anaphor *himsels* is required.

The existence of locally bound pronominals in Old English has the same explanation. Van Gelderen (2000) presents extensive evidence that in the relevant period the object received inherent, rather than structural Case. One of her important arguments is that Old-English lacked personal passives at that time. To what extent Old English has a different reflexivization pattern from Frisian or Dutch is an open issue. Prima facie it seems to show the same pattern as Frisian. I am not aware of any specific discussion of subject experiencer verbs showing that for such verbs it diverges from the Frisian pattern, but it would be important to check this.

Just like our insight in the processes licensing reflexives allowed us to understand prima facie surprising facts in Malayalam and Peranakan Javanese, the ingredients discussed in the present section also allow us to go back to the issue of finiteness and the role it plays in binding.

As is shown in detail in Reuland (2011), this process of Agree-chain formation with SE-anaphors can in principle cross clause boundaries. If so, it gives rise to long-distance binding. But whether it can in particular cases, depends both on the details of the functional structure and on properties of the syntactic configuration. Consider then the well-known example in (25) (Hellan 1988):

(25) Jon$_i$ bad **oss** [**PRO**$_1$ forsøke [å **PRO**$_2$ få ***deg*** [til ***PRO***$_3$ å snakke pent om seg$_i$]]]]]
Jon asked us (to) try to get you to talk nicely about SE
'John asked us to try to get you to talk nicely about him.'

The question is then how *seg* can skip PRO$_2$, and PRO$_3$ in its search for an antecedent. That is, why doesn't it have to go for the first possible antecedent, given that it may? I will show that the answer resides in the left periphery. Rizzi (1997) and Bianchi (2001) propose that finiteness is encoded by a functional head – Fin – in the left periphery. Adopting that proposal, we only need the assumption that in addition to the Fin head the left periphery contains minimally one –equidistant – Tense-related functional head (C_T) to derive the freedom observed. The crucial difference between infinitival clauses and finite clauses is that in infinitival clauses Fin is merged as unvalued, whereas in finite clauses Fin starts out with an intrinsic value. Thus, an infinitival clause is underspecified in two respects, Tense and Finiteness, represented in C_T and Fin, as in (26):

(26) Jon$_i$ bad **oss** [**PRO**$_1$ forsøke [å **PRO**$_2$ få ***deg*** [$_{CP2}$ til C_T Fin$_{(-)val}$ [***PRO***$_3$ å *T* *snakke pent om seg*$_i$]]]]]]
Jon asked us (to) try to get you to talk nicely about SE
'John asked us to try to get you to talk nicely about him.'

Consequently, the left periphery contains two potential linking pins with the higher-up structure. Neither of these linking pins is fully valued within the lower CP (CP$_2$). Finiteness will be valued the moment the controller is merged in the next higher clause, C_T will be valued the moment a higher up valued Tense is merged. Abstractly the relevant structure can be represented as in (27):

(27) $\ldots[_{CP1}\ C_T \ldots \text{Fin}\ [\ \boldsymbol{DP_{SU}}\ \mathbf{T}\ [\text{V}\ DP_{OBJ}\ [_{CP2}\ C_T \ldots Fin_{\pm val}\ [_{TP}\ PRO\ T \ldots .SE\ ]]]]]$

Let's assume now (following Reinhart 1983, and discussed in detail in Reuland 2011), that where grammar leaves options open, economy drives the choice. Locally within CP$_2$ both Fin (-val, before valuation) and C_T are equally good candidates for the *T...SE* chain to link up to, since neither choice leads to an immediate valuation for either SE or T. Forming a chain headed by Fin will lead to local binding by PRO (and indirectly by its controller), once the controller has been merged, but in the absence of look-ahead this is irrelevant at this point. Forming a chain headed by C_T is equally possible. And if so, this leads to bypassing the controlled PRO. The chain headed by C_T (and containing SE) may get chain-linked to T (via intermediate heads), and be valued, leading to binding of SE by a higher subject.[12] If the next higher clause is an infinitive

12. Technically 'linking' is effected by Agree-based probe-goal relations. Being (in part) unvalued both C_T and Fin are possible goals for higher-up probes. Being unvalued, the head of the lower T...SE chain is visible for probing by both C_T and Fin.

the same reasoning applies, and its subject may be bypassed as well. So, the optionality in the choice of an antecedent in long-distance binding results from an indeterminacy in the C-system when Fin is unvalued.[13]

If Fin is intrinsically valued, however (i.e. the sentence is finite), economy – requiring that SE be valued as soon as possible – induces the *T...SE* chain to link to Fin. Under this condition local binding is enforced, as shown in (28), and we don't have the optionality we saw in infinitival clauses.

(28) $\ldots[_{CP1}\ C_T \ldots \text{Fin}\ [\ DP_{SU}\ T\ [V\ DP_{OBJ}\ [_{CP2}\ C_T \ldots \boldsymbol{Fin}_{+val}\ [_{TP}\ \boldsymbol{DP\ T} \ldots \boldsymbol{SE}\ ]]]]]$

Thus, coming back to the discussion in the introductory section, finiteness plays a crucial role in understanding the contrast between infinitival and finite clauses in anaphor binding.

I will conclude this contribution with two case studies of prima facie puzzling anaphoric systems – one brief, the other more extensive – and show how they can straightforwardly be accommodated in the approach described.

5. The cases of Fijian and Chamorro

5.1 Fijian

Levinson (2000) brings up Fijian as a severe problem for the canonical binding theory, and he is right. It is as problematic for the canonical binding theory as Frisian. However, as we will see, from the theory developed here, Fijian brings nothing new. Levinson states the issue as follows, quoting Dixon (1988): " .... In the third person, a verb with the transitive marker *-a* and without an explicit object is interpreted as having unmarked reference to a third-singular object which is noncoreferential with the subject. If coreference or reflexivity is intended, a full object pronoun (e.g. *'ea*, third singular object) is required, and although this might be interpreted disjointedly, it encourages a coreferential reading:"

(29) sa va'a-.dodonu-.ta'ini' 'ea o Mika
ASP correct 3SG+OBJ Art Mike
'Mike corrected himself.' or 'Mike corrected him.'

At a first glance, this pattern is puzzling. How can a pronominal facilitate a reflexive interpretation? And why is there optionality? The crucial factor for an understanding

13. Reuland (2011) also shows how the differences in long-distance binding domains between Scandinavian, Dutch and German follow from the fact that in Dutch and German an 'extraposition' configuration – whatever its source – disrupts the configuration for chain formation. For reasons of space I refer to Reuland (2011) for the details.

is a fact Levinson mentions, but does not interpret (thanks to Dagmar Schadler for bringing this to my attention): without an explicit object the interpretation of (29) is necessarily non-coreferential. From this fact the analysis quite simply follows. According to Dixon's description, Fijian allows null-objects. Assuming that Fijian doesn't have a bundling operation applying to the verb *correct* (which makes it like English in this respect) assigning the interpretation *Mike (λx (x corrected x))* to *Mike corrected* $\varnothing_{pron}$ violates IDI. Hence it cannot receive this interpretation. The only way to license a reflexive interpretation is by protecting the variable. To achieve this nothing more is needed than an element that contributes complexity. The claim is that Fijian uses a pronominal element to do so. Such a use of a pronominal is not unique. As we already saw, also Malayalam uses a pronoun doubling strategy. The same holds true of, for instance, Caxur (see Toldova 1996). If so, the structure of (29) in the reflexive interpretation is in fact (30):

(30)	sa	va'a-.dodonu-.ta'ini'	[Ø	'ea]	o	Mika
	ASP	correct	3SG+OBJ	3SG+OBJ	Art	Mike
	'Mike corrected himself.'					

The pronoun protects the variable, just like in the other cases discussed. The reading with the object pronominal interpreted disjointly from the subject, simply follows if the pronominal is directly merged in object position. Although it should also be noted that presumably nothing enforces *'ea* to act as a reflexivizer if it has just the semantics of a pronoun.[14]

5.2 Chamorro

Chung (1989) presents an analysis of binding in Chamorro.[15] As she argues, Chamorro is a verb initial language, with the unmarked order Verb Subject Object Other. Her prime objective is to investigate null NPs in Chamorro in order to evaluate the classification empty categories in the framework of Chomsky (1982). But in order to be able to do so, she presents a detailed analysis of the Chamorro binding facts.

14. I refer to Schadler (2014) for an analysis of reflexivity in Fijian that is based on a more detailed investigation of the status of the object marker *-Ci*. This analysis was not yet available when the present article was written. It is in the same spirit as the analysis outlined in the main text, but capitalizes on the presence of *-Ci*, which is present when there is a pronominal, but absent in the case of a null object. As Schadler shows, *-Ci* both prevents a chain and licenses reflexivity.

15. Chamorro is an Austronesian language spoken on Guam and the Northern Mariana Islands.

As Chung puts it, Chamorro makes no thorough-going morphological distinction between anaphors and pronominals. Many sentences containing a Chamorro proform (which Chung refers to as *C-proform*) are ambiguous between an anaphor reading and a pronominal reading, as in (31):[16]

(31) Mamahlao si Miguel nu guiya
INFL.ashamed UNM Miguel OBL him
'Miguel$_i$ is ashamed of him$_j$ /himself$_i$.'

This would make Chamorro prima facie exceptional from the perspective of the canonical binding theory. Yet, Chung argues, Chamorro shows restrictions on binding that can only be explained if at some level an anaphor-pronominal distinction is present. Levinson (2000) argues that the assumption of a hidden distinction between pronominals and anaphors is non-explanatory, and hence cursorily dismisses Chung's analysis. However, the restrictions Chung describes are real; hence in the absence of an alternative explanation of the facts Levinson's dismissal is unfounded, and so are any further conclusions against the universality of binding principles as for instance in Evans and Levinson (2009).

From the current perspective Chamorro is interesting, since it would be important to see if the restrictions Chung observes could follow from the general approach to binding sketched above.

Let's start with the observation Chung starts her discussion with. With inanimates Chamorro does observe a pronominal–anaphor distinction:

(32) Ha-bäba guiʔ i petta, ya tayaʔ haʔ
INFL-open itself the door and INFL.not.exist indeed
taotao ch-um-onnik *pro*
person INFL-push
'The door$_i$ opened itself$_i$, and there was no one who pushed it$_i$.'

The object of reflexive *ha-bäba* 'open' is the C-proform *guiʔ*, the object of the transitive *ch-um-onnik* 'push' is a null-pronominal. As Chung puts it, 'inanimate anaphors are overt, whereas inanimate pronominals are null.' Note first of all, that even in his own terms this pattern shows that Levinson is overly rash in his dismissal of Chung's claim that Chamorro provides evidence for an anaphor-pronominal distinction. In this environment the distinction is not hidden, but overt. From the current perspective, of course, the question is what (32) tells us about our reinterpretation of the binding theory. More specifically, one would wonder why a null object could impose disjointness and why a full C-proform could be compatible with a reflexive interpretation. The

16. All Chamorro examples are from Chung (1989).

pattern looks less surprising the moment one sees that we have protection, just like what was observed in Fijian, but now showing up with inanimates.

Chung presents two arguments for the relevance of the notion of an anaphor in Chamorro. In her terms, there are several Chamorro-particular restrictions that specifically refer to C-proforms that are both *bound by the subject* and *bound within their 'governing category'* in Chomsky (1981)'s sense. Chung defines such forms as *anaphors*. For current purposes nothing much hinges on whether we call them anaphors or not. Crucial is that they exhibit local binding. Let's review them in turn.

5.2.1 *Restrictions on subject-object combinations*

As Chung shows, Chamorro has a restriction ruling out any clause that is transitive and has a 3rd person plural subject, which she formulates as the following filter:

(33) *V[Nom][Obj], order irrelevant, where [Nom] is third plural.

For current purposes it is enough to accept that some filter along these lines is operative, leaving open why it would hold. This filter has an interesting exception, namely it does not apply in the case of (34):

(34) Filter (33) is inapplicable if [Obj] contains an anaphor that is not bound within [Obj]

The joint workings of filters (33) and (34) are illustrated by the contrast in (35):

(35) a. Ma-faʔ mänggua? siha i famalaoʔan
INFL-ridicule them the women
'The women$_i$ ridiculed themselves$_i$/*them$_j$.'

b. Pära uma-faʔgasi siha ni häpbun i manäpplachaʔ
will INFL-was them OBL soap the dirty.ones
'The dirty ones$_i$ are going to wash themselves$_i$/*them$_j$.'

The examples in (35) show that the C-proform *siha* cannot be interpreted as a locally free pronominal. This is covered by the filter in (33). Surprisingly however, there is no restriction when *siha* bound by the local subject. This exception is captured by (34). The question is now why local binding would obviate the filter. Another way of putting the question is what intransitives, passives, that have no restriction on 3rd person plural subjects either, and cases with locally bound *siha* have in common. Chung does not address this question. However, from the perspective sketched above these are not so strange bedfellows. (35a,b) instantiate reflexive predicates. A way of licensing a reflexive predicate, as we saw, is by reducing an argument and bundling the thematic roles, essentially making the predicate intransitive. Just applying the model of Dutch and many other languages, *siha* would be present to check a residual structural case.

Chung notes, that (34) only applies if the binding is local. If a sentence such as (35a) is embedded it is ill-formed under a reading where *siha* is bound by the higher subject. This is to be expected, since in that case no reflexive predicate is formed.

Sentences of the type in (36) present an interesting further dimension to the puzzle.

(36) Ma-tätaitai [ennao na lepblu put siha] i famaguʔun
INFL-read-PROG that L book about them the children
'The children$_i$ are reading that book about themselves$_i$/*them$_j$.'

Here *siha* is not a direct argument of the main verb, but contained in a DP. In this case the exception condition in (34) applies as well: *that book about siha* counts as a full transitive object when *siha* is locally free, but does not do so when *siha* is bound by the subject of the local predicate. The question is, then, how binding of *siha* can 'mimick' detransitivization. I would like to suggest the following answer. We can characterize the bound reading of (36) as in (37):

(37) The children (λx (read x, fb(x))), where *fb* is a function assigning to each x the book about x.

Given (37) we can define a related property *fb.reading*, such that (37) is equivalent to (38):

(38) The children (λx (fb.read x)), where fb.read (x) is the property of reading a book about x.

In (38) we capitalized on the dependent character of *book about x* to create an equivalent expression that is essentially intransitive. The line sketched here is based on an operation in logical syntax, as conceived by Reinhart. A syntactic counterpart would involve incorporation of *book about* into the predicate. To determine which way to ultimately go more research would be needed. For the moment, let it suffice to conclude that this exception to (33), which prima facie seems so puzzling can in principle be accommodated using basic mechanisms of grammatical computation.

Going back to our starting point, whereas these results do not reconstruct the notion of an anaphor in the GB sense, they certainly show that licensing reflexivity, and in an indirect way enforcing it, reveals itself as a key notion in the grammar of Chamorro. Let's now turn to Chung's second argument.

5.2.2 *The subject effect*

Chung presents the following descriptive generalization covering the basic patterns of anaphora in Chamorro (formulated in terms of coindexing).

(39) If a C-proform NP_a is coindexed with a full NP, NP_b, then NP_b must either c-command NP_a at S-structure, or else precede it in surface word order.

I will take this descriptive generalization as my starting point, without attempting a further analysis here. Chung makes the interesting observation that the constraints on coindexing between the C-proform and its antecedent are stricter when the C-proform is contained in a subject. The examples in (40) and (41) serve as illustration:

(40) ??Mämpus guäguan pära si Maria [esti na lepblu
too INFL-expensive for UNM Maria this L book
put guiya]
about her
'This book about her$_i$ is too expensive for Maria$_i$.'

(41) *Ha-bisita si Juan [si nana-ña pro]
INFL-visit UNM Juan UNM mother-AGR
'His mother visited Juan.'

The antecedent *Maria* precedes the C-proform in (40) in accordance with (39), yet the coreferential interpretation is infelicitous. In (41) the (null) C-proform is preceded by *Juan*, and again the result is infelicitous. Chung sketches the offending configuration as in (42):

(42)

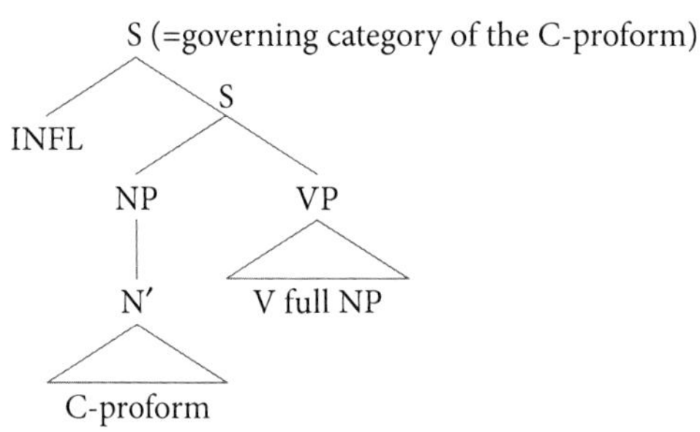

Note that order is not indicated. The structure should be read in such a way that it is neutral as to whether VP precedes the subject or not. If the VP precedes the subject, condition (39) should be satisfied, yet the result is not good. As a first go at the problem Chung sketches the following restriction:

(43) If a C-proform contained in the subject is coindexed with a full NP outside the subject, but within the governing category of the C-proform, then the C-proform must be an anaphor.

Thus, in (40), *guiya* within the subject must be an anaphor according to (43), and is subsequently ruled out, since it is not c-commanded by its prospective binder. So, what we have here is an intriguing decision fork: i. a particular option is forced by one principle; ii. the result is ruled out by another principle. As Chung notes, a principle such as (43) looks suspicious. Why would a language work like this? The definition of anaphor Chung uses is essentially contextual, but strictly speaking the conditions are not met in this structure. Chung notes that in all cases where (43) rules a particular binding configuration out there is an alternative to express the relevant meaning. For instance, the meaning of (41) is straightforwardly expressed by the passive in (44):

(44) B-in-isita si Juan as [nana-ña pro]
INFL-PASS-visit UNM Juan OBL mother-AGR
'Juan$_i$ was visited by his$_i$ mother.'

In this case, and similar cases Chung discusses, the C-proforms are both bound in their governing category, and bound by a subject, hence they qualify as anaphors under the contextual definition of anaphors she introduced. She then proposes that (43) can be replaced by a pragmatic strategy along the lines proposed in Reinhart (1983):

(45) a. If the meaning the speaker wants to convey can be encoded by two equally simple syntactic structures only one of which involves an anaphor, then the speaker should use the structure involving the anaphor if she intends her expressions to corefer.
b. Actives and the corresponding passives are equally simple syntactic structures.

Thus, (41) is ruled out by proxy. Since the C-proform in (41) is not (and cannot be) construed as an anaphor, it is rejected in favour of (44).

(45) involves a complex transderivational comparison. It goes far beyond the type of comparison in for instance Grodzinsky and Reinhart's (1993) Rule I that regulates coreference versus binding, as in (46), or Reuland (2001)'s Rule BV that prefers narrowly syntactic encoding by chain formation over variable binding where the option exists, given in (47).

(46) Rule I: Intrasentential Coreference
NP A cannot corefer with NP B if replacing A with C, C a variable A-bound by B, yields an indistinguishable interpretation.

(47) Rule BV: Bound variable representation (specific version)
NP A cannot be A-bound by NP B if replacing A with C, C an NP such that B heads an A-CHAIN tailed by C, yields an indistinguishable logical syntax representation.

For reasons discussed in Reinhart (2006) Rule I in this form overgenerates, although its transderivational character is minimal as compared to what is involved in (45). Rule BV in (47) compares derivation with *zich*-type anaphors that can be chain linked to derivations with pronominals that cannot. This requires a notion of economy that goes beyond the notion of economy of derivation in Chomsky (1995), which is strictly limited to derivations from one numeration. As already mentioned in Section 4.3, Reuland (2010 and 2011) pursues the idea that the relevant notion is cancellation in the sense of Chomsky (1995). The option of variable binding is blocked if the derivation leading to variable binding is a member of a set of alternatives that contains a cancelled derivation. For instance, derivations that lead to a feature chain with an impossible feature composition, such as a contradictory feature specification, or a violation of the PRD are cancelled; see the discussion of (23). A cancelled derivation blocks its local alternatives. Hence the option in (23) in which the antecedent just binds the pronominal is not considered.

Let's now see how this would help us understand the Chamorro facts. Consider again the structure in (42), changing some of the labels, but retaining the assumption that subject and predicate form a constituent that is a sister to INFL, here rendered as T:

(42)'

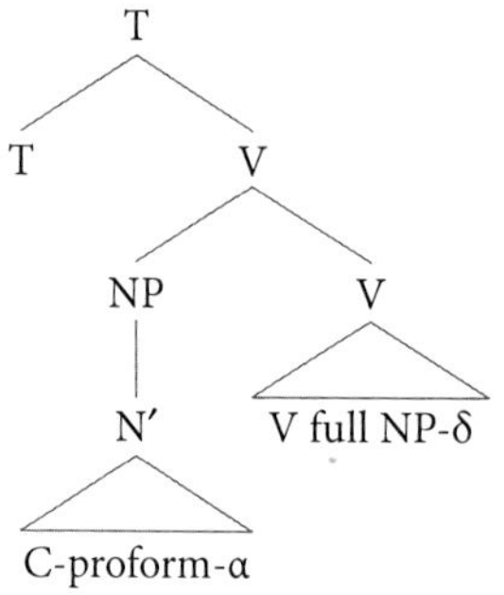

Although much of the fine grain of the structure is underdetermined by the data, let's assume that the C-proform is deficient in at least one relevant dimension, so that it can be probed by T (this is in line with the previous observation that it is not a full argument in reflexives for filter (33)). If α can be probed by T, it forms a feature chain with T. T, however, cannot probe NP-δ since the head of the VP intervenes. This entails that a syntactic encoding via a T-chain can only take place half-way and gets stuck, irrespective of whether or not NP-δ precedes the subject. Given this configuration, then, no binding dependency between α and δ can be established (nor a relation of coreference) since rejection by the grammar is final.[17]

17. Note the difference between this configuration and the Icelandic configuration discussed in Reuland (2005a, 2011):

(i) a. Det *ble* introdusert *en mann*$_i$ for *seg*$_i$ selv/*ham$_i$ selv
it became introduced a man to himself (Norwegian)
'A man was introduced to himself.'

b. Það *kom* *maður*$_i$ með börnin *sin*$_i$/*hans$_i$ (Icelandic)
There arrived a man with children SIG
'There arrived man with his children.'

In Icelandic the VP-internal argument is able to bind an argument it does not c-command due to the fact that it has an independent AGREE relation with T, which does c-command the anaphor, and hence can mediate in establishing the dependency.

Consequently, the fact that (44) is well-formed is entirely independent of the fact that (41) is ruled out. No comparison is needed. It is just the configuration that makes the dependency with the C-proform in (41) a near-miss. Indeed the C-proform is an "almost-anaphor", enough to reflect Chung's initial intuition, but not enough to end up bound. It is just the configuration that allows (44).

6. Conclusion

Although quite a bit of further work might be required to make the above account into a formal analysis, it already clearly shows that the binding facts of Chamorro, interesting as they are, require no theoretical tools that are not independently needed. In this case, what we need is IDI and protection, incorporation, feature deficiency, a probe-goal relation, and economy. And following the trail back, the same can be said about reflexives in languages like Fijian, Frisian or Old English, or the absence of the requirement to enforce reflexivization in Peranakan Javanese or Malayalam; only here we see a different feature composition, hence a different selection of general principles that get involved. In recent years detailed analyses have been provided of other languages with puzzling properties, such as locally bound pronominals in Tegi Khanty (Volkova 2014, Volkova and Reuland 2014), Village Jambi (Kartono 2013) and Mashan Zhuang (Schadler 2014), or non-enforcing reflexives and reflexives with split antecedents in a variety of Uralic languages (Volkova 2014), but also in Austronesian languages spoken in Indonesia (Kartono 2013; Schadler 2014). The upshot is that, contra the claims in Evans and Levinson (2009), the endeavour to determine significant properties of UG is making excellent progress.

References

Bianchi, Valentina. 2001. On finiteness as logophoric anchoring. In *Temps et point de vue/Tense and Point of View*, Jacqueline Guéron & Liliane Tasmowski (eds.), 213–246. Nanterre: Université Paris X.

Bošković, Željko. 1997. *The Syntax of Nonfinite Complementation: An Economy Approach* [Linguistic Inquiry Monograph 32]. Cambridge MA: The MIT Press.

Chomsky, Noam. 1981. *Lectures on Government and Binding*. Dordrecht: Foris.

Chomsky, Noam. 1982. *Some Concepts and Consequences of the Theory of Government and Binding*. Cambridge MA: The MIT Press.

Chomsky, Noam. 1995. *The Minimalist Program*. Cambridge MA: The MIT Press.

Chomsky, Noam 2008. On phases. In *Foundational Issues in Linguistic Theory: Essays in Honor of Jean-Roger Vergnaud*, Robert Freidin, Carlos Otero & Maria-Luisa Zubizarreta (eds.), 133–166. Cambridge MA: The MIT Press.

Chung, Sandra. 1989. On the notion "null anaphor" in Chamorro. In *The Null Subject Parameter,* Osvaldo Jaeggli & Ken Safir (eds.), 143–184. Dordrecht: Kluwer. doi:10.1007/978-94-009-2540-3_5

Cole, Peter, Hermon, Gabriella, Tjung, Yassir, Sim, Chang-Yong & Kim, Chonghyuk. 2008. A binding theory exempt anaphor. In Ekkehard König & Volker Gast (eds.), 577–591.

Dixon, Robert M.W. 1988. *A Grammar of Boumaa Fijian*. Chicago IL: Chicago University Press.

Evans, Nicholas & Levinson, Stephen. 2009. The myth of language universals: Language diversity and its importance for cognitive science. *Behavioral and Brain Sciences* 32: 429–492. doi:10.1017/S0140525X0999094X

Everaert, Martin. 1986. *The Syntax of Reflexivization*. Dordrecht: Foris.

Everaert, Martin. 1991. Contextual determination of the anaphor/pronominal distinction. In Jan Koster & Eric Reuland (eds.), 77–118. doi:10.1017/CBO9780511627835.005

Gast, Volker & Haas, Florian. 2008. On reflexive and reciprocal readings of anaphors in German and other European languages. In Ekkehard König & Volker Gast (eds.), 307–347.

van Gelderen, Elly. 2000. *A History of English Reflexive Pronouns: Person, Self, and Interpretability* [Linguistik Aktuell/Linguistics Today 39], Amsterdam: John Benjamins. doi:10.1075/la.39

Grodzinsky, Yosef & Reinhart, Tanya. 1993. The innateness of binding and coreference. *Linguistic Inquiry* 24: 69–101.

Hellan, Lars.1988. *Anaphora in Norwegian and the Theory of Grammar*. Dordrecht: Foris.

Hoekstra, Jarich. 1994. Pronouns and case: On the distribution of Frisian *harren* and *se* 'them'. *Leuvense Bijdragen* 83: 47–65.

Keenan, Edward. 1988. On semantics and the binding theory. In *Explaining Language Universals*, John Hawkins (ed.). Oxford: Blackwell.

Jackendoff, Ray. 1992. Mme. Tussaud meets the binding theory. *Natural Language & Linguistic Theory* 10: 1–33. doi:10.1007/BF00135357

Jayaseelan, K.A. 1997. Anaphors as pronouns. *Studia Linguistica* 51(2): 186–234. doi:10.1111/1467-9582.00012

Kartono, Bambang. 2013. A Puzzle in Binding: Half Reflexives and Locally Bound Pronouns. A Comparative Study of Anaphoric Systems in Indonesian, Javanese, Palembangnese, City Jambi and Village Jambi. MA thesis, Utrecht University.

König, Ekkehard & Gast Volker (eds.). 2008. *Reciprocals and Reflexives: Theoretical and Typological Explorations*. Berlin: Mouton. doi:10.1515/9783110199147

Koster, Jan. 1985. Reflexives in Dutch. In *Grammatical Representation,* Jacqueline Guéron, Hans-Georg Obenauer & Jean Yves Pollock (eds.), 141–168. Dordrecht: Foris.

Koster, Jan & Reuland, Eric (eds.). 1991. *Long Distance Anaphora*. Cambridge: CUP. doi:10.1017/CBO9780511627835

Levinson, Stephen. 2000. *Presumptive Meanings*. Cambridge MA: The MIT Press.

Lødrup, Helge. 2009. Animacy and long distance binding in Norwegian. *Nordic Journal of Linguistics* 32: 111–136. doi:10.1017/S0332586509002054

Manzini, Maria Rita & Wexler, Kenneth. 1987. Parameters, Binding Theory, and learnability. *Linguistic Inquiry* 18: 413–444.

Marelj, Marijana & Reuland, Eric. 2016. Deriving reflexives – Deriving the lexicon syntax parameter. In *Concepts, Syntax, and their Interface: The Theta System,* Martin Everaert, Marijnana Marelj & Eric Reuland (eds.). Cambridge MA: The MIT Press.

Pesetsky, David & Torrego, Esther. 2007. The syntax of valuation and the interpretability of features. In *Phrasal and Clausal Architecture: Syntactic Derivation and Interpretation* [Linguistik Aktuell/Linguistics Today 101], Simin Karimi, Vida Samiian & Wendy K. Wilkins (eds.), 262–294. Amsterdam: John Benjamins. doi:10.1075/la.101.14pes

Pica, Pierre. 1991. On the interaction between antecedent-government and binding: The case of long-distance reflexivization. In Jan Koster & Eric Reuland (eds.), 119–135. doi:10.1017/CBO9780511627835.006

Reinhart, Tanya. 1983. *Anaphora and Semantic Interpretation*. London: Croom Helm.

Reinhart, Tanya. 2006. *Interface Strategies: Optimal and Costly Computations*. Cambridge MA: The MIT Press.

Reinhart, Tanya & Reuland, Eric. 1991. Anaphors and logophors: An argument structure perspective. In Jan Koster & Eric Reuland (eds.), 283–321. doi:10.1017/CBO9780511627835.015

Reinhart, Tanya & Reuland, Eric. 1993. Reflexivity. *Linguistic Inquiry* 24(4): 657–720.

Reinhart, Tanya & Siloni, Tal. 2005. Thematic arity operations and parametric variations. *Linguistic Inquiry* 36(3): 389–436. doi:10.1162/0024389054396881

Reuland, Eric. 2001. Primitives of binding. *Linguistic Inquiry* 32(2): 439–492. doi:10.1162/002438901750372522

Reuland, Eric. 2005a. Agreeing to bind. In *Organizing Grammar: Linguistic Studies in Honor of Henk van Riemsdijk*, Hans Broekhuis, Norbert Corver, Riny Huybregts, Ursula Kleinhenz & Jan Koster (eds.). Berlin: Walter de Gruyter.

Reuland, Eric. 2005b. Binding conditions: How are they derived? In *Proceedings of the HPSG05 Conference*, Stefan Müller (ed.). Stanford CA: CSLI. ⟨http://csli-publications.stanford.edu/⟩

Reuland, Eric. 2008. Anaphoric dependencies: How are they encoded? Towards a derivation-based typology. In Ekkehard König & Volker Gast (eds.), 499–557.

Reuland, Eric. 2010. Minimal versus not so minimal pronouns: Feature transmission, feature deletion, and the role of economy in the language system. In *The Linguistics Enterprise: From Knowledge of Language to Knowledge in Linguistics* [Linguistik Aktuell/Linguistics Today 150], Martin Everaert, Tom Lentz, Hannah de Mulder, Øystein Nilsen & Arjen Zondervan (eds.), 257–283. Amsterdam: John Benjamins. doi:10.1075/la.150.11reu

Reuland, Eric. 2011. *Anaphora and Language Design*. Cambridge MA: The MIT Press.

Reuland, Eric & Reinhart, Tanya. 1995. Pronouns, anaphors and case. In *Studies in Comparative Germanic Syntax*, Hubert Haider, Susan Olsen & Sten Vikner (eds.), 241–269. Dordrecht: Kluwer. doi:10.1007/978-94-015-8416-6_11

Reuland, Eric & Sigurjónsdóttir, Sigríður. 1997. Long distance binding in Icelandic: Syntax or discourse? In *Atomism in Binding*, Hans Bennis, Pierre Pica & Johan Rooryck (eds.), 323–334. Dordrecht: Foris.

Reuland, Eric & Winter, Yoad. 2009. Binding without identity: Towards a unified semantics for bound and exempt anaphors. In *Lecture Notes in Artificial Intelligence*, Lalitha Devi Sobha, António Branco & Ruslan Mitkov (eds.), 69–79. Berlin: Springer.

Rizzi, Luigi. 1997. The fine structure of the left periphery. In *Elements of Grammar*, Liliane Haegeman (ed.). Dordrecht: Kluwer.

Safir, Kenneth. 2004. *The Syntax of Anaphora*. Oxford: OUP. doi:10.1093/acprof:oso/9780195166132.001.0001

Schadler, Dagmar. 2014. *Reflexivity: Licensing or Enforcing*. Utrecht: LOT International Dissertation Series.

Schladt, Mathias. 2000. The typology and grammaticalization of reflexives. In *Reflexives:Forms and Functions* [Typological Studies in Language 40], Zygmunt Frajzyngier & Traci Walker (eds.), 103–124. Amsterdam: John Benjamins. doi:10.1075/tsl.40.05sch

Sigurðsson, Halldór Ármann. 1986. Moods and (long-distance) reflexives in Icelandic. *Working Papers in Scandinavian Syntax* 25. Trondheim.

Sigurðsson, Halldór Ármann. 1990. Long distance reflexives and moods in Icelandic. In *Modern Icelandic Syntax*, Joan Maling & Annie Zaenen (eds.), 309–346. New York NY: Academic Press.

Toldova, Svetlana. 1996. Materialy k voprosu o povedenii mestoimenija *wuž* v caxskom dialekte caxurskogo jazyka. Ms, Moskva.

Thráinsson, Höskuldur. 1976a. Reflexives and subjunctives in Icelandic. In *NELS* 6, 225–239 Amherst MA: GLSA.

Thráinsson, Höskuldur. 1976b. Some arguments against the interpretive theory of pronouns and reflexives. In *Harvard Studies in Syntax and Semantics*, Jorge Hankamer & Judith Aissen (eds.), 573–624. Cambridge MA: Harvard University.

Thráinsson, Höskuldur. 1991. Long distance reflexives and the typology of NPs. In Jan Koster & Eric Reuland (eds.), 49–75. doi:10.1017/CBO9780511627835.004

Vikner, Sten. 1984. Anaphors in Danish as Compared to English Seen from the Point of View of the Government-binding Theory. MA thesis, University of London.

Vikner, Sten. 1985. Parameters of binder and of binding category in Danish. *Working Papers in Scandinavian Syntax* 23. Trondheim: University of Trondheim.

Volkova, Anna. 2014. *Licensing Reflexivity: Unity and Variation among Selected Uralic Languages.* Utrecht: LOT International Dissertation Series.

Volkova, Anna & Reuland, Eric. 2014. Reflexivity without reflexives? *The Linguistic Review* 31(3–4): 587–633. doi:10.1515/tlr-2014-0012

Finiteness, inflection, and the syntax your morphology can afford*

Kristin Melum Eide
Norwegian University of Science and Technology

In this paper English and Norwegian are compared with respect to a range of syntactic constructions (negated clauses, negative inversion, polarity questions, declaratives, subjunctives, *why-not-* constructions and infinitives). The paper also discusses preterit-participle mix-ups in English and relates these to the behaviour of main verbs in the investigated constructions. It is argued that in both languages these constructions require either an explicitly encoded finiteness feature, or, for the second set of constructions, the explicitly encoded absence of such a feature. English auxiliaries and main verbs differ in their respective feature specifications as regards finiteness, hence main verbs are banned from many of the positions where auxiliaries appear, and vice versa. English main verbs are bereft of a productive morphologically expressed finiteness distinction (except for in a few, but frequent irregular main verbs distinguishing preterits from participles), whereas auxiliaries *have* and *be* exhibit full paradigms of finite and non-finite forms. The modals and auxiliary *do,* on the other hand, exist only as finite forms and are hence banned from positions where non-finiteness is explicitly required by a given syntactic operation or construction. Hence, the finiteness feature is unevenly distributed across verbs and auxiliaries in English, but evenly distributed in all verbal categories in Norwegian, where all main verbs, modals and auxiliaries have full paradigms of finite and non-finite forms. This state of events, it is claimed, gives rise to the observed parametric variation between the Norwegian and English verbal systems.

Keywords: verbs; auxiliaries; Norwegian; English; Old English; participle levelling; Rich Agreement Hypothesis; *do*-support

* I want to thank the two reviewers for this paper whose insightful comments and wise suggestions made me rethink and rewrite this paper substantially.

DOI 10.1075/la.231.05eid

1. Introduction

> Dear Ann Landers:
>
> Have Americans forgotten there is such a thing as verb tense? I am shocked when I hear people say 'woulda came', 'coulda went', 'shoulda did', 'woulda took', 'had went', 'hadn't came', and so on […]. I heard a narrator say, 'I seen' in a political commercial, and a TV reporter say, 'We haven't spoke'… A TV anchorwoman said 'had threw it…[.]'. I am a secretary for almost 50 years and am thankful that, with only a high-school education, my English is impeccable. You will do a lot of folks a big favor if you print this letter and bring it to their attention.
>
> E.E.
> Wood Ridge, N.J.[1]

Educated readers and others like E.E. are regularly horrified when their fellow Americans use the past participle as if it were a preterit, and to some ears even worse, use the preterit as if it were a past participle. This "uneducated use" of the preterit and past participle forms is by no means confined to certain variants of American English; the trend is also very widespread in different dialects and spoken variants of British English (Cf. Edwards 1993; Sampson 2002) as well as English in Australia (e.g. Eisikovits 1987). According to one common explanation, this particular mix-up of preterit and past participial forms is related to the general erosion of inflection in the English language; e.g. Pinker (2000: 87) gives as "the main reason" for this decline the fact that "*all* distinctions in English inflection have been declining for the past thousand years" with the result that "syntax has been shouldering the load formerly borne by morphology".

There is no objecting to the fact that inflection has been eroding in the English language for centuries, as is of course the case with English's neighbouring Germanic languages, like Norwegian. Morphological markers of e.g. mood and agreement are no longer productive in Norwegian; in fact, as regards person and number agreement, inflections in Norwegian and the other Mainland Scandinavian languages are even more reduced than in English, since at least English maintains the present tense 3rd person singular *-s* in opposition to other forms, whereas in Norwegian the verb form is the same for all persons and numbers (cf. Section 2 below).

On this background however, it remains a puzzling (but thus far ignored) fact that letters to the editor of Norwegian newspapers, or letters like the one quoted above to Norwegian columnists similar to Ann Landers never address this particular mix-up of preterit and the past participle. That is not to say that Norwegian writers are any less annoyed by their fellow Norwegians and their sloppy use of the Norwegian language

1. From Ann Landers' syndicated column, February 1999, quoted here from Pinker (2000: 86).

than E.E. in his or her quest for proper English. Norwegian (self-appointed) "language mavens", (cf. Pinker 1994), are for instance extremely concerned with the fact that young people assign a weak inflection (i.e. with a dental suffix encoding 'past') to verbs that are prescribed to be strong verbs (i.e. with a vowel change, i.e. *Ablaut*, encoding 'past'); writing for instance *skjærte* – *skjært* 'cutPRET, cutPART' instead of *skar* – *skåret* 'cutPRET, cutPART' for the verb *skjære* 'cutINF'.[2] Another classic complaint is that Norwegian journalists (and other scribes) are unable to maintain the prescribed morphological distinction between weak transitive verbs and their strong intransitive counterparts where such weak-strong pairs exist; e.g. like in the verb *henge* 'hangINF', which has a weak transitive version *hengte* 'hangPRET' and a strong intransitive version with Ablaut, *hang* 'hangPRET'. Journalists (and others) tend to mix up these two, to the dismay of the aforementioned language mavens.

That is to say, there is absolutely no reason to believe that Norwegian language users are intrinsically any more patient with their fellow Norwegians as regards linguistic shortcomings, at least in written discourse. And yet, Norwegian language users obviously do not give the language mavens the exact same type of grief as their English counterparts. It seems that Norwegian language users are somehow bereft of the trigger for this particular mix-up of preterit and past participle forms.

On the other hand, since users of English in America, the British Isles, and Australia all show this particular linguistic behaviour in their spoken variants of English, this points to an underlying trigger for this mix-up residing in the English language system itself, not simply a sociolinguistic fact about certain users of English in certain environments. That is, there ought to be an explanation for this difference between English on one hand and Norwegian on the other, where this particular trigger is isolated and identified, and it should be present in English and lacking in Norwegian (and the other Mainland Scandinavian languages). Moreover, it seems that knowing English as a first or second language also affects the ability to separate between participles and preterits in Norwegian as a second or third language (Næss 2006; Wik 2014), since language users with a certain proficiency in English mix up these forms in Norwegian more often than learners who do not master English. Again, it seems that something residing in the English language itself acts as a trigger for mixing up these forms, even to the extent that it affects the way you learn and use Norwegian verb forms.

I claim in this paper that the particular trigger is related, not to general erosion of morphological inflections, since Norwegian and English have both been subject to this general erosion, but to the loss or rather the decline of one particular distinction in English, which happens to still be maintained and very much productive in Norwegian.

2. I will use the abbreviations INF, PRES, PRET and PART for the forms of the infinitive, the present, the preterit and the past participle, respectively.

I refer to this as "the productive morphological finiteness distinction (M-finiteness)", since this is the primary and primitive morphological distinction encoding a paradigmatic opposition between overtly finite and non-finite forms in Germanic. The distinction cannot be reduced to either tense or agreement, nor to a combination of the two. In short, it is not a derivative, but a primitive opposition expressed in productive paradigms and primarily morphological in nature (cf. Eide 2009a, b).

The term M(orphological)-finiteness was introduced by Lasser (1997:77) to emphasize the morphosyntactic side of finiteness, "the overt form that finiteness takes", in opposition to the interpretational side of finiteness, "the invisible function that finiteness serves" (cf. also Gretsch and Perdue 2007). This invisible function has semantic, pragmatic and contextual properties and is discussed in some detail in the introductory chapter of this volume. Authors often refer to it as the "anchoring function" of finiteness, and many relate this aspect of finiteness to clausal semantic independence. Gretsch and Perdue (2007:433) claim that it is "the condition for an independent interpretation of a sentence: an independently interpretable sentence is semantically finite. Thus semantic finiteness is related to the utterance and concerns all questions of reference [...]. This [is] the "anchoring" of the sentence"; "the act of appropriately embedding an utterance in the context" (Gretsch & Perdue 2007:437). Finiteness in such approaches is most often seen as the anchoring of the event, or the situation described by the clause, to the utterance context, cf. Amritavalli (2014:284).

> Event anchoring is what is identified as "finiteness," or the ability of a clause to "stand alone." It is usual to assume that the anchoring in question is temporal anchoring (of the event time to speech time, via a reference time); and that its syntactic reflex is tense [...]. Finite clauses are described as carrying "independent tense" or "absolute tense," which is "deictic," because it locates "the time of a situation relative to the situation of the utterance" (loc. cit.).

Bianchi (2003) develops an analysis of finiteness as anchoring where both semantic and syntactic features of the category are discussed. Taking as her point of departure Holmberg and Platzack's (1995) view that the function of finiteness is to relate the predication to the time[3] of the utterance, she proposes that (p. 245)

> [T]he syntactic feature of finiteness encodes the logophoric anchoring of the clause [...]. [Finite clauses] are anchored directly to the Speech event, which constitutes the external "centre of deixis".

3. Note however that the semantic contribution of finiteness is crucially assumed by these authors to be different from that of a tense marker; instead "finiteness is a prerequisite for tense and mood" (Holmberg & Platzack 1995:23), and "a finite verb is not identical with a tensed verb; finite verb forms may have tense or lack it" (ibid.); the authors mention imperatives as a case in point.

In more recent approaches, it is acknowledged that languages may choose to signal this anchoring function of finiteness via a range of morphosyntactic exponents, not limited to tense; Ritter and Wiltschko (2005, 2009, 2014) argue that exponents of *location* (e.g. specific location auxiliaries) or person features encoding specific *event participants* may fulfil the anchoring function identified here as the (universal) semantic anchoring function of finiteness (cf. also Sigurðsson 2004 for an early discussion on the function of person markings in logophoricity and finiteness). In other languages mood or other related categories such as (finite) negation may be overt morphological exponents signaling the finiteness function (cf. Amritavalli 2014); in some languages subject-verb agreement seemingly is the designated finiteness marker, and in languages where morphological markers are scarce, the occurrence of a referentially independent lexical subject may suffice to signal the anchoring function of finiteness (cf. Reuland this volume and Eide this volume; cf. also Eide 2008).

The way Lasser (1997) uses the term M-finiteness, it is in principle applicable to any of the "overt forms that finiteness takes" in the inconclusive list of the previous paragraph. However, I will limit my use of the term M-finiteness in what follows to one specific exponent of finiteness; as encoding a set of independent verb forms standing in a productive paradigmatic opposition to dependent verb forms in Mainland Scandinavian. In previous work (Eide 2009a, b) I have discussed how the dependent (−finite) forms behave like temporal local anaphora requiring a local antecedent whereas the independent (+finite) forms behave like temporal pronouns. These temporal pronouns are capable of independent temporal reference (in their deictic use; but just like nominal pronouns they also act as pronominals in certain contexts). Not very much hinges on this assumption in the present paper. The important thing to note is that the preterit and present verb forms are overtly finite even though there is no person or number agreement in Mainland Scandinavian. Also, since both finite and non-finite forms by assumption encode tense (past versus non-past; cf. Eide 2002a, 2005, 2009a, b), tense also cannot be the distinguishing feature for finiteness in these languages. In keeping with the traditional terminology employed in Scandinavian grammars, I refer to the preterit and present forms as finite forms, and I am assuming that they are morphological exponents of the anchoring function of finiteness. To emphasize the morphological nature of this distinction, I will also refer to it as M-finiteness.

(1)

	+Finite	−Finite
+Past	**Preterit**	**Participle**
−Past	**Present**	**Infinitive**

One major claim of this paper is that English no longer productively employs this distinction for main verbs, although the finite feature is found with the auxiliaries (note however that only the auxiliaries *have* and *be* have forms to fill all four finite and non-finite cells; cf. Section 4; tables in (29) and (30)). The distribution of the M-finiteness distinction thus constitutes an observable and perhaps prosaic fact about Norwegian and English, unless we are able to tie this morphological distinction to specific syntactic traits. Cf. Holmberg & Roberts (2013: 112):

> First, morphological differences among languages are extremely easy to observe. Second, if we can show that there is a systematic relation between morphological structure and syntactic structure, the morphological differences may reflect more abstract syntactic differences among languages. These points are important not just in the obvious way for linguists interested in cataloguing and understanding the patterns in the world's languages, but also for language acquisition: The morphological differences are easy to observe not only for linguists but also for children acquiring their first language. Indeed, there is clear evidence from studies of children's language acquisition that they are highly sensitive to morphology, particularly inflectional morphology (Slobin, 1982; Wexler, 1998; Guasti, 2002). If the second idea is right, morphological properties may be an important cue employed in the acquisition of syntax (see Dresher, 1999; Lightfoot, 1999 on the notion of cues).

I will utilize the distinction that I call M-finiteness in the description and explanation of nine linguistic phenomena in English and Norwegian. These naturally cluster into three data sets. The first set of phenomena belongs to the cluster known as "residual V2" (Rizzi 1996); where English behaves in a manner resembling V2 (verb second) languages, except confined to certain constructions and with certain types of verbs (i.e. auxiliaries). The second data set relates to the inability of English modals to occur in non-finite form and the way auxiliaries *have* and *be* pattern with modals for some types of constructions while patterning with main verbs in certain other construction types. Thirdly, I relate these phenomena explicitly to the participle-for-preterit and the preterit-for-participle mix-up discussed above, making up the third data set. For each cluster of data, I compare modern English to modern Norwegian and show that observing the distribution of the M-finiteness feature adds to the description and explains crucial differences between the major verbal categories in the two languages, and also the different verb-auxiliary splits in English. In doing so, this approach targets the categorical feature "auxiliary" versus "main verb" in English and ascribes to them morphosyntactic features separating them from one another. These generalizations thus highlight causal relations between morphological oppositions and syntactic behaviour of verb classes, thus shedding light on issues of learnability, language change, and the syntax-morphology interface.

More specifically the paper addresses four very familiar questions, like (a) what distinguishes English main verbs from auxiliaries, allowing the latter to raise e.g. past negation; (b) what accounts for the different patterns of English auxiliary types in certain clause types; (c) how come language users mix up preterits and participles in many English varieties; and (perhaps more ambitiously) (d) what makes English different from its Germanic siblings, e.g. from Norwegian, leading to the lack of generalized V2 in English declaratives and the need for *do*-support? The analysis attempts to answer all these questions, resting on the different distribution of one single feature and the description of the aforementioned three data sets.

Many of these phenomena have received earlier and alternative explanations in the linguistic literature, although to my knowledge, nobody has tried to find a common underlying explanation to all these questions via a description of these three data sets. To the extent that this approach succeeds in simplifying the description and explanation of a wide range of seemingly unrelated phenomena, it thus complies with "the basic goal of all linguistic theories: to achieve greater empirical coverage and deeper explanation with fewer resources" (McCarthy & Prince 1999: 1).[4]

The paper is structured as follows. Section 2 I compares the relevant verbal morphology of modern English and Norwegian, observing the division between main verbs and (different types of) auxiliaries. Here I also present the English and Norwegian data sets for the nine different constructions and phenomena I investigate in this paper. Section 3 introduces the theory that serves as the fundament for my analysis of the relevant constructions, focussing on the notion of M-finiteness, its relation to lexically expressed finiteness, and its distribution across verbs and auxiliaries in Norwegian and modern English. In Section 4 I investigate each construction in turn, discussing certain previous analyses and presenting my analysis ("the diagnosis") for the phenomenon at hand, exploiting the notion of M-finiteness. Section 5 sums up and concludes the paper.

2. Verbs and auxiliaries in English and Norwegian

According to Pinker (2000: 33), "English inflection is famous among linguists for being so boring." Whereas the verb in Spanish comes in about fifty forms, and the Bantu language Kivunjo equips its verb with prefixes and suffixes that multiply out to half a million combinations per verb (ibid.), English main verbs come in only four forms; cf. (2a). Norwegian main verbs are also rather unexciting with five distinct forms, (2b). In addition, Norwegian has a present participle (e.g. *likende*),[5] but there is a general consensus that this is an adjectival form, not a verbal form; cf. for instance Faarlund, Lie and Vannebo (1997: 119).

4. "[T]he goal of P(rosodic) M(orphology) is the same as the rest of linguistic theory: to achieve greater empirical coverage and deeper explanation with fewer resources – in the happiest case, with no resources at all that are specific to the domain under investigation."

5. Norwegian has two written standards, *Bokmål* and *Nynorsk*. The examples in this paper are given in *Bokmål*.

(2) a. like – likes – liked – liking English
b. like – liker – likte – likt – lik Norwegian

The four forms in English perform "at least thirteen different roles"; (Pinker 2000: 33); *like* can be an infinitive (*to like*) or a present (*I like it*), an imperative (*like it!*) or a subjunctive (*I insist that he like it). Likes* is only used for the present tense, third person singular, whereas *liked* performs as past tense (*I liked it*), past participle (*I have always liked it*), as a passive participle (*She was being liked by everyone*), and a verbal adjective (*a much-liked novel*). The *-ing* form is used for four different purposes, as a progressive (*I am liking it*), a present participle (*I tried liking it*), a gerund (*her unexpected opening of the window*), and a verbal adjective (*a tree-hugging hippie*). The *-ing* form will not be the focus of interest in this paper.

The Norwegian form *like* is an infinitive (*å like* 'to like'); the form *liker* is the present form for all persons and numbers (*Jeg/du/hun/vi/dere/de liker det* 'I/you/she/we/you/they like it'); *likte* is the preterit form for all persons and numbers (*Jeg/du/hun/vi/dere/de likte det* 'I/you/she/we/you/they liked it'), *likt* is the past participle (*Jeg har alltid likt det* 'I have always liked it'), the passive participle (*Hun ble likt av alle* 'She was liked by everyone') and a verbal adjective (*en godt likt roman* 'a well-liked novel'). The imperative normally consists only in the stem (*lik det!* 'like it!'; cp. to the infinitive *like*), thus unlike English, Norwegian has an imperative which is usually distinct from the infinitive.[6] The imperative will also not be discussed in this paper, but cf. Eide (2002b; 2007) and Platzack and Rosengren (1998) for investigations into the Norwegian imperative.

2.1 Auxiliaries in English

English auxiliaries are often split into two groups (e.g. Hasselgård, Johansson & Lysvåg 1998: 160 ff.), modal auxiliaries and grammatical auxiliaries. The modal auxiliaries in English are *will, shall, may, can, must, ought to, dare* and *need (not)*, cf. e.g. Palmer (1986), Denison (1993). Unlike main verbs, modal auxiliaries in English have no *-s* forms and no non-finite forms ("are always tensed"), cf. Roberts (1985: 21), Hasselgård, Johansson & Lysvåg (1998: 161); Haegeman & Guéron (1999: 85) among many others; and modals are mutually exclusive with (auxiliary) *do;* cf. data adapted from Roberts (1985: 21) and Schütze (2003: 405). (Note that sequences of modals are grammatical in some varieties of modern English.)

6. Sometimes employing the stem as an imperative yields phonologically ill-formed results, for instance, when removing the infinitival ending yields a coda cluster with rising sonority as in *åpne*→ **.åpn.* 'open', *klatre*→ **.klatr.* 'climb'; cf. Rice (2003). In these cases, the imperative is usually identical to the infinitive.

(3) a. *He mays, musts, wills, cans, etc.
b. *He has may, must, will, can, etc. do it.
c. *They are canning to do it.
d. *They might could do it.
e. *He does/did (not) must do it (cp. He does/did (not) have to do it)
f. *He must do (not) go.

Jackendoff (1972) proposed that modals are no longer verbs in Modern English, but are always auxiliaries, and he sums up the differences as follows (1972: 100):

> Consider the differences. Modals do not undergo number agreement, though all verbs do. Modals do not occur together, and they do not appear in gerunds and infinitives.... Modals also differ from all main verbs but *be* and some uses of *have* in that they undergo subject-aux inversion, precede *not*, and block *do*-support.... Thus we can treat modals as verbs only if we are willing to concede that they represent a remarkable coincidence of a large number of purely syntactic aberrations.

As mentioned by Jackendoff, modals share some properties with other auxiliaries. The grammatical auxiliary verbs in Modern English are auxiliary *do* (partaking e.g. in inversion and negation, cf. below), auxiliary *have* (used to build perfective, complex tenses), and auxiliary *be* (used to form the progressive aspect and the passive voice). Each of these three occurs in lexical versions which share some important properties with their auxiliary counterparts, e.g. their morphology in Standard English. However, there are also differences; note that lexical *do* does not partake in inversion (4c), unlike lexical *be* and lexical *have,* although examples like (6c) are marginal or ungrammatical to many speakers and the variant with *do*-support is preferred.

(4) a. He does/did his homework.
b. Does/did he do his homework?
c. *Does/did he his homework?

(5) a. There is/was a solution.
b. *Does/did there be a solution?
c. Is/was there a solution?
d. It is/was raining.
e. *Does/did it be raining?
f. Is/was it raining?

(6) a. She has/had a lot of money.
b. Does/did she have a lot of money?
c. ??Has/had she a lot of money?
d. She has/had left him.
e. *Does/did she have left him?
f. Has/had she left him?

Unlike modal auxiliaries which must be replaced with phrasal equivalents (like *have to, be able to;* cf. (3e)) in non-finite contexts (i.e. when being governed by another verb or auxiliary), *have, be* and *do* have both finite and non-finite forms (cf. more detailed discussion below). *Be* of course has a quite elaborated paradigm of agreeing forms, with three different shapes in the present tense (*I am, you are, he/she/it is, we/you/they are*) and two in the preterit (*I/you/he/she/it was, we/you/they were*).

2.2 Auxiliaries in Norwegian

The Norwegian modal auxiliaries are *burde* 'ought to', *kunne* 'can', *måtte* 'must', *skulle* 'should', *ville* 'will, want to', *trenger ikke* 'need not' and *behøver ikke* 'need not'. Unlike English modals, Norwegian modals behave just like main verbs in most respects (Eide 2005: 55). Unlike main verbs, Norwegian modals have no present participles and no imperatives;[7] the latter fact is probably related to the fact that modals denote states with a low degree of controllability (Eide 2005: 20 ff). Norwegian modals have a full paradigm of finite and non-finite forms (although their preterit form is mostly identical to the infintive), they occur in clusters, show no agreement, but neither does any other finite verb in Norwegian; cf. above.[8] Modals take part in inversion (7d), but so do Norwegian main verbs (7e) and auxiliaries (7f).

(7) a. Han/vi må/kan/vil komme i morgen.
he/we must/can/will come tomorrow
'He/we must/can/will come tomorrow.'

b. Han har måttet/kunnet/villet svømme.
he has mustPART/canPART/willPART swim.
'He has had to/been able to/wanted to swim.'

c. Det må kunne finnes en løsning.
It must canINF findPASS a solution
'It must be possible to find a solution.'

d. Vil du komme i morgen?
want you come tomorrow
'Do you want to come tomorrow?'

7. Except marginally the modal *kunne*, e.g. *kunn dette diktet til i morgen* 'know this poem by tomorrow'; and notably when the modal takes a DP complement, i.e. behaves like a lexical verb; cf Eide (2005: 21)

8. A distinction is maintained in Nynorsk, "at least in principle" (Askedal 1994: 238), between the 2.P.SG imperative and the 2.P.PL plural imperative. Whereas the 2. person singular imperative usually consists simply of the verbal stem (cf. above), the plural imperative obligatorily has the ending *-e*; cf. e.g. the NN imperative singular *køyr, gut* 'drive, boy' versus the imperative plural *køyre, gutar* 'drive, boys'.

e. Kommer du i morgen?
come you tomorrow?
'Are you coming tomorrow?'

f. Blir/er/har/får Jon spist?
{become/be/have/get}PRES Jon eaten
'Is John being eaten?/ Is John eaten?/
Has John eaten?/ Will John get to have eaten?'

The non-modal auxiliaries in Norwegian are sometimes dubbed perfective auxiliaries (e.g. Åfarli & Eide 2003: 132 ff), since they mostly take past (or passive) participles as their complements. The group consists in members *bli* 'become' used as an inchoative copula and to form the passive, *være* 'be' is the stative copula and used as the auxiliary in stative passives; *ha* 'have' is used in complex tenses like the past and present perfect, and *få* 'get' acts as an inchoative counterpart to *ha* in certain constructions. Like Norwegian main verbs and modals, these auxiliaries have full paradigms of finite and non-finite forms, partake in question inversion and V2 and seem to be inseparable from main verbs and modals on purely syntactic or morphological grounds.

2.3 Main verbs and auxiliaries in nine different constructions[9]

Chomsky's (1955, 1957) analysis of English verbal morphology is considered one highly successful accomplishment of the Generative Enterprise; Lasnik (1999: 98):

> Much of the apparent chaos of this central portion of English morphosyntax was rendered systematic by the fundamental insight that the tense-agreement inflectional morpheme ("C") is syntactically independent, even though always a bound morpheme superficially.

"The apparent chaos" that Lasnik refers to in this quote is the topic of the remainder of this section. And although Chomsky's analysis of English verbal morphology is beyond any kind of doubt one of the most brilliant scientific achievements of the field of linguistics, several residual issues need to be resolved before it reaches its full explanatory power. For instance, we still need a robust explanation for the questions this paper addresses, to repeat: (a) what distinguishes English main verbs from auxiliaries, allowing the latter to raise e.g. past negation; (b) what accounts for the different patterns of auxiliary types in certain clause types; (c) how come language users mix up preterits and participles in many English varieties; and (d) what makes English different from

9. Positive imperatives, negative imperatives, and root *wh*-questions seemingly belong to the same cluster of phenomena and could be accounted for under the same analysis. In compliance with the advice from the reiewers, these sections were left out for reasons of space, but cf. Eide (2007) for discussion.

its Germanic siblings, e.g. from Norwegian, leading to the lack of generalized V2 in English declaratives and the need for *do*-support? This paper attempts to shed some light on all these questions in what follows. The first step towards an explanation is to carefully examine the empirical facts and observable differences between English and Norwegian syntax in the verbal domain.

2.3.1 Σ (*sigma*) *negation, negative inversion, and polarity questions*

Do-support in English negated clauses as a topic has occupied generative linguists for fifty years. In a sense, all the analyses are refinements of Chomsky (1955, 1957); cf. Lasnik (1999: 98). The basic facts to be explained are quite familiar; cf. e.g. Cormack and Smith (1998: 1, 2000: 50) and many others. Norwegian data are mine.

(8)				
	a.	John often snores.	g.	*Jon ofte snorker.[10]
	b.	*John not snores.	h.	*Jon ikke snorker.
	c.	*John snores not.	i.	Jon snorker (*snorke) ikke/ofte.
	d.	John did not snore	j.	*Jon gjorde ikke snorke.
	e.	John must not snore.	k.	Jon må (*måttet) ikke snorke.[11]
	f.	John has not/often snored.	l.	Jon har (*ha) ikke/ofte snorket.

In English negated declarative sentences, any auxiliary or modal may precede *not*, but a main verb cannot precede negation. In finite sentences where no other auxiliary is present, *do* must be inserted to license negation. A main verb is licensed with other adverbs like *often*, but cannot occur to the left of this adverb, unlike auxiliaries. Norwegian has no *do*-support with negation; inserting a corresponding verb *gjorde* 'doPRET' renders the clause ungrammatical (8j). Finite auxiliaries and modals license negation, just like in English, but so do finite main verbs, unlike in English. Non-finite verbs, modals and auxiliaries are unable to license this type of negation (8ikl). Unlike English, Norwegian has a verb second requirement in declaratives; cf. (8ghi).

Of course main verbs can be negated without *do*-support in English, cf. for instance *to*-infinitives (*We decided not to go*), and *why-not* constructions (*Why not accept the facts?*) where main verbs license negation (cf. Section 2.3.4 below). However, negation in English finite clauses is by assumption of a particular kind. This particular negation can be reduced to *n't*, unlike negation in other surroundings; cf. e.g. Zanuttini

10. Throughout this section I have chosen the corresponding words and expressions in Norwegian, so that the English sentences may serve as word-for-word glosses and translations for the Norwegian sentences.

11. Inserting a modal in infinitive here is problematic, since the infinitive is formally identical to the preterit. Thus the infinitival form *måtte* would be interpreted as the preterit *måtte* in the V2 position, as this position requires a finite verb. Similar problems arise for the data sets below; cf. (9g, 10g, 11i) etc.

(1996) and Schütze (2003: 11). The latter, following "quite common practice", refers to "the head in which sentential negation *not* is generated" as Σ (Gleitman 1965; Laka 1990). Correspondingly, I will refer to the "finite" type of negation as Σ negation.

Norwegian negation facts are less complex. With Σ negation, i.e. the type of negation occurring in declarative finite root clauses, any finite verb or auxiliary occurs to the left of negation; cf. the data in (8g–l) above. In subordinate clauses, the verb or auxiliary (usually) occurs to the right of negation, even in finite clauses (*…at Jon ikke snorker/har snorket/må snorke,* lit. 'that John not snores/has snored/must snore.'); cf. also Section 2.3.2 below.

A negative constituent like the English adverb *never* and the corresponding Norwegian adverb *aldri* can be preposed to the leftmost position of a declarative. This preposing triggers verb second, V2, in Norwegian and something resembling V2 in English. Just like with Σ negation, only modals and finite auxiliaries can occur to the left of the subject in these cases in English. Main verbs remain to the right of the subject and require *do*-support, cf. (9a–d). In Norwegian all modals, auxiliaries and main verbs may partake in this type of inversion, and *do*-support is ungrammatical (9e–h); again, the English examples may serve as glosses and translations for the Norwegian ones.

(9) a. *Never saw/see I a more beautiful sight.
b. Never did/do I see a more beautiful sight.
c. Never will/would I see a more beautiful sight.
d. Never have/had I seen a more beautiful sight.
e. Aldri så/ser (*se/*sett) jeg et vakrere syn.
f. *Aldri gjorde/gjør jeg se et vakrere syn.
g. Aldri vil/ville (*villet) jeg se et vakrere syn.
h. Aldri hadde/har (*ha/*hatt) jeg sett et vakrere syn.

Polarity questions (yes/no-questions) mirror the facts in negative inversion and Σ negation. In English only modals and finite auxiliaries occur to the left of the subject in these constructions (10a–d); in Norwegian any finite main verb, modal or auxiliary may invert and occur in the V1 position (10e–h), but not non-finite ones. Again, *do*-support is ungrammatical in Norwegian (10f).

(10) a. *Saw/see you that play?
b. Did/do you see that play?
c. Will/would you see that play?
d. Have/had you seen that play?
e. Så/ser (*se/*sett) du det stykket?
f. *Gjør/gjorde du se det stykket?
g. Skal/skulle (*skullet) du se det stykket?
h. Har/hadde (*ha/*hatt) du sett det stykket?

2.3.2 *Declarative main clauses*

As briefly mentioned above, Norwegian declarative main clauses are verb second and require a finite main verb, auxiliary or modal as their second constituent, whether the first constituent is the subject or some other fronted constituent. A non-finite main verb, auxiliary or modal renders the sentence ungrammatical (cf. (11g), (11i) and (11j)). English declaratives have no verb second requirement, as is widely discussed in the literature. In English only modals and auxiliaries occur to the left of a sentence adverb, main verbs remain to the right of the subject and sentence adverbials.

(11) a. John often plays bridge.
b. *John plays often bridge.
c. *John did/does often play bridge (ok if *do* is emphatic).
d. John will often play bridge.
e. John has often played bridge.
f. *Jon ofte spiller bridge.
g. Jon spiller/spilte (*spille/*spilt) ofte bridge.
h. *Jon gjør/gjorde ofte spille bridge.
i. Jon vil/ville (*villet) ofte spille bridge.
j. Jon har/hadde (*ha/*hatt) ofte spilt bridge.

As before, *do*-support is ungrammatical in these constructions in Norwegian (11h) and in this case even in English, unless *do* is emphatic (cf. 11c).

2.3.3 *Intermediate summery, seminal works, and brief discussion*

In modern English only modals, auxiliaries *have, be* and *do* occur to the left of Σ negation, to the left of the subject in negative and polarity question inversion, and to the left of sentence adverbs in declaratives. If no other auxiliary is present, the auxiliary *do* is inserted in these instances (i.e. *do*-support). In contrast, in Norwegian any finite main verb, modal or auxiliary occurs to the left of Σ negation, to the left of the subject in negative and polarity inversion, and to the left of sentence adverbs in root declaratives. Norwegian does not employ *do*-support in any of the relevant constructions, and inserting such a verb *gjøre* 'do' yields ungrammaticality. Likewise, Norwegian does not accept non-finite main verbs, auxiliaries or modals in the leftmost verbal position in any of these constructions.

The similarities and differences between English main verbs and auxiliaries have been a recurring topic in syntactic theories at least since Chomsky (1955, 1957). Although Chomsky (1957) lists auxiliaries, i.e. modals and *have* and *be,* as appearing under a common (albeit phrasal) node Aux (e.g. p. 111), he groups main verbs and auxiliaries together under a common 'v' in certain structural analyses (e.g. the rule of Auxiliary Transformation; p. 113, op. cit.). According to Lasnik (2000:68), Chomsky's (1957) treatment of auxiliary verbs in fact renders them as "belonging to no syntactic category at all." This led Ross to question Chomsky's analysis of auxiliaries. Ross (1969) claims that all English 'auxiliaries' in are in fact part of the natural class of verbs. Cf. also the quote from Jackendoff (1972) in Section 2.1. above where he claims that English modals cannot be verbs, because they are simply too different from main verbs.

Roberts (1985) suggests that the syntactic differences between auxiliaries and main verbs in English are due to a semantic property – the fact that auxiliaries lack Theta-properties (thematic, argument-selecting properties). As Lasnik (2000: 161) points out, however, "it is not obvious that auxiliary verbs (especially modals) don't have a theta-role to assign." Roberts (1985) concedes that modals do contribute to the clause something resembling a Theta-role and, to account for this effect, adopts Zubizarreta's (1982) analysis of modals as modifiers analogous to Jackendoff's (1972) agent-oriented adverbs. Roberts' analysis is in relevant respects also the analysis adopted by Pollock (1989); cf. Pollock (1989: 385, 386):

> "[*Have* and *be* and their French equivalents] have a unique status with respect to θ-theory: they arguably fail to assign any θ-role to the constituents they are subcategorized for.... That aspectual *be/être, have/avoir*, and 'passive' *be/être* are not θ-role assigners is not, I think, controversial."

Pollock's (1989) analysis is adopted by Chomsky in subsequent works even though instead of referring to the auxiliaries as lacking Theta-properties, Chomsky (1995: 198) characterizes them as "semantically vacuous":[12]

> Consider again the intuition that underlies Pollock's account: Raising of the auxiliaries reflects their semantic vacuity; they are placeholders for certain constructions, at most 'very light' verbs. Adopting the intuition (but not the accompanying technology), let us assume that such elements, lacking semantically relevant features, are not visible to L[ogical]F[orm] rules. If they have not raised overtly, they will not be able to raise by LF rules and the derivation will crash.

Although it might seem rather uncontroversial to assume that the auxiliaries *have* and *be* are semantically light and perhaps not Theta-assigners, modals always pose a problem for the generalization that raising is due to lack of thematic content. Modals seemingly do contribute something resembling a Theta-role in many contexts, especially on their root readings (obligation, permission, and volition). Thus, modals are simply not

12. Lasnik (1999: 103) on the alleged semantic vacuity for the auxiliary *be*: "First, it is not clear that *be* is always semantically vacuous, yet the syntactic behaviour of *be* in finite clauses is always the same. For example, it is reasonable to assume that in [(i)], *is* has the meaning of *exists*. Yet, as seen in (ii), it raises overtly nonetheless:

(i) There is a solution.

(ii) a. There is not a solution.
     b. Is there a solution?

semantically light enough for them to pattern with *have* and *be* on semantic grounds. On the other hand, there are also a number of syntactic differences between modals and the auxiliary *do*, on the one hand, and the auxiliaries *have* and *be* on the other that receive no explanation under the assumption that the special feature of auxiliaries is their common lack of Theta-properties (or indeed on any of the other approaches discussed in this section).

2.3.4 *Subjunctives/infinitives/small clauses/why-not-constructions*

Schütze (2003) addresses these issues, and quotes certain other authors who have concerned themselves with the differences, not (only) between main verbs and auxiliaries, but differences within the group of auxiliaries in English. Thus, Warner (1985: 68) groups finite *be* with modals in "a separate form-class which lacks verbal affixes" and Becker (2002) argues that finite *be* forms are not verbs. Schütze himself (ibid. p. 400) claims that *have* and *be* are indeed verbs, to the extent that they should be removed from the category AUX, whereas modals and *do* are Mood markers and not verbs (cf. also the previous subsection). As one empirical basis for this claim, Schütze (2003: 405–6) lists a number of contexts in English where there is a split between modals and the auxiliary *do* on the one hand and *have* and *be* on the other, e.g. subjunctives (12), *to*-infinitives (13), small clauses (14), *Why not* constructions (15), and others. Data and grammaticality judgements in all examples a–e are Schütze's (2003: 405 ff); I have added the main verb examples in f–g.

(12) Subjunctives
  a. It is vital that John be here on time.
  b. It is vital that John be smiling on the photograph.
  c. It is vital that Rover have eaten before we arrive.
  d. *It is vital that John do not be late.
  e. *It is vital that John will not come unprepared.[13]
  f. It is vital that John do the dishes.
  g. It is vital that he show up.

(13) *To*-infinitives
  a. It is important (for everyone) to be on time.
  b. It is important (for a movie star) to be smiling […].
  c. It is important (for every applicant) to have finished high school.
  d. *It is important (for us) to do not leave her alone.
  e. *It is important (for us) to can be alone.
  f. It is important (for him) to do the dishes.
  g. It is important (for him) to show up.

13. (14e) is grammatical on a non-subjunctive reading: 'The fact that John will not come unprepared is vital.'

(14) Small clauses
  a. I made him be alone for a while.
  b. The director made us be dancing when the curtain opened.
  c. ?The coach made her not have just eaten when she came to practice.
  d. *The conductor made us do not sing the harmony line.
  e. *The therapy made her can/could walk again. (cf...made her be able to walk…).
  f. I made him do the dishes.
  g. I made him show up.

(15) *Why (not)* constructions
  a. Why (not) be a responsible citizen?
  b. Why be working when you could be partying on the beach?
  c. ?Why not have made the appointment with her before she has a chance to make one with you?
  d. *Why do not go to the beach?
  e. *Why should/must stay home? (cf. ?Why be obliged to stay home?)
  f. Why not do the dishes?
  g. Why not show up?

Schütze (op.cit. p. 406) notes that "For *do* and modals to pattern together against *be* and *have* in so many environments clearly should not be a coincidence."[14] My added examples in (12)–(15), the f and g examples, simply illustrate that main verbs pattern with *have* and *be* in these constructions, and that lexical *do,* also being a main verb, patterns with other main verbs as well as *have* and *be.* In *Syntactic Structures* (Chomsky 1957), the element *do* is described as the substitute "bearer of an unaffixed affix" (cf. also the "stranded affix" filter of Lasnik 1981), and Chomsky states that the *do* appearing in these contexts is, at least morphologically,[15] "the same element as the main verb in *John does his homework*" (Chomsky 1957: 62). The f examples above show that lexical *do* patterns with main verbs, not with auxiliary *do* syntactically. This is also the case as regards inversion, cf. (4) above.

14. Schütze's own explanation is that *do* and modals belong to the category Mood, where *do* is an expression of the feature [indicative] in the Mood head M, "that is, this feature has two allomorphs, *do* and Ø […] Pronounce [indicative] as *do* if Tense (or another affix) is in need of a host; otherwise pronounce it as Ø."; (op.cit. p. 409). Schütze explains the pattern illustrated in (12) through (15) with the assumption that these clause types are either too small to contain a Mood projection at all (small clauses) or come with their own Ø Mood morpheme (subjunctives) blocking the insertion of the Mood heads, i.e. *do* or modals.

15. Lasnik (p.c.) suggests that Chomsky means morphologically, not necessarily syntactically. Cf. Sections 3 & 4 for the claim that main verb *do* and auxiliary *do* are in fact different even when it comes to morphology.

Norwegian does not have a progressive, and there is also no productive subjunctive. In constructions where other languages would typically employ the subjunctive, Norwegian uses modals, the present indicative, or the preterit indicative to mark "distal"[16] relations; i.e. in denoting situations "removed from reality". The Norwegian data sets corresponding to (12) through (15) thus lack the b-examples from English, and would use an indicative form instead of the subjunctives in (12). Again, any attempt of *do*-support, insertion of the verb *gjøre* 'do', is ungrammatical, unless it acts as a lexical verb; cf. examples corresponding to *do*-support in 16 c, 17c, and 18c versus examples of lexical *gjøre* 'do' in 16e, 17e, 17e, and 18e).

(16) *To*-infinitives

a. Det er viktig å være presis.
It is important to beINF on-time
'It is important to be on time.'

b. Det er viktig å ha fullført ungdomsskolen.
It is important to haveINF finished youth-school
'It is important to have finished high school.'

c. Det er viktig å (*gjøre) ikke (*gjøre) la henne
It is important to doINF not doINF letINF her
være alene.
be alone
'*It is important to do not leave her alone.'

d. Det er viktig å kunne være alene.
It is important to canINF be alone
'It is important to be able to be alone.'

e. Det er viktig å gjøre leksene.
It is important to doINF homeworkDEF
'It is important to do his homework.'

f. Det er viktig å vise seg der.
It is important to showINF REFL there
'It is important to show up there.'

(17) Small clauses

a. Jeg lot ham være alene en stund.
I let him be alone a while
'I let him be alone for a while.'

b. Treneren lot oss aldri ha spist akkurat før treningen.
CoachDEF let us never have eaten just before practice
'The coach never let us have just eaten before practice.'

16. Term due to Langacker (1978:855); cf. Eide (2010).

c. Dirigenten ba oss (*gjøre) ikke (*gjøre)
conductorDEF asked us doINF not doINF

synge førstestemmen
singINF harmony-lineDEF

'The conductor asked us not to sing the harmony line.'

d. Det var stort å se henne kunne gå igjen.
It was great to see her canINF walk again.
'It was fantastic to see her able to walk again.'

e. Jeg bad ham gjøre leksene.
I asked him doINF homeworkDEF
'I made him do his homework.'

g. Jeg bad ham vise seg der.
I asked him showINF REFL there.
'I asked him to show up there.'

(18) *Why (not)* constructions

a. Hvofor ikke være en ansvarlig borger?
why not beINF a responsible citizen?
'Why not be a responsible citizen?'

b. Hvorfor ikke ha gjort en avtale med henne
why not haveINF made an appointment with her

på forhånd?
on beforehand

'Why not have made an appointment with her on beforehand?'

c. Hvorfor ikke (*gjøre) gå på stranda?
Why not doINF goINF to beachDEF?
'Why not go to the beach?'

d. ?Hvorfor skulle/måtte være hjemme?
Why shouldINF/mustINF stay home
'Why be obliged to stay home?'

e. Hvorfor ikke gjøre leksene?
why not doINF homeworkDEF?
'Why not do your homework?'

g. Hvorfor ikke vise seg der?
why not showINF REFL there
'Why not show up there?'

Norwegian constructions corresponding to the English subjunctives in (12), as mentioned, would employ the indicative instead of a designated subjunctive form. In *å*-infinitives 'to-infinitives', small clauses and *Why not* constructions, Norwegian has forms that are unmistakably infinitival. Modals have infinitival forms and appear in these constructions like any other infinitival main verb or auxiliary, and any attempt of *do*-support in these constructions leads to ungrammatical results.

Note that in both the English and the Norwegian data sets negation precedes the verb or auxiliary in *why not* constructions, small clauses, and *to*-infinitives. For the English subjunctive the verb or auxiliary likewise follows the negation; the corresponding indicative clauses in Norwegian clearly employ finite verbs, but as mentioned above, negation precedes the verb, modal or auxiliary in Norwegian subordinate clauses, whether the verb is finite or not.

2.3.5 *Preterit-participle and participle-preterit mix-ups*

The type of preterit-participle mix ups that we find with irregular verbs in modern English, so offending to the ears of E.E. quoted in the introduction (and many others), has no obvious parallel in Norwegian. This feature of English has been investigated by sociolinguists, formal linguists and corpus linguists, and is reported from most parts of the world where some variant of Standard English is spoken by first language users. This mix-up is typically seen as non-standard, sub-standard, or dialectal (cf. e.g. Trudgill 2000: 23). Sampson (2002: 19) states that

> It has often been noted (e.g. Edwards 1993) that non-standard dialects show many differences from standard English in the forms used for past tenses and past participles of individual verbs. Dialect usage frequently has the same form for past tense and past participle of an irregular verb which has distinct forms in the standard language (e.g. *drove* for both parts of DRIVE, *done* for both parts of DO). The form used for these two forms is sometimes identical to the base form, e.g. *run*, and sometimes different from any standard form, e.g. *seed* as past tense/participle of SEE.

Sampson reports that Eisikovits (1987), who examines these phenomena in detail, assumes that the *system* of the nonstandard dialect is the same as the standard system; only the forms realizing the particular elements of the system are different. Sampson questions this assumption, but concludes that it is possible that sometimes nonstandard dialects make no distinction between past and perfect tenses and therefore has little use for separate forms, or maybe the contrast is expressed as *they done it* v. *they've done it* (op. cit. p. 20). "Eisikovits (1987) describes the English of inner-city Sydney; but, as Trudgill and Chambers (1991: 52) rightly say, many of her findings apply to other English dialects" (Sampson 2002: 19). The examples in (19abc) are taken from Sampson's paper and are thus attested in British English; Pinker (2000: 86) lists the examples in (19def), and describes the examples as "quite common" in American English and "absolutely standard outside the upper and middle classes".

(19) a. *You ever seen that?* (cf. Standard *Have you ever seen that?*)
b. *Er gone in.* (cf. Standard *She has gone in.*)
c. *They done it.* (cf. Standard *They have done it.*)
d. *I seen it.* (cf. Standard *I have seen it.*)
e. *She done it.* (cf. Standard *She has done it.*)
f. *They gone home.* (cf. Standard *They have gone home.*)

One very widespread explanation for these mix-ups is known as auxiliary-drop; the idea is that the auxiliary (often reduced to *'ve, 's* in rapid speech) makes it easy to miss; cf. e.g. Pinker (2000: 87), "*He's seen it,* in particular, is easily reanalysed as *He seen it.*". Although this explanation fits the data in (19), it cannot very straightforwardly explain the preterit-for-participle forms like those listed by E.E. quoted in the introduction; '*woulda came*', '*coulda went*', '*shoulda did*', '*woulda took*', '*had went*', '*hadn't came*', '*We haven't spoke*', '*had threw it*' etc. What one might do on a theory on purported auxiliary drop is to set up a causal chain where the dropped auxiliary triggers the general mix-up. In Section 4 below I will give a different explanation where "auxiliary drop" plays at most a very minor or secondary role in the mix-up of preterits and participles.

The preterit-participle mix-up is only relevant for irregular verbs, not regular verbs. The reason of course is that for regular verbs in modern English the preterit and the past participle are always identical already (cf. Section 2 above, cf. also the more detailed discussion in Section 4 below). Even for irregular verbs only half of them continue to distinguish the preterit from the participle in modern English (Pinker 2000: 86). Modals are also not mixed up, since they have no participial forms for a language user to mix up with the preterit. The auxiliary *have* is like regular verbs in that the preterit and the past participle are identical. *Be* is irregular and has special forms *was, were* in the preterit and *been* for the participle.[17] As for the verb *do,* we need to observe that although the main verb version of *do* and the auxiliary version of *do* behave very differently as regards syntactic distribution (cf. above) they seemingly share their morphological paradigm in Standard English. Trudgill (1999) notes that

> Standard English fails to distinguish between the auxiliary forms of the main verb *do* and its main verb forms. This is true both of present tense forms, where other dialects distinguish between auxiliary *I do, he do* and main verb *I does, he does* or similar, and the past tense, where most other dialects distinguish between auxiliary *did* and main verb *done,* as in *You done it, did you?*

Trudgill observes here that auxiliary *do* and main verb *do* do not share their morphological paradigm in "most other dialects". We will investigate this question further in

17. Although it seems that *be* is rather robust against the preterit-participle mix-up, a quick Google search comes up with examples from lyrics such as *Good as I Been to You* and *I've Was a Bad Boy This Year.*

Section 4 below, and conclude that the paradigms for auxiliary *do* and main verb *do* are in fact different even in Standard English, despite appearances. Let us note for now that certain non-standard dialects may use *done* in the function or at least in the place of a preterit for main verb *do*, but not for auxiliary *do*.

As stated above, the preterit-participle mix-ups plaguing the English language have no parallel in Norwegian. This is not because the preterit and the past participle are usually or even mostly identical in Norwegian (as in regular English verbs), because for the overwhelming majority of verbs there is an easily detectable distinction between preterits and past participles. That is, except for the most productive class of regular verbs, the *kaste*-class (*kaste* 'throw'). (20) shows the forms in the infinitive, present, preterit and past participle, respectively, for the verb *kaste* as compared to a different weak verb *like* 'like'.

(20) a. *kaste – kaster – kasta – kasta*
b. *like – liker – likte – likt*

In spite of the formal syncretism for the most productive class, the difference between preterits and past participles thus seems much more robust in Norwegian than in English. Correspondingly, native Norwegian language users rarely mix up preterit and participle forms for any type of verb. This is however quite different from those learning Norwegian as a second language.

According to Hagen (2001:52 ff), adult learners of Norwegian have a lot of problems in acquiring the finiteness distinction in Norwegian. To make matters worse, this is *the* morphosyntactic category to master in order to acquire the syntax of Norwegian clauses [my translation]:

> The list of frequent, non-native traits of the interlanguage of adult L2 learners of Norwegian is remarkably short, and includes the distribution of expletives, verb inversion (i.e. V2), adverbial placement in main and embedded clauses, and the copula requirement. All are traits where the rule of distribution needs to refer to the category finiteness for its formulation.

When adult second language learners of Norwegian mix up finite and non-finite forms (and they do this to some extent; cf. below), they mix up the preterit and the past participle, just like English language users do with irregular verbs; cf. the participle for preterit in (21a) and the preterit for participle in (21b). Adult L2 learners of Norwegian also mix up the present tense and the infinitive quite often (cf. (21cd)).[18]

18. These data are taken from ASK, the corpus of Norwegian second language learner texts collected by linguists at the university of Bergen, the AKSIS group; cf. ⟨http://ask.uib.no⟩. The data in (21) come from informants s0698, s0590, s0868, and s0977 respectively.

(21) a. Etter mange år fått hun en nyheter. (target *fikk* 'getPRET')
After many years getPART she a news
'After many years she got some news.'

b. [Jeg] hadde ikke fikk jobb. (target *fått* 'getPART')
I had not getPRET job
'I hadn't (yet) gotten a job.'

c. [Da] ønsker jeg at skal jeg får fin
then wish I that shall I getPRES fine
en jobb. (target *få* 'getINF')
one job
'Then I wish that I will get a nice job.'

d. Og etterpå få barna høre det
and afterwards getINF childrenDEF hear the
samme igjen. (target *får* 'getPRES')
same again
'And later the children get to hear the same again.'

The mix-up of the participle and the present, for instance, almost never happens (Wik 2014). Likewise, a preterit or a participle seldom replaces an infinitive. It seems that there is something about the participle and the preterit that makes them easy to mix up for second language learners of Norwegian. Incidentally, this mirrors the English pattern: It is the preterit and the participle that are replaced by each other; they are not replaced by a third form, e.g. by the present *-s* form, the bare verb form, or the *-ing*-form. Moreover, it seems that the finiteness distinction, the difference between finite and non-finite forms, is especially hard to grasp for second language learners of Norwegian who speak English as a first or second language. Næss (2006) investigated a set of informants who had English, Tamil, Thai, and Persian as a first language who produced sentences with double tense markings, cf. (22).

(22) a. Kan han snakker norsk?
canPRES he speakPRES Norwegian
'Does he speak Norwegian?'

b. Skal du spiser nå?
ShallPRES you eatPRES now?
'Will you eat now?'

c. Er du heter Kari?
BePRES you callPRES Kari?
'Are you called Kari?'

These speakers all knew English either as their first or second language, and they contrasted with another set of informants in the same study; the latter informants did not speak English (but had French, Swahili, and Russian as their first language) and interestingly did not make this type of error. This is corroborated by the findings reported in Wik (2014). Wik investigated 80 texts by second language learners of Norwegian (from the ASK corpus in Bergen) where 40 texts were produced by informants with English as their first language; the remaining 40 were produced by German informants. These texts are produced as a test for gaining access to Norwegian higher education and the informants are hence very proficient in Norwegian. Their error rate regarding verbal inflection was less than 10% for the English speakers and less than 7% for the German speakers. Nevertheless, Wik found that for the English speakers, mix-ups of finite forms with non-finite forms (infinitive for present and vice versa; participle for preterit and vice versa) account for 51% of the residual errors made in the domain of verbal inflection. For the German speakers the corresponding percentage was 37%. Thus it seems that knowing English as a first or second language contributes to negative transfer in language learning when it comes to detecting the finiteness distinction even in Norwegian.[19]

2.3.6 *Summary: Main vs. auxiliary verbs in nine constructions*

Summing up the patterns characterizing English and Norwegian main verb-auxiliary splits in these nine constructions, we find that Norwegian is an "extremely boring" language as compared to the English system with all its twists and quirks. We also see that sometimes English auxiliaries group against main verbs, sometimes modals and auxiliary *do* group against main verbs and *have* and *be*.[20] For the final construction, preterit-past participle mix-ups investigated in Section 2.3.5, it does not make very much sense to split the data into modals, auxiliaries and main verbs, since this mix-up happens almost exclusively with irregular main verbs in English. In Norwegian this mix-up does not occur for native speakers, but happens to some extent for second language learners. The facts summed up in the following table will serve as the empirical basis for our investigations to be discussed in Section 4.

19. Note that the German speakers on average had shorter Length of Residence than the English informants.

20. In fact, sometimes even auxiliary *be* requires *do*-support (in negative imperatives). The format of this paper does not allow for the detailed discussion needed to account for this fact within the theory outlined here. However, cf. Eide (2007) for some discussion.

Table 1. Summing up properties of verbs in nine constructions, Norwegian and English

	Norwegian	English		
		Modals/aux *do*	*have/be*	Main verbs
License Sigma Negation	all finite verbs	yes	yes	no; *do*-support
Raise in negative inversion	all finite verbs	yes	yes	no; *do*-support
Raise in polarity questions	all finite verbs	yes	yes	no; *do*-support
Raise in declaratives	all finite verbs	yes	yes	no
Appear in subjunctives	not productive	no	yes	yes
Appear in *to-/å*-infinitives	all non-finite verbs	no	yes	yes
Appear in small clauses	all non-finite verbs	no	yes	yes
Appear in *why (not)-/ hvorfor (ikke)*- constructions	all non-finite verbs	no	yes	yes
Preterit-participle mix-up	L1: no; L2: yes	no	no	irregular verbs

3. Morphological finiteness in Norwegian and English

My approach to finiteness emerges from Comrie's (1985: 36) observation that natural languages display examples of *absolute* and *relative tenses.* Absolute tenses (e.g. the preterit) typically take the moment of speech as their deictic centre and relative ones (e.g. participles) take some other contextually-given time point as their point of reference. While in many languages specific verb forms encode the distinction between absolute and relative tenses, note that there are also languages, e.g. Creoles, where the same verb form is used for both. What I refer to as the lack of formal distinctions between absolute and relative tense forms traditionally has been considered a lack of formal finiteness distinction in the literature on Creoles (cf. Romaine 1993; Muysken & Law 2001; the introduction chapter to this volume). In most Germanic languages the finiteness distinction is morphologically encoded. I argue that even in Germanic languages the distinction between finite and non-finite verb forms corresponds to the distinction between absolute and relative tense forms. Cf. Eide (2002a), (2005), (2009a, b), for the details of this approach; here I only include a brief outline.

As Comrie (1985: 48) observes, most European languages have only a two-way split in their tense systems, past vs. non-past, "with subdivisions within non-past (especially future as opposed to the present) being at best secondary; thus the so-called present tense in such languages is frequently used for future time reference." Pairing this assumption with my claim that the absolute-relative distinction equals the finiteness distinction in the relevant languages, we arrive at the paradigm in (1) above; repeated here as (23), for the garden variety Germanic language. Here each and every verb form encodes a tense element consisting of two pieces of information: [±Past] and [±Finite]. In this analysis, being tensed is an essential part of being a verb (present participles are adjectival, at least in Norwegian, cf. Faarlund, Lie & Vannebo 1997: 119).[21]

(23)

	+Finite	−Finite
+Past	**Preterit**	**Participle**
−Past	**Present**	**Infinitive**

In Section 2, example (2) above (repeated as (24) below) it was shown that both Norwegian and English have quite simple verb paradigms, with four forms in English and five in Norwegian.

(24) a. like – likes – liked – liking English
b. like – liker – likte – likt – lik Norwegian

Earlier stages of Norwegian and English of course had a much larger inventory of verb forms. Both languages have been subject to a general erosion of morphological inflections which affected e.g. mood and agreement markings; I argue in this section however that this erosion also affected one particular distinction in English which happens to be still maintained and very much productive in Norwegian. This is the morphological finiteness distinction; the productive morphological paradigm for the encoding of special forms for verbs bearing absolute and relative tense elements.

Unlike Creole languages Norwegian productively encodes finiteness with all types of verbs; any verb form in Norwegian is inherently specified with respect to finiteness.[22] A [+Finite] form like *spiser* 'eatPRES' or *spiste* 'eatPRET' has distinct morphology showing that it is a finite (i.e. typically absolute) tense form; no context needs to be provided to determine this. Likewise, *spise* 'eatINF' and *spist* 'eatPART' are unambiguously non-finite, regardless of context. In contrast, an out-of-context main verb in English, e.g. *love* or *loved,* could be either a finite (absolute) or a non-finite (relative)

21. I am also glossing over the fact that imperatives are often believed to lack any tense marking. However, they are often believed to encode a type of mood (e.g. jussive or deontic mood). It might be that the description of verbness requires either tense or mood for a lexical root to be encoded as a verb.

22. Note again the exception constituted by the *kaste*-class, where the preterit and the participle are identical. However, even for this class the finiteness distinction is maintained as an opposition within the paradigm, since the infinitive (*kaste*) and the present (*kaster*) are always different.

tense form. *Loved* may be either a preterit or a participle, *love* either a present or an infinitive (in fact, *love* might even be a subjunctive or an imperative (cf. Section 2)).

This could be an accidental fact of formal homonymy and need not point to anything profound separating English morphology from Norwegian morphology; although e.g. Carstairs (1987: 123) advocates the view that there is no such thing as "accidental" systematic homonymy within an inflectional paradigm: All systematic homonymies within inflectional paradigms are either syncretisms or "take-overs", where both are identified by Sauerland (1996: 20) as cases of impoverishment. Impoverishment means the deletion of specific morphosyntactic features in specific contexts; usually involving relevant paradigms within one and the same language.[23] However, it is certainly possible to compare paradigms of basic verb forms and expect the formal syncretism, e.g. the systematic correspondence of two forms, preterit and participle to one, generalized [+past] form, to involve the across-the-board deletion of one specific morphosyntactic feature. To see the consequences of this particular syncretism, we need to acknowledge that the infinitive and the past participle are genuine, full-fledged participants in the basic tense system, giving rise to a four-way tense paradigm with two finite and two non-finite forms; cf. the table in (23), repeated here as (25a). Over time, English (weak) main verbs developed into a system employing the collapsed paradigm in (25b); here the finiteness distinction, the distinction between absolute and relative tense forms, is lost.

(25)

a	+Finite	–Finite
+Past	**Preterit**	**Participle**
–Past	**Present**	**Infinitive**

⇨

b

+Past	**Preterit/Participle**
–Past	**Present/Infinitive**

This loss results in a paradigm employing one generalized [+Past] form and one generalized [–Past] form ("the bare form"). Old English, like present day Norwegian, had distinct forms for all four cells in this paradigm for both strong verbs like *singan* and weak verbs like *lufian*, cf. paradigm (26a). However, English is changing before our eyes, becoming more like the Creole languages mentioned earlier. The finiteness distinction starts to disappear in weak verbs, adhering to the collapsed paradigm in (26b). In (26b), one generalized [+Past] form covers the function of the preterit and the past participle, and one [–Past] form ("the bare form") covers the present and the infinitive.

23. "Impoverishment, first proposed in Bonet (1991), is an operation on the contents of morphemes prior to Spell-Out. In early work in D(istributed) M(orphology), Impoverishment simply involved the deletion of morphosyntactic features from morphemes in certain contexts. When certain features are deleted, the insertion of Vocabulary Items requiring those features for insertion cannot occur, and a less specified item will be inserted instead." Harley & Noyer (1999: 3). Cf. also Sauerland (1996).

(26)

a	+Finite	–Finite
+Past Old English Norwegian	**Preterit:** *sang, lufode* *sang, likte*	**Participle:** *gesungen, lufod* *sunget, likt*
–Past Old English Norwegian	**Present:** *singe, lufie* *synger, liker*	**Infinitive:** *singan, lufian* *synge, like*

b Weak verbs	
+Past Modern English	**Preterit/Participle:** *liked, killed, smiled*
–Past Modern English	**Present/Infinitive** *like, kill, smile*

c Standard strong verbs	+Finite	–Finite
+Past Modern English	**Preterit:** *went, saw,* *drove*	**Participle:** *gone, seen,* *driven*
–Past Modern English	**Present:** *go, see, drive*	**Infinitive:** *go, see, drive*

d Dialectal strong verbs	
+Past Non-standard English	**Preterit/Participle** *gone, seen, drove*[24]
–Past Non-standard English	**Present/Infinitive** *go, see, drive*

While English regular weak verbs have been inflected according to the collapsed paradigm in (26b) for centuries, irregular strong verbs have maintained a slightly more complex system. Although there is only one generalized [–Past] form, there are distinct forms for the preterit and the past participle; instead of a four-way system, there is a three-way system in Standard English; cf. (26c). Currently, these remains of the finiteness distinction in main verbs, hitherto maintained in strong irregular verbs, are disappearing from many variants and dialects of English, resulting in alignment with the rest of the system (26d). We return to these dialectal facts in Section 4.4 below.

English main verbs are by no means incapable of expressing the anchoring function of finiteness, and they are of course very much capable of performing e.g. the task of being the only verb in an independent utterance. Neither are they incapable of expressing absolute tense. Just like in the Creole languages mentioned earlier, the context will disambiguate the English tense form; the tense element of the structurally highest verb takes on the function of absolute tense, even when the verb is not morphologically specified for finiteness. Thus, the difference in the construal of temporal

24. Not all dialects of English take the same path in simplifying the paradigm. In some cases, the preterit form is the one covering both functions, e.g. *should-a-went*; in other cases, a new form, neither the original preterit nor the past participle, is employed as the [+past] form; cf. the quote from Sampson (2002:19) in Section 2.3.5 above.

chains in Norwegian and English boils down to the fact that in the typical Norwegian temporal chain the structurally highest verb is obligatorily [+Finite] morphologically. In the corresponding English temporal chain, the structurally highest verb takes on the absolute interpretation, but there is no requirement for a morphologically [+Finite] verb, except for certain contexts (to be discussed in Section 4). Otherwise, the forming of the temporal chain proceeds similarly in Norwegian and English: each verb links up to the previous event in the chain, taking the previous verb (or event) as its point of temporal reference (cf. Eide 2009a for the details).

Note that nothing has been said so far about the 3rd person singular, which has a distinct form even for main verbs in English. I am assuming that the 3PSg ending *-s* is an agreement marker that plays no role in the tense system. Admittedly, the *-s* form shows up in standard English when the verb is semantically finite, that is, when it fulfils the anchoring function and denotes an absolute tense. This is usually the same context where a lexical subject is licensed (cf. Cowper this volume). Traditionally this effect has been attributed to morphological finiteness, as finiteness was believed to equal tense + agreement. In the present approach, the relationship between agreement and finiteness is less rigid, and agreement is not an ingredient in finiteness, at least for Germanic languages (cf. also Åfarli this volume). The fact that [+FIN] and [+AGR] tend to occur in the same contexts can be attributed to the *Anaphor-agreement effect* of Rizzi (1990: 26):

(27) *The anaphor agreement effect:*
Anaphors do not occur in syntactic positions construed with agreement.[25]

In my theory (cf. Eide 2009a for the details), verb forms inherently encode tense elements and behave like temporal anaphors when non-finite and like temporal pronouns when finite. If temporal anaphors (non-finite verbs) are subject to Rizzi's restriction, we would expect non-finite verbs to be mutually exclusive with agreement, unless they show a particular type of anaphor-agreement (cf. Woolford 1999).[26] Finite (i.e. pronoun-like) verbs, on the other hand, would be expected to show more agreement. This would be true even for English main verbs in finite functions, i.e. when their tense element takes the speech event S as their point of reference. That is, I am not considering 3PSg *-s* a marker of morphological finiteness; although it occurs when a verb takes on

25. According to Eric Reuland (p.c.), there are languages where the anaphor agreement effect is lacking. He mentions Greek and Georgian among the languages that allow anaphors as subjects of agreeing verbs.

26. It may be fruitful to discuss agreeing infinitives in European Portuguese in this perspective, especially if we could argue that the type of agreement in these constructions is in fact an instance of Woolford's (1999) particular anaphor-agreement type, e.g. because it gives rise to other semantic effects than ordinary "finite" agreement.

an S-finite anchoring function, it does not encode morphological finiteness; it is only a secondary accessory to S-finiteness, a marker of agreement.

Norwegian has no subject-verb agreement, and yet it productively encodes the finiteness distinction with all types of main verbs, modals, and auxiliaries (cf. Section 2 for the data). English modals on the other hand have only finite forms; if a modal is needed in a non-finite context (e.g. as the complement of an auxiliary), a phrasal replacement like *have to, be able to, be allowed to,* etc. must be enrolled (**He has may/must/can do it*; cf. (2), Section 2.1 above). Auxiliary *do,* either it is emphatic *do* or the *do* occurring in *do*-support, also never occurs in non-finite forms (**He must do not go*; **She could have done not notice it*); cf. Section 2.1. *Be* is a special case with all its different agreeing forms, but there is no doubt that it maintains the finiteness distinction: *be* and *been* are the non-finite forms; *am/are/is* and *was/were* are the finite forms. *Have* encodes no morphologically overt finiteness distinction. It has a non-past form *have* and a past form *had,* apart from the 3PSg *has,* which is marked for agreement, but does not signify the morphological finiteness distinction; cf. above.

Summing up: Abstracting away from the *-s* form (which is considered here an agreement marker), very few verbs in modern English overtly encode a morphological finiteness opposition. Weak verbs do not, modals and auxiliary *do* do not; the latter because they have no non-finite forms. *Have* also does not overtly encode this opposition, because it patterns with weak main verbs morphologically. We are left with *be,* and some irregular main verbs to encode the finiteness opposition in their paradigms. And these verbs, even if they are frequent, they are few. Pinker (2000: 18) claims that there are only about 150 to 180 irregular verbs in modern English, and only half of them continue to distinguish the preterit from the participle in modern English; cf. Pinker (2000: 86). Even for these 75–90 verbs, the infinitive and the present are still identical (again, abstracting away from 3PSg *-s*).

3.1 Morphological finiteness versus lexical finiteness

We have already seen that there is a semantic-conceptual side to finiteness which is the anchoring function (cf. Section 1, and also the introductory chapter to this volume). Likewise, the presence or absence of this function in a clause may correlate with certain morphological distinctions in some languages, like the opposition between independent and dependent verbal forms in Norwegian (cf. the discussion above). Specific syntactic processes may make reference to specific features of those forms, like the operation of verb raising to V2 in most Germanic languages, where only the independent, [+finite] verb may gain access to the V2 position. In this section I want to point out that there is another relevant level for finiteness morphology. A lexical verb form may bear the visible markings of finiteness but nevertheless be banned from syntactic operations like verb raising to the V2 position. The English main verb *bit* is seemingly overtly specified as a [+past, +finite] form, but never undergoes raising to V2. Moreover, these residual visible markings of finiteness by no means implies that the finiteness distinction is productive for Modern English main verbs. This is comparable to morphological case in Norwegian, where case endings have not been productive for centuries; however, there are still a number of collocational preposition phrases, such as some headed by the preposition *til* 'to', where the old case marking, the genitive ending -*s*, is still obligatory: *til fjells* 'to the mountain', *til sjøs* 'to the sea', *til fots* 'on foot', *til knes* '(up) to one's knees', etc. Leaving out the -*s* leads to ungrammaticality: **til fjell, *til sjø, *til fot, *til kne*. It would be very misleading to conclude from these examples that Norwegian has a productive case system, but there obviously exists a blocking effect where the archaic genitival -*s* forms block the unmarked forms with no -*s*. This resembles the facts where a [+past] form also specified as [+participle] (or potentially as [+past, –finite] in the current approach), e.g. *eaten* blocks the insertion of a form **eated* (cf. Halle & Marantz 1993; Sauerland 1996 and others).

Also, we will see that in the case of *have* in English this auxiliary fulfils the syntactic requirements for verb raising without overtly encoding the finiteness distinction in its productive morphological paradigm. That means that the presence or absence of the syntactically relevant M-finiteness feature cannot always be directly read off a given lexical verb or auxiliary; the acquisition process evidently tolerates certain exceptions to the systematic relation between lexical finiteness marking and the visibility of an M-finite feature to syntactic operations like verb raising.

(28) a. **Lexical finiteness:** visible finiteness markings on the token level, overt markings on a lexical form; i.e. on a verb or auxiliary.
b. **Morphological finiteness:** a feature assigned to a verb or auxiliary, iff the verb or auxiliary is input to a productive morphological rule generating finite forms.

This separation allows for a description of English strong irregular verbs as being L-finite without being M-finite: They have overt markings distinguishing finite forms, e.g. [+past,+finite] *shrank* in opposition to [+past,–finite] *shrunk*, but their finiteness markings e.g. signified by vowel shift (*Ablaut*) are not generated by a productive morphological rule. Pinker (2000: 53) describes irregular verbs as "fossils of the long-dead rules"; they are memorized, not the output of a productive morphological operation. Cf. also Pinker (2000: 133):

> [I]rregular inflection depends on *memorized* words or forms *similar* to them, but regular inflection can apply to *any* word, regardless of whether the word is readily retrievable from memory. Regular inflection has that power because it is computed by a mental operation that does not *need* access to the contents of memory, namely, a symbol-processing operation rule, which applies to any instance of the symbol 'verb'.

The productive symbol-processing operation rule for generating e.g. past forms for English main verbs no longer makes use of the finiteness distinction; the rule simply adds the past suffix (some variant of *-ed*) to the base form with no reference to finiteness, creating a two-way tense opposition [±past]. One may envisage a causal chain for the decline of L-finiteness and the loss of productive M-finiteness for English main verbs: When L-finiteness dropped below a crucial level (e.g. via a general rule of feature impoverishment), i.e. for a crucial number of main verb tokens, M-finiteness was lost for that category. Thus the memorized [+past,+finite] form *shrank* and the [+past, –finite] form *shrunk* no longer correspond to separate slots in the paradigm generated by the productive rule. Therefore, the category "main verb" in modern English has the value [M-finiteness not encoded]; irrespective of their L-finite appearance.

Not so for the morphological rule generating Norwegian past tense verb forms. Since Norwegian verb forms are portmanteau suffixes where tense and finiteness are intrinsically linked, the verb form will simultaneously express [±past, ±finite]; there is no way to express only tense with no reference to finiteness. This is true for irregular verbs and regular verbs (cf. table in 26a), main verbs, modals and auxiliaries (cf. data in Section 2). Thus all categories subsumed by the term "verb" in Norwegian are assigned the value [M-finiteness encoded], since the productive symbol-processing operation rule will need to refer to finiteness for the formation of past forms. This entails that all L-finite verbs in Norwegian are also M-finite: their overt morphological marking corresponds to a slot in the paradigm generated by the productive morphological rule.[27]

I stipulate that all auxiliaries in English have the value [M-finiteness encoded]. Modals and auxiliary *do* always occur in finite forms; they have no non-finite versions. This entails that their paradigms do not encode the finiteness opposition *per ce*; but I will assume that their finite forms are still generated by a productive morphological rule, thus ascribing to them the feature of M-finiteness. Finally, we have the paradigms of *be* and *have*. By assumption, these auxiliaries also have M-finiteness encoded, i.e. their finite forms are generated by a productive rule, in this case making use of the four-way paradigm for tense and finiteness. However, *be* not only has distinct forms for all four cells in the paradigm, but a number of different forms for the present and the preterit. Since *be* functions as the copula (and has other semantically light functions), it is not unexpected that it has retained the AGR inflections longer than other verbs. On certain approaches, predication, as instantiated by e.g. the copula in fact amounts

27. This in a sense makes reference to paradigms as a built-in level of syntactic rules, in a way resembling the approach Minimalist Morphology of Wunderlich and Fabri (1994) and Wunderlich (1995). I would very much like to address whether Minimalist Morphology is a fruitful line of investigation for the present data sets, but for now I have to leave that interesting question for future research.

to an AGR relation; cf. e.g. Guéron & Hoekstra (1995). On my approach to finiteness, AGR features play no role in the instantiation of M-finiteness (although it is found as an accessory to S-finiteness; cf. the discussion of 3Psg *-s* above). Thus, the abundance of AGR-dictated forms of *be* is not a problem for my proposal. The paradigm of *have* is quite another matter. As seen in (29b), *have* seemingly inflects like its lexical sibling *have*, with no detectable distinction between the participle and the preterit or the infinitive and the present; compare to the paradigm of regular weak verb *love*.[28]

(29)

a.	+Finite	−Finite
+Past	**Preterit:** *was, were*	**Participle:** *been*
−Past	**Present:** *am, are is*	**Infinitive:** *be*

b.	+Finite	−Finite
+Past	**Preterit:** *had, loved*	**Participle:** *had, loved*
−Past	**Present:** *have, love*	**Infinitive:** *have, love*

In the case of *have*, we have an instance of an auxiliary lacking overt L-finite marking, but I stipulate that it is still input to a productive morphological rule referring to finiteness; i.e. it is assigned the value [M-finiteness encoded]. One way to solve the "problem" of lacking L-finiteness for auxiliary *have* is to invoke homonymy or to stipulate zero-morphemes encoding finiteness. However, it is likely that the "main-verb-like" inflection of *have* is related to its main verb twin *have*, and for the main verb twin, one would of course expect it to inflect like any other main verb.

Summing up, I have argued that the relevant paradigms of main verbs and auxiliaries in English and Norwegian are as in (30), where the reference to finiteness means [M-finiteness encoded].

(30)

+Past	**Preterit/Participle**
−Past	**Present/Infinitive**

a. English main verbs

[+Past,+Finite]	**Preterit**
[−Past, +Finite]	**Present**

b. English modals, auxiliary *do*

	+Finite	-Finite
+Past	**Preterit**	**Participle**
-Past	**Present**	**Infinitive**

c. English *have/be*, Norwegian main verbs, modals and auxiliaries.

As there is a discrepancy between L-finiteness and M-finiteness for some irregular verbs, and also for *have*, this blurs the relation between visible morphology and syntactic behaviour believed to be quite important to acquisition (cf. the quote from Holmberg and Roberts 2013 given earlier). However, we know that any language

28. The auxiliary *have* never occurs as a participle in standard English.

contains and tolerates irregularities to a great extent, and this does not usually hamper the acquisition process. Irregularities typically linger on in a language for very frequent phenomena that still provide robust input to the acquisition process, although over time such irregularities tend to align with the rest of the system. For an English-learning child the detection that modals and auxiliary *do* have only finite forms gives very reliable indicators to the behaviour of these auxiliaries, since they occur only in positions where M-finiteness is required (whereas they are banned from constructions banning M-finiteness, as we will see in Section 4). Likewise, detecting that the M-finite feature is irrelevant and not encoded with main verbs (via the acquisition of the productive rule generating the impoverished, two-way paradigm in (30b)) gives the child a direct account of the syntactic behaviour of main verbs.

4. Diagnosing the nine phenomena

In this section, I utilize the notion of M-finiteness to diagnose the differences between Norwegian and English in the twelve phenomena investigated in Section 2 above. The rather simple idea is that the relevant syntactic operations refer to M-finiteness (crucially, not L-finiteness) in their underlying rule formation; for many constructions only a [+M-finite] element satisfies the given operator; other rules ban [+M-finite] elements.

4.1 Σ (sigma) negation/Negative inversion/Polarity questions

As our Table 1 from 2.3.6 above reveals, the facts concerning verb distribution relative to Σ (sigma) negation, negative inversion, and polarity questions pattern together (cf. below). Therefore, a common explanation for the distribution of verbs and auxiliaries in these constructions is warranted.

	Norwegian	English		
		modals/aux *do*	*have/be*	main verbs
License Sigma Negation	all finite verbs	yes	yes	no; *do*-support
Raise in negative inversion	all finite verbs	yes	yes	no; *do*-support
Raise in polarity questions	all finite verbs	yes	yes	no; *do*-support

All these constructions have been subject to an industry of proposals; I will not make a point of discussing these here, only briefly refer to certain representative analyses. As regards Σ-negation, Cormack and Smith (1998, 2000) set out to explain the data in (31), forming the questions Q1–Q3:

(31) a. John often snores.
b. *John not snores.
c. John did/will/must not snore.
d. *John snores not.

Q1: Why is (31b) ungrammatical? In particular,
Q2: What accounts for the difference between *often* and *not* in (31a) vs. (31b)?
Q3: Why can an Aux or modal precede *not*, while a V cannot (31c) vs. (31d)?

Cormack and Smith (2000:65) point out that

> It is not easy to give a principled account of the relative positions of negation with respect to auxiliaries and main verbs in English. Baker (1991) went so far as to argue that it was impossible within 'core grammar'. Lasnik (1995) proposes quite different properties for main verbs and auxiliaries with respect to their relation to inflection. Roberts (1998) assigns to auxiliaries (including our $Modal_2$ auxiliaries) the curious property of consisting of nothing but Formal Features.

We might add that Pollock (1989) and Chomsky (1995) cf. Section 2.3.3 above, stipulate that auxiliaries, unlike main verbs, are semantically vacuous. This begs the question, what semantic distinction would include auxiliary *do, have* and *be*, and modals like *can* and *must* in one group, and simultaneously exclude 'be able to' and 'be obliged to'; the latter patterning with main verbs? And how come this purported semantic distinction does not separate main verbs from auxiliaries in Norwegian? The semantics of Norwegian modals and auxiliaries do not seem to differ in any relevant respect from their correspondents in English; appealing to semantic criteria in this case seems *ad hoc*.

Cormack and Smith (1998, 2000) assume that the polarity head POL (which can be realized as sentential negation) is an element of the category V, unlike the adverb *often;* this means that negation is in effect a verb (=answer to Q2). This verb must be inflected, and (very simplified) *not* is the inflection of POL; moreover, any Infl must be adjacent to its verb (Cormack & Smith 2000:72). Next, they stipulate that *not* is a default (or defective) inflection, to be checked by Tense. However, the main verb *snores* also has a tense inflection, a non-defective, non-default tense inflection, i.e. present tense. There is an "Infl-precedence constraint" which forces the most specified tense inflection to appear first, thus (31b) is ruled out (=Q1). Adverbs, like *often,* have no V-features and do not intervene in the relevant tense checking relation. The answer to Q3 is again that auxiliaries have specified tense inflections and so must precede the default inflection *not,* and main verbs V cannot precede *not* because when V tries to check its inflection features (which need to appear adjacent to the Tense operator T, and before *not,* because of the Infl-precedence constraint), the V-features of POL intervenes between V and its Infl; cf. (32) adapted from Cormack and Smith (2000:75).

(32) John T[PRES] INFL^{PRES} INFL^{DEF} Pol[[V][NOT]] V[SWIM]
swims *not*
X

Although this analysis seemingly accounts for the facts, it does so at a cost. In this approach, Vs and auxiliaries are different categories; negation is likewise a V, *not* is an inflection, and the analysis rests on a number of stipulations (such as the Infl-precedence constraint and seven other constraints).

In contrast, the present theory explains the distribution not only of English modals, auxiliaries and main verbs relative to Σ-negation, but also the distribution of Norwegian verbs and auxiliaries relative to this negation. In addition, our explanation is the same as for negative inversion and polarity questions in both languages.

(33) Σ-negation, negative inversion, and polarity questions in Norwegian and English are licensed only by a [+M-finite] verb or auxiliary.

The operation that licenses a verb or auxiliary to the left of Σ-negation, the operation that raises a verb or auxiliary past a subject in negative inversion, and the operation that raises a verb or auxiliary to the V1 position in polarity questions all require an M-finite element as input. All Norwegian main verbs and auxiliaries fulfil this requirement as long as they are finite (since L-finiteness equals M-finiteness in Norwegian). In English only modals and auxiliaries fulfil this requirement; main verbs are not M-finite and unless they are accompanied by a modal, an auxiliary, or emphatic *do,* main verbs need to enrol the M-finite auxiliary *do* for support to meet the M-finite requirement of the syntactic operation.

4.2 Declaratives

The distribution of verbs, modals, and auxiliaries in declaratives in Norwegian and English is quite similar to the distribution of these elements in the three previous constructions; cf. the relevant part below of table (1) in Section 2.3.6. The crucial difference is that main verbs need no *do*-support in declaratives in modern English.

	Norwegian	English		
		modals/aux *do*	*have/be*	main verbs
License Sigma Negation	all finite verbs	yes	yes	no; *do*-support
Raise in negative inversion	all finite verbs	yes	yes	no; *do*-support
Raise in polarity questions	all finite verbs	yes	yes	no; *do*-support
Raise in declaratives	all finite verbs	yes	yes	no

This was not always the case. According to Denison (1993: 264–5), *do*-support is attested in positive declaratives from the thirteenth century and shows up in negative declaratives a little later (starting in the fourteenth century). If *do*-support was introduced as a repair strategy to fulfil the M-finite requirement of certain syntactic operations, after main verbs could no longer provide finiteness, the insertion of *do* in positive declaratives was seemingly the first step in this process; cf. Denison (1993: 265) and McWhorter (2009: 169). Whereas *do*-support spread to other constructions requiring [+M-Finite] verbs, it eventually dropped out of positive declaratives, in which it was first introduced, and nowadays *do*-support with non-emphatic, positive declaratives is attested only "in certain dialects, registers, and in child English", cf. Schütze (2004).

Norwegian, like all Germanic languages except modern English, has generalized verb movement to the second position of the clause in declarative main clauses. According to McWhorter (2005: 287), quoting Hopper (1975: 82), the general consensus is that verb second, V2, was a Proto-Germanic feature. Until approximately the fifteenth century, i.e. throughout Old English (OE) and into Middle English (ME), English had generalized V2 (Roberts 2007: 58; among others). At some point, the V2 rule ceased to be obligatory; in Lightfoot's (2006) terms, the cue for V2 (which he formulates as $_{CP}$[XP $_{c}$V]) becomes an optional, not obligatory, grammatical trait for new native speakers, until finally, main verbs cannot raise to this position at all in modern English.

There have been many attempts to explain what caused this syntactic change in English and relate it to other, preferably morphological, changes in the verbal paradigm. To explain the relationship between loss of agreement and loss of V2, Roberts (1985: 32) suggests that "obligatory [V2] movement of main verbs should apply to languages with rich agreement systems only." However, the data from Norwegian are at odds with this claim: Norwegian has obligatory V2 with main verbs, but less agreement than English; in fact, Norwegian has no agreement at all in the relevant contexts. Roberts (1993: 120) modifies his earlier claims, emphasizing the difference between English and Mainland Scandinavian (MSc) as regards infinitival endings: MSc has retained and English has lost distinct infinitival endings, so the infinitive in English (unlike in MSc) is non-distinct from the imperative and many other verb forms.[29]

Noting that the loss of V2 is generally linked to the erosion of verbal inflectional morphology, McWhorter (2005: 287 ff) offers a comprehensive overview of the arguments and concludes that "overall, the explanations…lack explanatory power or falsifiability" and "it seems clear that the link [between verb movement and inflectional

29. In contrast, Solà (1996) suggests that English main verbs are inflected neither for tense nor for agreement and should be considered (present or past) participles. Thus, the lack of verb movement with main verbs stems from the presence of a null auxiliary that represents tense (and agreement) and blocks the movement of the main verb.

morphology] is too weak in itself to offer a conclusive explanation for what happened in English in comparison to its sisters."

I advocate that the relevant inflectional feature is not the eroded mood or agreement inflections; nor did the differing properties of tense between Norwegian and English cause the loss of V2 in English. Nor is it the expression of a subset of agreement markings (e.g. 1st and 2nd person; cf. Rohrbacher 1999: 116), tense, or mood markings. The relevant feature is the M-finiteness feature, which amounts to a morphological rule productively generating finite forms. It is the loss of this feature that made English main verbs behave differently from auxiliaries and from main verbs in other Germanic languages. The generalization in (34) captures the difference between Norwegian and English declarative root clauses:

(34) Norwegian declaratives require a [+M-finite] verb in the V2 position.
In English declaratives the presence of a [+M-finite] verb is optional.

Note that if a finite auxiliary is present in English, it needs to be structurally the highest verb. This can be derived from "the condition on A-chains" from Reuland and Reinhart (1995), on a theory where temporal forms are compared to nominal pronouns and anaphora (cf. Eide 2007, 2009a for the details). A [+finite] verb or auxiliary is like a temporal pronoun; hence is +R, and has independent reference; thus it needs to head its referential chain. Being [+M-finite], this auxiliary also has access to the "residual V2" position, unlike English main verbs.

(35) *Condition on A-chains* (Reuland & Reinhart 1995: 255):
A maximal A-chain ($\alpha_1, \ldots, \alpha_n$) contains exactly one link – α_1 – which is +R.

4.3 Subjunctives/*to*-infinitives/Small clauses/*Why (not)*-constructions

Norwegian has no productive subjunctive form, cf. Section 2.3.4, and uses instead an indicative form, either the present or the preterit; i.e. a finite form. In English however, the form used in subjunctives is formally indistinguishable from the infinitive; a fact which was pointed out already by Cobbett (1919: 159):

> Therefore, as the subjunctive, in all its persons, takes the infinitive of the Verb without any change at all, the Verb *to be* exhibits the use of this mode most clearly; for, instead of *I am, thou art, he is, we are*, the subjunctive requires, *I be, thou be, he be, we be* [.].

Like Cobbett, I assume that the subjunctive is in fact formally like the infinitive in English. This is also what I will assume for the verb heading the other constructions discussed in Section 2.3.4: *to*-infinitives, small clauses and *why (not)* constructions. They are all generated by a syntactic operation rejecting a [+M-finite] form:

(36) Subjunctives, infinitives, small clauses and *why (not)-* constructions ban [+M-finite] forms.

This explains why they pattern together; cf. the relevant part of Table 1 in Section 2.3.6:

	Norwegian	English		
		modals/aux *do*	*have/be*	main verbs
Appear in subjunctives	not productive	no	yes	yes
Appear in *to-/å*-infinitives	all non-finite verbs	no	yes	yes
Appear in small clauses	all non-finite verbs	no	yes	yes
Appear in *why (not)-/ hvorfor (ikke)-* constructions	all non-finite verbs	no	yes	yes

Recall from Section 3 that all verbs in Norwegian have non-finite forms; thus they will always have a licit version to enroll in environments where [+M-finite] elements are banned, like in infinitives, small clauses and *why (not)*-constructions. English modals and auxiliary *do,* on the other hand, have no non-finite versions. Thus, only *have* and *be,* which have both finite and, crucially, non-finite forms, and main verbs, where the inflectional paradigm is impoverished and hence unspecified for finiteness, are licit as the verbal heads of these constructions in modern English. Within Distributed Morphology it is a plausible assumption that when a feature is deleted (or impoverished), syntax can no longer refer to it (cf. for instance Sauerland 1996).

4.4 Preterit-participle and participle-preterit mix-ups

The introduction to this paper was concerned with the mix-up of preterit and participle forms in English. Native speakers of English all over the world use preterits where the normative grammars tell them to use past participles (‘*woulda came*’, ‘*coulda went*’, ‘*shoulda did*’, ‘*woulda took*’, ‘*had went*’, ‘*hadn't came*’, ‘*we haven't spoke*’, ‘*had threw it*’, ‘*here's what I would have wrote*’, etc.) and past participles where the grammars dictate the presence of preterits (‘*I seen it*’, ‘*she done it*’, ‘*they gone home*’, ‘*a man come into a bar*’, ‘*who drunk my beer?*’, etc.). These preterit-participle mix-ups plaguing the English language have no parallel in Norwegian, except for adults acquiring Norwegian as a second language. cf. Section 2.3.5. above.

This mix-up, I argue, should find its explanation in features of the English language system, since it is found in Englishes all over the world. This explanation should include answers to questions 1, 2, and 3 below; preferably also question 4.

1. What causes this mix-up in the first place?
2. How come it is the preterit and the participle which are mixed up? How come the preterit is not replaced with the bare form, an *-ing* form, or the *-s* form?
3. Why doesn't this mix-up happen in languages like (native) Norwegian?
4. How come this mix-up shows up in Norwegian as a second language?

Section 3 above already suggested where we might look for an answer to all these questions. The answers reside in the paradigms of tensed verb forms in English and Norwegian, respectively. Whereas Norwegian has retained the finiteness distinction, hence has morphological rules productively generating the four-way tense paradigm, in modern English this four-way paradigm has collapsed into a two-way distinction for main verbs, such that the tense distinction [±past] is retained, and the finiteness distinction is lost; cf. the paradigm in (26) above, repeated here as (37). The productive morphological rule generating tense forms thus makes no reference to finiteness in modern English; cf. (37b).

(37)

a	+Finite	−Finite
+Past Old English Norwegian	**Preterit:** *sang, lufode* *sang, likte*	**Participle:** *gesungen, lufod* *sunget, likt*
−Past Old English Norwegian	**Present:** *singe, lufie* *synger, liker*	**Infinitive:** *singan, lufian* *synge, like*

⇨

b Weak verbs	
+Past Modern English	**Preterit/Participle:** *liked, killed, smiled*
−Past Modern English	**Present/Infinitive** *like, kill, smile*

⇩

c Standard strong verbs	+Finite	−Finite
+Past Modern English	**Preterit:** *went, saw, drove*	**Participle:** *gone, seen, driven*
−Past Modern English	**Present:** *go, see, drive*	**Infinitive:** *go, see, drive*

⇨

d Dialectal strong verbs	
+Past Non-standard English	**Preterit/Participle** *gone, seen, drove*
−Past Non-standard English	**Present/Infinitive** *go, see, drive*

The answer to question 1 above is that this mix-up happens because this distinction depends on the language user's memory to maintain a distinction on the lexical level which no longer corresponds to the paradigm generated by the productive morphological rule. Thus, it is obvious that more and more irregular verbs will defect from the paradigm maintaining the finiteness distinction (37c) and settle for an alignment with the rest of the tensed verb-paradigm (as in (37d)). They will tend to collapse into the same two-way distinction that characterizes the productive morphological rule. According to Pinker (2000: 89), in modern English there are about "164 modern irregular verbs: 81 weak (ending in *t* or *d*), 83 strong [with Ablaut]. Compare this to Old English, with 325 strong verbs alone, and it is clear that English is indeed becoming 'weaker'." Thus, more and more verbs are becoming regular, but even the irregular ones will find it hard to keep up their finiteness distinction; i.e. the moribund distinction between preterits and participles. This is the natural completion of the process illustrated in (37). When the [+past] forms collapse into one form, there will be a competition between the preterit and the participle to take over the function of both forms; a type of mechanism that Pinker refers to (for a different set of forms) as "a game of musical chairs". Not all dialects of English take the same path in simplifying the paradigm. In some cases, the preterit form is the one covering both functions, e.g. *should-a-went*; in other cases, a new form, neither the original preterit nor the past participle (for instance *seed* as the past form of *saw*), is employed as the [+past] form; cf. Section 2.3.5 above. Our theory does not predict which form will win out; it only predicts the extinction of one form to the benefit of the other. Since both forms are [+past], which one survives and takes on the function of the other is in principle arbitrary, hence trivial.

Ad question 2, the reason the preterit and the participle are the ones getting mixed-up is that they are both [+past] forms, and the only feature separating them is the L-finiteness feature; finiteness expressed on a lexical level, but not corresponding to a slot in the productive morphological paradigm. Neither the preterit nor the participle are replaced by the bare form, the *-s* form or the *-ing* form because these forms encode [−past] relations; hence there would be a mismatch between the semantics (requiring 'past') and the form employed.

Ad questions 3 and 4, the reason this mix-up does not happen in Norwegian is that the finiteness distinction is a productive and active part of Norwegian language users' morphology. Thus the computational system recognizes and refers to finiteness in all verb forms; it recognizes the paradigm. Learners of Norwegian as a second language, however, mix up these forms; they also mix up presents and infinitives (cf. Wik 2014). It seems that second language acquirers have comparatively less difficulty in acquiring a feature which has a clear semantic base: Glahn et al. (2001) undertook a study of second language acquisition of Scandinavian DPs and found that number agreement (realized on adjectives) was easier to acquire for these informants than gender agreement. The authors conclude that number corresponds to a conceptually salient category, hence is easy to grasp, whereas gender no longer corresponds to a semantically based distinction and is much harder to acquire. This is mirrored in the categories tense and finiteness: Tense is conceptually easier to grasp than finiteness; while the latter encodes the distinction between independent and dependent forms, tense transparently places events on a time line, thus tense oppositions are acquired more effortlessly.

5. Summing up

In this paper I argued that a very important difference between Norwegian and English morphology is that in Norwegian all main verbs, modals, and auxiliaries encode the finiteness distinction ([±M-finite]); a distinction which is generated by a productive morphological paradigm for all verb types in the language; in English, however, main verbs have lost this distinction and finiteness is productively assigned to auxiliaries only.

	Norwegian	English			Diagnosis
		Modals/ aux *do*	*have/be*	Main verb	
License Σ-negation	all finite verbs	yes	yes	no; *do*-support	[+M-finite] verb obligatory
Raise in neg. inversion	all finite verbs	yes	yes	no; *do*-support	[+M-finite] verb obligatory
Raise in polarity questions	all finite verbs	yes	yes	no; *do*-support	[+M-finite] verb obligatory
Raise in declaratives	all finite verbs	yes	yes	no	[+M-finite] verb obligatory in Norw.; optional in English
Appear in subjunctives	not productive	no	yes	yes	[+M-finite] verb banned
Appear in *to*-infinitives	all non-finite verbs (INF)	no	yes	yes	[+M-finite] verb banned
Appear in small clauses	all non-finite verbs (INF)	no	yes	yes	[+M-finite] verb banned
Appear in *why (not)*-constr.	all non-finite verbs (INF)	no	yes	yes	[+M-finite] verb banned
Preterit-participle mix-up	L1: no; L2: yes	no	no	irregular verbs	Lack of M-finiteness in Eng. and L2 Norw. discrepancy between [+L-finite] marking and productive paradigm

Modals and *do* are always [+M-finite], hence are banned from constructions where finiteness is rejected by the syntactic operation building the given structure. Auxiliaries *have* and *be* have both finite and non-finite forms and are thus among the most versatile verbal elements in modern English. I utilize the distinction that I dubbed M-finiteness in the description and explanation of nine linguistic phenomena in English and Norwegian; the facts are summed up in the table, with the diagnosis for each construction.

These constructions naturally cluster into three data sets. One is the "residual V2" cluster of phenomena (Rizzi 1996). The second cluster regards the split between different types of auxiliaries, where *have* and *be* pattern with main verbs and against modals and auxiliary *do*. The third data set consists in the systematic mix-up of preterit and participial forms in modern English varieties and also in second language learners of Norwegian. However, in this investigation we have touched upon a range of related morphosyntactic phenomena, such as the lack of generalized V2 in English main clause declaratives which sets English apart from its Germanic siblings. We have also provided an explanation for the contribution of *do*, since this is a repair strategy for adding a required M-finite feature to a clause for the specific syntactic operations where this feature is required but otherwise left unfulfilled. According to McWhorter (2009: 172) "a search for languages in which *do* has developed into *semantically empty conjunction with all verbs* is challenging indeed", and he concludes that "English's usage of *do* is extremely odd" and crosslinguistically without any clear parallels.

Many attempts have been made to explain these facts. The present approach rests on the morphosyntactic category of finiteness, which happens to be distributed differently in English and Norwegian. In a sense, ascribing to certain types of auxiliaries (*have* and *be*) all four cells in the paradigm in (30), while others have only finite forms (modals and *do*) and main verbs have no finite feature whatsoever, only restates the facts about their syntactic behaviour. However, in comparison with Norwegian we can clearly see that the finiteness feature is the relevant feature for the different constructions. Thus, even if the M-finite feature has morphed into some other feature regulating the syntactic behaviour of verbal forms in English, it seems very obvious that this feature at some point in history started out as a finiteness feature.

References

Åfarli, Tor. A & Eide, Kristin Melum. 2003. *Norsk Generativ Syntaks*. Oslo: Novus.

Amritavalli, Raghavachari. 2014. Separating tense and finiteness: Anchoring in Dravidian. *Natural Language and Linguistic Theory* 32: 283–306. doi:10.1007/s11049-013-9219-3

Askedal, Jon Ole. 1994. Norwegian. In *The Germanic Languages*, Ekkehard König & Johan van der Auwera (eds.), 219–270. London: Routledge.

Baker, Carl Lee. 1991. The syntax of English *not*: The limits of core grammar. *Linguistic Inquiry* 22: 387–429.

Becker, Misha. 2002. English has two copulas. In *University of Pennsylvania Working Papers in Linguistics: Current Work in Linguistics*, Vol. 7.2, Elsi Kaiser (ed.), 1–27. Philadelphia PA: University of Pennsylvania.

Bianchi, Valentina. 2003. On finiteness as logophoric anchoring. In *Temps et points de vue/ Tense and Point of View*, Jacqueline Guéron & Liliane Tasmovski (eds.), 213–246. Nanterre: Université Paris X.

Bonet, Eulàlia. 1991. Morphology after Syntax: Pronominal Clitics in Romance Languages. Ph.D. dissertation, MIT.

Carstairs-McCarthy, Andrew. 1987. *Allomorphy in Inflection.* London: Croom Helm.

Chomsky, Noam. 1955. The logical structure of linguistic theory. Ms, Harvard University. Revised 1956 version published in part by Plenum, New York, 1975; and University of Chicago Press, Chicago 1985.

Chomsky, Noam. 1957. *Syntactic Structures.* The Hague: Mouton.

Chomsky, Noam. 1995. *The Minimalist Program.* Cambridge MA: The MIT Press.

Comrie, Bernard. 1985. *Tense.* Cambridge: CUP. doi:10.1017/CBO9781139165815

Cobbett, William. 1919. *The English Grammar of William Cobbett. Carefully revised and annotated by Alfred Ayres.* New York NY: D. Appleton and Company.

Cormack, Anabel & Smith, Neil. 1998. Negation, polarity, and verb movement. In *Working Papers in Linguistics* 10: 285–322. London: Phonetics and Linguistics, University College London.

Cormack, Anabel & Smith, Neil. 2000. Head movement and negation in English. *Transactions of the Philological Society* 98(1): 49–85. doi:10.1111/1467-968X.00058

Denison, David. 1993. *English Historical Syntax: Verbal Constructions.* London: Longman.

Dresher, Bezalel Elan.1999. Charting the learning path: Cues to parameter setting. *Linguistic Inquiry* 30: 27–68. doi:10.1162/002438999553959

Edwards, Viv. 1993. The grammar of Southern British English. In *Real English: The Grammar of English Dialects in the British Isles,* James Milroy & Lesley Milroy (eds.), 214–235. London: Longman.

Eide, Kristin Melum. 2002a. Norwegian Modals. Ph.D. dissertation, NTNU.

Eide, Kristin Melum. 2002b. Adjunction sites for negation in Norwegian: Modals and negation. *Nordic Journal of Linguistics* 25(2): 225–252. doi:10.1080/033258602321093373

Eide, Kristin Melum 2005. *Norwegian Modals* [Studies in Generative Grammar 74]. Berlin: Mouton de Gruyter.

Eide, Kristin Melum. 2007. Finiteness and inflection. (Draft) *Lingbuzz.*

Eide, Kristin Melum. 2008. Finiteness in Norwegian, English, … and Chinese? In *Comparative Grammar and Language Acquisition in the Age of Globalization: Norwegian and Chinese,* Tor A. Åfarli & Fufen Jin (eds.). Trondheim: Tapir.

Eide, Kristin Melum. 2009a. Tense, finiteness and the survive principle: Temporal chains in a crash-proof grammar. In *Towards a Derivational Syntax: Survive-minimalism* [Linguistik Aktuell/Linguistics Today 144], Michael Putnam (ed.), 91–132. Amsterdam: John Benjamins. doi:10.1075/la.144.05eid

Eide, Kristin Melum. 2009b. Finiteness: The haves and the have-nots. In *Advances in Comparative Germanic Syntax* [Linguistik Aktuell/Linguistics Today 141], Artemis Alexiadou, Jorge Hankamer, Thomas McFadden, Justin Nuger & Florian Schäfer (eds.), 357–390. Amsterdam: John Benjamins. doi:10.1075/la.141.15fin

Eide, Kristin Melum. 2010. Mood in Norwegian. In *Mood in the Languages of Europe* [Studies in Language Companion Series 120], Björn Rothstein & Rolf Thieroff (eds.), 56–70. Amsterdam: John Benjamins. doi:10.1075/slcs.120.03eid

Eiskovits, Edina 1987. Variation in the lexical verb in inner-Sydney English. *Australian Journal of Linguistics* 7: 1–24. doi:10.1080/07268608708599371

Faarlund, Jan Terje, Lie, Svein & Vannebo, Kjell Ivar. 1997. *Norsk referansegrammatikk.* Oslo: Universitetsforlaget.

Gleitman, Lila R. 1965. Coordinating conjunctions in English. *Language* 41: 260–293. doi:10.2307/411878

Glahn, Esther, Håkansson, Gisela, Hammarberg, Bjørn, Holmen, Anne, Hvenekilde, Anne, & Lund, Karen. 2001. Processability in Scandinavian second language acquisition. *Studies in Second Language Acquisition* 23(3): 389–416. doi:10.1017/S0272263101003047

Gretsch, Petra & Perdue, Clive. 2007. Finiteness in first and second language acquisition. In Irina Nikolaeva (ed.) 432–484.

Guasti, Maria Teresa. 2002. *Language Acquisition. The Growth of Grammar.* Cambridge MA: The MIT Press.

Guéron, Jacqueline & Hoekstra, Teun. 1995. The temporal interpretation of predication. In *Small Clauses. Syntax and Semantics,* Anna Cardinaletti & Maria Teresa Guasti (eds.), 77–107. New York NY: Academic Press.

Hagen, Jon Erik. 2001. Finittkategoriens kritiske karakter i norsk som andrespråk. In *Andrespråk, tospråklighet, norsk,* Anne Golden & Helene Uri (eds.). Oslo: Unipub Forlag.

Haegeman, Liliane & Guéron, Jacqueline. 1999. *English Grammar. A Generative Perspective.* Oxford: Blackwell.

Halle, Moritz & Marantz, Alec. 1993. Distributed morphology and the pieces of inflection. In *The View from Building 20. Essays in Linguistics in Honor of Sylvain Bromberger,* Kenneth Hale & Samuel Jay Keyser (eds.), 111–176. Cambridge MA: The MIT Press.

Harley, Heidi & Noyer, Rolf. 1999. Distributed morphology. *GLOT International* 4(4): 3–9.

Hasselgård, Hilde, Johansson, Stig & Lysvåg, Per. 1998. *English Grammar: Theory and Use.* Oslo: Universitetsforlaget.

Holmberg, Anders & Platzack, Christer. 1995. *The Role of Inflection in Scandinavian Syntax.* Oxford: OUP.

Holmberg, Anders & Roberts, Ian. 2013. The syntax-morphology relation. *Lingua* 130: 111–131. doi:10.1016/j.lingua.2012.10.006

Hopper, Paul J. 1975. *The Syntax of the Simple Sentence in Proto-Germanic.* The Hague: Mouton.

Jackendoff, Ray. 1972. *Semantic Interpretation in Generative Grammar.* Cambridge MA: The MIT Press.

Laka, Itziar. 1990. Negation in Syntax: On the Nature of Functional Categories and Projections. Ph.D. dissertation, MIT. Published as *On the Syntax of Negation*, 1994, New York NY: Garland.

Langacker, Ronald W. 1978. The form and meaning of the English Auxiliary. *Language* 54: 853–882. doi:10.2307/413237

Lasnik, Howard. 1981. Restricting the theory of transformations: A case study. In *Explanations in Linguistics,* Norbert Hornstein & David Lightfoot (eds.), 152–173. London: Longman.

Lasnik, Howard. 1995. Verbal morphology: Syntactic structures meets the Minimalist Program. In *Evolution and Revolution in Linguistic Theory: Essays in Honor of Carlos Otero*, Héctor Campos & Paula Kempchinsky (eds.), 251–275. Washington DC: Georgetown University Press.

Lasnik, Howard. 1999. *Minimalist Analysis.* Oxford: Blackwell.

Lasnik, Howard. 2000. *Syntactic Structures Revisited. Contemporary Lectures on Classic Transformational Theory.* Cambridge MA: The MIT Press.

Lasser, Ingeborg. 1997. *Finiteness in Adult and Child German* [MPI Series in Psycholinguistics 8]. Wageningen: Ponsen and Looijen.

Lightfoot, David.1999. *The Development of Language: Acquisition, Change, and Evolution.* Oxford: Blackwell.

Lightfoot, David. 2006. *How New Languages Emerge.* Cambridge: CUP. doi:10.1017/CBO9780511616204

McCarthy, John J. & Prince, Alan. 1999. Faithfulness and identity in prosodic morphology. In *The Prosody Morphology Interface*, René Kager, Harry van der Hulst & Wim Zonneveld (eds.), 218–309. Cambridge: CUP. Downloaded ROA: ⟨http://roa.rutgers.edu/files/216-0997/216-0997 MCCARTHY-0-0.PDF⟩. doi:10.1017/CBO9780511627729.008

McWhorter, John. 2005. *Defining Creole.* Oxford: OUP.

McWhorter, John. 2009. What else happened to English? A brief for the Celtic hypothesis. *English Language and Linguistics* 13: 163–191. doi:10.1017/S1360674309002974

Muysken, Pieter & Law, Paul. 2001. Creole Studies. A theoretical linguist's field guide. *GLOT International* 5(2): 47–57.

Næss, Stine M. 2006. Kan han snakker norsk? En generativ analyse av ja/nei-spørsmål i norsk som andrespråk (Can he Speak Norwegian? A Generative Analysis of Polarity Questions in Norwegian as a Second Language). MA thesis, NTNU.

Palmer, Frank R. 1986. *Mood and Modality.* Cambridge: CUP.

Pinker, Steven. 1994. *The Language Instinct. The New Science of Language and Mind.* London: Penguin Books.

Pinker, Steven. 2000. *Words and Rules. The Ingredients of Language.* London: Phoenix.

Platzack, Christer & Rosengren, Inger. 1998. On the subject of imperatives: A minimalist account of the imperative clause. *The Journal of Comparative Linguistics* 1: 177–224. doi:10.1023/A:1009747522177

Pollock, Jean-Yves. 1989. Verb Movement, UG and the Structure of IP. *Linguistic Inquiry* 20: 365–424.

Reuland, Eric & Reinhart, Tania. 1995. Pronouns, anaphors and case. In *Studies in Comparative Germanic Syntax*, Hubert Haider, Susan Olsen & Sten Vikner (eds.), 241 269. Dordrecht: Kluwer. doi:10.1007/978-94-015-8416-6_11

Rice, Curt. 2003. Dialectal variation in Norwegian imperatives. *Nordlyd* 31(2): 372–384.

Ritter, Elizabeth & Wiltschko, Martina. 2005. Anchoring Events to Utterances without Tense. WCFLL 2005. ⟨http://www.linguistics.ubc.ca/People/martina/papers/wccfl_ritter_wiltschko.pdf⟩

Ritter, Elizabeth & Wiltschko, Martina. 2009. Varieties of INFL: TENSE, LOCATION and PERSON. In *Alternatives to Cartography,* Jeroen van Craenenbroeck (ed.), 153–201. Berlin: De Gruyter. doi:10.1515/9783110217124.153

Ritter, Elizabeth & Wiltschko, Martina. 2014. The composition of INFL. An exploration of tense, tenseless languages, and tenseless constructions. *Natural Language and linguistic Theory* 32: 1331–1386. doi:10.1007/s11049-014-9248-6

Rizzi, Luigi. 1990. On the anaphor agreement effect. *Rivista di Linguistica* 2: 27–42.

Rizzi, Luigi. 1996. Residual verb second and the wh-criterion. In *Parameters and Functional Heads*, Adriana Belletti & Luigi Rizzi (eds.), 63–90. Oxford: OUP.

Roberts, Ian. 1985. Agreement parameters and the development of English modal auxiliaries. *Natural Language and Linguistic Theory* 3: 21–58. doi:10.1007/BF00205413

Roberts, Ian. 1993. *Verbs and Diachronic Syntax.* Dordrecht: Kluwer..

Roberts, Ian. 1998. Have/be raising, Move F, and procrastinate. *Linguistic Inquiry* 29: 113–125. doi:10.1162/002438998553671

Roberts, Ian. 2007. *Diachronic Syntax.* Oxford: OUP.

Rohrbacher, Bernhard Wolfgang. 1999. *Morphology-Driven Syntax: A Theory of V to I Raising and Pro-Drop* [Linguistik Aktuell/Linguistics Today 15]. Amsterdam: John Benjamins. doi:10.1075/la.15

Romaine, Susanne. 1993. *Pidgin and Creole Languages.* London: Longman.

Ross, John R. 1969. Auxiliaries as main verbs. In *Studies in Philosophical Linguistics,* William Todd (ed.), 77–102. Evanston IL: Great Expectations.
Sampson, Geoffrey. 2002. Regional variation in the English verb qualifier system. *English Language and Linguistics* 6: 17–30. doi:10.1017/S1360674302001028
Sauerland, Uli. 1996. The late insertion of Germanic inflection. Ms, second draft, MIT.
Schütze, Carson T. 2003. When is a verb not a verb? In *Proceedings of the 19th Scandinavian Conference on Linguistics*, Anne Dahl, Kristine Bentzen & Peter Svenonius (eds.). *Nordlyd* 31(2): 400–415.
Schütze, Carson T. 2004. Synchronic and diachronic microvariation in English do. *Lingua* 114(4): 495–516. doi:10.1016/S0024-3841(03)00070-6
Sigurðsson, Halldór Á. 2004. The syntax of person, tense, and speech features. *Italian Journal of Linguistics* 16: 219–251.
Slobin, Dan.1982. Universal and particular in the development of language. In *Language Acquisition: The State of the Art,* Eric Wanner & Lila Gleitman (eds.), 128–172. Cambridge: CUP.
Solà, Jaume. 1996. Morphology and word order in Germanic languages. In *Minimal Ideas. Syntactic Studies in the Minimalist Framework,* Werner Abraham, Samuel David Epstein, Höskuldur Thráinsson & C. Jan-Wouter Zwart (eds.), 217–251. Amsterdam: John Benjamins. doi:10.1075/la.12.12sol
Trudgill, Peter. 1999. Standard English: What it isn't. In *Standard English: The Widening Debate,* Tony Bex & Richard J. Watts (eds.), 117–128. London: Routledge.
Trudgill, Peter. 2000. *Sociolinguistics. An Introduction to Language and Society,* 4th edn. London: Penguin.
Trudgill Peter & Chambers, Jack K. (eds.). 1991. *Dialects of English: Studies in Grammatical Variation.* London: Longman.
Warner, Anthony R. 1985. *The Structuring of English Auxiliaries: A Phrase Structure Grammar.* Bloomington IN: IULC.
Wexler, Kenneth.1998.Very early parameter setting and the unique checking constraint: a new explanation of the optional infinitive stage. *Lingua* 106: 23–79. doi:10.1016/S0024-3841(98)00029-1
Wik, Marte Aakre. 2014. Om tempus og finitthet i norsk som andrespråk (On Tense and Finiteness in Norwegian as a Second Language). MA thesis, NTNU.
Woolford, Ellen. 1999. More on the anaphor agreement effect. *Linguistic Inquiry* 30: 257–287. doi:10.1162/002438999554057
Wunderlich, Dieter. 1995. Minimalist morphology: The role of paradigms. In *Yearbook of Morphology*, Geert Booij & Jaap van Marle (eds.), 93–114. Dordrecht: Kluwer.
Wunderlich, Dieter & Fabri, Ray. 1994. Minimalist morphology. Ms, University of Düsseldorf.
Zanuttini, Raffaella. 1996. On the relevance of tense for sentential negation. In *Parameters and Functional Heads: Essays in Comparative Syntax*, Adriana Belletti & Luigi Rizzi (eds.), 181–207. Oxford: OUP.
Zubizarreta, Maria Luisa. 1982. On the Relationship of the Lexicon to Syntax. Ph.D. dissertation, MIT.

PART II

Morphosyntactic exponents of (non-)finiteness

Agreement is not an essential ingredient of finiteness

Evidence from impersonal sentences in Norwegian dialects and in English*

Tor A. Åfarli
Norwegian University of Science and Technology

I argue in this article that agreement is *not* an essential ingredient of T/finiteness. Using the mechanism of valuation of unvalued features, I argue that unvalued agreement features in T only exist if there is visible subject – verb agreement in the language/dialect. Correspondingly, I argue that unvalued agreement features in participles only exist if there is visible subject – participle agreement. The likelihood that these assumptions are correct is demonstrated through a comparative analysis of expletive subjects and agreement relations in impersonal constructions in Norwegian dialects and in English.

Keywords: agreement; expletive subject; impersonal construction; participle; passive

1. Introduction

In generative grammar, finiteness is traditionally taken to imply T with a positive specification for tense, and a finite T is usually taken to contain agreement features (Raposo 1987: 92). Moreover, on a Greed approach to agreement feature checking, it is implied that there must always exist functional agreement features in T that the

* Earlier versions of this paper were presented at the Nordic Microcomparative Syntax (NORMS) Workshop at the University of Tromsø in 2006, and at the Sound Patterns of Syntax workshop at Ben Gurion University, Beer Sheva in 2007. Many thanks to the audiences at both occasions for useful comments. Some of the ideas contained in this paper were also printed in Working Papers in Scandinavian Syntax 79, 2007: 55–72, and in Groninger Arbeiten zur Germanistischen Linguistik (GAGL) 49, 2009: 167–181. Many thanks to Ghiath El-Marzouk and Anu Laanemets for their comments to the GAGL written version of the paper. Also many thanks to two anonymous reviewers for the present volume for very useful suggestions.

DOI 10.1075/la.231.06afa

agreement features of a subject DP can be checked against, making agreement an essential ingredient of T/finiteness.

Contrary to these assumptions, I claim in this article that agreement is *not* an essential ingredient of T/finiteness. Specifically, using a probe – goal approach and the mechanism of valuation of unvalued features, I argue that unvalued agreement features (i.e. agreement probes) in T only exist if there is visible subject – verb agreement in the language. I show that this assumption has explanatory power through a comparative analysis of expletive subjects and impersonal constructions in Norwegian dialects and in English.

The article is organized as follows. Section 2 presents the relevant data from Norwegian. Section 3 introduces a more or less standard analysis of expletives and verbal agreement in English in order to set the stage for an analysis of the Norwegian data. Then, in Section 4, the Norwegian data are analysed, and some important consequences of the analysis are further discussed in Section 5. Section 6 speculates on possible solutions to some remaining problems, and Section 7 concludes the article.

2. Norwegian data

In the Norwegian data, I focus mainly on impersonal passives. There are two main types of passives in Norwegian: first, a periphrastic passive, which consists of an auxiliary verb and a passive participle, and second the *s*-passive, which consists of the reflexive form of the verb (see Åfarli 1992). Both types have personal and impersonal passive versions. In this article, I investigate the periphrastic type only.

The passive participle in periphrastic passives shows agreement properties in some Norwegian dialects, but not in others. In addition, while some dialects allow two types of expletive subjects in impersonal periphrastic passives, others allow only one type of expletive subject in such passives. I will show that there is an interesting interaction between the agreement properties of the passive participle and the particular type of expletive subject that occurs in the sentence, but first I want to give brief introductions to the basic facts concerning passive participles and to the basic facts concerning expletive subjects in Norwegian dialects, starting with the participles.

Concerning the personal periphrastic passives, Norwegian dialects can be divided into two groups depending on the agreement properties of the passive participle (see Faarlund et al. 1997: 518; Sandøy 1988). In one group, the passive participle shows no agreement inflection and occurs invariably in the singular neuter form (i.e. the invariant non-inflected form). These are the dialects that, on the whole, correspond to the *Bokmål* written variety. The dialects of the *Oslo* area and the dialects in northern Norway exemplify these non-agreeing dialects. The other group comprises the dialects which roughly correspond to the *Nynorsk* written variety, and which are exemplified by the rural dialects in the western parts of Norway, and also by many dialects in the eastern and southern parts of Norway. In these dialects, the passive participle is inflected in agreement with the subject (depending on verb class) with regard to gender and/or number (see Sandøy 1988 for a detailed description of the various agreement subsystems). Active participles, on the other hand, are never inflected in either group and invariably occur in the invariant singular neuter form.

The two dialect groups are exemplified below. For simplification, I only show a masculine – neuter gender opposition in the examples, although Norwegian dialects also have a feminine gender that in some dialects has a designated agreeing participle form.

Dialects with non-agreeing participle:

(1) a. Elgen ble **skutt**. (subject is m, SG)
elk-the was shot
'The elk was shot.'

b. Dyret ble **skutt**. (subject is n, SG)
animal-the was shot
'The animal was shot.'

c. Elgene/dyrene ble **skutt**. (subject is m/n, PL)
elks-the/animals-the was shot
'the elks/the animals were shot.'

Dialects with agreeing participle:

(2) a. Elgen vart **skoten**. (subject and participle are m, SG)
elk-the was shot
'The elk was shot.'

b. Dyret vart **skote**. (subject and participle are n, SG)
animal-the was shot
'The animal was shot.'

c. Elgane/dyra vart **skotne**. (subject and participle are m/n, PL)
elks-the/animals-the was shot
'The elks/the animals were shot.'

As the above examples illustrate, the participle agrees with the subject in the agreeing dialects, but not in the non-agreeing dialects.

Consider now expletive subjects. Impersonal passives are quite common in all Norwegian dialects. The dialects can be divided into two groups according to the type of expletive subjects that they allow. One group allows *det* 'it' only, whereas the other group allows both *det* 'it' and *der* 'there' (as well as *her* 'here'). The geographical distribution of the two dialect groups is as follows: Both subject types are used in the southernmost part of Norway (*Sørlandet*) and most of western Norway (*Vestlandet*), and also in the southern part of northern Norway, whereas only the *det* 'it' type is used in eastern Norway, in the far northern part of western Norway, and in the northern part of northern Norway (Sandøy 1992: 101; Dahl 1974). Notice that the classification of dialects according to the agreeing/non-agreeing participle property, on the one hand, and the expletive subject types that are allowed, on the other hand, crosscuts each other so that there are both agreeing and non-agreeing dialects that show only one or both of the expletive subject types.

Expletive subjects do not only occur in impersonal passives, but also in other kinds of impersonal constructions. Dialects which allow only the *det* 'it' type, have this expletive subject in all types of impersonal constructions. Furthermore, dialects that allow both types of expletive subject, generally allow both types in most impersonal construction types, at least in the three main types that I will mention here, namely meteorological sentences, presentational sentences, and impersonal passive sentences (Dahl 1974: 82). Still, there may be some variation between the dialects that allow both types, so that one of the subject types may be more frequent than the other in a certain construction type in some dialects.

The general situation, namely that all dialects that in principle allow both subject types, also allow both types in all the three main types of impersonal constructions, is illustrated by the data in (3)–(8) below from the *Stavanger* dialect located in the southern part of western Norway. Notice that the examples with participles show no agreement, thereby indicating that the *Stavanger* dialect, being an urban dialect, belongs to the non-agreeing type. All data from the *Stavanger* dialect are taken from Aksnes (2003).

Meteorological sentences:

(3) a. **Det** reggne i Hunnedalen.
it rain in Hunnedalen
'It rains in Hunnedalen.'

b. **Der** reggne i Hunnedalen.
there rain in Hunnedalen
'It rains in Hunnedalen.'

(4) a. Snør **det** i Sirdalen?
snow it in Sirdalen
'Does it snow in Sirdalen?'

b. Snør **der** i Sirdalen?
snow there in Sirdalen
'Does it snow in Sirdalen?'

Presentational sentences:

(5) a. **Det** komme mange te oss på nyttårsaften.
it come many to us on New-Year's-Eve
'Many people will come to us on New Year's Eve.'

b. **Der** komme mange te oss på nyttårsaften.
there come many to us on New Year's Eve
'Many people will come to us on New Year's Eve.'

(6) a. **Det** e komt ein nye film om James Bond på kino.
it is come a new film about James Bond on cinema
'A new film about James Bond has come to the cinema.'

b. **Der** e komt ein nye film om James Bond på kino.
there is come a new film about James Bond on cinema
'A new film about James Bond has come to the cinema.'

Impersonal passive sentences:

(7) a. I går blei **det** stjåle ein bil på Madla.
yesterday was it stolen a car at Madla
'Yesterday a car was stolen at Madla.'

b. I går blei **der** stjåle ein bil på Madla.
yesterday was there stolen a car at Madla
'Yesterday a car was stolen at Madla.'

(8) a. På konserten i går blei **det** sunge ein fine sang.
at concert-the yesterday was it sung a nice song
'At the concert yesterday a nice song was sung.'

b. På konserten i går blei **der** sunge ein fine sang.
at concert-the yesterday was there sung a nice song
'At the concert yesterday a nice song was sung.'

The examples shown in (3)–(8) indicate that *det* 'it' and *der* 'there' are more or less in free variation in the *Stavanger* dialect. A similar conclusion is reached in Johnsen (1962: 7f.) for the *Kristiansand* dialect located in the far southern part of southern Norway. As already mentioned, I take this to be the general pattern for dialects allowing both subject types, but with one very crucial exception that I will come back to.

Consider now the relation between the expletive subject and participle agreement in agreeing dialects that allow only *det* as expletive subject and in dialects that allow both *det* and *der*. Recall first the basic agreement pattern in personal passives given earlier in (2), repeated here for convenience, cf. (9).

(9) a. Elgen vart **skoten**. (subject and participle are m, SG)
elk-the was shot
'The elk was shot.'

b. Dyret vart **skote**. (subject and participle are n, SG)
animal-the was shot
'The animal was shot.'

c. Elgane/dyra vart **skotne**. (subject and participle are m/n, PL)
elks-the/animals-the was shot
'The elks/the animals were shot.'

Those agreeing dialects that only allow *det* as expletive subject, as a rule show agreement with the expletive subject. In other words, since the expletive *det*-subject is the singular neuter form of the corresponding pronoun, the participle is also in the singular neuter form. Thus, these dialects show the pattern in (10) alongside the pattern in (9).

(10) a. Det var **skote** ein elg. (subject and participle are n, SG)
it was shot an elk
'An elk was shot.'

b. Det vart **skote** eit dyr. (subject and participle are n, SG)
it was shot an animal
'An animal was shot.'

c. Det vart **skote** fleire elgar/dyr. (subject and participle are n, SG)
it was shot many elks/animals
'Many elks/animals were shot.'

On the other hand, the dialects that allow both *det*- and *der*-type expletive subjects, tend to show agreement with the expletive subject if *det* is used, just like the dialects that allow only *det* as expletive subject shown in (10), but they show agreement with the post-verbal DP if *der* is used, as indicated in (11).

(11) a. Der vart **skoten** ein elg. (participle and postverbal DP are m, SG)
there was shot an elk
'An elk was shot.'

b. Der vart **skote** eit dyr. (participle and postverbal DP are n, SG)
there was shot an animal
'An animal was shot.'

c. Der vart **skotne** (participle and postverbal DP are m/n, PL)
there was shot
fleire elgar/dyr.
many elks/animals
'Many elks/animals were shot.'

Thus, the situation for the alternating *det*- and *der*-dialects is shown by (10) and (11) combined.

This general characterization of the dialects that allow both types of expletive subjects, is based on the investigations of the *Stryn* dialect (situated in the middle part of western Norway) reported in Christensen & Taraldsen (1989), and also on remarks about an older variety of the *Stavanger* dialect reported in Aksnes (2003: 106). Notice, however, that there is considerable variation among dialects regarding the co-variation between subject type and agreement (see Sandøy 1988), and some dialects seem to show unstable agreement patterns. However, until further empirical investigations are done, I take what is shown in (10) and (11) to be the basic pattern relevant for the alternating *det-* and *der*-dialects.

The dialects that allow expletive subjects of both the *det*-type and the *der*-type, are (superficially) similar to English, which is a language that also allows two types of expletive subjects (*it*/*there*). Moreover, English has subject – finite verb agreement, which is partly similar to the subject – participle agreement shown by the participle agreeing Norwegian dialects. I will, therefore, take a look at the relevant data from English, since they may provide a clue as to the theoretical analysis of the Norwegian *det-*/*der*-alternation.

3. Analysis: English

Consider the expletive subjects *it* and *there* in English. As is readily seen, the distribution of *det/der* in (3)–(8) is somewhat different from the distribution of *it/there* in the corresponding English sentences given in this section, even though the etymologies of *det/der* and *it/there* are parallel. In addition to their uses as expletive subjects, English *it* and Norwegian *det* may also be used as 3. person referential pronouns, and English *there* and Norwegian *der* may both be used as locative adverbs. Therefore, in spite of the difference in distribution between Norwegian and English expletive subjects, it seems reasonable to take the analysis of the English expletive subjects *it/there* as a point of departure in trying to develop an analysis for the corresponding Norwegian expletive subjects *det/der*.

The basic facts concerning expletive subjects in English are very clear. That is, if there is no postverbal associate DP, the expletive subject shows up as *it*. If, however, there is a postverbal associate DP, the expletive subject shows up as *there*. This is shown in (12a–b) and (12c–d), respectively.

(12) a. It is raining outside.
b. It snows heavily today.
c. There is rain outside.
d. There is snow in the mountains.

I will suggest an analysis of this distribution, adopting a primitive mechanism of valued and unvalued features (see for instance Adger 2003; Radford 2004). More specifically, I will make two assumptions. First, since English has subject – finite verb agreement, there are unvalued agreement features (Number-u, Person-u) in finite T that must be valued.[1] Second, the expletive subject *it* contains inherently valued Number and Person agreement features (Number-SG, Person-3), whereas the expletive subject *there* does not contain any agreement features at all. Similar assumptions, *mutatis mutandis*, are made in Groat (1995).

Consider the facts in (12) with these assumptions in mind. In (12a–b), unvalued T can only be valued by the expletive subject, since there are no other candidates around that can possibly value T. Therefore, the expletive subject must be of the type that has inherently valued agreement features, namely *it*. If *there* is chosen as expletive subject, T cannot be valued since *there* does not contain any agreement features, leading the derivation to crash, as in (13a–b).

(13) a. *There is raining outside.
     b. *There snows heavily today.

Turning to (12c–d), *there* cannot value unvalued T, and therefore a postverbal associate DP is required to value T. The examples in (14) indicate that agreement on T is valued by the postverbal associate DP. The only role played by the expletive subject *there* is, thus, to be a receiver of abstract case and/or to satisfy the EPP.[2]

(14) a. There is rain outside.
     b. There are raindrops outside.
     c. There is a dog in the street.
     d. There are some dogs in the street.

One problem with this analysis is why *it* cannot be (optionally) used as an expletive subject even in examples like (12c–d). Why is *there* preferred to *it* when a postverbal associate DP is present? In other words, why are examples like (15a–b) ungrammatical?

(15) a. *It is rain outside.
     b. *It is snow in the mountains.

This is a difficult problem, especially when comparable Norwegian data are taken into account. I will suggest a solution to the problem posed by (15a–b) in Section 6, after the relevant Norwegian data have been discussed.

1. In contemporary generative syntax, T is the head of the T(ense)-projection. T accomodates the tense feature of the clause, as well as other features like agreement. The T-projection is situated above the verb phrase, and the verb relates to T either by movement or by some other mechanism like the probe – goal relation that associates the finite verb with the relevant features, see Adger (2003), Radford (2004).

2. The EPP or the Extended Projection Principle is the requirement that a clause must have a subject, see e.g. Chomsky (1995), Adger (2003), Radford (2004).

4. Analysis: Norwegian

It is clear that the Norwegian expletive subjects *det/der* (at least in the *Stavanger* and *Kristiansand* dialects) do not behave like the English counterparts *it/there*, as evidenced by comparing the English patterns in the preceding section with the *Stavanger* data in (3)–(8). To exemplify, the meteorological sentences from the *Stavanger* dialect given earlier in (3) are repeated for convenience, cf. (16).

(16) a. **Det** reggne i Hunnedalen.
it rain in Hunnedalen
'It rains in Hunnedalen.'

b. **Der** reggne i Hunnedalen.
there rain in Hunnedalen
'It rains in Hunnedalen.'

The crucial difference is that meteorological sentences in Norwegian alternating dialects allow both *det* and *der* as expletive subjects, whereas comparable sentences in English only allow *it*. Tentatively assuming that T in Norwegian is like T in English in containing unvalued agreement features that have to be valued (an assumption that will be revised below), the a-version in (16) is as expected. However, the grammaticality of the b-version is unexpected. If Norwegian *der* is like English *there* in lacking agreement features altogether, T cannot be valued, and the derivation should crash for the same reason that the derivations of English (13a–b) crash.

One possible solution to this problem could be to assume that Norwegian *der*, as opposed to English *there*, does contain agreement features, i.e. that the two expletive subjects in Norwegian have the same feature specification. That would explain why the two subjects are in free variation in (16); both subjects would be equally good at valuing the unvalued agreement features that, for the time being, are assumed to be situated in T.

However, the assumption that *det* and *der* have the same feature specification in Norwegian raises a serious problem, since, in certain cases, the expletive subjects *det* and *der* do not seem to be in free variation in the Norwegian dialects that otherwise allow both subjects, contrary to the general pattern described in Section 2. Specifically, they are not in full free variation in clauses with subject – participle agreement. The *Stavanger* dialect has very little subject – participle agreement (but see below), but the *Stryn* dialect reported in Christensen and Taraldsen (1989) has a well-developed system of subject – participle agreement, as illustrated in (17a, b). These examples are adapted from Christensen and Taraldsen (*op. cit.*), where corresponding examples with presentational sentences are given.

(17) a. Der [Ø] er nett **skotne** [m, PL] (*skote) **nokre elgar** [m, PL]
there is just shot some elks
'Some elks are just shot.'

b. **Det** [n, SG] er nett **skote** [n, SG] (*skotne) nokre elgar [m, PL]
it is just shot some elks
'Some elks are just shot.'

Here, (17a) shows that if the expletive subject is *der*, participle agreement is obligatory with the postverbal associate DP. However, if the expletive subject is *det*, participle agreement is obligatory with the expletive subject. This clearly suggests, among other things, that *der* has no agreement features, like *there* in English, whereas *det*, like *it* in English, is specified for agreement features. Moreover, the data also indicate that the participle has unvalued agreement features that are valued by the postverbal associate DP in (17a), and by the expletive subject in (17b).

Now, even though *det/der* in the Stryn dialect have different feature specifications corresponding to *it/there* in English, one could still imagine that *det/der* in the Stavanger dialect have developed the same feature specification, namely that *der* has developed the same specification as *det*, thus accounting for the free variation seen in examples like (16) in that dialect. However, this would not help, because even the Stryn dialect has basically free variation between *det* and *der* if participle agreement is not involved (thus raising the same problems as (16) in the Stavanger dialect), and, besides, it can be positively argued even for the *Stavanger* dialect that *der* has no agreement features.

The *Stavanger* dialect generally has invariant non-agreeing participles (i.e. the singular neuter form), and, as expected, *det* and *der* are in free variation with these non-agreeing participles, as illustrated in (18) (now assuming different feature specifications for *det* and *der*). Notice that *Gen* and *Num* are abbreviations for the agreement categories gender and number, respectively.

(18) a. **Bilen** [Gen-m, Num-SG] blei **stjåle**.
car-the was stolen
'The car was stolen.'

b. **Det** [Gen-n, Num-SG] blei **stjåle** ein bil.
it was stolen a car
'A car was stolen.'

c. **Der** [Ø] blei **stjåle** ein bil.
there was stolen a car
'A car was stolen.'

However, some older speakers still use an agreeing participle, as illustrated in (19a), in which case the participle has unvalued agreement features that must be valued. Importantly, the choice of expletive subject does not appear to be free in such structures for these speakers. For instance, if the masculine singular form of the participle is used in an impersonal construction, only *der* seems to be allowed as an expletive subject, not *det*, as shown in (19b) vs. (19c), see Aksnes (2003: 106).

Notice that the feature specifications in square brackets indicate features associated with the items themselves (u = unvalued), and that the feature specifications in round brackets are the specifications assumed to be acquired by the participle as a result of valuation.

(19) a. **Bilen** [Gen-m, Num-SG] blei stjå**len** [Gen-u, Num-u].
(Gen-m, Num-SG)
car-the was stolen
'The car was stolen.'

b. ??Det [Gen-n,Num-SG] blei stjå**len** [Gen-u,Num-u]
(Gen-m, Num-SG)
it was stolen
ein bil [Gen-m,Num-SG].
a car
'A car was stolen.'

c. Der [Ø] blei stjå**len** [Gen-u, Num-u] **ein bil** [Gen-m, Num-SG].
(Gen-m, Num-SG)
there was stolen a car
'A car was stolen.'

This is exactly the situation found with agreeing participles in the *Stryn* dialect, as shown in (17a, b). It must therefore be concluded that the featural make-up of *der* (no agreement features) is the same in the *Stryn* and *Stavanger* dialects.

As for the parallel to English, notice that the participle – associate DP agreement in (17a) and (19c) resembles the finite verb – associate DP agreement found in English, whereas the grammaticality of (17b) and its equivalent in the older variety of the *Stavanger* dialect (not given here) is unexpected from an English perspective, cf. (15) in Section 3. Thus, the data from the *Stryn* and *Stavanger* dialects discussed above are interestingly parallel to the English data to some extent (agreement with the associate DP), but there are crucial differences as well (the grammaticality of the type in (17b) versus the ungrammaticality of (15)).

The task now is to develop an analysis of the Norwegian data, both from *Stavanger* and from *Stryn*, that can also be extended to the English data. As a first step in this effort, we must ask what the theoretical ramifications are of the facts we have been discussing. Actually, what the various patterns that we have seen above show, is that the rigid distributions of *it/there* in English and of *det/der* in Norwegian dialects are correlated with the presence of unvalued agreement features elsewhere in the structure. Given that situation, a reasonable hypothesis is that free variation as to the type of expletive subject allowed in many instances in Norwegian dialects is correlated with the absence of unvalued agreement features elsewhere in the structure. This is my basic theoretical claim, see also Åfarli (1998) for an earlier discussion of this claim.

Following this idea, I will assume that finite T in all Norwegian dialects, as opposed to finite T in English, does *not* contain unvalued agreement features (or any agreement features at all for that matter). This assumption is supported by the existence of visible subject – finite verb agreement in English and its non-existence in Norwegian. My basic assumptions concerning finite T and agreement are given in (20).

(20) a. Finite T in a given language/dialect may or may not contain (unvalued) verbal agreement features.
b. Finite T contains verbal agreement features only if such features are morphologically visible in the language/dialect (as a type).
c. Unvalued verbal agreement features in finite T must be valued by the agreement features of a DP.
d. The agreement features of DPs are inherently valued.

Furthermore, I assume that passive participles contain unvalued agreement features in some Norwegian dialects (including at least the *Stryn* dialect and older varieties of the *Stavanger* dialect), which is indicated by the presence of visible agreement morphology on the participle in these dialects. Thus, I would like to suggest a corresponding set of assumptions concerning passive participles, see (21).

(21) a. A passive participle in a given language/dialect may or may not contain (unvalued) verbal agreement features.
b. A passive participle contains verbal agreement features only if such features are morphologically visible in the language/dialect (as a type).
c. Unvalued verbal agreement features in a passive participle must be valued by the agreement features of a DP.
d. The agreement features of DPs are inherently valued.

I will now consider some interesting consequences of these assumptions.

5. Some consequences

The theoretical assumptions made in (20) and (21) above have the following consequences. First, consider English very briefly. Since English has visible subject – verb agreement with finite verbs, there are unvalued agreement features in T that must be valued by the inherent features of a DP, either an expletive *it* DP or a postverbal associate DP. This yields the facts in (12)–(15), but notice that (15) is still a problem (to be tackled in the next section).

As for Norwegian, there is generally no visible subject – verb agreement with finite verbs, so Norwegian has no agreement features in T. That means that the featural make-up of the expletive subject has no consequences, and therefore *det* (with inherent agreement features) and *der* (with no agreement features) are in free variation, as seen e.g. in the *Stavanger* dialect, cf. (3)–(8). My assumptions are also compatible with the possibility that a given dialect may use only one of the expletive subjects as its favoured expletive, a possibility that is realised in the many Norwegian dialects that allow only *det* as an expletive subject.

Turning to dialects, like the *Stryn* dialect, that have both types of expletive subject as well as participle agreement, we have noticed that *det* and *der* are not fully in free variation in sentences with participles, since the choice of expletive subject co-varies with the agreement morphology on the participle, cf. (17a, b). How should this co-variation be explained?

Recall that visible agreement morphology on the participle, according to (21), is taken as an indication that the participle is associated with unvalued agreement features that must be valued by the inherent features of a DP, either an expletive *det* DP or a postverbal associate DP. This is similar to the situation in English (except that in English it is T that has the unvalued features).

Let us now take a systematic look at the relevant data from the *Stryn*-type dialect and try to explain the patterns, exploiting the machinery that has been assumed in (21) and otherwise. Consider first the ungrammatical (22) with *der* as expletive subject and a non-agreeing participle. Recall that that the feature specifications in round brackets are the specifications taken to be acquired by the participle as a result of valuation.

(22) ***Der** [Ø] er **skote** [Gen-u, Num-u] (Gen-n, Num-SG) **nokre elgar** [Gen-m, Num-PL]
there is shot some elks
'Some elks are shot.'

In (22), since *der* does not contain any agreement features, only the postverbal DP can possibly value the unvalued features of the participle, but since the participle doesn't in fact agree with the associate DP (*skote* 'shot' is the n, SG form), proper valuation evidently has not taken place and the derivation crashes. (23), on the other hand, is identical to (22), except that the participle in fact agrees with the associate DP, and therefore proper valuation must have taken place and the derivation converges.

(23) **Der** [Ø] er **skotne** [Gen-u, Num-u] (Gen-m, Num-PL) **nokre elgar** [Gen-m, Num-PL]
there is shot some elks
'Some elks are shot.'

Furthermore, consider the corresponding structures with *det* as expletive subject instead of *der*. (24) is grammatical, and evidently the participle has been valued by *det* (both *det* and the participle are specified as Gen-n, Num-SG), which is of course possible since *det*, as opposed to *der*, has inherently specified agreement features.

(24) **Det** [Gen-n, Num-SG] er **skote** [Gen-u, Num-u] **nokre** **elgar** [Gen-m, Num-PL]
(Gen-n, Num-SG)
it is shot some elks
'Some elks are shot.'

In the approach followed here, only unvalued features must be valued/checked, so the inherent features of the associate DP need no checking, cf. (20/21d). However, as shown in (23), the features of an associate DP are in principle capable of valuing the unvalued features of the participle in Norwegian. Therefore, since the inherent features of *det* need no checking (by the same logic as the inherent features of the associate DP need no checking), it must be assumed that *det* and the associate DP compete for valuing the participle when both are present. Therefore, both (24), with the participle valued by *det*, and (25) below, with the participle valued by the associate DP, should have been grammatical. However, (25) is ungrammatical, which must mean that *det* somehow has priority over the associate DP in cases where the two DPs compete for valuation of the participle.

(25) ***Det** [Gen-n,Num-SG] er **skotne** [Gen-u,Num-u] **nokre** **elgar** [Gen-m,Num-PL]
(Gen-m, Num-PL)
it is shot some elks
'Some elks are shot.'

The fact that the expletive subject seems to have priority over the postverbal associate DP regarding valuation of the participle, as indicated by the contrast between (24) and (25), can be explained by assuming that the expletive subject is structurally closer than the associate DP to the site of the unvalued agreement features at the relevant point in the derivation. The relevant notion of closeness can be established on an analysis where the site of the unvalued agreement features is a designated functional head (call it F) that has the projection of the participle as its complement, and with the expletive subject generated as a specifier of the participle projection, and with the associate DP generated in the complement domain of the participle projection. The subject is subsequently raised to the specifier of FP and further up. On such an analysis, the subject is always closer to the unvalued features of the participle, now technically construed as the unvalued features of F, than the associate DP is, since the subject is closer in the search domain of the F probe. Therefore, if the subject has inherent agreement features, it will have priority over the postverbal associate DP as to valuation. In other words, it is only in cases where the expletive subject lacks inherent agreement features that the postverbal associate DP can value the participle. This would explain why (24) is grammatical and (25) is ungrammatical.

There is one snag, though, and that is that my own preliminary investigations of other Norwegian dialects that employ both *det* and *der* as expletive subjects as well as passive participles of the agreeing kind, indicate that these other dialects in fact allow the type in (25) alongside (24), see also Sandøy (1988: 109f.). Investigation of these dialects belongs to future work, and for the time being I will stick to the *Stryn*-type dialects, which seem to show the judgement pattern in (24)–(25).[3]

6. A remaining puzzle

Even though the analysis developed so far explains most of the English and Norwegian data, we are still left with one important puzzle, namely, given the situation in English, why is even (24) grammatical? In fact, among the structures (22)–(25), only (23) should have been grammatical from the view-point of English. This now relates to our unsolved problem from Section 3, which was why the examples in (15) are ungrammatical. These examples are repeated here for convenience, cf. (26).

(26) a. *It is rain outside.
b. *It is snow in the mountains.

The contrast in grammaticality between (26) and (24) is unexpected since both English and the *Stryn*-type dialects have two comparable types of expletive subject and both languages/dialects have unvalued verbal agreement features that may in principle be valued by the *it/det* type expletive subject or by a postverbal associate DP. Nevertheless, regarding the actual valuation patterns, the relevant Norwegian dialects are more permissive than English in allowing the type in (24). I will now take a closer look at this problem, trying at least to locate in which direction one should look in order to find a solution.

Notice first that among the Norwegian dialects that allow only *det* as expletive subject, there are dialects that have agreeing participles. This is the case for the dialect in *Halsa* in the far northern part of western Norway. In that dialect (22) and (23) are of course excluded (since the dialect lacks *der* as a possible expletive subject). Moreover, (25) is also excluded, and (24), with the participle agreeing with *det*, seems to be the only possibility. In other words, we have here a dialect with unvalued participles, and in an impersonal structure with a postverbal associate DP and with *det* as the only possible expletive subject, the expletive subject must value the participle, even though the postverbal DP is in principle available. This suggests one important thing that I want

3. A possible analysis of this variation concerning the grammaticality of (25) in different dialects could try to exploit the notion of structural closeness still further, trying out the parametric hypothesis that *det* is the DP that is structurally closest to the unvalued agreement features in dialects where (25) is ungrammatical, whereas the postverbal DP is structurally closest to the unvalued agreement features in dialects where (25) is grammatical. It would still be predicted that (22) must be ungrammatical in both instances.

to focus on, namely that the postverbal associate DP in an impersonal sentence in Norwegian is fully licensed on its own (e.g. without being involved in the valuing of the participle). The data from the other dialects that have been discussed are of course compatible with this assumption, too. Now, considering English, this assumption leaves the ungrammaticality of the English examples in (26) as a real puzzle, a problem that I will turn to now.

One thing that is similar in English and Norwegian is the following: If the finite verb or the participle unambiguously agrees with a postverbal associate DP, then the expletive subject must be of the type without inherent agreement features, i.e. the adverb type *there/der*. This is directly predicted by the analysis that has been proposed. However, a crucial difference between English and Norwegian is that English disallows the *it*-type expletive if there is a postverbal associate DP present in the structure, hence the ungrammaticality of (26), whereas Norwegian allows the *det*-type expletive even if there is a postverbal associate DP (as long as the participle agrees with the expletive), hence the grammaticality of (24).

Another way to state this difference is to say that English, unlike Norwegian, requires agreement with an associate DP, if such a DP is contained in the structure. I take this to mean that an associate DP in English cannot be licensed unless it agrees with T. Thus, if *it* is chosen as an expletive subject as it is in structures like (26), the expletive subject is forced to agree with T because it is the closest element, and the postverbal DP will not be involved in valuation, and it will therefore not be licensed. Hence, structures like (26) must be ungrammatical in English. In other words, in structures like (26), the presence of *there* is obligatory in order to force the unvalued agreement features of T to be valued by the associate DP so that the associate DP can be licensed. In Norwegian, on the other hand, a postverbal associate DP is licensed without being involved in agreement licensing (as suggested above), so there is no requirement that an associate DP must take part in agreement valuation in Norwegian. This explains the otherwise puzzling difference between English (26) and Norwegian (24).

The proposed difference between English and Norwegian in the licensing requirements of postverbal associate DPs is stipulated as a parametric difference in this analysis. However, notice that Norwegian is far more permissive than English in allowing postverbal associate DPs in impersonal construction than English is. This may be connected to the difference in licensing requirements proposed here. An investigation of these facts and their possible connection belongs to future work.

7. Summary and conclusion

English has unvalued agreement features in T, as evidenced by the fact that English shows subject – finite verb agreement. Further, it seems that an associate postverbal

DP in an impersonal presentational construction in English must be licensed by valuing unvalued T, unlike what is the case in Norwegian. This is the reason why *there* is obligatory as an expletive subject if the structure contains an associate DP. An analysis along these lines would solve the problem posed by the ungrammaticality of (15)/(26) in English.

Norwegian does not have visible subject – verb agreement, and therefore one can conclude that Norwegian has T without any (unvalued) agreement features. Thus, as far as T is concerned, *det* and *der* are in free variation in dialects of Norwegian that have both types of expletive subject. This situation is also compatible with the fact that many dialects only allow *det*. However, many Norwegian dialects have passive participles with unvalued agreement features. In these dialects, as a main rule, *det* and *der* co-vary with agreement morphology on the passive participle such that the presence of *det* forces agreement with *det*, whereas the presence of *der* forces agreement with the postverbal associate DP. (Only the first option is allowed for dialects that allow only *det*, but still have participle agreement.) The first option is allowed since in Norwegian, as opposed to English, associate postverbal DPs are licensed independently of agreement valuation. Notice that some dialects of Norwegian may also allow postverbal agreement even when *det* is the expletive subject, which is a possible parametric option that has to be investigated further both empirically and theoretically. Still, this parametric possibility is not in principle incompatible with the analysis proposed here.

The comparative analysis of the Norwegian and English data that I have defended here, relies on one important assumption, namely that agreement is *not* an essential ingredient of T/finiteness universally, as implied under a Greed analysis of agreement checking of DPs. Specifically, I have claimed that unvalued agreement features (i.e. agreement probes) in T or in participles only exist if there is visible subject – verb or subject – participle agreement in the language/dialect. I take it that the comparative analysis lends support to that particular assumption.

Also, another crucial assumption that is of course incompatible with a Greed analysis of agreement checking of DPs is that the agreement features inherent to a DP are not obligatorily checked or do not obligatorily take part in valuation, even though they may (sometimes) take part in the valuation of unvalued functional agreement features if such unvalued features are present in the structure. On the other hand, postverbal associate DPs in English still seem to be subject to obligatory checking/valuation against T. However, this is a special trait of English impersonal presentational structures and must not be taken as an indication that the inherent agreement features of DPs generally must be checked or must take part in valuation.

I think the investigation carried out here shows quite convincingly that agreement cannot be an essential ingredient of T/finiteness. This claim has quite far-reaching theoretical ramifications that should be pursued in future work, for instance regarding questions about the relation between agreement and case licensing. Also belonging to future work is the further empirical and theoretical investigation of the fascinating variation and complexity shown by Norwegian dialects as regards the phenomena that I have delved into in this article.

References

Adger, David. 2003. *Core Syntax: A Minimalist Approach*. Oxford: OUP.

Åfarli, Tor A. 1992. *The Syntax of Norwegian Passive Constructions* [Linguistik Aktuell/ Linguistics Today 7]. Amsterdam: John Benjamins. doi:10.1075/la.7

Åfarli, Tor A. 1998. Dialektsyntaks. In *MONS 7*, Jan Terje Faarlund, Brit Mæhlum & Torbjørn Nordgård (eds.), 270–293. Oslo: Novus.

Aksnes, Marita. 2003. Konstruksjoner med formelt subjekt i stavangerdialekten. MA thesis, Norwegian University of Science and Technology.

Chomsky, Noam. 1995. *The Minimalist Program*. Cambridge, MA: The MIT Press.

Christensen, Kirsti Koch & Taraldsen, Knut Tarald. 1989. Expletive chain formation and past participle agreement in Scandinavian dialects. In *Dialect Variation in the Theory of Grammar*, Paola Benincà (ed.), 53–83. Dordrecht: Foris.

Dahl, Torstein. 1974. Setninger med *der/her* som formelt subjekt i norske målføre og nynorsk skriftspråk. MA thesis, University of Oslo.

Faarlund, Jan Terje, Lie, Svein & Vannebo, Kjell Ivar. 1997. *Norsk referansegrammatikk*. Oslo: Universitetsforlaget.

Groat, Eric. 1995. English expletives: A minimalist approach. *Linguistic Inquiry* 26: 354–365.

Johnsen, Arnulf. 1962. *Syntaksen i Kristiansands bymål*. Oslo: Aschehoug.

Radford, Andrew. 2004. *Minimalist Syntax: Exploring the Structure of English*. Cambridge: CUP.

Raposo, Eduardo. 1987. Case Theory and Infl-to-Comp: The inflected infinitive in European Portuguese. *Linguistic Inquiry* 18: 85–109.

Sandøy, Helge. 1988. Samsvarsbøying av adjektiv og perfektum partisipp i norske dialektar. In *Nordiske studiar: Innlegg på den tredje nordiske dialektologkonferansen 1986*, Andreas Bjørkum & Arve Borg (eds.), 85–117. Oslo: Universitetsforlaget.

Sandøy, Helge. 1992. *Norsk dialektkunnskap*. Oslo: Novus.

Non-finiteness in Saamáka*

Marleen Susanne van de Vate & Tonjes Veenstra
ZAS Berlin

In this paper we demonstrate that the creole language Saamáka does exhibit the finite vs. non-finite distinction by analysing the semantic characteristics and syntactic distribution of complementizer *fu*. We adopt a Klein style analysis of finiteness and argue that clauses embedded under this complementizer lack the features Assertion and Topic Time, and, hence, that these clauses are non-finite. Based on this semantic analysis, we propose to split up the Fin-head and demonstrate that complementizer *fu* is base-generated in the higher Fin-position. As a result, we claim that our analysis calls for a richer lower C-domain than previously assumed in the literature.

Keywords: syntax-semantic interface; cartography; creole languages; finiteness; complementizers; temporal pronominals

1. Introduction

In this paper we discuss whether creole languages have non-finite clauses and in our discussion we focus on Saamáka,[1] an English/Portuguese-based creole spoken in Suriname. Mufwene and Dijkhoff (1989) claim that since finiteness is a purely

* The data discussed in this paper was collected during fieldwork trips to Pikin Slee, Suriname in 2008 and 2009 (totaling six months). Specifically designed questionnaires targeting tense and aspect interpretations were used for data elicitation with bilingual Saamáka – Dutch speakers. Data from narratives by and interviews with monolingual Saamáka speakers are also discussed in this paper. Marleen gratefully acknowledges the funding provided by HumFak, Universitetet i Tromsø. She would like to thank her consultants for their time and patience. Tonjes' participation in this project was made possible through the support by the Federal Ministry of Education and Research (BMBF) of Germany (grant number 01UG0711).

1. Saamáka is an English/Portuguese-based creole spoken along the Suriname River, Suriname. The substrate languages are the Gbe languages and Kikongo (Smith 1987). The language was created by slaves who fled the plantations towards the end of the 17th century (Price 1983). Currently, the language has 50.000 speakers (Aboh et al. 2013) who reside on the banks of the Suriname River, in Paramaribo, in French Guiana, and in The Netherlands. In the literature, the language is also referred to as Saramaccan.

DOI 10.1075/la.231.07van

morphological distinction and creole languages are morphologically poor, creole languages do not exhibit the finite vs. non-finite distinction. Bickerton (1981, 1984) and Byrne (1987) argue that in Saamáka all clauses are finite and that the language lacks complementizers. More recent work on Saamáka (Damonte 2002; Aboh 2006; Lefebvre & Loranger 2006, 2008; Veenstra 2008) has demonstrated that the language has (at least) two complementizers: indicative/declarative *táa* and subjunctive/irrealis *fu*, as exemplified in (1a) and (1b) respectively.[2]

(1a) Mi sísa píki mi dyusnu de táa dí gaanmá kó.
1SG sister tell me just.now there TAA DET Granman come
'My sister has told me just now that the Granman has arrived'.

(1b) Mi ké fu i gó.
1SG want FU 2SG go
'I want for you to go'.

Since clauses embedded under complementizer *táa* have been argued to be finite, they are left aside.[3]

In this paper we focus on the syntactic distribution and the semantic characteristics of complementizer *fu* and aim to determine whether clauses embedded under complementiser *fu* are finite or non-finite. Although the syntactic distribution of *fu* has been discussed in the literature (see Bickerton 1981, 1984; Byrne 1987; Damonte 2002; Aboh 2006; Lefebvre & Loranger 2006), its semantic characteristics have received much less attention. By adopting Klein's (1998; 2006; 2009) definition of finiteness i.e. a finite verb carries the features Assertion and Topic Time, we demonstrate that clauses embedded under *fu* lack the features Assertion and Topic Time, [-AST] and [-TT]. Consequently, we postulate that *fu*-clauses are non-finite and, hence, that Saamáka exhibits the finite vs. non-finite distinction.

As for the syntactic position of complementizer *fu*, we argue that it is base-generated in a position between the Force and Fin-position (in the sense of Rizzi 1997). The evidence for this comes primarily from the distribution of Topic and Focus in the left periphery. Aboh (2006) observes that focused elements can precede as well as follow complementizer *fu*, as illustrated in (2).

2. Abbreviations: SG = singular; PL = Plural; MOD = modal marker; PST = Past interpretation; IMP = Imperfective; NEG = Negation; BE = Copula; COMP = Complementizer; DET = Determiner; ART = Article; LOC = Locative; Q = Question marker; RQ = Rhetorical Question marker; NARR = Narrative marker; FU = Prepositional complementizer fu; IDEO = Ideophone; REL = relativizer; TAA = indicative complementizer.

3. We refer to Lefebvre and Loranger (2008) for an overview and discussion of complementiser *táa*.

(2a) Amato ké fu [a mátu] Ajawa kísi dí ogífou.
Amato want FU LOC jungle Ajawa catch DET owl
'Amato wants Ajawa to catch the owl IN THE JUNGLE' (Aboh, 2006, 35).

(2b) Amato ké [a mátu] fu Ajawa kísi dí ogífou.
Amato want LOC jungle FU A catch DET owl
'Amato wants Ajawa to catch the owl IN THE JUNGLE' (Aboh, 2006, 35).

We take this to mean that complementizer *fu* is not base-generated in the lowest position in the C-domain, as argued for by Damonte (2002). This tallies nicely with Van de Vate's (2011) proposal that it is the situational pronominal *bì* – which established an Anchor Time – that occupies the lowest C-position. However, we want to maintain the analysis of Damonte (2002) who argues that complementizer *fu* is situated in Fin. We, therefore, propose to split up the Fin-position. The two Fin-positions in our proposal have different semantic properties. The lower Fin-position is (directly) anchored to TP (in the sense of Bianchi 2003; Giorgi 2006). In this position, the situational pronominal *bì* is merged. The higher Fin-position, on the other hand, is a non-anchoring position where complementizer *fu* is situated. In between these two Fin-positions, focused elements can occur, just as in between the higher Fin-position and the Force-position. We argue that this calls for a richer lower C-domain than previously assumed in the literature.

This paper is organised as follows: Section 2 discusses the interpretation of *fu*-clauses. Section 3 presents an overview of previous literature on the finite vs. non-finite distinction in Saamáka. Our theoretical background assumptions regarding the semantic composition of finiteness are presented in Section 4. Section 5 presents our semantic and syntactic analysis of *fu*-clauses. Section 6 ends this paper with some concluding remarks.

2. Characteristics of fu

The morpheme *fu*[4] is a multifunctional element which can be used as a possessive preposition, a modal morpheme expressing obligation,[5] and a complementizer, as illustrated in (3)–(5) respectively.

4. The morpheme is pronounced as *fu* or *u*. Furthermore, certain morphemes can fuse with personal pronouns. Complementizer *fu* can fuse with second person singular pronoun *i* (this results in *fii* and with third person singular pronoun *a* (this results in *faa*).

5. The modal use of *fu* is highly debatable. Byrne (1987) and Aboh (2006) worked with consultants who accepted this use of *fu*, while the consultants with whom Veenstra (1996), McWhorter (1997), Lefebvre and Loranger (2006) and van de Vate (2011) worked rejected this use of *fu*. Further research is necessary to establish whether these differences in grammatical judgments are the result of several Saamáka varieties.

(3) Dí lògòsò gó nján dí húku paú fu dí míi gíngi a
DET turtle go eat DET hook stick FU DET child sturdy 3SG
butá a búka
put down LOC mouth
'The turtle has taken the child's fishing rod sturdy in his mouth'.

(4) Dí wómi fu woóko a dí bakáa wósu.
DET man FU work LOC DET white.man house
'The man should work at the white man's house' (Byrne, 1987, 114).

(5) Dí sondí bì hebi nóo yoó ké hói hen
DET thing PST heavy NARR 2SG.MOD want hold 3SG
fu á kai
FU 3SG.NEG fall
'The thing was heavy and therefore you would want to hold it so that it would not fall'.

Since this paper focuses on the question whether Saamáka has non-finite clauses, the prepositional and modal use of *fu* are left aside.[6] In this paper we discuss the use of *fu* as a complementizer.

2.1 Characteristics of clauses embedded under *fu*

First, the subject of an embedded *fu*-clause is optional. It can be overtly expressed, as in (6) and (7), or covertly, as in (8).

(6) Senni$_i$ ta pakiséi fu Freddy$_j$ hén kíi dí ganía.
Senni IMP consider FU Freddy 3SG kill DET chicken
'Senni is considering that Freddy, he should kill the chicken (but he hasn't done it (yet))'.

(7) Dí$_i$ tódo djómbo fu a$_i$ gó a watá.
DET frog jump FU 3SG go LOC water
'The frog jumped so that he will go into the water'.

(8) Mi$_i$ gó wóoko mi góon súku sondí u $\emptyset_{i/*j}$ nyán.
1SG go work 1SG garden search thing FU eat
'I went to work in my (vegetable) garden to look for something I could eat'.

6. We refer the interested reader to Lefebvre and Loranger (2006) for an overview of the different meanings and usages of *fu*.

When the embedded subject is covert, it is obligatorily coreferential with the subject of the main clause, whereas an overt subject can be coreferential with the main clause subject or with an external referent (see also Byrne 1987; Veenstra 2008).

Second, the eventuality[7] of an embedded clause is interpreted as that it has not been realised. This gives rise to an irrealis interpretation, as illustrated in (9) and (10).

(9) Akí dí wómimíi hópo wán sondí faa gó náki dí dágu.
here DET child lift ART thing FU=3SG go hit DET dog
'Here the boy has gotten something so that he should hit the dog'.

(10) Mi paamúsi dí míi u kó heépi hén.
1SG promise DET child FU come help 3SG
'I promised the child to help him' (Veenstra, 2008, 11).

Third, (11) and (12) illustrate that *fu* cannot be taken as a complement of verbs that convey a reading in which the truth-value of the embedded clause seems to hold according to the agent.[8]

(11) *Senni bì méni fu Freddy hén kíi dí ganía.
Senni PST remember FU Freddy 3SG kill DET chicken
Intended interpretation: 'Senni remembered that Freddy killed the chicken'.

(12) *Senni biíbi fu Freddy dé a lío.
Senni belief FU Freddy BE LOC river
Intended interpretation: 'Senni believes that Freddy is near the river'.

Fourth, (13) and (14) demonstrate that an embedded eventuality can be modified by the morpheme *bì*, regardless of whether the subject is overt or covert. The morpheme *bì* gives rise to a past interpretation of the eventuality. The examples below express an eventuality in the past which has not been realised, but it could have been realised.

7. The term eventuality is used as cover-term for states, events and processes. The term state refers to stative eventualities, and the term event to event/process eventualities throughout this study (in the sense of Bach 1986).

8. Both sentences are grammatical when *fu* is substituted by complementizer *táa*, as illustrated below.

(i) Senni bì méni táa Freddy hén kíi dí ganía.
Senni PST remember TAA Freddy 3SG kill DET chicken
'Senni remembered that Freddy, he killed the chicken'.

(ii) Senni biíbi táa Freddy dé a lío.
Senni belief TAA Freddy BE LOC river
'Senni beliefs that Freddy is near the river'.

(13) A góa wósu faa bì nján.
3SG go LOC house FU=3SG PST eat
'He went home with the intention of eating (but he didn't)'
(Bickerton, 1984, 8).

(14) Mi poobá fu bì léi dí tóngo.
1SG try FU PST learn DET language
'I tried to learn the language (but I didn't succeed)'.

Other tense, aspect and modality (TAM) morphemes can also occur in a *fu*-clause, as exemplified for the necessity modal *musu* and the possibility modal *sa* in (15) and (16) respectively.

(15) Akí dí míi púu búku fu a musu gó a dí
here DET child pull throwers FU 3SG MOD go LOC DET
dágu báka.
dog back
'Here the child pulled out his pants for he must go after the dog'.

(16) Mi ké dí tyúba pasá fu mi sa gó a Saamáka.
1SG want DET rain pass FU 1SG MOD go LOC S
'I want the rain to stop so that I can go to Saramacca'.

The presence of *musu* in (15) gives rise to an obligation reading, while the presence of *sa* in (16) gives rise to a general ability reading. The eventuality in both embedded clauses has not taken place at the time of utterance. Imperfective morpheme *ta* can also occur in a fu-clause, as illustrated in (17).

(17) Té wán písi nóo telefón ó kó. Nóo de taá fu
until ART place NARR telephone MOD come NARR 3PL TAA FU
tooná bái báka. Eé yoó ábi tú of ún méni yoó
return buy back if 2SG.MOD have two or how many 2SG.MOD
ábi. Nóo fii ta béli nó?
have NARR FU.2SG IMP call Q
'At a certain moment the telephone mast will come. Then they will say to buy it (= top-up card for prepaid mobile phone) again. If you want two or how many you want. Then you should be calling all the time, isn't it?'

In (17), *ta* conveys a habitual reading, and, as in the previous examples, the eventuality has not been realised at the time of utterance.

To summarize, clauses embedded under complementiser *fu* have the following characteristics. The embedded eventuality is interpreted as not been realised. A *fu*-clause has a future interpretation when there are no TAM morphemes present. When the morpheme *bì* modifies the embedded eventuality, a *fu*-clause has a past interpretation.

In combination with other TAM morphemes, a *fu*-clause conveys a future interpretation. The embedded subject can be both overtly and covertly expressed.

3. Lack of infinitival clauses in Saamáka: Discussion of Bickerton and Byrne

In this section, we present an overview of the discussion in Bickerton (1981, 1984) and Byrne (1987) on finiteness in Saamáka. Both linguists have argued that Saamáka lacks complementizers as well as non-finite clauses.

Bickerton claims that *fu* has the following characteristics (1984, 8/9):

- It marks complements of uncertainty or non-accomplishments, as in (18) and (19).
- It functions as a modal verb, as in (4) above and in (20).
- It introduces tensed (i.e. finite) complement clauses, as in (18) and (19).
- It functions as a main verb and is itself tensed, as in (19) and (20).

(18) A gó a wósu faa bì nján.
3SG go LOC house FU=3SG PST eat
'He went home with the intention of eating (but he didn't)' (Bickerton, 1984, 181).

(19) A gó a wósu bì faa nján.
3SG go LOC house PST FU=3SG eat
'He went home with the intention of eating (but he didn't)' (Bickerton, 1984, 181).

(20) Dí wómi bì fu woóko a dí bakáa wósu.
DET man PST FU work LOC DET white.man house
'The man should have worked at the white man's house' (Byrne, 1987, 114).

Bickerton and Byrne argue that *fu* is a finite verb, because (1) *fu* can be tensed, as illustrated in (19) and (20) above, and (2) *fu* can be fronted,[9] as illustrated in (21).

(21) Fu i fu naki di mii.
FU 2SG FU hit DET child
'You should hit the child' (Bickerton, 1984, 181).

Furthermore, Byrne argues that a sentence containing *fu* is bi-clausal. This is regardless of whether *fu* functions as a semi-modal verb, as illustrated in (4) and (20) above,

9. Veenstra (1996) argues that in Saamáka fronting is a diagnostic to establish whether an element is a verb or not.

or as a semi-complementizer, as illustrated in (18) and (19) above. The underlying structure of a *fu*-clause, as proposed by Byrne, is presented in (22).

(22) $[_{S'} [_{S}$ NP$_{i}$ INFL fu $[_{S'} [_{S}$ pro$_{i}$ INFL VP]]]] (Byrne, 1987, 131)

To summarize, Bickerton and Byrne claim that *fu* is a main verb which subcategorizes for a S-complement and which is introduced by a S-node.

The analysis of the morpheme *bì* is important for both Bickerton's and Byrne's analysis of *fu* as well as for our analysis. Bickerton and Byrne analyse this morpheme as a past tense morpheme. If the morpheme *bì* is indeed a past tense morpheme, one would have to argue that clauses embedded under *fu* are finite, because this morpheme can occur in a clause embedded under *fu*, as illustrated in (18) above. However, we postulate in Section 5.2.1 that *bì* is not a past tense morpheme, but a temporal pronominal (in the sense of Partee 1984 and Enç 1987). Consequently, in our analysis the presence of the morpheme *bì* does not necessarily indicate that a sentence is finite. In other words, examples like (18) do not demonstrate that *fu*-clauses are finite.

In Section 5, we argue against Bickerton and Byrne and postulate that *fu* is not a verb, but a complementizer (following Damonte 2002; Aboh 2006; Lefebvre & Loranger 2006; Veenstra 2008). Furthermore, by assuming that finiteness is marked by the features Assertion and Topic Time (in the sense of Klein 1998), we propose that Saamáka does have non-finite clauses.

4. Semantic composition of finiteness

In Klein's (1992; 1994) system of temporal interpretation, three time spans are distinguished: Time of Utterance (TU), Topic Time (TT) and Time of Situation (TSit). The former refers to the moment when an utterance is made. Topic Time refers to the time for which a particular utterance makes an assertion. It refers to a time span to which the assertion made is constrained. Time of Situation is the time at which an eventuality occurs (Klein 1992, 535–538). Tense expresses a temporal ordering relation between Time of Utterance and Topic Time, while Aspect expresses a temporal ordering relation between Topic Time and Time of Situation.

Klein (1998; 2006; 2009) argues that finiteness is not merely a morphological category. The crucial elements of finiteness are Topic Time and Assertion. A finite verb carries the features Topic Time and Assertion (AST), while a non-finite verb does not carry these features. Topic Time provides the time span for which an assertion holds, while Assertion determines the illocutionary force of a sentence. Assertion is a set of modal features which mark whether the eventuality described by an utterance is obtained. Klein argues that Assertion is linked to Topic Time in the following way: 'The finite component simply defines a time span, which can be placed somewhere on the temporal axis. This is what is called here "topic time". In declarative main clauses, this TT is the time for which the claim is made – the time to which the abstract element AST is linked' (Klein, 1998, 233). Assertion does not necessarily indicate the truth-value of a situation, but it indicates that Topic Time follows/contains/is contained in Time of Situation.

Finiteness (FIN) is formed by three variables; *lex, mod* and *t*. The former refers to the description/interpretation of the verb. The variable *mod* refers to the sentence modality (this might be AST or some other sentence modality). The variable *t* specifies the time span for which the assertion holds; i.e. TT.

(23) FIN*[lex, t; AST] (INF*[V, arguments, optional elements]) (Klein, 1998, 240).

Structurally the sentence consists of three elements: Topic Component, Sentence Base and a Finiteness element. The crucial component of Topic Component is Topic Time. Other components can be Topic Place, Topic World and Topic Entity (this last one is realised by the subject). The Topic Component specifies the eventuality that is expressed by the utterance. Sentence Base (= INF) conveys the content of Assertion (= the eventuality). It hosts the non-finite verb and the verbal argument(s). The Finiteness element (= FIN) relates Sentence Base to Topic Component (Klein, 2006, 266).

Utterance		
Topic Component	**FIN**	**Sentence Base**
topic topic topic (topic time place world entity)		V_S and arguments

Since Finiteness consists of the components Topic Time and Assertion (i.e. FIN [TT, AST]), it depends on the value of these two features whether a verb is marked or unmarked for finiteness.[10] This is illustrated by an example from German. In (24), the lexically empty element *es* is the subject of the sentence. It fills the Topic Component. The subject does not provide information regarding Topic Time. The verb is the finiteness marker and *hatte* is the tense bearing verb. The example has a past interpretation; i.e. Topic Time is situated prior to the Time of Utterance. The Sentence Base is filled by the argument *jemand für dich angerufen* which is the non-finite component of the example.

(24) Es hatte jemand für dich angerufen.
it has-PST someone for you called (Klein, 2006, 267)

10. INF has a topic and a focus component. However, FIN only applies to the focus component of INF (see Klein 1998).

The English example in (25) is a declarative sentence. AST has the value declarative, while *bought* is the tense bearing verb. It has a past interpretation. Hence, the time interval at which the eventuality, *bought salt*, is asserted prior to the Time of Utterance.

(25) Mary bought salt. (Becker, 2005, 268).

The verb *bought* carries the features Topic Time and Assertion. Hence, (25) is finite. The semantic structure of (25) is presented in (26).

(26) FIN [AST, TT](INF[BUY(MARY, SALT)]) (Becker, 2005, 268)

In a language like English, Topic Time and Assertion are realised by the same syntactic head, however, these two functions are not similar and need to be considered separately. In, for example, Vietnamese these two functions are realised by different heads and are, thus, realised separately (see Duffield 2007 for discussion).

5. Decomposition of *fu*-clauses

This section aims to establish whether *fu*-clauses are finite or non-finite. Following Klein's (1998; 2006; 2009) analysis, we assume that a finite verb carries the features Topic Time and Assertion, whereas a non-finite verb does not carry these features. In this section, we demonstrate that an embedded *fu*-clause lacks both features and is, therefore, non-finite. Section 5.1 addresses the question of whether *fu*-clauses carry the feature Assertion, while Section 5.2 addresses the question of whether *fu*-clauses carry the feature Topic Time.

5.1 Do *fu*-clauses carry the feature assertion?

Assertion is a structural notion which determines the illocutionary force of a sentence. It involves linking of propositional material, i.e. INF, to a particular Topic Time. In Section 2, it was demonstrated that an eventuality embedded under complementizer *fu* has not been obtained, as illustrated in (9) which is repeated below as (27). The embedded eventuality, *gó náki dí dágu* (='go hit the dog'), is not asserted at the Time of Utterance.

(27) Akí dí wómimíi hópo wán sondí faa gó náki dí dágu.
here DET child lift ART thing FU=3SG go hit DET dog
'Here the boy has gotten something so that he should hit the dog'.

As exemplified in (14), repeated below as (28), the morpheme *bì* can be embedded under *fu* while *bì* modifies the embedded eventuality. The presence of *bì* gives rise to a past interpretation of the embedded eventuality. In (28), the embedded eventuality has not taken place at the Time of Utterance and, therefore, is not asserted. This is another piece of evidence that *fu*-clauses embed eventualities that are not asserted.

(28) Mi poobá fu bì léi dí tóngo.
1SG try FU PST learn DET language
'I tried to learn the language (but I didn't succeed)'.

Another example in favour of the argument that an eventuality embedded under *fu* is not asserted are presented in examples (11) and (12), repeated below as (29) and (30). These examples illustrated that *fu* cannot be taken as a complement of verbs which convey a reading in which the truth value of the embedded eventuality holds according to the agent.

(29) *Senni bì méni fu Freddy hén kíi dí ganía.
Senni PST remember FU Freddy 3SG kill DET chicken
Intended interpretation: 'Senni remembered that Freddy killed the chicken'.

(30) *Senni biíbi fu Freddy dé a lío.
Senni belief FU Freddy BE LOC river
Intended interpretation: 'Senni believes that Freddy is near the river'.

Based on the data presented in this section, we conclude that eventualities embedded under *fu* have not obtained at Time of Utterance, i.e. these eventualities are not asserted.

Recall that Klein (1998, 2006, 2009) postulates that Assertion is linked to Topic Time. Therefore, it is important to establish whether *fu*-clauses lack Topic Time, in order to argue that *fu*-clauses are non-finite. This is the focus of the next section.

5.2 Do *fu*-clauses carry the feature Topic Time?

The absence of Topic Time implies that the time span to which an eventuality is constrained is not made explicit and/or does not exist. Since Tense orders Topic Time to the Time of Utterance and Aspect orders Topic Time to the Time of Situation, a sentence without a Topic Time does not have a Tense head nor an Aspect head. Before we demonstrate that *fu*-clauses lack a Topic Time (Section 5.2.2), it is important to decompose the morpheme *bì* (Section 5.2.1).

5.2.1 *Decomposing the morpheme* bì

The morpheme *bì* can convey a simple past reading, as illustrated in (31).

(31) Dí wómi bì gó a mátu nóo hén wán píngo kó
DET man PST go LOC forest NARR NARR ART wild.pig come
nyá én nóo hén a kíi én.
eat 3SG NARR NARR 3SG kill 3SG
'The man went to the forest, a wild pig attacked him and he, the man, killed it'.

Based on this example one might analyse *bì* as a past tense morpheme. Such an analysis would imply that a sentence containing this morpheme would have a Topic Time because Tense expresses a temporal ordering relation between Topic Time and Time of Utterance (in the sense of Klein 1992, 1994; Demirdache & Uribe-Etxebarria 2000). Since the morpheme *bì* can be embedded under complementiser *fu*, such an analysis would therefore imply that *fu*-clauses would have a Topic Time and that they would be finite. However, the morpheme *bì* has a couple of characteristics which cannot be accounted for under a past tense analysis. We therefore postulate that *bì* is not a past tense morpheme but a temporal pronominal (in the sense of Partee 1984; Enç 1987, 2004; Kratzer 1998). This temporal pronominal establishes the Anchor Time directly and makes it not be the time of utterance but some other contextually relevant past time (see van de Vate 2011, 2013b). In other words in our analysis, the temporal pronominal *bì* does not express a temporal ordering relation between Topic Time and Time of Utterance. Hence, it is not a past tense morpheme. As a consequence, a sentence containing the temporal pronominal *bì* does not necessarily have a Topic Time (although a Topic Time is not excluded either) and is not necessarily finite (although this is not excluded either).

5.2.1.1 Characteristics of *bì*. The morpheme *bì* can convey a simple past reading regardless of whether the verb is stative or eventive, as illustrated in (32) and (33) respectively.

(32) Lathoya bì suáki ma a béte.
Lathoya PST ill but 3SG better
'Lathoya was ill, but she is better now'.

(33) Context: What did the girl do yesterday?
Dí muyéemíi bì kandá.
DET girl PST sing
'The girl sang'.

Bì can also convey a past-before-past reading regardless of whether the verb is stative or eventive, as illustrated in (34) and (35) respectively.

(34) Éside Senni bì ta woóko. A dí wíki dí bì pasá
yesterday Senni PST IMP work LOC DET week REL PST pass
de a bì suáki.
there 3SG PST ill
'Yesterday Senni was working. The week before, he had been ill'.

(35) Éside dí Freddy kó a wósu a bì wéi. A bì
yesterday when Freddy come LOC house 3SG PST tired. 3SG PST
woóko taánga.
work strong
'Yesterday when Freddy came home, he was tired. He had worked hard'.

The morpheme *bì* cannot modify an eventuality which is situated in the past of an anchor time located in the future i.e. a past-in-the-future reading, as illustrated in (36). Therefore, the morpheme *bì* can only expresses a past reading with regard to some other time which is restricted to be non-future i.e. it's reading is inconsistent with a past from a future perspective.

(36) Context: I am having a conversation with a pregnant woman and I tell her that in a year from now I will return to Pikin Slee. She replies to me:
*Té i toonáá kó nóo mi bì palí.
when 2SG return come NARR 1SG PST give.birth
Intended reading: 'By the time you have returned, I will have given birth.'

The morpheme *bì* is optional and can be omitted, as illustrated in (37).[11]

(37a) Yoó dá u to? Únfa dí gaánwáta bigí u kó únfa
3SG.MOD give 1PL right how DET flood start FU come how
i dú.
2SG do
F: 'You will give us something, right? When the flood started to come, what did you do?'

(37b) Mé bì dé akí.
1SG.NEG PST BE here
S: 'I was not here.'

(37c) Oh yá bì dé akí?
oh 2SG.NEG PST BE here
F: 'Oh, you were not here?'

(37d) Mi dé a Semoisi.
1SG BE LOC Semoisi
S: 'I was in Semoisi.'

(37e) Oh yá bì dé akí nó?
oh 2SG.NEG PST BE here RQ
M: 'Oh, you were not here?'

(37f) Nóno mi dé a Semoisi. Dí a kó a dóu té.
no 1SG BE LOC Semoisi when 3SG come 3SG arrive until
S: 'No, I was in Semoisi. When it came, it reached up to there.'

11. Abbreviations: F = Fonteni, my guide and interpreter; S = Sina, an elderly monolingual woman and main narrator; M = Marleen. Please note that the Saamáka of the author is that of a second language learner who has not acquired the language completely.

Unmarked stative verbs in Saamáka convey a present interpretation.[12] In order for stative verbs to convey a past interpretation they need to be modified by the morpheme *bì*. It would be expected that under a past tense analysis of *bì*, all stative verbs have to be embedded by *bì* to convey a past interpretation. As (37) demonstrates this is not obligatory. In line (37-d), the copula *dé* is unmarked. Under a past tense analysis of *bì*, a present interpretation of the copula would be expected. However, the discourse context makes it clear that the speaker is not referring to the present moment, but to where she was when her narrative took place.

That *bì* can be omitted is also demonstrated with a bi-clausal sentence. In (38), imperfective morpheme *ta* modifies both eventualities, while *bì* only modifies one eventuality. The imperfective morpheme conveys a present interpretation in an out-of-the-blue context (and without the presence of other TAM marking). It requires *bì* to convey a past interpretation of the eventuality. In (38), both eventualities fall under the scope of *bì*, whereas only the second eventuality is modified by *bì*. Both eventualities convey a past interpretation and are interpreted as occurring simultaneously. For the temporal interpretation of this sentence, it is irrelevant which of the eventualities is modified by the morpheme *bì*.

(38a) Dí muyée ta nái koósu nóo a bì ta kondá wán sondí
DET woman IMP sew cloth NARR 3SG PST IMP tell ART thing
a déé sembe.
LOC DET.PL person
'The woman was sewing cloth(s) while she was telling something to the others'.

12. In Saamáka, utterances containing an unmarked stative verb have a present interpretation, while those containing an unmarked dynamic verb have a past interpretation, as illustrated below.

(ia) Dí wómi sábi néngétóngo.
DET man know Sranan
'The man knows Sranan'.

(ib) Dí wómi mbéi wán bóto.
DET man make ART boat
'The man has made a boat'.

To account for this difference in temporal interpretation, van de Vate (2011, 2013a) postulates that the language has a morphologically null perfect morpheme. This analysis exploits the independently acknowledged difference between states and events concerning the inability of the latter to co-occur with a point-like present tense. The 'perfect' must be inserted in these contexts to create a derived resultant state, creating the illusion of a 'past tense' in many interpretational contexts.

(38b) Event e_1 O Event e_2 < TU

To summarize, *bì* can convey both a simple past and a past-before-past interpretation. Furthermore, *bì* is insensitive to aktionsart: The pattern of distribution is not determined by whether a predicate is stative or eventive. Finally, *bì* is discourse sensitive: The presence of *bì* can be optional. A past tense analysis cannot explain all of these characteristics. Therefore, we propose a different analysis.

Examples as (37) and (38) indicate that the morpheme *bì* is discourse sensitive; i.e. that it can be omitted. Under the hypothesis that *bì* is a past tense morpheme, discourse sensitivity and omission is unexpected and cannot be accounted for in a formal theory. Following Stowell (1996), we assume that Tense is a universal feature. Consequently, TP is always present in the underlying structure of a clause. We postulate that Saamáka has a null Tense head which expresses PRESENT tense (following van de Vate 2013a). It is expected that if *bì* would be a past tense morpheme which is situated in TP ánd *bì* would not modify an eventuality, the temporal ordering relation expressed by Tense would be PRESENT. As (37) and (38) have demonstrated, this expectation is not borne out. Predicates which give rise to a present interpretation in an out-of-the-blue context and require the morpheme *bì* for a past interpretation, can be interpreted with a past interpretation in contexts as in example (37) and (38).

We postulate that *bì* is a temporal pronominal which establishes the Anchor Time directly and makes it not be the time of utterance but some contextually relevant past moment (in the sense of Partee 1984; Enç 1987, 2004; Kratzer 1998). All eventualities are anchored to this Anchor Time and fall under the scope of this Anchor Time (unless they are interrupted by a different storyline after which the Anchor Time needs to be reestablished when the narrative continues). This Anchor Time is restricted to be situated prior to the Time of Utterance. This entails that the eventuality is located before the Time of Utterance (and thus the past interpretation of *bì* is explained). The morpheme *bì* ranges over times and it expresses 'not now' (in the sense of Iatridou 2000). In a cartographic approach to language structure, it would be situated under a Fin-head. The morpheme *bì* can, in principle, co-occur with a Topic Time. The morpheme does not have a feature which would exclude this (van de Vate 2011, 2013b).

5.2.2 *Availability of Topic Time in* fu-*clauses*

In this section we establish that *fu*-clauses do not have a Topic Time. Our argument is as follows. First, in Section 5.1, we argued that the eventuality embedded under complementizer *fu* has not (yet) obtained, and therefore no Assertion is made. As a consequence, Topic Time is not necessary to relate the eventuality to Time of Utterance or to situate the eventuality on a timeline. Secondly, in Section 5.2.1, we postulated that the morpheme *bì* is not a past tense morpheme, but a temporal pronominal which establishes the anchor time directly. Consequently, a sentence containing *bì* does not necessarily have a Topic Time. Our analysis implies that examples like (28) above, in which *bì* occurs under complementiser *fu*, do not indicate that *fu*-clauses have a Topic Time. The occurrence of *bì* under *fu* gives merely rise to the interpretation of a potential eventuality prior to the Time of Utterance which has not obtained. No indication of the presence of a Topic Time is made.

5.3 Semantic decomposition of *fu*

In (2), which is repeated below as (39), we are interested in the embedded clause *fu* i gó (='for you to go'). It expresses the desire of the speaker and has an irrealis interpretation, i.e. the eventuality has not occurred (yet) at the time of utterance.

(39) Mi ké fu i gó.
1SG want FU 2SG go
'I want for you to go'.

Recall that Topic Time provides the time span for which an assertion holds, while Assertion determines the illocutionary force of a sentence. Structurally a sentence consists of a Topic Component (which specifies the eventuality, components are Topic Time, Topic Entity, Topic World), a Sentence Base (which host the non-finite elements and it conveys the content of the Assertion, i.e. the eventuality) and a Finiteness element (which relates the Sentence Base to the Topic Component).

The Topic Component of (39) is filled by the second person pronoun *i* (=Topic Entity) while the Topic Component is not filled by a Topic Time. This latter fact is crucial for our semantic analysis. The embedded clause makes no assertion that the eventuality *gó* has obtained at a Topic Time. The lack of a Topic Time indicates that the eventuality cannot be linked to a time span for which the Assertion of the eventuality holds. Therefore, we argue that the embedded clause in (39) does not carry the features Topic Time and Assertion, and is thus non-finite.

5.4 Syntactic decomposition of *fu*

As for the syntactic position of complementizer *fu*, there are two existing proposals in the literature, Damonte (2002) and Aboh (2006). Both assume a cartographic approach to the C-domain (in the sense of Rizzi 1997; Cinque 1999). According to this approach, the C-domain is split into (minimally) the following positions:

(40) [CP Force Top Foc Fin [IP]]

Damonte argues that complementizer *fu* is base-generated in the lower C-domain and that it occupies the Fin-position. Aboh, on the other hand, claims that there are two *fu* complementizers: (1) '*deontic modal particle*' which is situated in the Fin-position

(FU_2 in Aboh's terminology)[13] and (2) '*irrealis complementizer*' which is situated in the Force-position (FU_1 in Aboh's terminology).

We follow Damonte's (2002) analysis in positing that there is only one complementizer *fu*. We propose that the complementizer *fu* is base-generated in a position between the Force- and Fin-position. This calls for a richer lower C-Domain than previously assumed in the literature.

Both Aboh's and Damonte's proposals account for the complementizer use of *fu*, but they situate *fu* in different positions: Force and Fin respectively. We can rule out the high position for *fu*, as in Aboh's (2006) proposal, on the ground that it can co-occur with complementizer *taá*, which according to both Aboh and Damonte occupies Force. All our consultants accept the following examples. Please note that none of our consultants have the modal use of *fu*, i.e. FU_2, in their grammar and therefore only complementizer *fu*.

(41) I táki táa fu a náki dí dágu.
3SG say TAA FU 3SG hit DET dog
'You told him to hit the dog' (Veenstra, 1996, 116).

Interestingly, even some speakers consulted by Aboh (2006) allow for such examples. In these examples his informants do not assign a deontic interpretation to *fu*. If they would assign this interpretation to the morpheme, this would be an indication that FU_2 is involved. As Aboh (2006, 31) notes, '[t]he star in between parentheses indicates that certain speakers disallow these constructions with the given interpretation'. Instead, one speaker volunteered (43) to convey a deontic interpretation.

(42) Mi táki táa fu Amato nján dí bakúba.
1SG say TAA FU Amato eat DET banana
(*) 'I said that Amato should eat the banana'.
'I told Amato to eat the banana' (Aboh, 2006, 31).

(43) Mi táki táa fu Amato musu nján dí bakúba.
1SG say TAA FU Amato MOD eat DET banana
'I said that Amato must eat the banana' (Aboh, 2006, 31).

The deontic interpretation of (43) is due to the necessity modal *musu*, and not to *fu*. Our interpretation of this fact is that in (42) and (43) are dealing with the irrealis

13. As discussed in Section 2, the modal use of *fu*, i.e. FU_2, is highly debatable. The consultants we worked with all reject this use of *fu*. Since further research is necessary to establish whether these differences in grammatical judgments are the result of several Saamáka varieties or due to different fieldwork settings and techniques, we, for the moment, assume that our consultants have a grammar without FU_2. This means that there is only one *fu* which functions as an irrealis complementizer

complementizer *fu* (and not with FU$_2$, the deontic modal particle, as Aboh analyses it). The conclusion, therefore, is that since *fu* can co-occur with complementizer *táa,* it cannot be situated in the Force-position. The analysis of Damonte (2002) accounts for the distribution of *fu* much better. He demonstrates that even though *táa* and *fu* precede the subject, focused elements may precede *fu*, as illustrated (44), but not complementizer *táa*, as illustrated in (45).

(44) A ké [a mátu] fu a kísi dí ogífou.
3SG want LOC jungle FU 3SG catch DET owl
'He wants him to catch the owl IN THE JUNGLE (Byrne, 1987, 138).

(45a) A táki táa [a dí kéiki] di mujée bì gó.
3SG say TAA LOC DET church DET woman PST go
'He said that the woman had gone TO THE CHURCH' (Byrne, 1987, 149).

(45b) *A táki [a dí kéiki] táa dí mujée bì gó.
3SG say LOC DET church TAA DET woman PST go
(Byrne, 1987, 149)

These facts follow if *táa* is situated in Force and *fu* in Fin, but, as Aboh observes, focused elements can precede as well as follow complementizer *fu*. The relevant data are presented in (2) which is repeated as (46).

(46a) Amato ké fu [a mátu] Ajawa kísi dí ogífou.
Amato want FU LOC jungle Ajawa catch DET owl
'Amato wants Ajawa to catch the owl IN THE JUNGLE' (Aboh, 2006, 35).

(46b) Amato ké [a mátu] fu Ajawa kísi dí ogífou.
Amato want LOC jungle FU Ajawa catch DET owl
'Amato wants Ajawa to catch the owl IN THE JUNGLE' (Aboh, 2006, 35).

Aboh notes that two of his consultants consider (46a) marginal and prefer (46b). Our consultants also allow for both orders, as illustrated in (6) which is repeated as (47).

(47) Senni$_i$ ta pakiséi fu [Freddy$_j$ hén] kíi dí ganía.
Senni IMP consider FU Freddy 3SG kill DET chicken
'Senni is considering that Freddy, he should kill the chicken (but he hasn't done it (yet))'.

We take this to mean that *fu* is not base-generated in the lowest position in the C- domain. This tallies nicely with our proposal in Section 5.2.1 that it is the temporal pronominal *bì* that occupies the lowest C-position. In the proposals of both Damonte and Aboh, this lowest position is the Fin-head. We want to maintain the analysis that *fu* is situated in some Fin-related position. We, therefore, propose to split up the Fin-position. The two Fin-positions in our proposal have different properties. The lower Fin-position is (directly) anchored to TP (in the sense of Bianchi 2003; Giorgi 2006).

In this position, *bì*, which is a temporal pronominal and establishes an Anchor Time, is merged. The higher Fin-position is a non-anchoring position where complementizer *fu* is situated. In between these two Fin-positions, focused elements can occur, just as between the higher Fin-position and Force (this can account for examples (46) and (47)). The lower Fin-position is the lowest head position in the C-domain. Thus, the syntax of *fu*-clauses in Saamáka points towards a richer lower C-Domain than previously assumed in the literature.

6. Summary

The aim of this paper was to establish whether Saamáka has non-finite clauses. We adopted a Klein (1998, 2006, 2009) style analysis of finiteness. Klein argues that a finite verb carries the features Assertion and Topic Time. This paper discussed clauses embedded under complementizer *fu*. Following Klein's characteristics, we postulated that *fu*-clauses lack the features Assertion and Topic Time and are, thus, non-finite. This is contra Bickerton (1981, 1984) and Byrne (1987) who have argued that Saamáka lacks complementizers and that all clauses are finite.

Secondly, we postulated that complementizer *fu* is situated under Fin (see also Damonte 2002). Temporal pronominal *bì* is also located in Fin. Since *fu* and *bì* can co-occur, i.e. are not mutually exclusive, they cannot be situated under the same functional head. Their semantic characteristics are also quite different. This would make it illogical for them to be situated under the same functional head. *Fu* has the features [-AST] and [-TT], whereas *bì* is neutral towards these features i.e. [±AST] and [±TT]. Secondly, *bì* establishes an Anchor Time, while *fu* does not establish an anchor. As a consequence, we argue for a more elaborate C-domain than previously assumed in the literature; one which hosts two Fin heads: one for *fu* and one for *bì*.

This paper has demonstrated the importance of semantic analyses for a cartographic approach to language structure. Additionally, the data presented in this paper suggests that more cross-linguistic research is necessary in order to establish the semantic characteristics of elements located in the C-domain.

References

Aboh, Enoch, 2006. Complementation in Saramaccan and Gungbe: The case of C-type particles. *Natural Language & Linguistic Theory* 24: 1–55. doi:10.1007/s11049-005-1815-4

Aboh, Enoch, Smith, Norval S.H. & Veenstra, Tonjes. 2013. Saramaccan. In *Atlas of Pidgin and Creole language structure*, Martin Haspelmath, Magnus Huber, Philippe Maurer & Susanne Michaelis (eds.), 27–38. Oxford: OUP.

Bach, Emmon. 1986. The algebra of events. *Linguistics and Philosophy* 9: 5–16.

Becker, Angelika. 2005. The semantic knowledge base for the acquisition of negation and the acquisition of finiteness. In *The Structure of Learner Varieties*, Henriëtte Henriks (ed.), 263–314. Berlin: Mouton de Gruyter. doi:10.1515/9783110909593.263

Bianchi, Valentina. 2003. On finiteness as logophoric anchoring. In *Temps et point de vue*, Jacqueline Gúeron & Liliane Tasmowski (eds.), 213–246. Nanterre: Université Paris X.

Bickerton, Derek. 1981. *Roots of Language*. Ann Arbor MI: Karoma Publishers.

Bickerton, Derek. 1984. The Language Bioprogram Hypothesis. *The Behavioral and Brain Sciences 7*: 173–188. doi:10.1017/S0140525X00044149

Byrne, Francis. 1987. *Grammatical Relations in a Radical Creole. Verb Complementation in Saramaccan* [Creole Language Library 3]. Amsterdam: John Benjamins. doi:10.1075/cll.3

Cinque, Guglielmo. 1999. *Adverbs and Functional Heads: A Cross-linguistic Perspective*. Oxford: OUP.

Damonte, Federico. 2002. The complementizer layer in Saramaccan. In *Current Issues in Generative Grammar. 10th Colloquium on Generative Grammar, Selected Papers*, Manuel Leonetti, Olga Fernadez Soriano & Victoria Escandell Vidal (eds.), 31–50. Alcalá de Henares: Universidad Alcalá de Henares.

Demirdache, Hamida & Uribe-Etxebarria, Myriam. 2000. The primitives of temporal relations. In *Step by step: Essays on Minimalist Syntax in Honor of Howard Lasnik*, Roger Martin, David Michaels & Juan Uriagereka (eds.), 157–186. Cambridge MA: The MIT Press.

Duffield, Nigel. 2007. Aspects of Vietnamese clausal structure: Separating tense from assertion. *Linguistics* 45: 765–814. doi:10.1515/LING.2007.023

Enç Mürvet. 1987. Anchoring conditions for Tense. *Linguistic Inquiry* 18(4): 633- 657.

Enç, Mürvet. 2004. Rethinking past tense. In *The Syntax of Time*, Jacqueline Guéron & Jacqueline Lecarme (eds.), 203–215. Cambridge MA: The MIT Press.

Giorgi, Alessandra. 2006. From temporal anchoring to long distance anaphors. *Natural Language & Linguistic Theory* 24: 1009–1047. doi:10.1007/s11049-006-9004-7

Iatridou, Sabine. 2000. The grammatical ingredients of counterfactuality. *Linguistic Inquiry* 31: 231–270. doi:10.1162/002438900554352

Klein, Wolfgang. 1992. The present perfect puzzle. *Language* 68: 525–552. doi:10.2307/415793

Klein, Wolfgang. 1994. *Time in Language*. London: Routledge.

Klein, Wolfgang. 1998. Assertion and finiteness. In *Issues in the Theory of Language Acquisition*, Norbert Dittmar & Zvi Penner (eds.), 225–245. Bern: Peter Lang.

Klein, Wolfgang. 2006. On finiteness. In *Semantics in Acquisition*, Veerle van Geenhoven (ed.), 245–272. Dordrecht: Springer. doi:10.1007/1-4020-4485-2_10

Klein, Wolfgang. 2009. Finiteness, universal grammar and the language faculty. In *Crosslinguistic Approaches to the Psychology of Language: Research in the Tradition of Dan Isaac Slobin*, Jinsheng Guo, Elena Lieven, Nancy Budwig, Susan Ervin-Tripp, Keiko Nakamura & Seyda Ozcaliskan (eds.), 333–344. New York NY: Psychology Press.

Kratzer, Angelika. 1998. More structural analogies between pronouns and tenses. In *Proceedings of SALT VIII*. Cambridge MA: MIT.

Lefebvre, Claire & Loranger, Virginie. 2006. On the properties of Saramaccan FU: Synchronic and diachronic perspectives. *Journal of Pidgin and Creole Studies* 21: 275–335. doi:10.1075/jpcl.21.2.02lef

Lefebvre, Claire & Loranger, Virginie. 2008. A synchronic and diachronic account of the multifunctionality of Saramaccan taá. *Linguistics* 46: 1167–1228. doi:10.1515/LING.2008.037

McWhorter, John. 1997. *Towards a New Model of Creole Genesis*. Bern: Peter Lang.

Mufwene, Salikoko & Dijkhoff, Marta. 1989. On the so-called 'infinitive' in Atlantic Creoles. *Lingua* 77: 297–330. doi:10.1016/0024-3841(89)90043-0

Partee, Barbara. 1984. Nominal and temporal anaphora. *Linguistics and Philosophy* 7: 243–286. doi:10.1007/BF00627707

Price, Richard. 1983. *First time*. Baltimore MD: John Hopkins University Press.

Rizzi, Luigi. 1997. The fine structure of the left periphery. In *Elements of Grammar*, Liliane Haegeman (ed.), 281–337. Dordrecht: Kluwer. doi:10.1007/978-94-011-5420-8_7

Smith, Norval. 1987. The Genesis of the Creole Languages of Suriname. Ph.D. dissertation, University of Amsterdam.

Stowell, Tim. 1996. The phrase structure of tense. In *Phrase Structure and the Lexicon*, Johan Rooryck & Laurie Ann Zaring (eds.), 277–292. Dordrecht: Kluwer. doi:10.1007/978-94-015-8617-7_10

van de Vate, Marleen Susanne. 2011. Tense, Aspect and Modality in a Radical Creole: The Case of Saamáka. Ph.D. dissertation, University of Tromsø.

van de Vate, Marleen Susanne. 2013a. An account of the stative vs. dynamic split in Saamáka. *Lingua* 129: 129–149. doi:10.1016/j.lingua.2012.07.004

van de Vate, Marleen Susanne. 2013b. To bi or not to bi: A pronominal analysis for past. *Journal of Portuguese Linguistics* 12(1): 63–82.

Veenstra, Tonjes. 1996. *Serial Verbs in Saramaccan. Predication and Creole Genesis*. The Hague: HAG.

Veenstra, Tonjes. 2008. Relexification and reconstitution of predicate classes: The case of sentence-embedding. Paper presented at *Syntax under Lexical Rule*. Berlin: ZAS.

Finiteness and response particles in West Flemish

Liliane Haegeman[1,2] & Andrew Weir[3]
[1]Ghent University / [2]FWO Odysseus / [3]NTNU Norwegian University of Science and Technology*

The empirical focus of the chapter is the morphosyntax of the morphologically marked response particles *ja* and *neen* in the Lapscheure dialect of West Flemish. Building on Krifka (2013)'s analysis of the corresponding German response particles *ja/nein* as TP pro-forms, we analyze morphologically marked Flemish *ja/neen* as TP pro-forms. First we show that the morphological marking on these particles is *sui generis*: it does not correspond to the marking found on verbs nor does it correspond to a clitic form of the subject pronoun. We develop a cartographic analysis of the syntax of the morphologically marked response particles in the dialect, endorsing Rizzi and Shlonsky (2006, 2007)'s proposal that a finite TP is dominated by a specialized projection for the subject, SubjP, a criterial projection. The pronominal marking on *ja/neen* is an instantiation of finiteness. If all finite clauses have SubjP then the finite TP pro-form realized by morphologically marked *ja/neen* is also dominated by (the criterial) SubjP. In the absence of an overt subject, following Rizzi and Shlonsky (2006, 2007), we assume that the Subject Criterion is satisfied by nominal φ-features generated on Fin and that morphologically marked *ja/neen* moves to Fin in order to license these features. Our analysis predicts that West Flemish morphologically marked *ja/neen* are a root phenomenon. In addition to the variant with pronominal marking, there is also a bare variant of the *ja/neen* pro-forms. The presence and absence of the pronominal marking on *ja/neen* correlates fairly closely with the distribution of finite and non-finite clauses, and we correlate the presence vs. absence of pronominal marking with a finiteness opposition.

Keywords: West Flemish; *yes/no*; pronominal marking; pro-form; cartography; SubjP; subject criterion; FinP; root phenomenon

* This research is funded by FWO Belgium as part of project 2009-Odysseus-Haegeman-G091409. We thank the audience at the 29th Comparative Germanic Syntax Workshop and at the SynCart seminar in Geneva on 5 February 2015 for their comments.

DOI 10.1075/la.231.08hae

1. Introduction: The domain of finiteness

The literature on morphological finiteness is generally focussed on finiteness encoding on verbal elements, where verbs (both lexical verbs and auxiliaries) are taken to come in finite and non-finite varieties. Finiteness has also been shown to impact on the morphology of subject pronouns: specifically nominative case is often related to finiteness (but see Mensching 2000; Szabolcsi 2005; Eide 2009; Cowper this volume, among many others). Recently, for instance, Cowper (this volume) reaches the following conclusion: "the traditional understanding of finiteness, namely that it consists of the ability to assign structural (nominative) case to a subject, and the possibility of having φ-feature agreement encoded on the verb, is essentially correct." (Cowper this volume: 74). Finiteness has also been related to the functional architecture of the clause, with proposals that it is encoded in FinP, the lowest functional projection of the articulated CP (Rizzi 1997; Adger 2007).

Less attention has so far been paid to the fact that constituents which are at first sight not verbal in nature may also appear to come in finite vs. non-finite variants. One case in point is the response particles *yes/no* in some Flemish dialects of Dutch. In many Flemish dialects these particles display what looks like verbal agreement marking and combine with what looks like a nominative subject clitic, which seems to suggest that finiteness can be encoded outside the 'verbal domain'. In these dialects, the morphological marking on the response particles is that associated with the verbal domain. However, there are also dialects in which the pronominal marking on the particles is *sui generis*. The Lapscheure dialect of West Flemish is one case in point: response particles come in two forms, morphologically marked response particles and their bare alternatives. This paper proposes an analysis of this morphological marking in terms of finiteness. One significant ingredient of our analysis will be the claim that the morphological marking on the response particles cannot be equated to other manifestations of finiteness in the dialect. Our conclusion on the nature of the morphological marking on the Lapscheure response particles departs significantly from the existing literature on morphologically marked response particles in other Flemish dialects. However, in spite of the fact that the marking in the Lapscheure dialect is not isomorphic to that found in the verbal domain, the pronominal marking does reflect finiteness restrictions: the bare forms are restricted to what would be non-finite domains, while the marked forms pattern with finite root clauses. The precise implementation of our analysis also leads to the conclusion that finiteness and (nominative) case marking are not intrinsically linked.

The focus of the paper is the morphologically marked response particles *ja* and *neen* in the Lapscheure dialect. Building on Krifka (2013)'s analysis of the German response particles *ja/nein* as TP pro-forms, we analyze the Flemish response particles as TP pro-forms. We develop a cartographic analysis of the syntax of the morphologically marked response particles, in which a crucial role is played by the functional projection SubjP and the associated Subject Criterion (Rizzi & Shlonsky 2006, 2007).

We also show that the presence and absence of the morphological marking on *ja/neen* correlates closely with the distribution of finite and non-finite clauses, and we propose that the presence or absence of morphological marking is therefore to be understood in terms of a finiteness opposition. Though space prevents us from going into this point in detail, closer examination of the 'non-finite' variant of *ja/neen* will provide support for the hypothesis that non-finite infinitival clauses do not constitute one homogeneous class (see a.o. Landau 2004; Wurmbrand 2014 for recent discussion).

1.1 The empirical data: Finite response particles

Response particles in the Lapscheure dialect of West Flemish show morphological marking which at first sight looks like pronominal marking. In (1a), for instance, the response particle *ja* has an ending *-k* which, as shown by the gloss, corresponds to the first person, while in (1b) the particle is accompanied by *-g*, which corresponds to the second person. These endings are also found on the response particle *nee.*

(1) a. Q: Oa-j gelyk?
Had-you right?
'Were you right?'
A: Ja-k. /Nee-k.
Yes-I/No-I [Lapscheure]

b. Q: Oan-k gelyk?
Had-I right?
'Was I right?'
A: Ja-g. /Nee-g.
Yes-you/No-you [Lapscheure]

Morphological marking on response particles is found in many Flemish dialects of Dutch, although with considerable dialectal variation; see Paardekooper (1993), Barbiers, Bennis, De Vogelaer, Devos & van der Ham (2005) and De Vogelaer and van der Auwera (2010) for a survey of the variation and for references. We concentrate on the Lapscheure dialect, but where relevant we will point out differences with other dialects. Though there is some literature on the specific forms and possible derivations of the response particles with pronominal marking, virtually no attention has been paid to the fact that the dialects in question also have bare response particles, lacking pronominal marking. One attested example is (2), and this pattern would also be licit in the dialect we are focussing on here:

(2) A: Boer, ga je der weer uitvallen, de?
Farmer, go you there again out drop, PRT?
'Are you going to quit again?'

B: k zeggen: "Kgeloven van ja."
I say: "I believe of *ja*"
(UGhent, Dialect recording Oostkerke 29.12.66)

The forms with pronominal marking and those without are in near-complementary distribution. Whilst in cases like (1) the bare form of the particle *ja* is possible, it is a *non sequitur. Ja* in (3) is not a polarity reply but would convey something like 'I can understand you', and is perhaps to be compared to English 'okay' (see also Krifka 2013); witness the fact that it does not alternate with a bare form of *nee*. On the other hand, as shown in (4), a variant of (2), the bare forms *ja* and *nee* do not alternate with a form with pronominal marking, even though they do function as a polarity response:

(3) a. Q: Oa-j gelyk?
Had-you right?
'Were you right?'
A: #Ja./*Nee.
Yes /No [Lapscheure]
b. Q: Oan-k gelyk?
Had-I right?
'Was I right?'
A: #Ja./*Nee.
Yes /No. [Lapscheure]

(4) A: Ga je der weer uitvallen, de?
Go you there again out drop, PRT?
B: *Kgeloven van ja-k/ nee-k.
I.believe of yes-I/ no-I

Observe that the preposition *van* can also introduce non-finite clauses, as illustrated in (5):

(5) kpeinzen van em doa te zien
I.think of him there to see
'I expect to see him there.'

There therefore appears to be a correlation between the distribution of 'bare' *ja/neen* and non-finite clauses, and pronominally marked *ja/nee* and finite clauses, respectively. We will therefore propose that the presence/absence of the pronominal marking on the response particles correlates with finiteness, and we will provide an account for the distribution of the morphologically marked forms of the response particles and their unmarked counterparts.

In the course of the elaboration of the analysis of the morphologically marked particles, we will also turn to the properties of 'reversal' answers. In the dialect, a response particle which 'reverses' a declarative statement bears the pronominal marking but in addition it bears extra morphology, instantiated by a schwa, which we will refer to as 'reversal schwa'. This is illustrated in (6): while the 'agreeing' response whose polarity is the same as that of the declarative is *ja-s*, with third person feminine marking, a response that reverses the polarity of the positive 'antecedent' clause must be expressed by *nee-s-e*, which has third person feminine marking as well as the extra schwa. With a positive antecedent, the reversal schwa does not occur in an agreeing response with the particle *ja* and is obligatory in a disagreeing response with the particle *neen*. With a negative antecedent, reversal or disagreement is expressed by the reversal schwa on *ja*, and in an agreeing response the particle *nee* is incompatible with the reversal schwa. The relevant pattern is illustrated in (6) and (7). For completeness' sake, note also that bare *ja/neen* are also unavailable in these contexts.[1] Overt marking of reversal by *-e* is only generally available in response to statements (with declarative word order) (Devos & Vandekerkhove 2005).

(6) Marie goa morgent kommen.
Marie goes tomorrow come
'Marie will come tomorrow.'

A_{SAME}: Ja-s.
yes-3SG.F
'yes she will.'

A_{SAME}: *Ja-s-e.
yes-3SG.F-RVRS

A_{SAME}: *Ja.

$A_{REVERSE}$: *Nee-s.
no-3SG.F

$A_{REVERSE}$: Nee-s-e.
no-3SG.F-RVRS
'No she won't.'

$A_{REVERSE}$: *Neen.

(7) Marie goa morgent niet kommen.
Marie goes tomorrow not come
'Marie won't come tomorrow.'

A_{SAME}: Nee-s.
no-3SG.F

1. This is a simplification: as discussed above, *ja* is licit to indicate that the speaker has heard the statement, but it cannot function as a polarity response particle.

A_{SAME}: *Nee-s-e.
no-3SG.F-RVRS
'No she won't.'

A_{SAME}: *Ja.

$A_{REVERSE}$: *Ja-s.
yes-3SG.F
'yes she will.'

$A_{REVERSE}$: Ja-s-e.
yes-3SG.F-RVRS

$A_{REVERSE}$: *Neen.

Though they have been signalled occasionally (De Vogelaer 2005; Barbiers et al. 2005; Devos 1986; Devos & Vandekerckhove 2005), to the best of our knowledge the Flemish reversal forms have not been analyzed in detail in the literature.

1.2 Aim and scope of the paper

Our paper has a number of different goals. A first goal is that of documentation: we will provide a detailed survey of the morphology and distribution of the response particles, and we will inventorize the contexts in which the morphologically marked and the bare varieties of *ja/nee* can occur. The latter point has, as far as we know, not been systematically undertaken in the literature. A second goal is to provide a syntactic analysis for the distribution of the morphologically marked and the bare (i.e. non-morphologically marked) particles. Though these particles constitute one word utterances, we will argue that they have the syntax of full clauses.

Response particles such as German *ja/nein* have been independently argued to be TP pro-forms (e.g. Krifka 2013). We will show that West Flemish *ja/nee* are also amenable to such an analysis. But we also argue that, as full TPs show a finite/non-finite opposition, so too should TP pro-forms. We will argue that the presence or absence of pronominal marking on *ja/nee* represents a finiteness opposition: TP pro-forms can be finite or nonfinite, with pronominal marking appearing only on the finite forms.

To implement our analysis of the pronominal marking on the TP pro-forms, we will adopt the cartographic approach to clause structure, and in particular the assumption that finiteness is encoded syntactically in a designated left peripheral head (see Rizzi 1997) and the assumption that the canonical subject position of finite clauses is to be set apart from the specifier of TP. We will argue that morphologically marked *ja/nee* bear agreement morphology and move to Fin in order to license the presence of φ-features on Fin which are required to satisfy the Subject Criterion (Rizzi 2006; Rizzi & Shlonsky 2007).

1.3 Organization of the paper

The paper is organized as follows: Section 2 presents the data on the form and distribution of morphologically marked and bare response particles in the Lapscheure dialect. Section 3 argues against accounts of the morphological marking on *ja/nee* in terms of PF ellipsis or invoking null TP pro-forms and presents the ingredients of the analysis to be pursued here, notably Krifka's proposal that response particles be seen as TP pro-forms. This section also presents arguments against analyzing the pronominal marking on *ja/neen* as a manifestation of (enclitic) subject pronouns. Section 4 presents the syntax of morphologically marked response particles, showing that they pattern distributionally with root V2 clauses, whose derivation they also largely mirror. The account is framed in the cartographic approach (Rizzi 1997) and makes crucial use of Rizzi's SubjectP (Rizzi 2006) and of Rizzi and Shlonsky's (2006, 2007) hypotheses about the role of FinP in facilitating subject extraction. Section 5 turns to the distribution of bare response particles and relates the opposition between morphologically marked and bare particles to a finiteness opposition. The section also provides evidence for a non-unitary treatment of non-finite clauses. Section 6 is a summary of the paper.

2. The data

2.1 Response particles in Lapscheure West Flemish

In (1, 6, 7) we have illustrated morphological marking on the response particles for first, second and third person, i.e. with referential subjects. As shown in (8), the marking is also obligatory with non-referential subjects. (8a) illustrates the case of weather verbs: as can be seen the response particles also bear what looks like a pronominal form corresponding to the non-referential subject in the question. In (8b) we illustrate the existential pattern, with the non-referential subject clitic *der* in the canonical (postverbal) subject position of the *yes-no* question. In response particles, a non-referential *-t* ending shows up on the particle. We return to this form presently (Section 2.2). As before, the marking is obligatory: omission of the endings would render the responses in (8) ungrammatical.

(8) a. Q: Goa t morgent regenen?
Goes it tomorrow rain
'Will it rain tomorrow?'

A: Ja-t. / Nee-t.
yes-3SG no-3SG
'Yes (it will)/No (it won't).'

b. Q: Goa der morgent eentween kommen?
Goes there tomorrow someone come
'Will there be someone coming tomorrow?'

A: Ja-t. / Nee-t.
yes-3SG.EXPL no-3SG.EXPL
'Yes (there will)/No (there won't).'

In Table 1 we provide a survey of the finiteness paradigm for the response particles.[2]

Table 1. Finiteness morphology on response particles

PERSON/NMB	*Yes*	*No*
1SG	Ja-k	Nee-k
2SG	Ja-g	Nee-g
3SG MASC	Ja-j	Nee-j
3SG FEM	Ja-s	Nee-s
3SG NEUT	Ja-t	Nee-t
1PL	Ja-m	Nee-m
2PL	Ja-g	Nee-g
3PL	Ja-s	Nee-s

2.2 Morphological marking and subject clitics

A type of morphological marking on *yes/no* is common in many dialects of Dutch (Barbiers et al. 2005 and references cited), but its exact morphological status is not clear. The dialect survey in Barbiers et al. (2005), which is based on the questionnaires used to compile the *Syntactic Atlas of the Dutch Dialects* (SAND), shows a lot of variation in the form of the marking following *ja/nee* (2005: 53–5), and no fully clear generalization emerges.

> The clitics ... look like obvious reduced forms of the weak pronouns *'k, je, ie, ze, 't, we, je* and *ze* ('I, you, he, she, it, we, you and they' respectively), which are attested in Standard Dutch as well. But in many cases, it is not immediately clear what might be the nature of a certain pronoun following *ja* ('yes') or *nee* ('no'). (Barbiers et al. 2005: 53)

2. In isolation, *ja* is pronounced [ja]. When the pronominal marking is attached, regular phonological processes in West Flemish result in the pronunciation *joa* [jɔ:] e.g. *joa-k* [jɔ:k]. We continue to write *ja* for clarity.

In the Wambeek dialect investigated by van Craenenbroeck (2010), the response particles are associated with a pronominal element, which, according to van Craenenbroeck, is "identical to the clitic pronoun that is right-adjoined to the complementizer in embedded clauses" (van Craenenbroeck 2010: 217). The form of the clitic that is right-adjacent to the complementizer is also that found to the right of the finite verb in V2 clauses. We will come back to this point in Section 3.2.1, where we will illustrate the data. We will show that in the Lapscheure dialect under consideration here the morphological marking on the particles cannot be equated with the post-complementizer or post-V2 clitic.

For completeness' sake, we add that in other Flemish dialects, in addition to what looks like pronominal marking, *ja/nee* also carry what looks like verbal agreement (the same as that found on complementizers or on the finite verbs in Flemish dialects). This is illustrated in (9). The dialect we are focussing on does not display this agreement.

(9) a. A: Èèn Piet en Jan gewonnen?
have Pete and John won
B: Ja-n-s.
yes-AGR.PL-they$_{\text{CLITIC}}$

b. Kpeize da-n Piet en Jan gewonnen èèn.
I.think that-AGR.PL Pete and John won have
(van Craenenbroeck 2010: 217, Waregem Dutch)

c. Dat doet-n niet.
That does-he$_{\text{CLITIC}}$ not
'He doesn't do that.' (ex: van Craenenbroeck 2010: 142)

In the Lapscheure dialect, (i) there is no such verbal agreement on finite response particles, and (ii) the pronominal marking does not match perfectly with the clitics that appear to the right of verbs or complementizers (see esp. Devos 1986). In order to detect this we need to take a closer look at the forms of the clitic subject in the dialect of Lapscheure (see Haegeman 1990 for full description). In general, in the dialect we are describing, the post-V and post-C subject clitics look identical to the pronominal marking on *ja/neen*, as illustrated for the first person in (10); the first-person clitic and marking on *ja/neen* are in all cases realized as a velar voiceless stop [k], orthographically represented as ⟨k⟩. This form of the clitic is also found in a pre-verbal position.

(10) a. Toen een-k eur gezien. Post V: [k]
then have-I her seen

b. dan-k eur gezien eet Post C: [k]
that-I her seen have

c. Ja-k. Post *ja/nee*: [k]
Nee-k.

d. K'een eur gezien. Initial: [k]
I have her seen

Post-V and post-C clitics, however, are distinct from the second person singular and third person expletive marking on *ja/nee* (11) and (12). As seen in (11), the post-V/C second person clitic is realized as a palatal approximant, [j], represented orthographically as ⟨j⟩. The morphological marking on *ja/neen* is a voiceless velar fricative [x], which we represent orthographically as ⟨g⟩. The pronominal marking on *ja/neen* is similar to the pre-V/C form of the subject clitic, which is a voiced glottal approximant [ɦ], as shown in (11d).

(11)	a.	Toen ee-j/*g eur gezien. then have-you her seen	Post V: [j]
	b.	da-j/*g eur gezien eet that-you her seen have	Post C: [j]
	c.	Ja-g/*j. Nee-g/*j.	Post *ja/nee*: [x]
	d.	G/*j'eet eur gezien. you have her seen	Initial: [ɦ]

So, the pronominal marking on *ja/neen* in this dialect is different from that discussed by van Craenenbroeck for Wambeek Dutch and illustrated in Section 3.2.1. Rather than being like the post-V or post-C subject clitic, if anything, the morphological marking in the Lapscheure dialect is reminiscent of the preverbal one. The same is true for existential patterns already illustrated in (8) and repeated here in (12). In postverbal position and to the right of the complementizer, the expletive *der* is used. However, the pronominal marking on *ja/neen* takes the form *-t*. Again, this form is more like that in preverbal position, in which the expletive used in existential patterns is a clitic form of the third person neuter pronoun *t*,[3] similar to German *es*, used in the same position.

(12)	a.	Toen is ter/*t veel volk geweest. then is there/*it much people been 'that there were many people'	Post V: [dər/tər]
	b.	dat der/*t veel volk geweest is that there/*it much people been has 'that there were many people'	Post C: [dər/tər]
	c.	Joa-t/*der. Nee-t/*der.	Post *ja/nee*: [t]
	d.	T/*der is veel volk geweest. it/*there is much people been 'There was a large crowd.'	Initial: [t]

3. Note that while the pronominal marking on *ja/neen* probably has a diachronic relation with the pre-verbal clitic forms, our hypothesis is that synchronically they are not to be identified. See Section 3.4 and Haegeman & Weir (2015) for further discussion.

As illustrated above, the morphologically marked response particles can be used all by themselves as a response to a polarity question. The response particles can also be accompanied by a full clause, explicitizing the answer further, possibly providing additional information. If a full clause is used, subject marking is present on *ja/neen* and then the subject appears again in the main clause, whether as a subject pronoun (13a, c) or a full DP (13b). Observe that both the morphological marking on the particle *and* a second instantiation of the overt subject are obligatory. Utterances in which the subject is only expressed once, by the morphological marking on the subject in (13d), by the preverbal clitic subject in (13e) or by a full DP (13f) are all strongly ungrammatical.

(13) Q: Goa Marie morgent kommen?
Goes Marie tomorrow come
'Is Marie coming tomorrow?

a. A: Ja-s ze goat morgent kommen.
yes-3SG.F she goes tomorrow come

b. A: Ja-s Marie goat morgent kommen.
yes-3SG.F Marie goes tomorrow come

c. A: Ja-s morgent goa-ze kommen.
yes-3SG.F tomorrow goes=she come

d. A: *Ja-s goat morgent kommen.
yes-3SG.F goes tomorrow come

e. A: *Ja ze goat morgent kommen.
yes she goes tomorrow come

f. A: *Ja Marie goat morgent kommen.
yes Marie goes tomorrow come

In (13), the morphological marking *-s* on the response particle encodes third person feminine. On the basis of such data it might be concluded that the morphological marking on *ja/neen* always matches the features of the subject of the preceding *yes/no* question. For instance, in (13a) above the subject of the question is a third person feminine DP *Marie*, and the response particles are associated with the ending *-s*, corresponding to what seems like the clitic form of the third person pronoun *ze* ('she'). As can be seen in our first examples, though, this is, however, not quite an accurate characterization of the facts. The precise feature composition of the morphological marking is not determined by the subject of the *yes/no* question, but rather the morphological features are those of what would be the subject of the full answer to the *yes/no* question. In (1a) above, for instance, the subject of the polarity question is the second person, cf. the clitic *j* ('you') on the finite verb; the reply to this would have a first person subject, hence the response particle will be associated with a first person ending *-k*.

So far, the responses with finite *ja/neen* all had as their antecedents a root clause. For completeness' sake, note that morphological marking on *ja/neen* does not necessarily match the subject of a matrix antecedent. This is shown in (14). While the first reply (A1) targets the matrix polar question, the second reply (A2) targets the indirect polar question. The choice of either reply depends on what is 'at issue': the main clause ('do you know' in (14)) or the embedded clause. Depending on the target clause, the response particle gets the appropriate morphological marking.

(14) Q: Weet-je gie of da Valère a thus is?
know.2SG you if that Valère already home is
'Do you know if Valère is already home?'

A1: Ja-k./Nee-k.
yes-1SG/no-1SG
'I (don't) know.'

A2: Ja-j./Nee-j.
yes-3SG.M/no-3SG.M
'He is (not) home.'

2.3 Bare *ja/neen*

As already mentioned in relation to (1), bare *ja* without morphological marking is not as such ungrammatical in the dialect. It has a number of uses, which we will list here. As a reaction to a polar question, as for instance in (1), *ja* is basically a *non sequitur*; it is not a reply to the polar question, rather, it means something like 'I can hear you', 'I understand the question'. In this use, *ja* does not alternate with *neen* and the morphological marking on *ja* is ungrammatical. There are a number of other contexts in which bare *ja* does not function as a reply to a polar question and in which it does not alternate with bare *neen*. In these uses too morphological marking on *ja* is ungrammatical. Typical instances are answering the door, or responding to a call or an address, when the particle is used as an interjection similar in interpretation to 'well', in an agreement to a course of action, or as a response to an imperative. In the latter two uses, bare ja again corresponds to English *okay*.

(15) a Answering the door: Ja/*Ja-k/ *Neen/*Nee-k.

b. A: Marie!
B: Ja/*Ja-k/*Nee-(k).

c. Ja,/*Ja-k/*Nee-(k), wat moet ik nu zeggen?
JA/JA-1SG/Nee-1SG, what must I now say
'Well, what can I say to that?'

d. A: k'gaan t'achtnoene werekommen we!
I go in the afternoon back come PRT

B: 'kzeggen. "Ja, 't is goed 'e."
I say: JA it is good PRT
(Dialect recording Ghent University, Oostkerke 29.12.60)

e. Response to imperatives:
A: Pakt da mo mee.
Take that PRT with
R: Ja/??Ja-k.

We will set the above examples aside, since they do not involve a response to a polar question or to the polarity of a declarative antecedent and they could arguably involve an altogether different use of the particles. In a number of other contexts, however, both bare *ja* and bare *neen* can appear in responses to polar questions or to the content of declaratives and in these the morphological marking is ungrammatical. A first important restriction is that while, as we have shown, the response particles may take the polarity of an embedded clause as their antecedent (see (14)), *ja/neen*, marked or bare, cannot be embedded under complementizers like *dat* which introduce finite clauses. This is shown in (16).[4]

(16) A: Is Valère geweest?
is V. been
'Has Valère been?'
B: *Kpeinzen dat ja/ja-j.
I.think that yes/yes-3SG.M
intended: 'I think so.'

However, as we have already shown in examples (2) and (4), bare *ja/neen*, though not their morphologically marked counterparts, can (sometimes somewhat marginally) be embedded under *van*. Importantly, *van* can also introduce a non-finite clause in West Flemish, as was shown in (5) (on this use of *van* in Dutch and Flemish see van Craenenbroeck 2002; Hoeksema 2006, 2008).

(17) a. Ze peinst van ja/*ja-s.
she thinks of yes/yes-3SG.F
b. Ze peinst van neen/*nee-s.
she thinks of no/*no-3SG.F

Finally, bare *ja/neen* – but not morphologically marked *ja/neen* – also appear under *van* in construction with motion verbs such *knikken* 'nod' and *schudden* 'shake', *gebaren* 'gesture', *teken doen* 'gesture'.

(18) a. Ze knikte van ja/*ja-s.
she nodded of yes/yes-3SG.F
'She nodded her head yes.'

4. For a discussion of cross-linguistic variation in the embeddability of *yes/no* see Authier (2013: 347–8) and the references cited there.

b. Ze schudde van neen/*nee-s.
she shook of no/*no-3sg.f
'She shook her head no.'

c. Ze gebaarde van ja/neen/*ja-s/*nee-s.
she gestured of yes/no/yes-3sg.f/no-3sg.f

d. Ze deed teken van ja/neen/*ja-s/*nee-s.
she made sign of yes/no/yes-3sg.f/no-3sg.f

What emerges from the inventory above is that, if we put the non-polarity use of root *ja* aside, morphologically marked and bare *ja/neen* are in strict complementary distribution, very much as would be the case with finite/non-finite forms of a verb. In contexts where morphologically marked *ja/neen* is possible, it is obligatory; in contexts where bare *ja/neen* is possible, the morphologically marked variant is excluded. Neither form is available in finite embedded clauses.

For completeness sake, we add that the reversal schwa (*ja-s-e/nee-s-e*) only occurs with morphologically marked *ja/neen*; there is no bare counterpart of reversal particles.

3. The ingredients of the analysis

From the discussion in the preceding sections we retain that morphologically marked and bare *ja/neen* are in complementary distribution, and that their distribution correlates with finiteness. The reversal variants of *ja/neen* are morphologically marked and we will develop a syntactic account of reversal *ja/neen* built on the account for morphologically marked *ja/neen*. Henceforth, when we refer to morphologically marked *ja/neen* this will include reversal *ja/neen*.

One point emerging quite clearly is that while interpretively *ja/neen* may target the polarity of embedded antecedent propositions (14), the morphologically marked variants of *ja/neen* themselves are not embeddable. Even though descriptively they consist of just one word, then, morphologically marked *ja/neen* have the distribution of root clauses. In this respect morphologically marked *ja/neen* align not just with finite clauses per se, but with finite V2 clauses which in the West Flemish (WF) dialect are not embeddable. In our account the syntax of morphologically marked *ja/neen* will be assimilated to that of V2 root clauses. Before examining the distribution of morphologically marked and bare *ja/neen*, we provide an account of the nature of the pronominal marking on morphologically marked *ja/neen*. We first consider some possible accounts that we believe do not capture the relevant data, before turning to our own analysis.

3.1 Against a PF ellipsis account

In line with the recent literature on response particles (see e.g. Kramer & Rawlins (2011), Holmberg (2013) and Servidio (2014) a.o.) we might interpret the data in terms of an ellipsis account. Recall that superficially the morphological marking on the response particles in the dialect we are looking at is closely similar to the pre-verbal clitics in a V2 clause (cf. (10–12)). So one might envisage a derivation in which *ja/neen* are base generated in a relatively high left-peripheral position, say PolFocP, and are in construction with a full V2 clause with subsequent encliticization of a pre-verbal subject pronoun to *ja/neen*, and PF-deletion of the rest of the clause. Such an account is proposed in Devos (1986: 169) and a formal rendering of her proposal is represented very schematically in (19).

(19) Is Valère geweest? –[Ja-j$_1$ [$_{FinP}$ ⟨t$_1$ is geweest⟩]]
is Valère been yes-3SG.M is been
'Has Valère been? – Yes.'

This account would assimilate *ja/neen* responses to analyses of fragment answers (Merchant 2004) as in (20a) or sluicing (Merchant 2001) as in (20b), both of which are derived by PF-deletion of a clause.

(20) a. What did John eat? – Chips ⟨he ate t⟩.
b. John ate something, but I don't know what ⟨he ate t⟩.

van Craenenbroeck (2010) provides a number of arguments against a straightforward clausal PF-deletion analysis of polarity particles, at least for Flemish morphologically marked *ja/neen*. Further arguments are given in Haegeman and Weir (2015). For reasons of space, we will only point out some of these arguments here and we refer the interested reader to the literature. One argument against the PF-deletion approach is that it is usually optional, as shown for sluicing in (21):

(21) John ate something, but I don't know what he ate.

However, the absence of clausemate material is never optional for morphologically marked *ja/neen*. The purported overt source for the structure proposed in (19), given in (22a), would be ungrammatical.

(22) a. Is Valère geweest? – *Ja-j is geweest.

Rather the overt version would be as in (22b) or (22c), with an intonation break between the morphologically marked *ja/neen* and the following full V2 clause:

(22) b. Ja-j, j'is geweest.
c. Ja-j, Valère is geweest.

As already suggested by the intonation break, these examples look like two separate root clauses: in WF root clauses a preverbal clitic never co-occurs with a second preverbal clitic, with a preverbal strong pronoun or with a preverbal full DP:

(22) d. *Je je is geweest.
e. *Je jij is geweest.
f. *Je Valère is geweest.

If the presence of the morphological marking on *ja-j* is taken to suggest that there is some form of clausal structure here, it must be the case then that this clausal structure is *obligatorily* silent. This would require at least a modification of a simple PF deletion account.

We also note that in patterns which are less controversially analyzed as PF-deletion, such as sluicing, there is no morphological marking in the relevant dialects (as discussed by van Craenenbroeck (2010: 231); see also Lobeck (1995) and Merchant (2001)).

(23) Z'èèn eentwien gezien, maar k'en weten nie wien(*s).
they.have someone seen but I.NEG know not who(-they$_{\text{CLITIC}}$)
[Lapscheure]

It does not seem to generally be the case, then, that subject marking/subject clitics can 'survive' PF-deletion of a clause in the way that an ellipsis analysis would suggest. This is also true in a case where a fragment answer answers a polar question, e.g.

(24) Q: Ee-g genoeg geld?
have.you enough money?
A: Misschienst(*-k).
possibly(-1SG)

These data suggest that morphologically marked *ja/neen* are to be treated as separate from fragment answers or regular instances of PF ellipsis such as sluicing.

3.2 A TP pro-form

3.2.1 *Morphologically marked* ja/neen *in Wambeek Dutch*

In the Wambeek dialect, investigated by van Craenenbroeck (2010), the response particles are associated with morphological marking. This marking is illustrated in *jo-n* in (25a). The third person masculine marking *-n* on *jo* ('yes') is "identical to the clitic pronoun that is right-adjoined to the complementizer in embedded clauses" (van Craenenbroeck 2010: 217), as illustrated in (25b). The form of the clitic that is right-adjacent to the complementizer is also that found to the right of the finite verb in V2 clauses as shown in (25c).

(25) a. A: Kom Jef mergen?
comes Jeff tomorrow
'Is Jeff coming tomorrow?'

B: Jo-n.
yes-he$_{\text{CLITIC}}$

b. Ik paus dat-n mergen komt.
I think that-he$_{\text{CLITIC}}$ tomorrow comes

c. Dat doet-n niet.
That does-he$_{\text{CLITIC}}$ not
'He doesn't do that.' (van Craenenbroeck 2010, 142)

In his analysis of the Wambeek Dutch morphologically marked response particles, van Craenenbroeck (2010) also argues against the PF-deletion approach. He proposes that morphologically marked *ja/neen* are base generated in the left periphery and that a null TP pro-form is dominated by an $\text{Agr}_\text{S}\text{P}$ projection, whose specifier is the subject clitic. This subject clitic right-adjoins to C in the same way that postverbal subject clitics adjoin to C or adjoin to the finite V in the V2 pattern.[5,6]

(26) (from van Craenenbroeck (2010)'s (23))

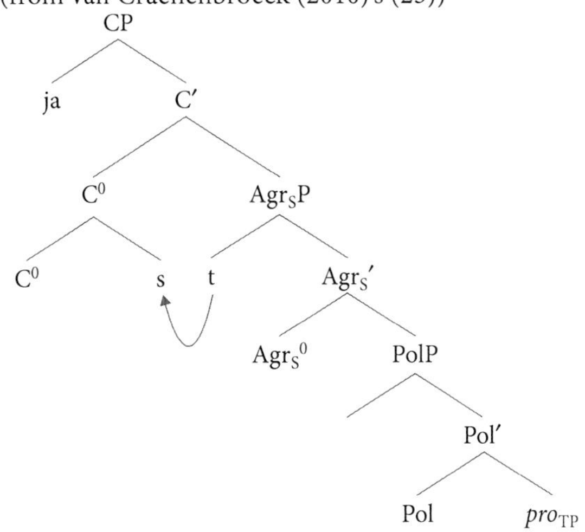

5. For more details on the motivation of the analysis as well as on its semantics, we refer to van Craenenbroeck's own work. van Craenenbroeck actually does assume PF-deletion of $\text{Agr}_\text{S}\text{P}$. This is (a) to ensure that no material which might be base-generated in Pol^0 (which immediately dominates the TP pro-form) or $\text{Agr}_\text{S}{}^0$ is pronounced, and (b) to license the TP pro-form, which would otherwise be ungoverned; PF-deletion is a form of 'rescue by ellipsis'. See van Craenenbroeck for full details. However, the silence of the TP part of the clause is derived by the use of a TP pro-form.

6. The TP pro-form analysis accounts for another difference between *ja/neen* and other forms of 'clausal silence' such as fragment answers and sluicing, namely that while the latter allow for extraction from the ellipsis site, extraction from what would be the ellipsis site is not available with finite *ja/neen*. See van Craenenbroeck (2010). This effect is also found in WF.

In the spirit of van Craenenbroeck's analysis, we endorse the idea that a TP pro-form is involved in morphologically marked *ja/neen* constructions. However, empirical differences between the morphological marking in *ja/neen* in the dialect we are investigating and that in the Wambeek dialect prevent us from fully adopting his analysis and we will therefore elaborate an alternative. For some conceptual objections to van Craenenbroeck's analysis we refer to Haegeman and Weir (2015).

For the Wambeek data, postulating that *ja* is in [Spec, C] and that the subject clitic right-adjoins to C correctly predicts that morphological marking on *ja/neen* is isomorphic with the form that shows up after complementizers, or after verbs in V2 position. However, as already discussed in Section 2.2, in the dialect we are concerned with, the morphological marking on the polarity particles does not always resemble the post-C/V form of the clitic (Devos 1986). We repeat some of the relevant data in (27); see also (11) and (12).

(27) a. da-j/*g eur gezien eet post-C: [j]
that-you her seen have

b. Ja-g/*j. post-*ja*: [x]

Note that since the TP pro-form in (26) is by hypothesis opaque, the subject clitics on *ja/neen* must originate TP-externally and for this reason van Craenenbroeck (2010) invokes a specialised projection, labelled Agr_SP, which hosts subject clitics. Because Agr_SP lacked a semantic reflex (Chomsky 1995: 349–355), its status in the theory was challenged, a point van Craenenbroeck acknowledges. He in fact suggests tentatively that the appearance of a subject clitic in this high position may perhaps be taken as empirical support for the existence of Agr_SP (2010: 249). We will endorse van Craenenbroeck's hypothesis that there is a dedicated projection for the subject but we will reinterpret it as Rizzi (2006)'s SubjP. However, differently from van Craenenbroeck, we do not assume that the morphological marking in *ja/neen* originates in SubjP.

3.3 Morphologically marked *ja/neen*, TP pro-forms and V2

Rather than postulating that morphologically marked *ja/neen* are merged in the CP area and are in construction with a null TP pro-form, we follow Krifka (2013)'s analysis of *ja/nein* in German and we propose that morphologically marked *ja/neen* themselves *are* the TP pro-forms. For a semantic analysis of this proposal we refer to Haegeman and Weir (2015). This hypothesis is schematically represented in (28): TP is realized as *ja/neen* (depending on polarity) and moves to a left-peripheral position. The fact that morphologically marked *ja/neen* cannot occur in construction with clausal material is explained: morphologically marked *ja/neen are* themselves the clauses, or more accurately, they are TP pro-forms. We discuss the landing site of *ja/neen* and the nature of the morphological marking below.

(28)

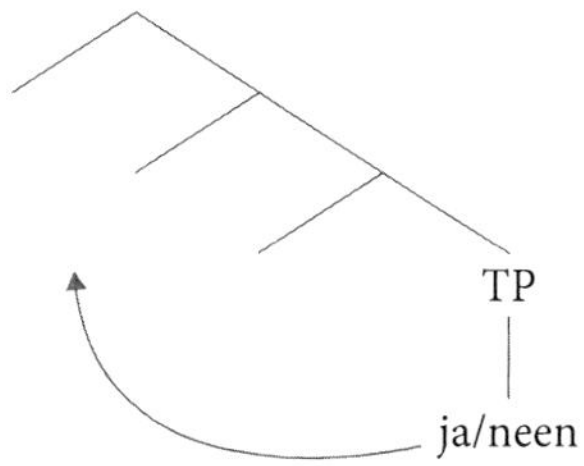

In the previous discussion we tacitly assumed that morphologically marked *ja/neen* are incompatible with clause-mate material (26). This incompatibility will immediately follow from (28), because *ja/neen* are themselves the clause. However, the assumption is actually a simplification: reversal *ja/neen*, which is always morphologically marked, can co-occur with the auxiliary *doen* 'do'.

(29) a. Marie goa morgent kommen.
Marie goes tomorrow come
'Marie will come tomorrow.'

$\text{A}_{\text{REVERSE}}$: Nee-s-e doet.[7]
no-3SG.F-RVRS does
'No she won't.'

b. Marie goa morgent nie kommen.
Marie goes tomorrow not come
'Marie won't come tomorrow.'

$\text{A}_{\text{REVERSE}}$: Ja-s-e doet.
yes-3SG.F-RVRS does
'Yes she will.'

The patterns in (29) alternate with Short Do Replies in (30) (SDRs; see also van Craenenbroeck 2010), in which reversals are expressed simply by means of *doet* ('do');

(30) a. Q: Marie goa morgent kommen.
Marie goes tomorrow come
'Marie will come tomorrow.'

$\text{A}_{\text{REVERSE}}$: Ze doet/Z'en doet
She does/she.NEG does
'No she won't.'

7. In the Lapscheure dialect both *ja-s-e* and *nee-s-e* combine with *doet*. In the Wambeek dialect, only *jou* ('yes') can combine with SDR (van Craenenbroeck 2010: 131). There is considerable variation in the judgements across dialects (van Craenenbroeck 2010: 275, Note 8).

b. Q: Marie goa morgent nie kommen.
Marie goes tomorrow not come
'Marie won't come tomorrow.'
$A_{REVERSE}$: Ze doet/ Z'en doet.
she does/she.NEG does
'Yes she will.'

SDRs have the syntax of subject initial V2 sentences. We assume, following Haegeman (1996), that V2 is a requirement to fill the Fin head in an articulated left periphery (see also Roberts 2004; van Craenenbroeck and Haegeman 2007). SDR clauses are V2 clauses with the finite verb (here *doet* 'does') in Fin and the subject in SpecFin (see Haegeman (1996) for more discussion). Assuming that morphologically marked *ja/neen* originates as a TP pro-form, and that this is also true for (morphologically marked) reversal *ja/neen*, and given that reversal *ja/neen* precedes *doen*, we postulate that *ja/neen* moves to the left, as schematized in (31a):

(31) a.

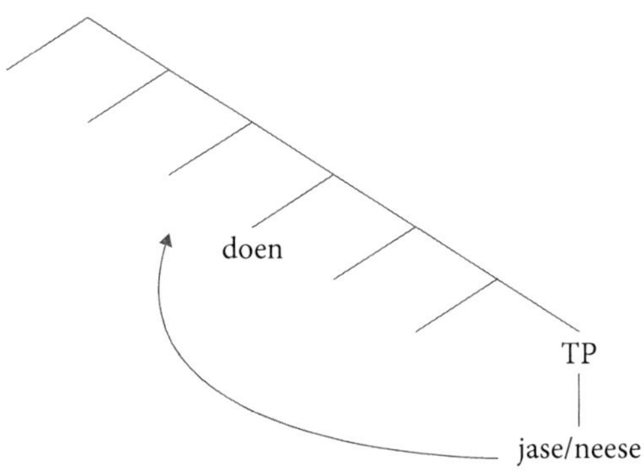

The derivation in (31a) comes down to saying that morphologically marked reversal *jase/neese* undergoes movement to the left periphery. We will assume that a similar derivation holds for neutral morphologically marked *ja/neen* and that this particle also moves to the left periphery. Details of the trigger for the movement and the precise landing sites in (31a) and (31b) will be discussed in Sections 4.2–4.

(31) b.

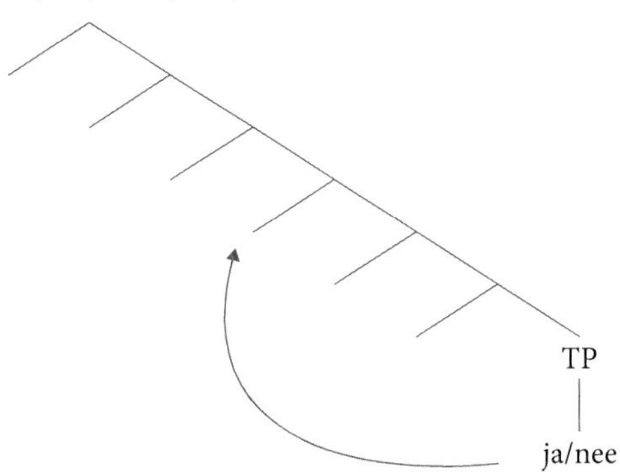

3.4 The nature of morphological marking on *ja/neen*

The question that now arises is what the nature of the morphological marking is. At first sight it might appear as if we can analyze the morphological marking on *ja/neen* as an instantiation of the preverbal clitic in V2 clauses. Thus, based on (31b) we might propose a derivation much along the lines of van Craenenbroeck (2010) according to which what would be a preverbal clitic in a V2 pattern right adjoins to the polarity particle.

(32)

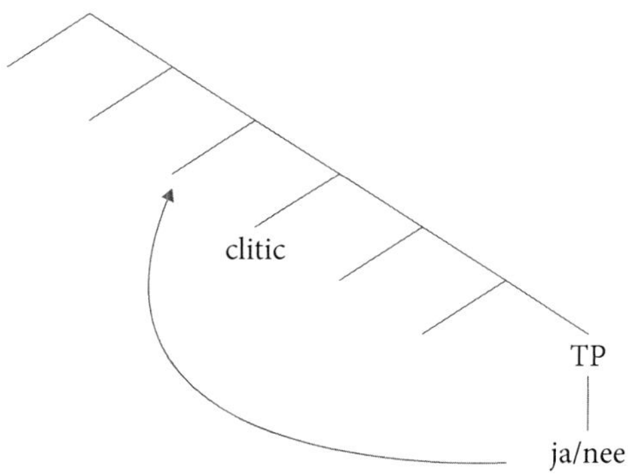

However, a closer look at the phonological properties of the morphological marking shows there are some flaws in this proposal. Consider the following. West Flemish unvoiced consonants generally voice intervocalically at word boundaries and at derivational morphology boundaries (De Schutter & Taeldeman 1986; Simon 2010):

(33)	a.	*goat* 'goes'	[ɦɔ:t]	→	*goat André*	[ɦɔ:dandre]
	b.	*zus* 'sister'	[zʌs]	→	*zuseke* 'sister-DIM'	[zʌzəkə]
	c.	*vis* 'fish'	[vɪs]	→	*vishaak* 'fish-hook'	[vɪzɔ:k]

However, when morphological marking on *ja/neen* is realized by voiceless consonants, these consonants do *not* become voiced when the reversal schwa *e* is attached. Consider the paradigm for the dialect we are interested in Table 2.

Third person singular feminine and third person plural agreeing *ja/neen* have a final voiceless [s]. When followed by the discourse particle *eh*, the final [s] on *ja* becomes voiced, as shown in column 6. This is expected: word-final voiceless fricatives undergo intervocalic voicing. However, when reversal schwa appears after this voiceless [s], it does *not* become voiced, as shown in column 5.

Similarly, second person singular and plural agreeing *ja/neen* end in a final voiceless [x]. When the morphologically marked particles are followed by the discourse particle *eh* the final [x] on *ja* becomes voiced [ɣ], as shown in column 6. This is the result of the expected intervocalic voicing. However, when reversal schwa appears on *ja/nee*, the voiceless fricative [x] of the second person marking does *not* become voiced. (34) and (35) summarize the observed patterns.

Table 2. Voicing alternations in pronominal marking in Lapscheure

	1 pre-V		2 post-V		3 post-C		4 *ja*		5 *ja*+RV		6 *ja*+PRT	
1SG	k-goan		goan-k		dan-k		ja-k		ja-ke		ja-k-eh	
2SG	ge-goat	[ɦ]	goa-j	[j]	da-j	[j]	ja-[x]	[jɔ:x]	ja-[x]e	[jɔ:xə]	ja-g-eh	[jɔ:ɣe]
3SGM	je-goat		goat-je	[tʃ]	dat-je	[tʃ]	ja-j		ja-je		ja-j-eh	
3SGF	ze-goat	[z]	goa-[s]e		da-[s]e		ja-s	[jɔ:s]	ja-[s]e	[jɔ:sə]	ja-z-eh	[jɔ:ze]
3SGN	t-goat		goat-t		dat-t		ja-t		ja-te		ja-t-eh	
3EX	t-goat		goat-er		dat-er		ja-t		ja-te		ja-t-eh	
1PL	me-goan		goa-me		da-me		ja-m		ja-me		ja-m-eh	
2PL	ge-goat	[ɦ]	goa-j		da-j		ja-[x]	[jɔ:x]	ja-[x]e	[jɔ:xə]	ja-g-eh	[jɔ:ɣe]
3PL	ze-goan	[z]	goan-ze	[z]	dan-ze	[z]	ja-[s]	[jɔ:s]	ja-[s]e	[jɔ:sə]	ja-z-eh	[jɔ:ze]

(34) a. *ja-s* 'yes-3SG.F' [jɔ:s]
→ *ja-s-e* 'yes-3SG.F-RVRS' [jɔ:sə] NOT *[jɔ:zə]
b. *ja-s eh* 'yes-3SG.F PRT' [jɔ:ze]

(35) a. *ja-g* 'yes-2SG' [jɔ:x]
→ *ja-g-e* 'yes-2SG-RVRS' [jɔ:xə] NOT *[jɔ:ɣə]
b. *ja-g eh* 'yes-2SG PRT' [jɔ:ɣe]

This leads to the perhaps surprising conclusion that, since it does not trigger intervocalic voicing, the reversal schwa *e* is an integral part of the word *ja-s-e*, i.e. *e* is not derivational morphology, nor is *-e* a separate word of its own. The hypothesis that the reversal schwa in *ja-s-e* is an integral part of the word has consequences for the analysis of the pronominal marking. If this marking originated as a clitic pronoun, this clitic would have to somehow 'infix' between the head *ja* and the reversal schwa. To the best of our knowledge, such clitic infixation does not have a precedent elsewhere in the dialect: for example, post-complementizer clitics appear after the agreement morphology, not before.

(36) dan ze / *da-ze-n Valère kennen
that-AGR.pl they / that-they-AGR.PL Valère know
'that they know Valère'

We interpret 'reversal schwa' as an instance of inflectional morphology because it does not trigger intervocalic voicing.[8] Since the pronominal marking on *ja/neen* occurs

8. De Vogelaer (2005: 126, 134, 147–8) suggests that the *ja/neen* with morphological marking are considered as residues of earlier stages of the language and that their internal structure is not syntactically derived. Though we agree with this proposal we do assume that the marking remains syntactically relevant.

internally to 'reversal schwa', we analyze the marking on *ja/neen* also as a form of inflectional morphology, more specifically agreement morphology. This morphology is *sui generis*: it is only found on the polarity particles. We argue, then, that even in the absence of verbal agreement on *ja/neen* in this dialect (cf. the discussion of (9a)), there is nevertheless agreement. It is likely that the agreement has developed from a subject clitic source much in the way that agreement markers in some Italian dialects have developed from subject clitics (see also Rizzi (1982) and many others after him, for French see Culbertson (2010) and the references cited there). We will not pursue this line here but hope to return to it in future research.

Recall that we postulate that *ja/neen* is a TP pro-form and moves to the left periphery. We argue that the movement of morphologically marked *ja/neen* can be seen as similar to the T-to-C movement of the finite verb which derives the V2 pattern. Thus our proposal is tantamount to saying that one-word utterances consisting of response particles are in fact full finite clauses. In the next section we make an explicit proposal for the derivation.

4. The syntax of morphologically marked *ja/neen*

In this section we spell out the derivation of polarity responses. The core of our proposal is the assumption that *ja/neen* are TP pro-forms which move to the left periphery. The movement is analogous to that which places the finite verb in the C domain, giving rise to Verb Second. In this section we flesh out the details of the syntactic analysis of morphologically marked *ja/neen*.

We also have to account for the restriction that the morphological marking on *ja/neen* is subject-oriented, i.e. why the φ-features encoded on *ja/neen* correspond to the φ-features of the subject of the full clausal continuation in the response. This property suggests that subjecthood is a key component in the derivation, a point that was also reflected in van Craenenbroeck's (2010) analysis, where a designated projection for the canonical subject, there labelled SpecAgr$_S$P, was assumed. In order to bring out the privileged role of the clausal subject we will subscribe to recent proposals by Rizzi (2006) and also Rizzi and Shlonsky (2006, 2007) who postulate subjecthood as a primitive in the functional hierarchy.

4.1 Background assumptions: Cartography and SubjP

Following a.o. Rizzi (1997) and Rizzi and Shlonsky (2006, 2007) we adopt the articulated functional structure in (37). A specialized functional projection for subjects, the Subject Phrase (for motivation see Cardinaletti 1997, 2004; Rizzi 2006; Rizzi & Shlonsky 2006, 2007) dominates TP. SubjP corresponds to what used to be Agr$_S$P in earlier versions of the theory (Pollock 1989; Chomsky 1993) and was discarded in later Minimalist work (Chomsky 1995: 349–355). In Rizzi's conception, unlike its precursor Agr_SP, SubjP is interpreted: it serves the discourse function of encoding the 'subject of predication' of the clause.[9] Following Rizzi (1997), FinP is the lowest projection in the CP-domain and encodes the finiteness of the clause. V2 is seen as a requirement to fill the left peripheral Fin head, the lowest head in the articulated CP area (Haegeman (1996), Roberts (2004) and van Craenenbroeck & Haegeman (2006)).

(37)

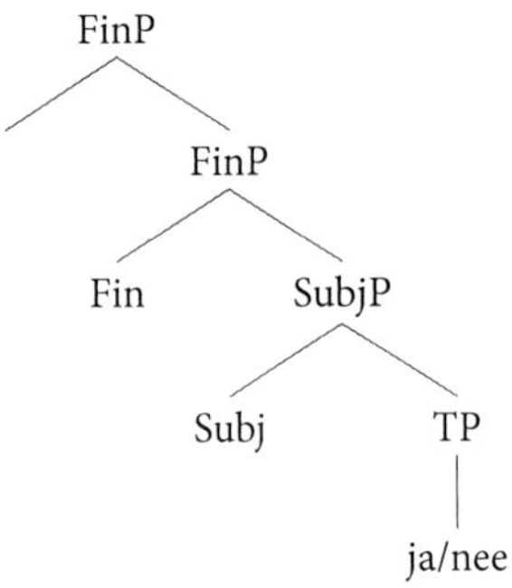

Following Rizzi (2006) and Rizzi and Shlonsky (2006, 2007) we also assume that SubjP is a criterial projection. A criterial requirement is defined as in (38a) (R&S 2007: 138, their (53)), where X is a head and A is a constituent:

(38) a. For [+F] a criterial feature, X+F is in a Spec-head configuration with A+F.

In effect, the Subject Criterion is one way of encoding of the requirement that clauses must have subjects. Criterial configurations ([*wh*] (or [Int]), [Top], [Foc], [Rel] and [Subj]) lead to freezing of the constituent in the specifier position. As a result of Criterial Freezing, a constituent in [Spec, SubjP] is frozen in place. This is illustrated by the well-known subject-object asymmetry in the case of long extraction in French interrogatives (40).

9. On the semantic side, there is more to develop here, because expletives can occupy [Spec, SubjP]. We assume, following Rizzi (2006) and Rizzi and Shlonsky (2007), that the necessity to fill [Spec, SubjP] (Rizzi's Subject Criterion) is a formal requirement that can be satisfied by an expletive. On the semantic side, we could imagine that an expletive simply has no content (i.e. a sentence containing an expletive in subject position simply has no subject of predication), or alternatively perhaps that an expletive can express a situation or event argument as subject of predication. We leave detailed discussion of this aside here, although see Rizzi (2006) and Rizzi & Shlonsky (2007) for some discussion.

(39) a.

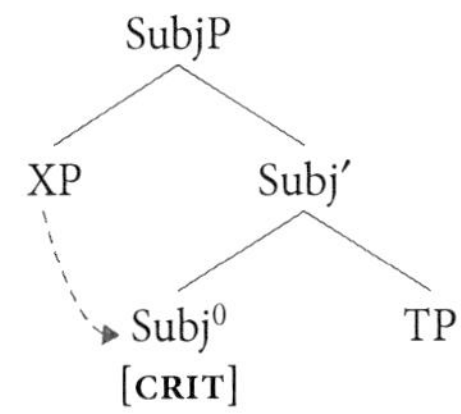

(40) a. *Qui$_i$ crois-tu que [$_{SubjP}$ t$_i$ va partir]?
who think-you that will leave

b. Que$_i$ crois-tu que [$_{SubjP}$ Jean a fait t$_i$]?
what think-you that Jean has done
'What do you think (that) John did?'

To allow subjects to escape from finite clauses, as in French (40c), it is assumed that the Subject Criterion can also be satisfied by an alternative mechanism. In French, the implementation of such a mechanism is reflected in the so-called *que/qui* alternation, whereby the finite complementizer *que* is replaced by *qui*:

(40) c. Qui crois-tu qui va partir?
who think-you *qui* will leave
'Who do you think will leave?'

Rizzi and Shlonsky (2007:138) propose that the form *qui* (40c) spells out Fin enriched with nominal (φ) features (Taraldsen 2001). In (41) we represent this instantiation of Fin as Fin+Phi. For Rizzi and Shlonsky, Fin+Phi satisfies the Subject Criterion by virtue of its local relation with the head Subj; this leads to them restating the criterial condition as in (38b).

(41)

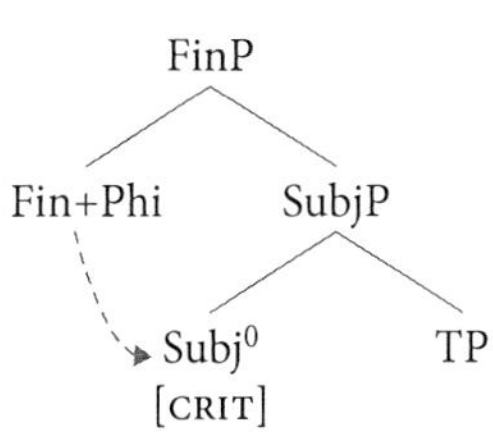

(38) b. For [+F] a criterial feature, X+*F* is locally c-commanded by A+*F*.

In addition, in Rizzi and Shlonsky's implementation, the φ-features on Fin+Phi have to be independently and locally checked by a constituent with (matching) φ-features in [Spec, FinP]. In the French subject extraction case, the moved subject *wh*-phrase will ensure this checking: on its way to its higher criterial landing site, the *wh*-phrase transits through [Spec, FinP] and checks the φ-features of Fin+Phi. (42) summarizes the derivation.

(42)

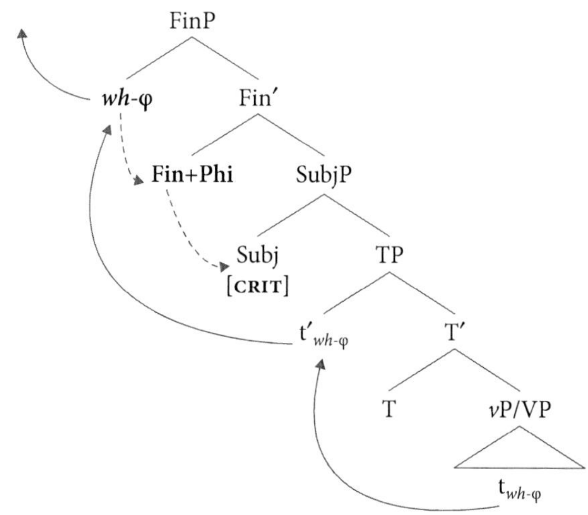

We will adopt Rizzi and Shlonsky's implementation in our own analysis.

4.2 Morphologically marked *ja/neen* and the satisfaction of V2

Let us assume that *ja/neen* is inserted as a TP pro-form in the functional structure in (37). In *ja/neen* responses there is no filler for the specifier of SubjP. In line with Rizzi and Shlonsky (2007)'s analysis of subject extraction, we assume that the Subject Criterion can be satisfied by nominal φ-features present on Fin. We assume that, along with φ-features, a pronominal index (here represented as *n*) can be generated in Fin, which is given the role of the 'subject of predication' (i.e. it is the semantic 'argument' of the Subj head). Like Rizzi and Shlonsky, we assume that the φ-features of Fin themselves must be checked locally. We argue that this is achieved precisely by the morphological marking on *ja/neen*. *Ja/neen* are inserted with their φ-features and move to check Fin's φ-features. One underlying assumption is that single words such as *ja/neen* dominated by XP may pattern either as X^0 or as XP (cf. Muysken 1982; Muysken & van Riemsdijk 1986). If *ja/neen* are in fact TP/T^0 then the movement of *ja/neen* to Fin instantiates the regular case of T-to-C in the V2 languages.

(43)

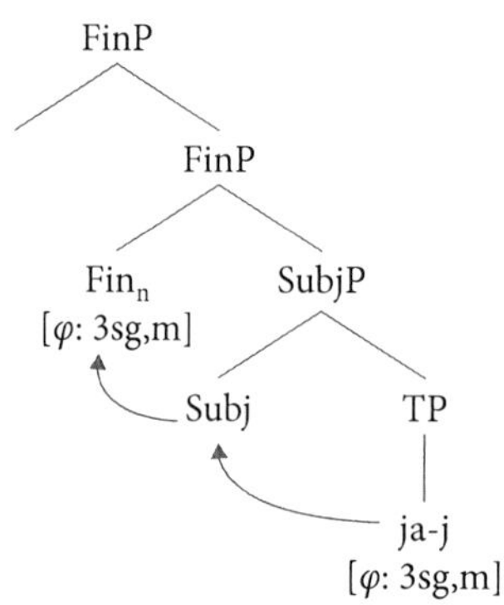

Recall that the Subj head anchors the subject of predication. This restriction ensures that the φ-features on *ja/nee* (and the matching φ-features on Fin which are being checked) must be those that would be appropriate for the subject if a full clause were used.

In a nutshell, the derivation of pronominally marked *ja/neen* responses hinges crucially on the assumption that *ja* and *neen* are TP pro-forms, and that TP is dominated by SubjP. In the absence of an overt subject, SubjP necessitates the presence of an enriched Fin, which itself in turn triggers movement of the morphologically marked *ja/nee* TP pro-form to the left periphery.

4.3 The syntax of reversal *ja-s-e* and *nee-s-e*

The reversal particles serve to 'reverse' the polarity of the antecedent declarative. Suppose that polarity reversal is encoded by a Verum Focus feature that needs to be checked in a left-peripheral PolFoc projection.[10] We assume that the particles are also inserted as TP pro-forms. Like neutral *ja-s/nee-s*, *ja-s-e/nee-s-e* raise first to Fin to check the latter's φ-features, and then onwards to check the Verum Focus feature:

(44)

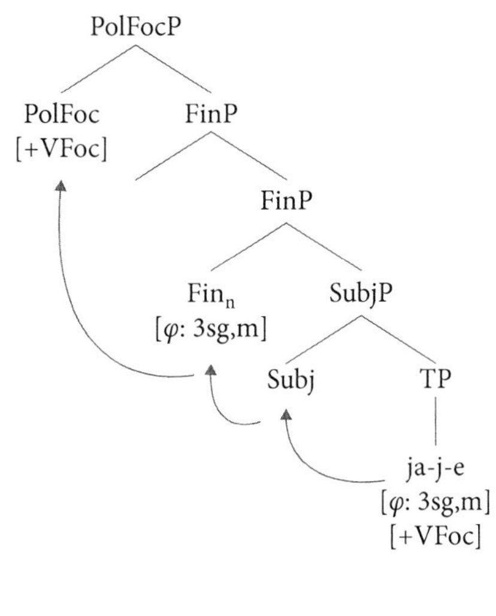

10. This can be seen as a cartographic implementation of Holmberg's (2001, 2007, 2013) left-peripheral ΣP/C_{POLFOC}/FocP. Holmberg proposes that *yes/no* response particles are base-generated in such a projection (an assumption also made by van Craenenbroeck (2010)), while we propose that – at least for West Flemish – they move there to check features, in a similar way to how Holmberg proposes that verb phrases can move to this position in Finnish and various other languages. In as much as our proposal involves the movement of a TP constituent to a left-peripheral position, it resembles Holmberg's analysis of Finnish.

4.4 Reversal *ja/nee* and SDR

In our representations in (43) and (44), morphologically marked *ja/neen* head-move through Fin to check the φ-features on Fin. Recall from (29) that the 'emphatic'/reversal forms with the reversal schwa can also co-occur with the verb *doen* as used in SDR. We outline the essence of the analysis of this pattern here but refer to Haegeman and Weir (2015) for a slightly more articulated derivation. (45) is the relevant example:

(45) Ja-s-e doet.
yes-3SG.F-RVRS does

Our assumption is that *doen* is merged outside the reversal TP pro-form *jase/neese*, which itself does not have internal structure, and that *jase/neese* moves past it. However, if, like the neutral form of the response particle in (43), *jase/neese* undergoes head movement, then the resulting derivation in (46) would violate the Head Movement constraint (Travis 1984).

(46)

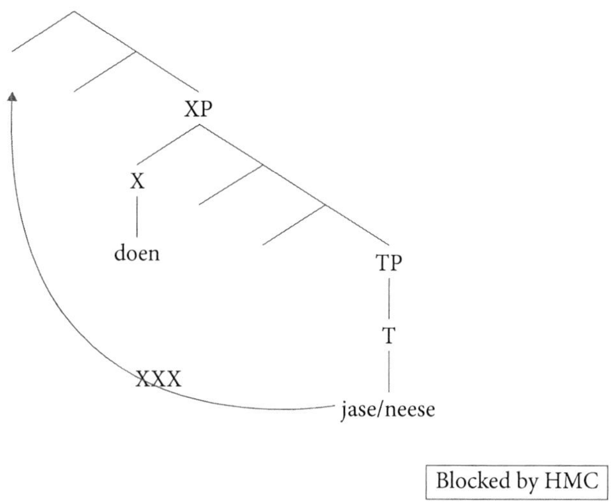

Exploiting the XP/X^0 ambiguity of one-word items (cf. Muysken 1982), we propose that in (45) *doet* fills Fin (and hence also satisfies V2) and that reversal *jase/neese* undergoes phrasal movement to [Spec,FinP] and onwards to [Spec,PolFocP]. Support for this derivation comes from the distribution of the discourse particle *ba* in *ja/nee* responses. (For the distribution of discourse particles with *ja/nee* see also Smessaert 1995; Devos & Vandekerckhove 2005; for similar restrictions in Wambeek Dutch see Footnote 8 and van Craenenbroeck 2010).

Consider first (47a) and (47b). Both are reversal responses to the content of the declarative. There is no discernable semantic difference between the two, except that *doet* sounds slightly redundant, as the reversal is expressed by both the schwa on morphologically marked *ja* and by *doet*. As shown in (47c) and (47d) the discourse particle *ba* is compatible with reversal *ja/neen* but it is in complementary distribution with *doet*. It is unlikely that the contrast between (47c) and (47d) is due to some semantic effect, given that (47a) and (47b) have the same interpretation.

(47) Hij komt morgent niet.
he comes tomorrow not
'He isn't coming tomorrow.'

a. Ja-j-e.
yes-3SG.M-RVRS
'Yes he *is*.'

b. Ja-j-e doet.
yes-3SG.M-RVRS does
'Yes he *is*.'

c. Ba ja-j-e.
BA yes-3SG.M-RVRS
'But he *is*.'

d. *Ba ja-j-e doet.
BA yes-3SG.M-RVRS does

We propose that (47d) is ungrammatical for syntactic reasons. We assume that *ba* is generated in the Spec of the left peripheral projection (say PolFocP) that attracts the reversal particle. This entails that the only way for *ba* to be compatible with the reversal particle is for the latter to move to the head of the projection. But if this is the case then the particle must undergo head movement, and this is incompatible with the presence of *doet* in Fin.

(48)

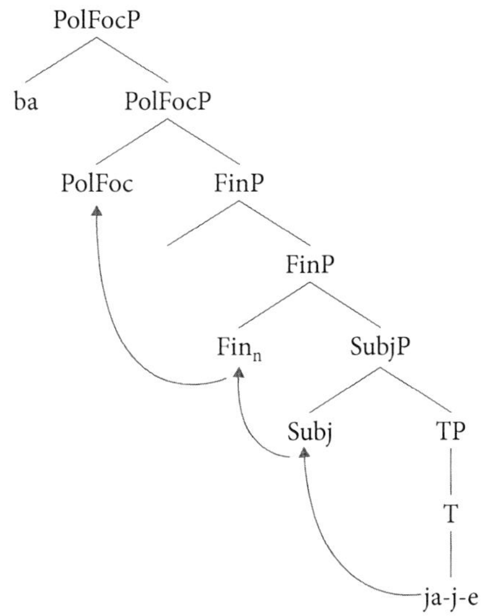

Thus the ambivalence of the TP pro-form in fact is at the basis of the fact that *ba* and *doet* are in complementary distribution.

5. The distribution of bare *ja/nee*

5.1 The data

So far, our discussion has focussed on the morphologically marked forms of the response particles in the Lapscheure dialect. However, as already pointed out in Section 2.3, the response particles also show up in a bare form. In this section we will look at the morphologically marked/bare alternation in more detail. To the best of our knowledge, this piece of the puzzle has not been discussed at all in the literature. We will concentrate on those instances in which there is an alternation in polarity between bare *ja* and *neen.* We tentatively assume that the uses of bare *ja* in which it does not alternate with *neen* (see Section 2.3, examples (15)) represent a distinct use as a discourse particle and we set this aside here. For reasons of space we illustrate our discussion with examples with *ja,* but in the appropriate context this alternates with *neen.*

Bare *ja/neen* can convey polarity in domains embedded under the preposition *van* in two kinds of cases, neither of which allows a morphologically marked version of *ja/neen* as an alternative: in construction with verbs of gesture such as *knikken* 'nod' and *schudden* 'shake' (and some other verbs of 'motion of the body' like *gebaren* 'gesture', *teken doen* 'gesture'):

(49) Ze knikte van ja/*ja-s.
she nodded of yes/yes-3SG.F

And in construction with bridge verbs such as *zeggen* 'say', *peinzen* 'think', *geloven* 'believe', etc. (see van Craenenbroeck 2002):

(50) Ze peinst van ja/*ja-s.
she thinks of yes/yes-3SG.F

Distributionally, these two cases pattern differently, reflecting a different status. Under *knikken/schudden* etc., *van ja/van neen* appear in the middle field and cannot extrapose, and thus pattern with nominal/PP arguments. Conversely, in clauses embedded under bridge verbs, *van ja/van neen* obligatorily extrapose to the right and thus pattern with clausal arguments.

(51) a. omdat ze van ja knikte
because she of yes nodded

b. *omdat ze knikte van ja

c. omdat ze peinst van ja
because she thinks of yes

d. *omdat ze van ja peinst

A second difference is that under verbs of gesture *ja/neen* do not alternate with *wel/niet*; this alternation is available under bridge verbs.

(52) a. *omdat ze van wel knikte
because she of wel nodded

b. omdat ze peinst van wel
because she thinks of wel

We propose that when in construction with the 'verbs of gesturing' like *knikken* 'nod' and *schudden* 'shake', *van ja/van neen* represents a nominal use of *ja/neen*, in the same way as we see in (53) below.

(53) a. Laat jenen ja nen ja zyn en jenen neen nen neen.
let your yes a yes be and your no a no
'Let your yes be yes, and your no, no.' (Matthew 5:37)

b. Den neen in Schotland was te verwachten.
the no in Scotland was to expect
'Scotland's no (vote) was to be expected.'

By contrast, under bridge verbs *van ja* 'of yes'/*van neen* 'of no' has clausal distribution. In this context, 'clausal' *van ja/neen* has the response function and picks up on the polarity of a preceding (root or embedded) polar question.

(54) A: Goa Valere kommen?
Goes Valere come
'Is Valere coming?'

B: Kpeinzen van ja.
I think of *ja*
'I think so.'

B': *Kpeinzen van ja-j.
I think of *ja*-3.SG

(55) A: Weet-je gie of da Valere ga kommen?
know.2SG you whether that Valere goes come
'Do you know if Valere is coming?'

B: Kpeinzen van ja.
I believe of *ja*
'I think so.'

B': *Kpeinzen van ja-j.
I believe of *ja*-3.SG

We propose that, when embedded under bridge verbs such as *peinzen* 'think' or *geloven* 'believe', bare *ja/van neen* corresponds to the TP pro-form that we have argued for above. This hypothesis gives rise to at least three questions, which we will deal with below:

- If 'clausal', bare *ja/neen* is available in response to polar questions in *van*-complements of bridge verbs, why is bare *ja/neen* not possible in root clauses, where the morphologically marked forms are the only option on the relevant interpretation?
- More generally, why can't the TP pro-form show up in response to polar questions in other contexts where TPs appear independently, such as in embedded finite clauses? I.e. why is *ja/neen* ungrammatical in (56), regardless of whether it is morphologically marked or not?

(56) A: Is Valère geweest?
is V. been
'Has Valère been?'

B: *Kpeinzen dat (je) ja(-j).
I.think that he yes(-3.SG)
intended: 'I think so.'

- What rules out the person marking in non-finite contexts, such as *peinzen/geloven van ja/*ja-k*?

5.2 Morphological marking on ja/neen and finiteness

The analysis which we have elaborated for the syntax of morphologically marked *ja/neen* in fact is tantamount to saying that morphologically marked *ja/neen* has the syntax of a finite clause, i.e. a clause with a finite TP. Our overall answer to the questions that emerge in the preceding section is then that, in the same way that verbs bear φ-features in finite contexts but do not bear φ-features in non-finite contexts, the presence or absence of morphological marking on *ja/neen* in fact must be interpreted in terms of a *finiteness opposition*. The hypothesis is that bare *ja/neen* corresponds to a non-finite TP and that, hence, the distribution of morphologically marked *ja/neen* and bare *ja/neen* is a function of finiteness.

5.2.1 *Finite clauses: Root contexts*

By assumption, root contexts are finite, and so only morphologically marked (i.e. 'finite') *ja/neen* are acceptable in root contexts.

(57) Q: Goa Marie da doen?
Goes Marie that do?
'Will Mary do that?'

A: Ja-s./#Ja.
yes-3SG.F/ja

We assume that morphologically marked *ja/neen* correspond to a finite TP and that the finite TP is dominated by SubjP. Hence, the subject criterion is activated, and it is satisfied in the way discussed in the preceding sections.

(58)

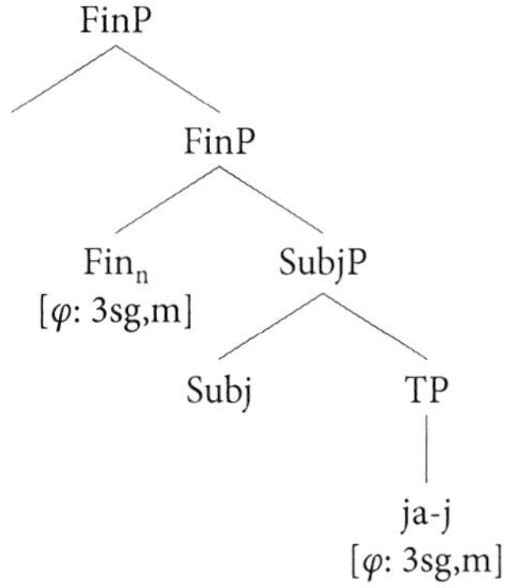

5.2.2 *Finite clauses: Embedded contexts*

We might expect that the morphologically marked (=finite) TP pro-form could also show up in finite complement clauses, say those introduced by the complementizer *dat* under bridge verbs. In fact, regardless of the presence vs. absence of morphological marking and regardless of the presence of the complementizer *dat*, in such contexts no form of *ja/neen* is acceptable. Below we will discuss these examples in turn.

(59) A: Is Valère geweest?
is V. been
'Has Valère been?'

a. B: *Kpeinzen dat ja/neen.
I.think that yes/no

b. B: *Kpeinzen dat ja-j/ nee-j
I.think that yes-3SG.M/no-3SG.M

c. B: *Kpeinzen dat je ja/neen/ja-j/nee-j.
I.think that he yes/no

d. B: *Kpeinzen ja-j/ nee-j
I.think yes-3SG.M/no-3SG.M

(59a) is straightforwardly ruled out: by hypothesis, the complementizer *dat* selects for a finite clause and bare *ja/neen* is a non-finite form. (59a) is ungrammatical for the same reason that (59a') is ungrammatical.

(59) a'. B: *Kpeinzen dat Valère niet (te) kommen.
I.think that V. not (to) come

(59b) cannot be ruled out this way, however, since by our hypothesis morphologically marked *ja-j* is 'finite'. Recall that we assume that morphologically marked *ja/neen* constitute a TP pro-form dominated by SubjP and that, in the absence of an overt subject, the Subject Criterion is satisfied by nominal φ-features on Fin. We suggest that (59b) is ruled out by the fact that the nominal φ-features on Fin would need to be licensed by the movement of φ-marked TP into a local configuration. However, in (59b), the TP pro-form *ja-j/nee-j* cannot move to Fin to check the latter's φ-features, because movement to Fin (i.e. verb-second) does not take place in embedded clauses in West Flemish. Whatever rules this out in general also rules it out in (59b).[11] Observe furthermore that phrasal movement to SpecFin of *ja-j/nee-j* is also excluded, because – again for independent reasons – finite embedded clauses in WF are incompatible with any movement to the left periphery.

(60)

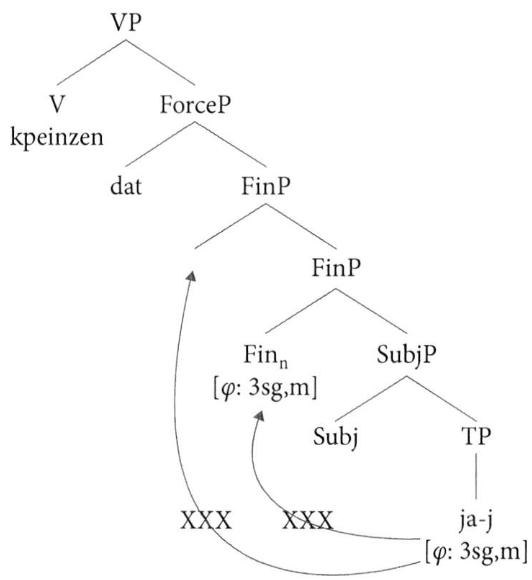

(59c) illustrates another alternative: base-generating a subject pronoun in [Spec, SubjP] and pairing it with morphologically marked *ja/neen*.

11. Admittedly the restrictions on embedded V2 still need to be independently accounted for. Observe that the WF agreement features on the complementizer cannot be straightforwardly equated with the nominal features on Fin which are needed to satisfy the Subject Criterion as complementizer agreement is generally obligatory in all embedded clauses and the features associated with complementizer agreement cannot be used to independently satisfy the Subject Criterion. This requires further work.

For arguments against Feature Inheritance see Haegeman and van Koppen (2012), who have shown that the features on C need not be identical to those on T.

(61)

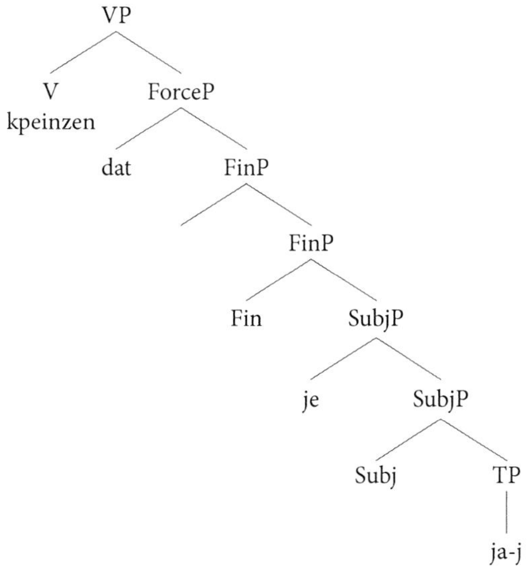

Here, the selectional requirement of *dat* is satisfied since morphologically marked *ja/neen* is finite, and the Subject Criterion would be satisfied directly by the base-generated pronoun, without there being any need for nominal phi-features on Fin, or movement to Fin to TP to check φ-features. We propose that this is independently ruled out because a subject pronoun base-generated in [Spec, SubjP] has no means of getting Case.[12] Observe that in terms of our account these data would then pose a challenge for the traditional view which postulates that finiteness and nominative case licensing are intrinsically linked (see Cowper this volume, cited in Section 1). Note that subject pronouns do not appear in constructions with morphologically marked *ja/nee* in root contexts either (whether before or after), so on our analysis the 'finiteness' of *ja/nee* does not in general suffice to license the presence of an overt subject pronoun.

(62) Q: Is Valère geweest?
A: *Je joaj./Joaj je./Neej je./Je neej.

(59d), lacking *dat*, embeds the morphologically marked variant of the response particles directly under a bridge verb. This would be tantamount to embedding a root clause. As discussed, though, the dialect in question precludes such embedded root phenomena, including embedded V2 or the absence of overt complementizers.

12. This entails that the agreeing complementizer cannot all by itself license nominative case (pace Haegeman & van Koppen 2012) and that incorporation of the clitic to C is also insufficient for case licensing.

There is therefore no way of generating the morphologically marked pro-form *ja* in embedded finite *dat*-clauses: in such patterns an overt subject pronoun is unavailable and satisfying the Subject Criterion via movement of morphologically marked *ja/neen* to [Spec, FinP] would violate whatever rules out movement to the embedded left periphery in West Flemish. We predict, then, that morphologically marked *ja/neen* cannot show up anywhere that finite TPs can, but rather only in root position (and when they are in root position, they must be 'finite', i.e. morphologically marked).

5.2.3 *Clausal van*

As discussed, bare *ja/neen* can appear in construction with bridge verbs. Based on its distribution we assume that *van ja/neen* is clausal. As shown in (5), repeated below as (63a) *van* can embed a non-finite clause in West Flemish, but not a finite clause, regardless of whether the complementizer *dat* is present.

(63) a. kpeinzen van em morgen te zien
I-think of him tomorrow to see
'I think I'll see him tomorrow.'

b. *kpeinzen van dan-k em morgen goan zien
I-think van that-I him tomorrow will see

c. *kpeinzen van ik em morgen goan zien
I-think van I him tomorrow will see

We will thus assume that *van* selects a non-finite clausal complement,[13] and so *van* can only select for non-finite (that is, not morphologically marked) *ja/neen*. This is what we see:

(64) A: Goa-j em morgen zien?
Goes you him tomorrow see

B. kpeinzen van ja/*ja-k.
I think of yes/yes-1SG.F

For completeness' sake we add that in addition to bridge verbs illustrated above, non-finite clausal *van ja* also appears under a set of one argument verbs with an expletive subject, such as 'it could be that', 'it seems that'. As was the case with the preceding cases, *van ja/neen* is extraposed and cannot remain in the middle field, and *ja/neen* alternates with *wel/niet*.

13. This is a shortcut. In particular it is not clear that clausal *van* in *van ja/neen* can be assimilated to control *van*. See Servidio (2014:90 ff), for a detailed discussion of the contrast between Italian non-finite *di* and *di* in *credo di sì*.

(65) A: Is Valère geweest?
is V. been
'Has Valère been?'

a. B: t zou keunen van ja.
it may can of *ja*
'It could be.'

b. B: *t zou van ja keunen
it may of *ja* can

c. B: t zou keunen van wel.
it may can of well

The distributional restrictions on bare/morphologically marked *ja/neen* are identical to those discussed above.

(66) A: Is Valère geweest?
is V. been
'Has Valère been?'

a. B: *t zou keunen (dat) ja/neen.
it may be that yes/no

b. B: *t zou keunen (dat) ja-j/nee-j
it may be that yes-3SG.M/no-3SG.M

c. B': *t zou keunen (dat) je ja/neen/ja-j/nee-j.
it may be that he yes/no

At this point the full inventory of verbs selecting clausal *van ja/van neen* needs to be established.

5.2.4 *Non-finite clauses*

We propose that bare *ja/neen* are pro-forms for a non-finite TP and thus we correctly predict that they do not appear in contexts that require a finite TP. However, it is not the case that bare *ja/neen* can show up in all contexts in which non-finite TPs can be found. We provide a survey of the crucial data here. It emerges that only the prepositional complementizer *van* can embed *ja/neen*, and that even with this complementizer there are restrictions.

In addition to *van*, the dialect also uses the non-finite complementizer *vur* ('for') to introduce control pattens; *vur* does not allow embedding of *ja/nee* to alternate with a control pattern. Observe that in this context *wel* is also not available:

(67) S: Eet-je t gelezen?
has=he it read
'Has he read it?'

A: j'ee geprobeerd vur het te lezen.
he has tried C it to read
'He has tried to read it.'

A': *j'ee geprobeerd vur ja.
he has tried C yes

A': *j'ee geprobeerd vur wel.
he has tried C well

The restriction is not just related to the choice of complementizer. In the control context *vur* may actually alternate with *van*. In such a context, *van* itself also does not allow embedding of *ja/nee*.

(68) S: Eet-je t gelezen?
has.he it read
'Has he read it?'

A: j'ee geprobeerd van het te lezen.
he has tried C it to read
'He has tried to read it.'

A': *j'ee geprobeerd van ja.
he has tried C yes

A': *j'ee geprobeerd van wel.
he has tried C well

The restriction is related to the nature of the infinitival complement. In (63a), *peinzen* ('think') has an epistemic interpretation and embeds a propositional (control) complement. In (69) below, the non-finite control complement of *peinzen* has an intentional reading, meaning 'I intend to', 'I plan to'. With this irrealis interpretation, the *van ja* complement is not available. In (69b) the response *peinzen van ja* is not quite felicitous, as it would have to mean: 'I think it will be the case', 'I expect that to be the case', and would seem to suggest that the future activity is not within the subject's direct control.

(69) a. Kpeinzen van morgen no de cinema te goan.
I-think of tomorrow to the cinema to go
'I'm thinking of going to the cinema tomorrow.' (=I intend to)

b. A: Goa-j morgen no de cinema?
Go-you tomorrow to the cinema
'Are you going to the cinema tomorrow?'

B: #kpeinzen van ja.
I-think of yes

Under non-bridge verbs, non-finite clauses with what seem to be realis readings are (perhaps marginally) possible, and they would be introduced by *van*, as shown in (70a). In such contexts, though, non-finite *van ja* cannot appear.

(70) a. ?Kzyn blye van da morgen niet meer te moeten doen.
I.am glad of that tomorrow not more to have.to do
'I am glad I don't have to do that tomorrow.'

b. Q: Moet je dat morgen nog doen?
must you that tomorrow yet do
'Do you still have to do that tomorrow?'

A: *Kzyn blye van neen.
I.am glad of no
(intended: 'I'm glad that I don't.')

The data discussed here are relevant in the wider context of the discussion of finiteness marking, and in particular they provide confirmation for proposals in the literature that non-finite clauses, and specifically control clauses, are not a homogeneous group, which means in turn that the opposition finite vs. non-finite is too coarse (see a.o. Landau 2004, Wurmbrand 2014, Cowper this volume). Non-finite *ja* and *neen* seem to be limited as pro-forms for one particular clause type, that of the propositional (i.e. realis) complements to bridge verbs (see also van Craenenbroeck (2002) and Hoeksema (2006, 2008) for discussion).

Various avenues suggest themselves for understanding and formalizing this restriction. At this point we do not take a stance and we only sketch two major routes that could be envisaged. One line of approach would be purely semantic: one might propose that *ja* and *neen* are anaphoric to the Question under Discussion (Roberts 2012/1996), that they can only be understood as propositional/realis, and that this is the reason why they cannot appear in control/intentional contexts, or under factive predicates which 'background' their clausal complements. Another more cartographic approach might be to speculate that the interpretive distinctions which are identified are syntactically encoded and that, in a more fine grained structure (cf. Cinque 1999; Wurmbrand 2014), the response particles are the pro-forms of a specialized functional projection which is present in realis complements but not irrealis, control, or factive complements, and whose precise nature remains as yet to be determined. See also Servidio (2014: 90–91) for discussion on the cartography of *di sì* in Italian. We leave this issue for future work.

6. Summary of the paper

The empirical focus of the paper is the morphosyntax of the morphologically marked response particles *ja* and *neen* in the Lapscheure dialect. Building on Krifka (2013)'s analysis of the German response particles *ja/nein* as TP pro-forms, we also analyze morphologically marked Flemish *ja/neen* as TP pro-forms.

In the first part of the paper we first argue that the morphological marking on these particles is *sui generis*: it does not correspond to the marking found on verbs nor does it correspond to a clitic form of the subject pronoun. We develop a cartographic analysis of the syntax of the morphologically marked response particles in the dialect. We endorse Rizzi and Shlonsky (2006, 2007)'s proposal that a finite TP is dominated by SubjP. We assume that the pronominal marking on morphologically marked *ja/neen* is an instantiation of finiteness. This means that the finite TP pro-form realized by morphologically marked *ja/neen* is dominated by SubjP, a criterial projection. In the absence of an overt subject, the Subject Criterion (Rizzi & Shlonsky 2006, 2007) is satisfied by nominal φ-features generated on Fin. Morphologically marked *ja/neen* has to move to Fin in order to license these features. Our analysis predicts that West Flemish morphologically marked *ja/neen* are a root phenomenon.

As 'verbal' TPs come in finite and non-finite variants, we might expect that TP pro-forms also should, and we have shown that this is indeed the case: in addition to the variant with pronominal marking, there is also a bare variant of the *ja/neen* pro-forms. We have shown that presence and absence of the pronominal marking on *ja/neen* correlates fairly closely with the distribution of finite and non-finite clauses, and we propose that the pronominal marking is therefore to be understood in terms of a finiteness opposition. Closer examination of the non-finite variant of *ja/neen* provides support for the hypothesis that non-finite infinitival clauses do not constitute one homogeneous class, an issue which itself should be addressed in future work.

References

Adger, David. 2007. Three domains of finiteness: A minimalist perspective. In *Finiteness. Theoretical and Empirical Foundations*, Irina Nikolaeva (ed.), 23–58. Oxford: OUP.

Authier, Jean-Marc. 2013. Phase-edge features and the syntax of polarity particles. *Linguistic Inquiry* 44(3): 345–89.

Barbiers, Sjef, Bennis, Hans, De Vogelaer, Gunther, Devos, Magda & van der Ham, Margreet. 2005. *Syntactic Atlas of the Dutch Dialects*, Vol. I: *Commentary*. Amsterdam: AUP.

Cardinaletti, Anna. 1997. Subjects and clause structure. In *The New Comparative Syntax*, Liliane Haegeman (ed.), 33–63. London: Longman.

Cardinaletti, Anna. 2004. Towards a cartography of subject positions. In *The Structure of CP and IP* [The Cartography of Syntactic Structures 2], Luigi Rizzi (ed.), 115–165. Oxford: OUP.

Chomsky, Noam. 1993. A minimalist program for linguistic theory. In *The View from Building 20. Essays in Linguistics in Honor of Sylvain Bromberger*, Kenneth Hale & Samuel Jay Keyser (eds.), 1–52. Cambridge MA: The MIT Press.

Chomsky, Noam. 1995. *The Minimalist Program*. Cambridge MA: The MIT Press.

Cinque, Guglielmo. 1999. *Adverbs and functional heads*. Oxford: OUP.

Cowper, Elizabeth. This volume. Finiteness and pseudofiniteness.

van Craenenbroeck, Jeroen. 2002. *Van* as a marker of dissociation: Microvariation in Dutch. In *Studies in Comparative Germanic Syntax* [Linguistik Aktuell/Linguistics Today 53], C. Jan-Wouter Zwart & Werner Abraham (eds.), 41–68. Amsterdam: John Benjamins.

van Craenenbroeck, Jeroen. 2010. *Ellipsis in Dutch dialects*. Oxford: OUP.

van Craenenbroeck, Jeroen & Haegeman, Liliane. 2007. The derivation of subject-initial V2. *Linguistic Inquiry* 38(1): 167–178.

Culbertson, Jennifer. 2010. Convergent evidence for categorial change in French: from subject clitic to agreement marker. *Language* 86(1): 85–132.

De Schutter, Georges & Taeldeman, Johan. 1986. Assimilatie van stem in de zuidelijke Nederlandse dialekten. In *Vruchten van z'n akker: opstellen van (oud-) medewerkers en oud-studenten voor Prof. V.F. Vanacker,* Magda Devos & Johan Taeldeman (eds.), 91–133. Ghent: Seminaire voor Nederlands Taalkunde.

De Vogelaer, Gunther. 2005. Subjectsmarkering in de Nederlandse en Friese Dialecten. Ph.D. dissertation, Ghent University.

De Vogelaer, Gunther & van der Auwera, Johan. 2010. When typological rara generate rarissima: Analogical extension of verbal agreement in Dutch dialects. In *Rara & Rarissima. Collecting and Interpreting Unusual Characteristics of Human Language,* Jan Wohlgemuth & Michael Cysouw (eds.), 47–73. Berlin: De Gruyter Mouton.

Devos, Magda. 1986. Het persoonlijk voornaamwoord 2e pers enk in het Westvlaams. Geografie en historiek. In *Vruchten van z'n akker: opstellen van (oud-) medewerkers en oud-studenten voor Prof. V.F. Vanacker,* Magda Devos & Johan Taeldeman (eds.), 167–189. Ghent: Seminaire voor Nederlands Taalkunde.

Devos, Magda & Vandekerckhove, Reinhild. 2005. *Taal in stad en land. West-vlaams.* Tielt: Lannoo.

Eide, Kristin Melum. 2009. Finiteness: the haves and the have-nots. In *Advances in Comparative Germanic Syntax* [Linguistik Aktuell/Linguistics Today 141], Artemis Alexiadou, Jorge Hankamer, Thomas McFadden, Justin Nuger & Florian Schäfer (eds.), 357–90. Amsterdam: John Benjamins.

Haegeman, Liliane. 1990. Subject pronouns and subject clitics in West-Flemish. *The Linguistic Review* 7(4): 333–364.

Haegeman, Liliane. 1996. Verb second, the split CP and null subjects in early Dutch finite clauses. *GenGenP.* ⟨http://ling.auf.net/lingBuzz/001059⟩

Haegeman, Liliane & van Koppen, Marjo. 2012. Complementizer agreement and the relation between C^0 and T^0. *Linguistic Inquiry* 43(3): 441–454.

Haegeman, Liliane & Weir, Andrew. 2015. The cartography of *yes* and *no* in West Flemish. In *Discourse-oriented Syntax* [Linguistik Aktuell/Linguistics Today 226], Josef Bayer, Roland Hinterhölzl & Andreas Trotzke (eds.), 175–210. Amsterdam: John Benjamins.

Hoeksema, Jack. 2006. Hij zei van niet, maar knikte van ja: Distributie en diachronie van bijwoorden van polariteit ingeleid door *van. Tabu* 35(3–4):135–158.

Hoeksema, Jack. 2008. *Van* + bijwoord van polariteit: Een geval van verplichte PP extrapositie? *Tabu* 37(1–2):69–74.

Holmberg, Anders. 2001. The syntax of yes and no in Finnish. *Studia Linguistica* 55(2): 141–175.

Holmberg, Anders. 2007. Null subjects and polarity focus. *Studia Linguistica* 61(3): 212–236.

Holmberg, Anders. 2013. The syntax of answers to polar questions in English and Swedish. *Lingua* 128: 31–50.

Kramer, Ruth & Rawlins, Kyle. 2011. Polarity particles: an ellipsis account. In *Proceedings of NELS 39*, Suzi Lima, Kevin Mullin & Brian Smith (eds.). Amherst MA: GLSA.

Krifka, Manfred. 2013. Response particles as propositional anaphors. In *Proceedings of SALT 23*, Todd Snider (ed.), 1–18. Ithaca NY: CLC Publications.

Landau, Idan. 2004. The scale of finiteness and the calculus of control. *Natural Language and Linguistic Theory* 22: 811–77.

Lobeck, Anne. 1995. *Ellipsis: Functional Heads, Licensing and Identification*. Oxford: OUP.

Mensching, Guido. 2000. *Infinitive Constructions with Specified Subjects: A Syntactic Analysis of the Romance Languages*. Oxford: OUP.

Merchant, Jason. 2001. *The Syntax of Silence*. Oxford: OUP.

Merchant, Jason. 2004. Fragments and ellipsis. *Linguistics and Philosophy* 27(6): 661–738.

Muysken, Pieter. 1982. Parameterizing the notion 'head'. *Journal of Linguistic Research* 2: 57–75.

Muysken, Pieter & van Riemsdijk, Henk. 1986. Projecting features and featuring projections. In *Features and Projections*, Pieter Muysken & Henk van Riemsdijk (eds.), 1–30. Dordrecht: Foris.

Paardekooper, Piet C. 1993. Jaak/neenik enz. *Tabu* 23(3): 143–173.

Pollock, Jean-Yves. 1989. Verb movement, Universal Grammar, and the structure of IP. *Linguistic Inquiry* 20(3): 365–424.

Rizzi, Luigi. 1982. *Issues in Italian Syntax*. Dordrecht: Foris.

Rizzi, Luigi. 1997. The fine structure of the left periphery. In *Elements of Grammar*, Liliane Haegeman (ed.). Dordrecht: Kluwer.

Rizzi, Luigi. 2006. On the form of chains: Criterial positions and ECP effects. In *Wh-movement: Moving on*, Lisa Lai-shen Cheng & Norbert Corver (eds.), 97–133. Cambridge MA: The MIT Press.

Rizzi, Luigi & Shlonsky, Ur. 2006. Satisfying the subject criterion by a non-subject: English locative inversion and heavy NP shift. In *Phases of Interpretation*, Mara Frascarelli (ed.), 341–361. Berlin: Mouton de Gruyter.

Rizzi, Luigi & Shlonsky, Ur. 2007. Strategies of subject extraction. In *Interfaces + Recursion = Language? Chomsky's Minimalism and the View from Syntax-semantics*, Hans-Martin Gärtner & Uli Sauerland (eds.), 115–160. Berlin: Mouton de Gruyter.

Roberts, Craige. (2012/1996). Information structure in discourse: Towards an integrated formal theory of pragmatics. *Semantics & Pragmatics* 5: 1–69. Originally published in *OSU Working Papers in Linguistics 49: Papers in semantics*, Jae-Hak Yoon & Andreas Kathol (eds.). Columbus OH: The Ohio State University.

Roberts, Ian. 2004. The C-system in Brythonic Celtic languages, V2, and the EPP. In *The structure of CP and IP: The Cartography of Syntactic Structures*, Vol. 2, Luigi Rizzi (ed.), 297–328. Oxford: OUP.

Servidio, Emilio. 2014. Polarity Particles in Italian: Focus, Fragments, Tags. Ph.D. dissertation, University of Siena.

Simon, Ellen. 2010. Phonological transfer of voicing and devoicing rules: Evidence from L1 Dutch and L2 English conversational speech. *Language Sciences* 32(1): 63–86.

Smessaert, Hans. 1995. Morfo-syntaxis van het Westvlaamse *bè-jaa-k-gie*. *Tabu* 25(1): 45–60.

Szabolcsi, Anna. 2005. Overt infinitival subjects (if that's what they are). *Organizing Grammar: Linguistic Studies in Honor of Henk van Riemsdijk*, Hans Broekhuis, Norbert Corver, Riny Huybregts, Ursula Kleinhenz & Jan Koster (eds.), 618–25. Berlin: Mouton de Gruyter.

Taraldsen, Knut Tarald. 2001. Subject extraction, the distribution of expletives and stylistic inversion. In *Subject Inversion in Romance and the Theory of Universal Grammar*, Aafke Hulk & Jean-Yves Pollock (eds.), 163–182. Oxford: OUP.
Travis, Lisa. (1984). Parameters and Effects of Word Order Variation. Ph.D. dissertation, MIT.
Wurmbrand, Susi. 2014. Tense and aspect in English infinitives. *Linguistic Inquiry* 45: 403–447.

PART III

Finiteness in language acquisition

Word order and finiteness in acquisition

A study of Norwegian and English *Wh*-questions*

Marit Westergaard
UiT – The Arctic University of Norway

Children acquiring languages such as English, German or Dutch typically go through a phase where they produce non-finite root clauses, often referred to as the Optional Infinitive (OI) stage. But there is a difference between English on the one hand and the other Germanic languages on the other with respect to the occurrence of non-finite *wh*-questions: while there is a high number of OIs in English in this context, non-finite *wh*-questions are virtually non-existent in child data of e.g. German or Swedish. This is often argued to be due to the early setting of the V2 parameter. Comparing Norwegian and English child data on *wh*-questions, this paper argues that there is no such parameter and that children instead are sensitive to fine syntactic distinctions in the input called micro-cues. On this view, both English and Norwegian have restricted V2 in *wh*-questions. The paper also shows that there is no causal correlation between finiteness morphology and word order in this context. Children's non-finite root clauses are argued to generally be caused by a problem realizing auxiliaries, in both languages, and the difference between English and Norwegian is due to the type of verb required in *wh*-questions (auxiliaries vs. lexical verbs).

Keywords: auxiliaries; English; Norwegian; verb second; *wh*-questions

1. Introduction

This paper addresses the issue of syntax-morphology correlations, more specifically, the relationship between syntactic movement and finiteness morphology. It is often claimed that the two are closely connected – in syntactic structure, in diachronic development and in acquisition. This has led to a large body of work arguing that

* A considerably shorter paper using some of the data and argumentation in the present article has been published as Westergaard and Bentzen (2010). I thank Kristine Bentzen for collaboration on the work in Section 5 of this paper.

DOI 10.1075/la.231.09wes

the connection between morphology and syntax is a causal relationship in the sense that overt morphological marking triggers syntactic movement. There is also a considerable literature arguing against such a causal relationship. In this paper I explore this issue by considering the acquisition of finiteness morphology and verb movement resulting in verb second (V2) word order in *wh*-questions in Norwegian, comparing it with subject-auxiliary inversion in English. Based on child language data from both languages, I argue against a causal syntax-morphology correlation in the case of verb movement and finiteness. This paper also takes the view that, when children produce non-finite root clauses, this is not a sign of a deficit in their grammar related to tense and agreement. Instead, it shows that child grammar is affected by economy principles in the acquisition process and that with respect to omissions, children have specific problems with functional elements, e.g. auxiliaries.

Young children's production of non-finite root clauses, often referred to as Optional Infinitives (OIs) or Root Infinitives (RIs), has been discussed extensively in the literature (see e.g. Wexler 1994, 1999 and Rizzi 1993/94, 2000). In much previous research on the acquisition of English and V2 languages such as Dutch and German, it has been argued that there is a difference between English on the one hand and V2 languages on the other with respect to the production of non-finite root clauses in *wh*-questions. This difference is typically linked to the V2 phenomenon, i.e. verb movement (to the C-position). In previous studies, it has been found that, while non-finite root clauses may frequently occur in English *wh*-questions, as in examples (1)–(2), illustrating an infinitive and a progressive participle respectively, they are virtually non-existent in this clause type in the other Germanic languages. Thus, while non-finite root clauses may appear in other clause types, *wh*-questions in V2 languages are generally finite, as illustrated by the Swedish examples in (3)–(4). The child data to be presented in this paper (Section 4) show that this generalization also holds for Norwegian, illustrated in examples (5)–(6).

(1) what the dolly have? (Eve 1;11)

(2) what you doing? (Eve 2;0)

(3) *Docka* ***rita*** *här.* (Sara 2;5, Josefsson 2004: 120)
doll draw.INF here
'(The) doll (should/must) draw here.'

(4) *Hur* ***gör*** *apa då?* (Tor 2;5, Santelmann 2004: 272)
how does.PRES monkey.DEF then
'How does the monkey go then?'

(5) ... *han ikke* ***røre*** *klossen.* (Ina 2;4.1)
he not touch.INF brick.DEF
'He (should/must) not touch the brick.'

(6) *kor skal den være henne?* (Ole 2;7.20)
where shall it be LOC
'Where should this go?'

According to Wexler's (1999) model of Optional Infinitives (OIs), the reason for this difference between English and the other Germanic languages is that the V2 parameter is set very early, and this movement operation only applies to finite verbs. Thus, children learning a V2 language such as German or Dutch will only provide finite structures in *wh*-questions. In the Truncation model of Rizzi (1993/94, 2000) this result is due to the fact that, when the CP is present (and filled by the *wh*-element), then no other projection below the CP may be missing. This means that the IP domain and consequently finiteness must necessarily be present in *wh*-questions. One problem for these analyses, in my view, is that English in fact does have verb movement in questions (in the form of subject-auxiliary inversion), and it is therefore difficult to relate the distinction between English and the other Germanic languages in this clause type to syntactic movement.

In Westergaard (2008, 2009a, b), it is argued that there is no V2 parameter, and that V2 effects should be explained as the result of a number of micro-cues, small pieces of syntactic structure present in speakers' I-language grammars. One important argument for this claim is the considerable variation that is found across languages and dialects with respect to the V2 phenomenon. That is, there may be different V2 requirements dependent on linguistic context – clause type, verb class, type of initial element as well as factors of information structure. Another argument is that children are sensitive to this micro-variation from early on, producing V2 and non-V2 in appropriate contexts. The micro-cues are formed in the child's I-language grammar as a result of an interaction between innate categories and principles and exposure to the relevant input. In this model, English is also a type of V2 language, in that it has V2 effects in *wh*- and *yes/no*-questions in the form of subject-auxiliary inversion, while Norwegian is another type of V2 language, where this word order is dependent on various factors (see e.g. Westergaard 2009b). On this view, English and Norwegian both have V2 word order in *wh*-questions, exactly the environment where they differ with respect to the expression of finiteness in early child language. The difference between the two languages in relation to the existence of non-finite root clauses therefore cannot be due to syntactic movement *per se*.

In this paper I provide several arguments against a causal correlation between syntax and morphology in this area of the grammar. Instead, I argue that the differences between English and Norwegian child language with respect to finiteness morphology in *wh*-questions is due to a difference in the subcategory that verb movement applies to in the two languages. While in Norwegian, all verbs move to second position, this movement operation only applies to auxiliaries in English, i.e. functional elements that are typically acquired relatively late, in all clause types. Furthermore, I argue that non-finite root clauses in child Norwegian, which predominantly have a modal meaning, are due to the same problem as that experienced by English children, viz. a difficulty in the realization of auxiliaries. The difference between the two languages with respect to finiteness in *wh*-questions is then shown to be due to a difference in the typical proportion of modals and other auxiliaries appearing in this clause type at an early stage. It should be noted here that I do not adopt the model of finiteness taken in Eide (2009, this volume), but take a more traditional approach, where finiteness morphology is simply considered to be the expression of tense and/or agreement on the verb.

The paper is organized as follows: The next section gives a brief introduction to the alleged relationship between syntactic movement and finiteness morphology, with a focus on this correlation in previous acquisition work. It also gives a brief overview of the word order patterns and verbal morphology in the target languages for the children in this study, Standard English and a dialect of Norwegian (Tromsø). I then discuss some child data from English in Section 3 and a corpus of three Norwegian children acquiring the Tromsø dialect in Section 4. It is shown that the English-speaking children have a problem with auxiliaries (but not the copula *be*), which are often missing from *wh*-questions, and that occasional non-inverted examples in the child data appear only with finite verbs. Similarly, the Norwegian children are found to produce target-consistent V2 as well as non-V2 questions almost exclusively with finite verbs. Based on these findings from the child data I draw the conclusion that there cannot be a causal relationship between word order and finiteness morphology in early child language. Section 6 discusses the difference between English and Norwegian child data with respect to the expression of finiteness in *wh*-questions, and provides extensive new data from several children, showing that this difference is due to the proportion (and type) of auxiliaries present in early *wh*-questions in the two languages.

2. Background

2.1 The syntax-morphology interface

The relationship between verbal morphology and syntactic structure has been the topic of much debate, not only in the field of language acquisition, but also within general syntactic theory and models of diachronic language change. It has been commonly assumed in much of the literature that there is a clear correlation between syntactic verb movement and overt verbal morphology. This has led to what is known as the Rich Agreement Hypothesis (RAH), which in its strongest version claims that there is a causal and bi-directional relationship between overt morphological agreement and V-to-I movement, see e.g. Rohrbacher (1999). This has also been claimed by e.g. Pollock (1989) for the distinction between French and English and Vikner (1995) on the differences between Icelandic and the Mainland North Germanic languages.

Other accounts have questioned these claims and generally taken a more skeptical approach to the strong correlation between word order and verbal morphology, see e.g. the collection of papers in Lightfoot (2002). Bobaljik and Thrainsson (1998) propose a weaker (unidirectional) approach to the syntax-morphology correlation and argue that morphology is simply a reflection of syntactic structure, not necessarily its cause. That is, rich agreement causes verb movement, but verb movement may also be triggered by other factors. Bobaljik (2002), citing Lardiere (2000) and Meisel (1994), also claims that acquisition data in general do not support an approach where children use verbal morphology as a cue for syntactic parameter setting. This would also correspond to claims made in Bentzen (2003, 2005, 2007) that there is occasional V-to-I movement in embedded clauses in Norwegian dialects, although there is no morphological agreement in these cases. Wiklund, Hrafnbjargarson, Bentzen and Hróarsdóttir (2007) also question the weaker version of the Rich Agreement Hypothesis, in that they show that, in certain varieties of Icelandic, there may be lack of verb movement despite the presence of agreement.

In the next section we turn to a more detailed discussion of the syntax-morphology correlation in language acquisition, more specifically the acquisition of V2 word order.

2.2 Acquisition research on V2 and tense/agreement morphology

As verb movement generally only applies to finite verbs, the acquisition of V2 has often been linked to the mastery of verbal morphology. Clahsen (1986), for example, shows that subject-verb agreement is not fully mastered until around the age of 34–36 months in German child language. He also argues that the acquisition of agreement is developmentally linked to V2 word order. At the stage when the agreement paradigm falls into place, there is an increase in the use of V2 from 40% to nearly 90% in the German child data he investigated. Clahsen therefore argues that the acquisition of agreement is a prerequisite for verb movement.[1] These findings are reported also in e.g. Clahsen & Muysken (1986, 1989) and Clahsen (1988), and the same argument is made for a developmental correlation between the acquisition of agreement and the production of V2. Furthermore, in Clahsen and Penke (1992) it is claimed that in particular the 2sg ending *-st* serves as a lexical trigger for the setting of the V2 parameter in German child language. For the purposes of the present paper, it is interesting that Clahsen and Penke also discuss the situation

1. Clahsen also argues that the production of overt subjects is related to the mastery of agreement markings, as the number of subjectless sentences decreases sharply at the stage when agreement endings are acquired.

in the Mainland North Germanic languages, where there is no agreement at all on the verb. They admit that the triggering relationship between subject-verb agreement and verb movement thus cannot hold universally, but simply conclude that in "languages without subject-verb agreement, generalized V2 … has to be triggered in a different way" (p. 215). In this connection one may note that Verrips and Weissenborn (1992), based on bilingual German-French data, argue that it is finiteness that is of primary importance in this respect, not agreement, and that finiteness and V2 word order are available to children independently of their knowledge of agreement morphology.

The idea that tense/agreement morphology and syntactic movement are causally related has been further developed in the Optional Infinitive (OI) hypothesis advocated by Poeppel and Wexler (1993) and Wexler (1994). This hypothesis argues that children go through a stage in which they may produce root clauses with uninflected verbs, due to an option in child grammar to leave tense underspecified. This has especially been found to be the case in V2 languages such as Dutch and German. In Harris and Wexler (1996), this hypothesis is also argued to hold for English, as they show that tense is used more often in affirmative than medial-NEG sentences (43% vs. 9.6%). They relate this finding to the OI stage: as the tense feature is missing, dummy *do* will not be inserted in negative sentences, and since English is not a language with verb movement (V-to-I or V2), there is nothing that causes the verb to move across negation either.

Wexler (1999) argues for a maturational model where parameters are generally set early, whereas some universal principles emerge late. The OI stage is explained as young children's adherence to a restriction in UG called the Unique Checking Constraint (UCC), which causes them to check the D-feature of the subject only once and thus to omit either tense or agreement.[2] Learners of V2 languages set the V2 parameter early, as argued by e.g. Poeppel and Wexler (1993) for German and Santelmann (1995) for Swedish, but the presence of this developmental UG constraint in their grammar (the UCC) makes it possible for them to optionally leave the verb non-finite. In the early work, e.g. Wexler (1994), the OI hypothesis was contrasted with an analysis with missing modals. However, Wexler (1999) seems to specifically include such cases within the OI stage, since an OI language is defined as "one in which in early development a substantial proportion of root clauses (that in the adult grammar are required to be finite) are produced by the child in non-finite form" (p. 55). This means

2. The UCC is defined in the following way (Wexler 1999, p. 59):

Unique Checking Constraint (UCC) (on kids in OI-stage)
The D-feature of DP can only check against one functional category.

that when tense or agreement is omitted, verb inflections as well as auxiliaries will be lacking in children's clauses.

Rizzi (1993/94, 1999), on the other hand, assumes a truncation model to explain the non-target forms of early child language. That is to say, although the full set of functional projections are assumed to be available from the onset of language acquisition, young children may optionally truncate a clausal structure at some point in the hierarchy (normally either IP or VP). When this happens, all projections above the truncation point will be missing. This means that, unlike the tense omission model, the truncation analysis predicts that, when tense is missing, there will be no CP layer present in the clause either. This captures the fact that root infinitives are generally not found in *wh*-questions and non-subject-initial declaratives in V2 languages, illustrated in examples (3) and (4) above. In Rizzi (1993/94), truncation is argued to be possible in child grammar because children lack a principle, present in the adult grammar, requiring root clauses to be CPs. This principle is assumed to be subject to maturation, which will take place around age 2;5. Rizzi (2000) suggests that the generalization 'root=CP', which is a clear restriction in the adult language, is only a tendency in the child grammar. Thus, what children need to learn is that truncation is restricted to certain registers. The truncation model accounts well for the findings in child V2 languages such as Dutch and German, but fares less well with findings in child English. In order to explain the occurrence of RIs in *wh*-questions in child English, Guasti (2000) proposes an analysis within a Split-CP model (Rizzi 1997), with truncation of the highest projection (ForceP) and the presence of a null auxiliary in the head of the next projection, the FocP.

Not all studies from this time agree that there is a causal relationship between word order and verbal morphology, e.g. Atkinson (1998), Lasser (1997) or Bohnacker (1999). Already in Jordens (1990), arguments are presented against Clahsen's approach to the German data as well as de Haan's (1987) similar analysis of child Dutch, claiming that the acquisition of V2 is not a sudden development dependent on the acquisition of subject-verb agreement. According to Jordens (1990), the two processes only appear to be related. Based on a re-examination of some of the German and Dutch data, Jordens (1990) shows that children go through a relatively long period of time when there are clear distributional differences in the child data in that finite verbs predominantly appear in first/second position and non-finite verbs in final position, as illustrated by the following examples from de Haan (1987), cited in Jordens (1990:1415–1416):

(7) *papa* ***slaapt*** *nog.* (Tim, age 25.5–27.5) (Dutch)
daddy sleep.PRES still
'Daddy is still sleeping.'

(8) *ik ook* ***doen.*** (Tim, age 25.5–27.5)
I also do.INF
'I also (want to?) do (this).

Investigating his own daughter Jasmijn, Jordens (1990) finds that she also systematically uses finite forms in second position (often modals and auxiliaries) and non-finite forms in final position (infinitives and participles), already from a relatively early age (approximately 23–24 months). Jordens also argues that the position of the verb in Jasmijn's early data is dependent on the semantic category of the verb. More specifically, stative verbs are used exclusively in second position, while resultative verbs may occur either in second position with finite morphology or in final position with past participle morphology and activity verbs in final position with either infinitive or past participle morphology. He then argues that the early verb-final structures in Dutch and German child language are precursors to complete predicates with discontinuous word order. This means that sentences like (8), where the verb is in final position, are not examples of word order mistakes where the children have failed to move the verb. Jordens (1990) also finds that these verb-final structures rapidly disappear from the child's production at the stage where there is a simultaneous increase in clauses with modals and other auxiliaries.

Several proposals have been presented, also for other languages, arguing that there is a modal or another auxiliary missing in these root non-finite clauses, e.g. Plunkett and Strömquist (1990), Boser et al. (1992), Behrens (1993), Ingram and Thompson (1996) and Josefsson (1999). Wijnen, Kempen and Gillis (2001) explore the possibility that the predominance of infinitive forms in child Dutch is a result of the input. They conclude that the frequency of infinitive constructions in child-directed speech is too low to account for this, but that the salience of the infinitive in final position may contribute to children's early preference for root infinitives. Like Jordens (1990), Hoekstra and Hyams (1998) also focus on the different verb types appearing in finite and non-finite root clauses in child language and the modal interpretation that is typically found in root infinitives in Dutch and many other languages, but not in English child language. Discussing an analysis with a missing modal, they conclude that, despite its merits, it must be discarded due to certain shortcomings. One of these is the difference between the proportion of non-finite root clauses in *wh*-questions and other clause types in V2 languages. In Section 4 below, I show that this distinction in Norwegian child language is due to other factors, more specifically the types of verbs typically appearing in early *wh*-questions. Finally, Blom (2007) presents naturalistic and experimental data confirming the difference between the interpretation of root infinitives in Dutch and English child language, although she shows that this difference is smaller than previously assumed. Adopting an approach in terms of Distributed Morphology, she argues that non-finite verb forms are underspecified in child language and may thus be inserted in various syntactic contexts. Thus, she views morphology as distinct from syntax.

In the next section we take a closer look at the word order variation found in *wh*-questions in the adult language in English and Norwegian.

2.3 Wh-questions in English and Norwegian

Norwegian is often referred to as a classical V2 language with verb movement across the subject in most main clause questions and (non-subject-initial) declaratives. This is illustrated in (9)–(10). English, on the other hand, only shows residual V2-effects in the form of subject-auxiliary inversion in main clause questions (Rizzi 1996), also applying to the copula, see (11)–(12).

(9) ***Likte du*** *denne boka?*
liked you this book
'Did you like this book?'

(10) *Denne boka* ***likte jeg*** *virkelig godt.*
this book liked I really well
'This book I liked really well.'

(11) **Have you** read this book?

(12) What else **was there** to do?

But V2 is somewhat restricted also in Norwegian. First, it does not apply in all clause types, as exclamatives and most embedded clauses require non-V2. Second, and more important for this paper, word order in *wh*-questions is variable in many dialects, see e.g. Vangsnes (2005). In the dialect spoken by the children in this study (Tromsø), V2 is only required when the *wh*-element is phrasal, i.e. disyllabic or longer, as illustrated in (13). When the *wh*-word is monosyllabic (i.e. a *wh*-head, see Westergaard 2008, 2009a, b), on the other hand, the choice of V2 vs. non-V2 is dependent on information structure, non-V2 being chosen when the subject is given information (typically a pronoun) and V2 when the subject is new and/or focused information (most often a full DP), see Westergaard (2003, 2009a, b). V2 word order also tends to appear with the verb *være* 'be'. The importance of information structure for the choice of word order is illustrated in examples (14a, b) from one of the adult investigators in the acquisition corpus: In the first question, the subject (*skoan hannes* 'his shoes') is mentioned for the first time and appears in postverbal position (V2). In the follow-up question the subject is given information and can therefore be referred to by a pronoun and appear in preverbal position (non-V2).

(13) *Korfor* ***kommer han*** *ikkje?* **Korfor han ikkje kommer?*
why comes he not why he not comes
'Why isn't he coming?'

(14) a. *kor* ***er skoan*** ***hannes*** *henne?* (INV, file Ole.17) V2
where are shoe.DEF/PL his LOC
'Where are his shoes?'

b. *kor dem er henne?* Non-V2
where they are LOC
'Where are they?'

In my view, both Norwegian and English are mixed V2 grammars in that there is variation between V2 and non-V2 in both languages, dependent on clause type, verb class, type of initial element, as well as information structure, see Westergaard (2008, 2009b). Children acquiring the two languages cannot simply set a parameter for a positive value in one case and a negative value in the other (±V2), but need to pay attention to various linguistically relevant factors that affect the choice of word order in different contexts. This is what is referred to as micro-cues in Westergaard (2009a, c), i.e. small pieces of I-language structure that are produced in the children's grammars on exposure to the relevant input. More specifically, while Norwegian and English are similar in that both have V2 word order in *wh*-questions, they are different in that English-speaking children need to restrict V2 to certain verb types (auxiliaries and *be*), while Norwegian children need to make distinctions depending on the type of *wh*-element and restrict V2 to certain subject types (those conveying new and/or focused information).

Another similarity between English and Norwegian is that finiteness morphology is fairly impoverished. English verbs mark agreement only on 3rd person sg. subjects (*-s*), and modals have no morphological marking at all. In comparison, the verb in Norwegian has no person or number agreement. Both languages have tense marking on the verb, in English the familiar past tense and past participle *-ed* on regular verbs, and in Norwegian two different endings, *-a* and *-t(e)*, reflecting the two regular weak classes which make up about 96% of all verbs in the language, according to Endresen and Simonsen (2001). In addition there are various irregular past tense and participle forms in both languages. This is illustrated for Norwegian (Tromsø dialect) in Table 1, which gives an overview of verbal morphology in the two major verb classes (WL – large weak class, WS – small weak class) and a few examples of irregular morphology.

Table 1. Overview of verb forms in the Tromsø dialect

	Infinitive	**Present**	**Past**	**Past part.**	**Imperative**
WL class	kast-e 'throw'	kast-e	kast-a	kast-a	kast-Ø
WS class	lek-e 'play'	lek-e	lek-te	lek-t	lek-Ø
Irregular	drikk-e 'drink'	drikk-Ø	drakk-Ø	drukk-et/-e	drikk-Ø
	komm-e 'come'	komm-er	kom-Ø	komm-et	kom-Ø
	si-Ø 'say'	si-r	sa-Ø	sag-t	si-Ø

Furthermore, apart from the 3rd person SG. form, the present tense in English is identical to the infinitive, and it might be predicted that children initially find it hard to distinguish between the two, i.e. between a finite and a non-finite form. In the Tromsø dialect of Norwegian, this might be even more difficult, since the present tense ending *-er* of the standard language has been reduced to *-e* in the dialect for virtually all regular verbs in the two major weak classes, cf. columns 2 and 3 in Table 1. This makes the infinitive and the present tense forms of these verbs identical in all cases. Norwegian is thus different from V2 languages such as German and Dutch where infinitive morphology is distinct from the bare form.

This means that, if finiteness morphology really serves as a trigger for verb movement, then this triggering mechanism must be extremely weak, both in English and in Norwegian. On such an account, therefore, one might expect to see a certain delay in the acquisition of verb movement, as compared with other Germanic languages. This is not the case, as has been shown both for English (e.g. Radford 1992) and Norwegian (Westergaard 2009a). This will also be clear from the data discussed in the next two sections.

Finally, there is one difference between English and Norwegian that will turn out to be relevant for the present study, viz. the frequency of auxiliaries in *wh*-questions. As already mentioned, only auxiliaries and *be* undergo verb movement to second position in English questions, while in Norwegian any lexical verb may appear there. Since subject-auxiliary inversion is a syntactic requirement in English, the language must also create a dummy auxiliary in the form of *do*-support when there is no other auxiliary present. And finally, the existence of progressive aspect in English makes the use of the auxiliary *be* quite frequent in everyday spontaneous speech. This means that English *wh*-questions involve an auxiliary much more frequently in the input to children than the Norwegian data. These frequencies should also be reflected in the child data, English-speaking children producing (or attempting to produce) a considerably higher percentage of *wh*-questions with auxiliaries than Norwegian-speaking children. In the next two sections, we consider some child data from both languages.

3. Finiteness morphology and verb movement in English child language

In this section we investigate data from seven English-speaking children, all from the CHILDES database (MacWhinney 2000). Two of the children are American, while five children are speakers of British English.

(15) **Brown corpus** (Brown 1973): Adam (3;0.11–3;5.1), Sarah (2;9.6–5;1.6)
Manchester corpus (Theakston et al. 2001): Warren (1;10.6–2;9.20), Anne (1;10.7–2;9.10), Ruth (1;11.15–2;11.21), Liz (1;11.9–2;10.18), Nicole (2;0.25–3;0.10)

As mentioned in the Introduction, auxiliaries are functional elements and for this reason generally late acquired. It is also well known that English-speaking children produce a high proportion of auxiliary-less structures in all clause types for a relatively extended period of time, and examples are frequently found in English child data. This is illustrated in the declaratives in (16)–(17), showing the lack of auxiliary *be* and dummy *do* respectively.

(16) I **going** sit. (Adam 2;6.17)

(17) tha(t) no(t) **hurt**. (Sarah 3;1.24)

Furthermore, non-finite and verbless *wh*-questions (lacking an auxiliary or the copula) are also frequent, as illustrated in (18)–(23):

(18) what he **doing**? (Adam 3;0.11)

(19) where my spoon **gone**? (Warren 2;0.17)

(20) where me **sit**? (Anne 2;3.28)

(21) why you **get** another one? (Liz 2;8.14)

(22) what you **looking** for? (Ruth 2;7.24)

(23) what the name, Caroline? (Nicole 2;9.17)

According to Radford (1992) and Roeper (1999), as soon as auxiliaries appear in English child data, they are typically target-consistently inverted, as illustrated by the examples in (24)–(25). There is also early inversion with copula *be*, as in example (26):

(24) what **do I** see? (Eve 2;0)

(25) Sue # what **are you** folding? (Eve 2;1)

(26) where **is a box**? (Adam 3;0.11)

However, as first pointed out by Klima and Bellugi (1966), some English-speaking children go through a stage where there is occasional lack of inversion in *wh*-questions, especially questions involving modals, illustrated in examples (27)–(28) from Adam's data.

(27) why **I can** keep dem? (Adam 3;2.21)

(28) why **he can't** hit? (Adam 3;4.01)

This phenomenon has been studied extensively, see e.g. Labov & Labov (1978), Stromswold (1990), Radford (1994), Guasti, Thornton & Wexler (1995), Guasti (1996), Rowland & Pine (2000, 2003), Berk (2003), and Thornton (2008). In the latter two, it is argued that the main cause of this word order distinction is that the question word *why* is significantly different from other *wh*-elements, occurring more frequently without verb movement. In Guasti, Thornton and Wexler (1995) and Guasti (1996) it is argued that the presence of negation is the cause of the problem for English-speaking children: While they in general produce target-consistent word order in affirmative questions, they make a considerable number of verb placement errors in negative questions, as in (28).

Since two different word orders are attested in some English-speaking children's data, one might ask whether verb movement at this stage is somehow related to finiteness morphology on the verb. The answer to this question seems to be no: In sentences with non-inverted word order the unmoved auxiliary is always finite, i.e. there are no examples attested where non-finite auxiliaries appear in post-subject position. This is in many cases necessarily so, since non-inversion typically appears with modals, and modals have no non-finite forms in present-day English.[3] Thornton (2008) has also found non-inversion with the question word *why* up to the age of 5–6 in the production of some English-speaking children, and it seems obvious that these children do not have any problem with finiteness at this stage. Thus, the lack of subject-auxiliary inversion cannot be related to missing finiteness on the auxiliary. There are also occasional examples in the child data where (target-consistently) uninverted lexical verbs are also finite, as illustrated in (29)–(32):

(29) where he **went**? (Anne 2;5.2)

(30) what dey **said**? (Adam 3;2.9)

(31) what it **looks** like now? (Sarah 4;2.28)

(32) what four **means**? (Sarah 4;5.29)

Within the model of Role and Reference grammar, Van Valin (2002) has argued for an alternative version of the correspondence between syntactic movement and finiteness. More specifically, he argues that the lack of inversion with auxiliaries, typically modals, is due to the fact that modals have no clear finiteness morphology in English, lacking 3rd person SG *-s*. Modals are therefore presumably not perceived as clearly tensed by children and are consequently not inverted. Similarly, this should explain the lack of inversion with negative auxiliaries (since they always end in *n't*). But if this were the case, we would expect to see modals not moving to a position above negation in declaratives either (V-to-I movement) – also a movement process that only applies to finite forms of auxiliaries and *be*. Such examples (e.g. *I not can go*) seem to be unattested in English child data. Considering Adam's data in detail, we find that his first example of a modal together with a full (non-contracted) version of the negation *not*

3. In Norwegian, where the modals do have a non-finite form, they never appear in non-finite root clauses (e.g. **han ikke kunne gjøre det* 'he not could.INF do it'). This seems to be evidence that children very early recognize the appropriate modals as finite verbs, despite the lack of finiteness morphology (see Section 4 below, and Westergaard 2009a).

shows target-consistent word order, see (33). Other auxiliaries also appear above negation, as in (34). This means that Aux-Neg word order is in place as soon as the relevant elements appear in child language data.

(33) I **may not**. (Adam 3;2.21)

(34) I'**m not** going put some more +... (Adam 3;3.18)

Another argument against there being a finiteness/movement correlation in this case is that, as reported in many studies (see above), English-speaking children who have a problem with inversion in *wh*-questions typically do invert in *yes/no*-questions, illustrated by the following example from Adam:

(35) **Can you** # play with me? (Adam 3; 3.18)

Furthermore, it has sometimes been noted that there is typically a distinction between the copula and auxiliaries with respect to inversion. Investigating Adam's data between the ages of 3;2 and 3;5, Westergaard (2009c) finds that, while the copula is inverted 96.4% (455/472) of the time, auxiliaries are inverted only 34.2% (35/73). This distinction also holds for omissions in *wh*-questions: while the copula is missing only 36.8% (261/710) in Adam's data at this time, auxiliaries are missing as often as 83.6% (588/703). Furthermore, a discrepancy between the copula and other verbs with respect to verb movement has also been found in Swedish child language (Waldmann 2008), as well as in declaratives in Norwegian child data (Westergaard 2009a). This would be surprising on an account that analyzes the lack of finiteness marking as the result of a grammatical deficit (e.g. the UCC). Table 2 shows that a similar discrepancy between auxiliaries and the copula is also found in *wh*-questions in the data of other English-speaking children. It also shows that there is a difference in the development of finiteness marking involving the two verbal categories: At an early stage, the copula is missing almost as often as auxiliaries, but these omissions quickly disappear, and at a later stage (varying among different children), there is a considerable difference between the proportion of auxiliary and copula omissions.

Table 2. The overt realization of copula vs. auxiliaries in *wh*-questions in English child data

	Age	Missing copula	Missing auxiliary
Sarah	2;9–3;8	73.7% (84/114)	94% (47/50)
	3;8–5;1	4.5% (7/156)	50% (127/254)
Warren	1;10–2;3	91.9% (34/37)	95.2% (20/21)
	2;3–2;9	21.0% (47/224)	45.1% (32/71)
Liz	1;10–2;3	17.4% (36/207)	33.3% (24/72)
	2;3–2;9	4.4% (7/158)	36.2% (38/105)

Westergaard (2009c) provides an account of the lack of inversion in specific cases in terms of children's sensitivity to fine distinctions in syntax (micro-cues), which prevents them from generalizing a rule from one (sub-)category to another. This is argued to be what is responsible for children generally being conservative learners (see Snyder 2007 for a recent discussion). In addition to preventing overgeneralization errors in syntax, this ability to recognize micro-cues also sometimes causes children to 'undergeneralize' a syntactic rule, making even finer distinctions than the target grammar. In the case of English, for example, this results in a difference between *be* and auxiliaries with respect to inversion and omissions in *wh*-questions.[4] This model may also explain why English-speaking children make a distinction between *why* and other question words. That is, V2 with *be* doesn't automatically generalize to aux, and V2 with *what* does not immediately generalize to *why*. Thus, English, Norwegian and Swedish children are argued to have smaller V2 grammars than the corresponding adult languages.

Given the child data investigated in this section, I argue that the occurrence of non-finite root clauses produced by English-speaking children is not due to a problem related to the realization of finiteness *per se*. I also argue that there is no direct link between the production of non-finite root clauses and verb movement (subject-auxiliary inversion). That is, non-inversion or non-finite *wh*-questions are not caused by a lack of finiteness, but rather by a problem realizing auxiliaries combined with a conservative approach to rule generalization.

4. Finiteness and verb movement in Norwegian child language

The investigation of *wh*-questions in the Norwegian child data is based on a corpus of three Norwegian children (Ina, Ann and Ole) between the ages of approximately 1;8 and 3;3, illustrated in the overview in (36) (see Anderssen 2006 for further information about the corpus).

(36) **Tromsø corpus** (Anderssen 2006): Ina (1;8.20–3;3.18), Ann (1;8.20–3;0.1), Ole (1;9.10–2;11.23).

Westergaard (2003, 2009a, c) shows that both V2 and non-V2 word orders are in place from early on. The children also produce the two word orders in appropriate contexts, e.g. only V2 with disyllabic *wh*-elements, as in (37), cf. example (13) above.

4. An anonymous reviewer asks whether it s justified to generalize over the different auxiliaries and suggests that there may be relevant distinctions also at a further micro-level. The micro-cue model clearly opens up for this possibility. In fact, it it shown in Section 5 below that English-speaking children have considerably more problems with the auxiliaries *be* and *do* than the modals (cf. Tables 6 and 8).

(37) *korfor får den ikkje mat?* (Ole 2;8.5) V2
why get.PRES it not food
'Why doesn't it get any food?'

In questions with monosyllabic *wh*-elements, where both word orders are possible in the adult language (cf. example (14) above), the children are also target-consistent with respect to the verb and subject types appearing with the two word orders. Table 3 provides an overview of all complete non-subject *wh*-questions produced by the three children in the corpus (i.e. questions containing a *wh*-element, a verb and a subject).[5] Examples (38) and (39) illustrate that V2 is preferred with full DP subjects (and *be*) and non-V2 with pronominal subjects, as in the adult language.

Table 3. Percentage of V2 in questions with monosyllabic wh-elements, three Norwegian children

Wh-word	Ina.01–23, age 1;8.20–2;10.12	Ann.01–21, age 1;8.20–3;0.1	Ole.01–22, age 1;9.10–2;11.23	Total
ka 'what'	34.7% (43/124)	25.4% (18/71)	100% (3/3)	198
kor 'where'	88.7% (126/142)	78.3% (65/83)	100% (42/42)	267
kem 'who'	69.2% (18/26)	63.6% (7/11)	100% (2/2)	39
Total	64.0% (187/292)	54.5% (90/165)	100% (47/47)	504

(38) *kor er Ann sin dukke hen?* (Ann 1;11.0) V2
where be.PRES Ann POSS doll LOC
'Where is Ann's doll?

(39) *ka du gjør?* (Ann 2;3.9) Non-V2
what you do.PRES
'What are you doing?'

5. Ole does not produce a single complete *wh*-question with non-V2 word order. However, in so-called *wh*-less questions, he produces questions with and without verb movement, with the same subject and verb preferences as in the adult data – i.e. verb movement with full DP subjects and no verb movement with pronominal subjects, see (i)–(ii).

(i) *er doktoren?* (Ole.02, age 1;10.0)
be.PRES doctor.DEF
'(Where) is the doctor?' Target: Kor er doktoren?

(ii) *den gjør der?* (Ole.02, age 1;10.0)
that do.PRES there
'(What) is that doing there?' Target: Ka den gjør der?

If there were a causal correspondence between finiteness morphology and syntactic movement in child language, we would expect to find the V2 examples appearing with finite verbs and the non-V2 questions with non-finite verbs, at least at an early stage. However, this is not the case. The children's verb types appearing with the two word orders are illustrated in Table 4, where the corpus has been divided into three periods in order to illustrate some development. The verbs occurring in *wh*-questions are almost exclusively finite, or they are ambiguous, meaning that they belong to one of the weak verb patterns where the infinitive and the present tense forms are identical (cf. Section 2.3). The only difference between *wh*-questions with V2 and non-V2 is that the latter type occurs much more often with ambiguous verb forms. This is simply a function of V2 being preferred with the verb *være* 'be', for reasons of information structure (see Westergaard 2003, 2009a), while non-V2 is chosen when the verb is any other verb, often one which belongs to the weak verb classes.

Table 4. The number of finite, ambiguous and non-finite verb forms in the three Norwegian children's wh-questions, with V2 and non-V2 word order

	V2			Non-v2		
Files	Fin	Amb	Non-f	Fin	Amb	Non-f
Ina.01–10	43	6	0	12	5	0
Ina.11–16	89	2	0	17	5	1
Ina.17–23	47	0	0	31	32	2
Total	**179**	**8**	**0**	**60**	**42**	**3**
Ann.01–10	11	0	0	9	1	0
Ann.11–16	42	1	0	16	15	0
Ann.17–21	36	0	0	34	0	0
Total	**89**	**1**	**0**	**59**	**16**	**0**
Ole.01–10	3	0	0	0	0	0
Ole.11–16	7	0	0	0	0	0
Ole.17–22	37	0	0	0	0	0
Total	**47**	**0**	**0**	**0**	**0**	**0**

In the whole corpus, there are only three examples of clearly non-finite *wh*-questions, illustrated in (40)–(42), all three produced by Ina.[6] One example contains an infinitive, while the other two have past participle forms. In all three cases it seems reasonable

6. There is also one example in Ina's data and one in Ann's involving the verb *si* 'say', where they have produced the bare form instead of the standard present tense *si(e)r* with non-V2, see

to assume that there is an auxiliary missing, a modal in (40) and the perfective *have* in (41)–(42), as suggested by the translations. The three examples of non-finite root clauses are of course necessarily non-V2, since, given that there is no auxiliary, there is no element that may or may not undergo movement. The non-finite verb is in target-consistent post-subject position.

(40) *kor æ* ***legge*** *den hen?* (Ina.16, age 2;7.8)
where I lay.INF it LOC
'Where (should) I put it?'

(41) *ka* ***reven*** ***gjort?*** (Ina.18, age)
what fox.DEF done
'What (has) the fox done?'

(42) *ka* ***æ fått*** *den?* (Ina.22, age 2;10.2)
what I got that
'What (have) I got there?'

This means that, as predicted by both the OI and the Truncation models, the number of non-finite root clauses is very low, making up only 0.6% (3/504) of the total number of *wh*-questions. In comparison, these Norwegian children relatively frequently produce non-finite root clauses in *yes/no*-questions and subject-initial declaratives with negation, typically also lacking the subject, as shown in (43)–(44). According to Westergaard (2009a), these appear between 5.1% and 22.5% in the child data. On an account that there is a causal correlation between finiteness and verb movement, the distinction in the Norwegian child data between *wh*-questions and *yes/no*-questions with respect to finiteness is somewhat surprising, just like in the English data (cf. Section 3). The V2 requirement holds completely consistently in *yes/no*-questions, while *wh*-questions allow both V2 and non-V2 in the Tromsø dialect, as we have seen. Yet, it is the former clause type that displays examples of non-finite root clauses.

(43) *tegne den?* (Ina, 2;0.5)
draw that
'(Can I) draw that?'

(44) *ikke være sånn.* (Ole, 1;10.0)
not be such
'(It should) not be like that.'

---

example (i). However, this bare form is also occasionally found in the data of some the adults in the corpus and may thus be considered a dialect variant of the present tense of this verb.

(i) *ka du si?* (Ann.11, age 2;4.0)
what you say.PRES
'What are you saying?'

Examples such as (43)–(44) often have a modal meaning, cf. the translations. Crucially, therefore, I interpret these structures to be cases where there is an auxiliary missing, not examples where there is no verb movement due to the lack of finiteness morphology on the verb. Thus, this corresponds to what has been argued by others questioning the causal correlation between finiteness morphology and verb movement (see Section 2.2). Some evidence supporting this position is that non-finite root clauses are sometimes preceded or followed by the same sentence with the auxiliary provided, as in the follow-up to example (5), which was provided in the Introduction.

(5') a. ... *han ikke* ***røre*** *klossen.* (Ina.11, age 2;4.1)
he not touch.INF brick.DEF
'He (should/must/may) not touch the brick.'

b. *han* ***kan*** *ikke* ***røre*** *klossen.* (Ina.11, age 2;4.1)
he can not touch brick.DEF
'He may not touch the brick.'

Despite this distinction between *wh*-questions and these other clause types, my account for the occurrence of non-finite root clauses is the same in both cases, viz. a problem realizing auxiliaries (often modals). The difference between *wh*-questions and other clause types is thus one of frequency. We may now ask why there is a difference between *wh*-questions on the one hand and subject-initial declaratives and *yes/no*-questions on the other with respect to the occurrence of non-finite root clauses. Could it be that the latter two clause types for some reason involve more auxiliaries, especially modals? A detailed investigation of the Norwegian child data reveals that in fact they do: Subject-initial declaratives with negation (which is the context investigated) often appear with modals, e.g. *kan ikke* 'cannot', *vil ikke* 'will not', *må ikke* 'must not', etc. And in early *yes/no*-questions modals are attested as often as 40–65%, see Westergaard (2009a).

In comparison, modals and other auxiliaries are virtually non-attested in *wh*-questions. A detailed investigation of the verb types typically appearing in Norwegian children's *wh*-questions reveals that the copula is by far the most frequent verb. Lexical verbs such as *ha* 'have', *gjøre* 'do' and *hete* 'be-called' also appear relatively frequently in this clause type. Auxiliaries are correspondingly rare, especially in early files. It is important to stress that the children do not attempt to produce such clauses either – in fact, most of the earliest *wh*-questions are with the verb *be*.

More specifically, Ina produces only 7 examples of an auxiliary in *wh*-questions (5 modals, 2 with perfective *have*), spread across the corpus (the first in file 5, age 2;0.5). This means that only 3.4% (10/292) of her complete *wh*-questions have an auxiliary (overt or missing). As noted above, Ann and Ole do not produce a single example of a non-finite *wh*-question. An investigation of the number of auxiliaries in their data reveals that Ole uses altogether 5 (all modals) while Ann produces 21 (15 modals, 6 perfective *have*) – making up 10.6% (5/47) and 12.7% (21/165) for the two of them respectively. These *wh*-questions appear with both V2 and non-V2. But the crucial fact is the following: Most of the *wh*-questions with auxiliaries appear in the latest files in the corpus, as 4 of Ole's 5 examples are attested in files 19 and 20 (age 2;10.0–2;10.15), while 17 of Ann's 21 examples appear after file 17 (age 2:8.4). And at this stage, the number of non-finite root clauses in other clause types is negligible: In subject-initial declaratives these examples tend to disappear around file 16 (age 2;7.8) for Ina, file 14 (age 2;6.0) for Ann, and file 12 (age 2;5.18) for Ole, and in *yes/no*-questions somewhat earlier than this (see Westergaard 2009a). This means that, by the time these Norwegian children start producing auxiliaries in *wh*-questions, they are already at a stage where these are no longer missing to any large extent in other clause types.

Finally, it could be mentioned that the Norwegian children also produce some verbless *wh*-questions. The verb missing is in all cases the copula, and these examples are thus similar to the ones where *be* is missing in English child data. The examples occur in the production of all three children, although not to a very large extent in Ole's data, where only one such example is attested, making up 2.1% (1/48). Ina produces 22 (7%, 22/314) and Ann five (2.9%, 5/170) – examples are given in (45)–(46). Most of these verbless questions occur in the children's early files (e.g. 18 of Ina's 22 examples are in files 3–9). However, the verb *være* 'be' is very frequent in the children's production and also appears early in *wh*-questions as well as other clause types. Just as in the English child data, therefore, there seems to be a distinction between missing *be* and missing auxiliaries in early Norwegian child language, in that *be* falls into place earlier than the auxiliaries.

(45) *ka* *det*? (Ina.03, age 1;10.23)
what that
'What (is) that?'

(46) *kor* *dem*? (Ann.07, age 2;1.7)
where they
'Where (are) they?'

Summarizing, we have seen in this section that the Norwegian children have both V2 and non-V2 word orders in place in *wh*-questions from early on and that finiteness morphology is not only a feature of questions with V2 word order, as also questions with non-V2 almost exclusively appear with finite verbs. Similarly, in the previous section, we saw that occasional non-inverted *wh*-questions in English child data involve finite verbs only. Furthermore, the clear difference between the copula and auxiliaries indicates that the problem for English-speaking children is related to the realization of auxiliaries. In this section, this is argued to be the case also in non-finite root clauses in Norwegian child language, as well as in the occasional non-finite *wh*-questions. Thus, I have argued that non-finite verbs are intended to be infinitive (or in some cases a participle form), and also intended to be in situ. That is, it is not a verb that lacks finiteness morphology and therefore does not move, or reversely, does not move and therefore lacks morphology. The alleged causal connection between finiteness morphology and verb movement therefore does not seem to hold in the acquisition of subject-auxiliary inversion or V2 word order in English and Norwegian, and the distinction between the two languages is reduced to one of frequency. This is discussed in the next section.

5. Discussion: The difference between English and Norwegian *wh*-questions

In the two previous sections we have considered child language data from English and Norwegian and argued that there cannot be a causal correlation between finiteness morphology and syntactic verb movement, resulting in V2 word order in *wh*-questions. This is generally due to the fact that verbs are virtually exclusively finite in Norwegian *wh*-questions, regardless of word order, V2 or non-V2 (both grammatical in the target language). Similarly, English-speaking children who produce certain non-inverted examples in *wh*-questions do not produce non-finite auxiliaries in such cases. The distinction between the copula and auxiliaries also shows that the main problem for English-speaking children is in the realization of auxiliaries. Since auxiliaries are often missing in all clause types in English, there is no reason why they should not be missing also from *wh*-questions. Thus, as we are not assuming that there is any correlation between finiteness and syntactic movement, we need no extra explanation for non-finite *wh*-questions in English child language. When English non-finite *wh*-questions have a modal meaning, there is a modal missing – in other cases it may be dummy *do* or progressive *be* that is intended. And given the analysis adopted in this paper of non-finite root clauses in general, with a modal or other auxiliary missing, this is what I argue is the problem for Norwegian children too. This is the case in all clause types, and the problem with the realization of auxiliaries is unrelated to the position of the finite verb and the issue of verb movement.

What could be the cause of the difference between English and Norwegian in *wh*-questions then? That is, why are examples such as (2) relatively frequent in English child language, while examples such as (40) are virtually non-existent in Norwegian child data?

(2') what you doing? (Eve.14, age 2;0)

(40') *kor æ legge den hen?* (Ina.16, age 2;7.8)
where I lay.INF it LOC
'Where (should) I put it?'

In the Norwegian child corpus investigated here, the only failed attempts at producing an auxiliary in *wh*-questions are the three examples in (40)–(42). But in order to explain why non-finite examples are infrequent in Norwegian *wh*-questions, we need to consider the number of these non-finite *wh*-questions in relation to the number of examples that have an overt modal or auxiliary. That is, how often do the children actually produce (or attempt to produce) a *wh*-question with an auxiliary?

As shown in Section 2, inversion is required with different verbs in the two languages (see the overview in (47)): While in Norwegian, all verbs may invert – lexical verbs as well as auxiliaries, i.e. perfective *have* and modals, only auxiliaries and the copula invert in English. Furthermore, English has two auxiliaries that do not exist in Norwegian, progressive *be* and dummy *do*. This means that, while Norwegian children encounter problematic elements in only some *wh*-questions (those which involve auxiliaries), English-speaking children are faced with these problems in all *wh*-questions (except those involving the copula).

(47) **English:** modals, *have*, *do*, *be* + copula
Norwegian: modals, *have* + all lexical verbs

In order to investigate whether this may be the reason for the difference between English and Norwegian child language with respect to finiteness in *wh*-questions, we will first have a look at the distribution of the various auxiliaries in English child language. Table 5 shows an overview of the use of auxiliaries in *wh*-questions in the data of the seven children investigated in Section 3. The data have been searched for all *wh*-questions, and every single example has been individually considered with respect to overt or missing auxiliaries. If the auxiliary is missing, a present participle (*-ing*) is considered to be a *be* context, a past participle is considered to be a *have* context and an infinitive considered to be a modal or *do* context, depending on the linguistic environment of the *wh*-question. In the table, a distinction is made between *do* and *be* contexts on the one hand (those that are only found in English) and *have* and modals on the other, i.e. those auxiliaries that are also relevant for Norwegian.

Table 5. Type of auxiliary contexts in English *wh*-questions

	***do* + *be* contexts**	***have* + modal contexts**
Adam	89.4% (734/821)	10.6% (87/821)
Sarah	91.2% (279/306)	8.8% (27/306)
Ruth	92.6% (63/68)	7.4% (5/68)
Nicole	73.1% (76/104)	26.9% (28/104)
Anne	57.1% (121/212)	42.9% (91/212)
Warren	55.4% (51/92)	44.6% (41/92)
Liz	49.7% (88/177)	50.3% (89/177)
Total	79.3% (1412/1780)	20.7% (368/1780)

It is clear from Table 5 that the auxiliaries *do* and *be* are the most frequent ones, making up almost 80% of the total.[7] A closer investigation of these examples shows that these two auxiliaries also make up the core of English-speaking children's problems with auxiliary realization: Table 6 shows how often the auxiliary is missing in *do* and *be* contexts, as well as how much these omissions account for in relation to the total number of omissions in *wh*-questions in the English child data. As we see, both *do* and *be* are missing approximately 70% of the time, and more importantly, these omissions make up close to 90% of all auxiliary omissions in *wh*-questions in the child data. As these auxiliaries are not relevant for Norwegian-speaking children, it seems that these figures should account for most of the difference between the two child groups with respect to finiteness in *wh*-questions.

Table 6. Missing auxiliaries *do* and *be* in English *wh*-questions and the percentage of this in relation to all missing auxiliaries

	Missing of all *do*	Missing of all *be*	% of all missing aux
Adam	74.3% (375/505)	88.6% (203/229)	95.7% (578/604)
Sarah	64.5% (147/228)	54.9% (28/51)	94.6% (175/185)
Ruth	100.0% (11/11)	97.9% (47/48)	92.5% (62/67)
Nicole	93.3% (28/30)	60.9% (28/46)	69.1% (56/81)
Anne	41.1% (30/73)	50.0% (24/48)	62.8% (54/86)
Warren	30.8% (4/31)	55.3% (21/38)	48.1% (25/52)
Liz	36.4% (8/22)	53.0% (35/66)	69.4% (43/62)
Total	67% (603/900)	73.4% (386/526)	87.3% (993/1137)

But we also need to have a closer look at the contexts for *have* and modals in the child data. As shown in Table 7, these auxiliary types are fairly infrequent in both English and Norwegian *wh*-questions: The modals make up less than 10% for all the children (average around 5–6%), while there is more variation with respect to perfective *have*. As noted in Footnote 7, the British children (especially Anne, Warren and Liz) produce more *have* contexts than the American children, presumably because British English uses perfective *have* in contexts where American English would prefer the simple past tense.

7. Some of the British children (especially Anne, Warren and Liz) produce a lower percentage of *do* and *be* contexts than the American children. This is due to a much higher proportion of perfective *have* in their data (cf. Table 7), presumably caused by a difference between the two varieties of English with respect to contexts for the present perfective vs. the simple past.

Table 7. *Have* and modal contexts in English and Norwegian *wh*-questions

	***Have* contexts**	**Modal contexts**
Adam	2.9% (24/821)	7.7% (63/821)
Sarah	0.3% (1/306)	8.5% (26/306)
Ruth	7.4% (5/68)	0.0% (0/68)
Nicole	26.0% (27/104)	1.0% (1/104)
Anne	38.7% (82/212)	4.2% (9/212)
Warren	44.6% (41/92)	0.0% (0/92)
Liz	48.6% (86/177)	1.7% (3/177)
Total	14.9% (266/1780)	5.7% (102/1780)
Ina	1.4% (4/292)	2.0% (6/292)
Ann	3.6% (6/165)	9.1% (15/165)
Ole	0.0% (0/47)	10.6% (5/47)
Total	2% (10/504)	5.2% (26/504)

Furthermore, as shown in Table 8, these auxiliaries are not as often missing as *do* and *be* (cf. Table 6). This is especially the case for modals.

Table 8. Missing *have* and modals in English and Norwegian *wh*-questions

	***Have* contexts**	**Modal contexts**
Adam	91.7% (22/24)	6.3% (4/63)
Sarah	0.0% (0/1)	38.5% (10/26)
Ruth	100.0% (5/5)	–
Nicole	92.6% (25/27)	0.0% (0/1)
Anne	37.8% (31/82)	11.1% (1/9)
Warren	65.9% (27/41)	–
Liz	22.1% (19/86)	0.0% (0/3)
Total	48.5% (129/266)	15.2% (15/99)
Ina	50.0% (2/4)	16.7% (1/6)
Ann	0.0% (0/6)	0.0% (0/15)
Ole	–	0.0% (0/5)
Total	20% (2/10)	3.9% (1/26)

In this section it has been argued that the difference between English and Norwegian with respect to the frequency of non-finite *wh*-questions is not due to a qualitative difference in the child grammars related to finiteness and verb movement. Instead, this is shown to be due to a difference in the type of verb that moves in these questions – all verbs in Norwegian, but only auxiliaries (and *be*) in English. This means that English-speaking children encounter functional elements in all *wh*-questions except those involving the copula, while Norwegian children face these problematic elements only in *wh*-questions containing auxiliaries. As noted in Section 4, the copula is the most frequent verb in early *wh*-questions, as well as a few other lexical verbs. Furthermore, the auxiliaries produced by two of the children (Ann and Ole) appear so late in the corpus that non-finite root clauses are hardly attested any more in other clause types. Investigating the child that does produce occasional non-finite *wh*-questions, Ina, it turns out that she produces only 7 examples of auxiliaries. This means that only 3.4% (10/292) of her complete *wh*-questions contain an auxiliary (overt or missing). But this also means that her three failed attempts at producing an auxiliary make up 30% (3/10) – considerably more than the 0.6% we calculated above for non-finite root clauses in relation to all *wh*-questions. Although numbers are very small and caution is required, this indicates that Ina is no longer that different from what is found in the data from English-speaking children.

The account of young children's non-finite root clauses presented in this paper is similar in spirit to what is argued in Phillips (1995). Comparing the occurrence of non-finite *wh*-questions in the data of English and French children, he finds that such examples are virtually non-attested in the French child data. He also argues that this is not due to a grammar deficit, but to the type of verb that typically appears in *wh*-questions in the two languages. Interestingly, however, the French children produce almost exclusively auxiliaries in this clause type. Given that auxiliaries are always finite in young children's production data (see e.g. Wexler 1994 and Section 3 above), this fact should account for the lack of non-finite *wh*-questions in French. This is of course the opposite of what has been found in *wh*-questions in the Norwegian child data, where auxiliaries are hardly attested at all. I have no explanation for the discrepancy between French and Norwegian with respect to the occurrence of auxiliaries in *wh*-questions, nor why auxiliaries seem to be easier to acquire in French than in Norwegian. Nevertheless, the two accounts are not contradictory: In languages where auxiliaries are difficult to learn (Norwegian, English), non-finite root clauses will appear in early child language due to omission of the auxiliary. Once auxiliaries appear, however (early in French, somewhat later in English and Norwegian), they will always be finite. Thus, the fact that neither French nor Norwegian children produce non-finite *wh*-questions can be accounted for by the high frequency of auxiliaries (always finite) in this context in French and the corresponding lack of auxiliaries in early child Norwegian.

6. Summary and conclusion

In this paper I have argued that the alleged causal correlation between finiteness morphology and syntactic movement does not hold with respect to the acquisition of V2 word order. Evidence for this is provided by child data on *wh*-questions in English and a dialect of Norwegian, both considered in this paper to be mixed V2 grammars. Finiteness is shown to be in place in both languages irrespective of verb movement, also in occasional non-inverted examples in English and target-consistent non-V2 examples in Norwegian. The difference between the two languages with respect to the number of non-finite *wh*-questions is related to a difference in the restriction on V2, which is limited to auxiliaries (and *be*) in English, a category that is typically late acquired, in all clause types. In Norwegian, on the other hand, any verb can move to second position in *wh*-questions. Non-finite root clauses, often attested in subject-initial declaratives and *yes/no*-questions in Norwegian child data, are argued to be due to the same problem as in English child language, viz. a problem realizing auxiliaries. The lack of non-finite examples in *wh*-questions in Norwegian child data is shown to simply be due to auxiliaries being virtually non-existent in this clause type. Instead, most of the Norwegian children's early *wh*-questions involve the copula or frequent lexical verbs. The paper has also presented extensive child data showing that the auxiliaries *do* and *be*, which are not relevant for Norwegian, pose the biggest challenge for English-speaking children, accounting for approximately 90% of the non-finite *wh*-questions produced. Modal contexts, on the other hand, are shown to be very rare in *wh*-questions both in English and in Norwegian. This means that Norwegian-speaking children are faced with problematic auxiliary contexts in *wh*-questions much less frequently than English-speaking children. Consequently, while non-finite wh-questions are relatively frequent in English child language, they are hardly attested in Norwegian child data.

References

Anderssen, Merete. 2006. The Acquisition of Compositional Definiteness in Norwegian. Ph.D. dissertation, University of Tromsø.

Atkinson, Martin. 1998. Now, hang on a minute: Some reflections on emerging orthodoxies. In Clahsen (ed.), 451–499.

Behrens, Heike. 1993. Temporal Reference in German Child Language: Form and Function of Early Verb Use. Ph.D. dissertation, University of Amsterdam.

Bentzen, Kristine. 2003. V-to-I Movement in the absence of morphological cues: evidence from Northern Norwegian. In *Proceedings from the 19th Scandinavian Conference of Linguistics*, Peter Svenonius, Anne Dahl & Marit R. Westergaard (eds.). *Nordlyd* 31(3): 573–588.

Bentzen, Kristine. 2005. What's the better move? On verb placement in Standard and Northern Norwegian. *Nordic Journal of Linguistics* 28(2): 153–188. doi:10.1017/S0332586505001411

Bentzen, Kristine. 2007. The degree of verb movement in embedded clauses in three varieties of Norwegian. In *Scandinavian Dialect Syntax 2005*, Kristine Bentzen & Øystein A. Vangsnes (eds.). *Nordlyd* 34: 127–146.
Berk, Stephanie. 2003. Why 'why' is different? In *Proceedings of the 27th Annual Boston University Conference on Language Development*, Barbara Beachley, Amanda Brown & Frances Conlin (eds.),127–137. Somerville MA: Cascadilla Press.
Blom, Elma. 2007. Modality, infinitives, and finite bare verbs in Dutch and English child language. *Language Acquisition* 14(1): 75–113. doi:10.1080/10489220701331821
Bobaljik, Jonathan David. 2002. Realizing Germanic inflection: Why morphology does not drive syntax. *Journal of Comparative Germanic Linguistics* 6: 129–167. doi:10.1023/A:1023669927250
Bobaljik, Jonathan David & Thráinsson, Höskuldur. 1998. Two heads aren't always better than one. *Syntax* 1(1): 37–71. doi:10.1111/1467-9612.00003
Bohnacker, Ute. 1999. Icelandic plus English: Language Differentiation and Functional Categories in a Successively Bilingual Child. Ph.D. dissertation, University of Durham.
Boser, Katharina, Lust, Barbara C., Santelmann, Lynn & Whitman, John. 1992. The syntax of V2 in early child German grammar: The Strong Continuity Hypothesis. *Proceedings of the Northeastern Linguistic Society* 22: 51–66.
Brown, Roger. 1973. *A First Language: The Early Stages.* Cambridge MA: Harvard University Press. doi:10.4159/harvard.9780674732469
Clahsen, Harald. 1986. Verb inflections in German child language: Acquisition of agreement markings and the functions they encode. *Linguistics* 24: 79–121. doi:10.1515/ling.1986.24.1.79
Clahsen, Harald. 1988. Parameterized grammatical theory and language acquisition: A study of the acquisition of verb placement and inflection by children and adults. In *Linguistic Theory in Second Language Acquisition*, Suzanne Flynn & Wayne O'Neil (eds.), 47–75. Dordrecht: Kluwer. doi:10.1007/978-94-009-2733-9_4
Clahsen, Harald & Muysken, Pieter. 1986. The availability of Universal Grammar to adult and child learners – A study of the acquisition of German word order. *Second Language Research* 2(2): 93–119. doi:10.1177/026765838600200201
Clahsen, Harald & Muysken, Pieter. 1989. The UG paradox in L2 acquisition. *Second Language Research* 5(1): 1–29. doi:10.1177/026765838900500101
Clahsen, Harald & Penke, Martina. 1992. The acquisition of agreement morphology and its syntactic consequences: New evidence on German child language from the Simone-corpus. In *The Acquisition of Verb Placement: Functional Categories and V2 Phenomena in Language Acquisition*, Jürgen M. Meisel (ed.), 181–223. Dordrecht: Kluwer.
de Haan, Germen. 1987. A theory-bound approach to the acquisition of verb placement in Dutch. In Germen de Haan & Wim Zonneveld (eds.), *Formal Parameters of Generative Grammar*, 15–30. Dordrecht: ICG.
Endresen, Rolf Theil & Simonsen, Hanne Gram. 2001. The Norwegian verb. In *A Cognitive Approach to the Verb: Morphological and Constructional Perspectives*, Hanne Gram Simonsen & Rolf Theil Endresen (eds.), 73–94. Berlin: Mouton de Gruyter.
Eide, Kristin Melum. 2009. Finiteness: The haves and the have-nots. In *Advances in Comparative Germanic Syntax* [Linguistik Aktuell/Linguistics Today 141], Artemis Alexiadou, Jorge Hankamer, Thomas McFadden, Justin Nuger & Florian Schäfer (eds.), 357–390 Amsterdam: John Benjamins. doi:10.1075/la.141.15fin
Guasti, Maria Teresa. 1996. Acquisition of Italian interrogatives. In Clahsen (ed.), 241–270.

Guasti, Maria Teresa. 2000. An excursion into interrogatives in Early English and Italian. In *The Acquisition of Syntax: Studies in Comparative Developmental Linguistics*, Marc-Ariel Friedemann & Luigi Rizzi (eds.), 105–128, Harlow: Longman.

Guasti, Maria Teresa, Thornton, Rosalind & Wexler, Ken. 1995. Negation in children's questions: The case of English. In *BUCLD 19: Proceedings of the 19th Annual Boston University Conference on Language Development*, Dawn MacLaughlin & Susan McEwen (eds.), 228–240. Somerville MA: Cascadilla Press.

Harris, Tony & Wexler, Ken. 1996. The optional-infinitive stage in child English: Evidence from negation. In Clahsen (ed.), 1–42.

Hoekstra, Teun & Hyams, Nina. 1998. Aspects of root infinitives. *Lingua* 106: 81–112. doi:10.1016/S0024-3841(98)00030-8

Ingram, David & Thompson, William. 1996. Early syntactic acquisition in German: Evidence for the Modal Hypothesis. *Language* 72(1): 97–120. doi:10.2307/416795

Jordens, Peter. 1990. The acquisition of verb placement in Dutch and German. *Linguistics* 28: 1407–1448.

Josefsson, Gunlög. 1999. Non-finite root clauses in Swedish child language. *Working Papers in Scandinavian Syntax* 63: 105–150.

Josefsson, Gunlög. 2004. Input and output: Sentence patterns in child and adult Swedish. In *The Acquisition of Swedish Grammar* [Language Acquisition and Language Disorders 33], Gunlög Josefsson, Christer Platzack & Gisela Håkansson (eds.), 95–133. Amsterdam: John Benjamins. doi:10.1075/lald.33.05jos

Klima, Edward S. & Bellugi[-Klima], Ursula. 1966. Syntactic regularities in the speech of children. In *Psycholinguistic Papers*, John Lyons & Roger J. Wales (eds.), 183–208. Edinburgh: EUP. Also published in Lust, Barbara C. & Foley, Claire (eds.). 2004. *First Language Acquisition: The Essential Readings*, 344–366. Malden MA: Blackwell.

Labov, William & Labov, Teresa. 1978. Learning the syntax of questions. In *Recent Advances in the Psychology of Language: Formal and Experimental Approaches*, Robin N. Campbell & Philip T. Smith (eds.). New York NY: Plenum.

Lardiere, Donna. 2000. Mapping features to forms in second language acquisition. In *Second Language Acquisition and Linguistic Theory*, John Archibald (ed.), 102–129. Oxford: Blackwell.

Lasser, Ingeborg. 1997. Finiteness in Adult and Child Language. Ph.D. dissertation, City University of New York.

Lightfoot, David. 2002. *Syntactic Effects of Morphological Change*. Oxford: Oxford University Press. doi:10.1093/acprof:oso/9780199250691.001.0001

Meisel, Jürgen M. 1994. Getting FAT: Finiteness, agreement and tense in early grammars. In *Bilingual First Language Acquisition: French and German Grammatical Development*, [*Language Acquisition and Language Disorders* 7], Jürgen M. Meisel (ed.), 89–129. Amsterdam: John Benjamins. doi:10.1075/lald.7.06mei

MacWhinney, Brian. 2000. *The CHILDES Project: Tools for Analyzing Talk*, Vol. 2: *The Database*, 3rd edn. Mahwah NJ: Lawrence Erlbaum Associates.

Phillips, Colin. 1995. Syntax at age two: Cross-linguistic differences. In *Papers on Language Processing and Acquisition* [MIT Working Papers in Linguistics 26], Carson T. Schütze, Jennifer B. Ganger & Kevin Broihier (eds.), 325–382. Cambridge MA: MITWPL.

Plunkett, Kim & Strömqvist, Sven. 1990. The Acquisition of Scandinavian Languages. *Gothenburg Papers in Theoretical Linguistics* 59.

Poeppel, David & Wexler, Ken. 1993. The Full Competence Hypothesis of clause structure in early German. *Language* 69: 1–33. doi:10.2307/416414

Pollock, Jean-Yves. 1989. Verb movement, universal grammar and the structure of IP. *Linguistic Inquiry* 20(3): 365–425.

Radford, Andrew. 1992. The acquisition of the morphosyntax of finite verbs in English. In *The Acquisition of Verb Placement: Functional Categories and V2 Phenomena in Language Acquisition*, Jürgen M. Meisel (ed.), 23–62. Dordrecht: Kluwer.

Radford, Andrew 1994. The syntax of questions in child English. *Journal of Child Language* 21: 211–236. doi:10.1017/S0305000900008722

Rizzi, Luigi. 1993/94. Some notes on linguistic theory and language development: The case of root infinitives. *Language Acquisition* 3(4): 371–393. doi:10.1207/s15327817la0304_2

Rizzi, Luigi. 1996. Residual verb second and the *wh*-criterion. In *Parameters and Functional Heads*, Adriana Belletti & Luigi Rizzi (eds.), 63–90. Oxford: OUP.

Rizzi, Luigi. 1997. The fine structure of the left periphery. In *Elements of Grammar: Handbook of Generative Syntax*, Liliane Haegeman (ed.), 281–337. Dordrecht: Kluwer.

Rizzi, Luigi. 2000. Remarks on early null subjects. In *The Acquisition of Syntax: Studies in Comparative Developmental Linguistics*, Marc-Ariel Friedemann & Luigi Rizzi (eds.), 269–292. Harlow: Longman.

Roeper, Tom. 1999. Universal Bilingualism. *Bilingualism: Language and Cognition* 2(3), 169–186.

Rohrbacher, Bernhard Wolfgang. 1999. *Morphology-Driven Syntax: A Theory of V to I Raising and Pro-drop* [Linguistik Aktuell/Linguistics Today 15]. Amsterdam: John Benjamins. doi:10.1075/la.15

Rowland, Caroline F. & Pine, Julian M. 2000. Subject-auxiliary inversion errors and *wh*-question acquisition: 'What children do know?' *Journal of Child Language* 27: 157–181. doi:10.1017/S0305000999004055

Rowland, Caroline F. & Pine, Julian M. 2003. The development of inversion in *wh*-questions: A reply to Van Valin. *Journal of Child Language* 30: 197–212. doi:10.1017/S0305000902005445

Santelmann, Lynn. 1995. The Acquisition of Verb Second Grammar in Child Swedish: Continuity of Universal Grammar in WH-questions, Topicalizations and Verb Raising. Ph.D. dissertation, Cornell University.

Santelmann, Lynn. 2004. The acquisition of Swedish *wh*-questions. In Gunlög Josefsson, Christer Platzack and Gisela Håkansson (eds.), *The Acquisition of Swedish Grammar*, 261–307. Amsterdam: John Benjamins.

Snyder, William. 2007. *Child Language: The Parametric Approach.* Oxford: OUP.

Stromswold, Karin. 1990. Learnability and the Acquisition of Auxiliaries. Ph.D. dissertation, MIT.

Theakston, Anna L., Lieven, Elena V.M., Pine, Julian M. & Rowland, Caroline F. 2001. The role of performance limitations in the acquisition of verb-argument structure: An alternative account. *Journal of Child Language* 28: 127–152. doi:10.1017/S0305000900004608

Thornton, Rosalind. 2008. Why continuity? *Natural Language and Linguistic Theory* 26: 107–146. doi:10.1007/s11049-007-9031-z

Vangsnes, Øystein A. 2005. Microparameters for Norwegian *wh*-grammars. *Linguistic Variation Yearbook* 5: 187–226. doi:10.1075/livy.5.07van

Van Valin, Robert D. 2002. The development of subject-auxiliary inversion in English *wh*-questions: An alternative analysis. *Journal of Child Language* 29: 161–175. doi:10.1017/S0305000901004974

Vikner, Sten. 1995. *Verb Movement and Expletive Subjects in the Germanic Languages.* Oxford: OUP.

Verrips, Maaike & Weissenborn, Jürgen. 1992. Routes to verb placement in early German and French: The independence of finiteness and agreement. In *The Acquisition of Verb Placement: Functional Categories and V2 Phenomena in Language Acquisition*, Jürgen Meisel (ed.), 283–331. Dordrecht: Kluwer.

Waldmann, Christian. 2008. *Input och output: Ordföljd i svenska barns huvudsatser och bisatser* (Input and Output: Word Order in Swedish Children's Main and Embedded Clauses). Ph.D. dissertation, University of Lund.

Westergaard, Marit R. 2003. Word order in *wh*-questions in a North Norwegian dialect: Some evidence from an acquisition study. *Nordic Journal of Linguistics* 26(1): 81–109. doi:10.1017/S0332586503001021

Westergaard, Marit. 2008. Acquisition and change: On the robustness of the triggering experience for word order cues. *Lingua* 118(12): 1841–1863. doi:10.1016/j.lingua.2008.05.003

Westergaard, Marit. 2009a. *The Acquisition of Word Order: Micro-cues, Information Structure and Economy* [Linguistik Aktuell/Linguistics Today 145]. Amsterdam: John Benjamins. doi:10.1075/la.145

Westergaard, Marit. 2009b. Microvariation as diachrony: A view from acquisition. *Journal of Comparative Germanic Linguistics* 12(1): 49–79. doi:10.1007/s10828-009-9025-9

Westergaard, Marit. 2009c. Usage-based vs. rule-based learning: The acquisition of word order in *wh*-questions in English and Norwegian. *Journal of Child Language* 36(5): 1023–1051. doi:10.1017/S0305000909009349

Westergaard, Marit & Bentzen, Kristine. 2010. Word order and finiteness in the acquisition of English and Norwegian *wh*-questions. In *BUCLD 34: Proceedings of the 34th Annual Boston University Conference on Language Development*, Vol 2, Katie Franich, Kate M. Iserman & Lauren L. Keil (eds.), 457–467. Somerville MA: Cascadilla Press.

Wexler, Kenneth. 1994. Optional infinitives, head movement and the economy of derivation. In *Verb Movement*, David Lightfoot & Norbert Hornstein (eds.), 305–350. Cambridge: CUP. doi:10.1017/CBO9780511627705.016

Wexler, Kenneth. 1999. Very early parameter setting and the unique checking constraint: a new explanation of the optional infinitive stage. In *Language Acquisition: Knowledge Representation and Processing*, Antonella Sorace, Caroline Heycock & Richard Shillock (eds.). Special issue of *Lingua*, 23–79.

Wijnen, Frank, Kempen, Masja & Gillis, Steven. 2001. Root infinitives in Dutch early child language: An effect of input? *Journal of Child Language* 28(3): 629–660. doi:10.1017/S0305000901004809

Wiklund, Anna-Lena, Hrafnbjargarson, Gunnar Hrafn, Bentzen, Kristine & Hróarsdóttir, Þorbjörg. 2007. Rethinking Scandinavian verb movement. *Journal of Comparative Germanic Linguistics* 10(3): 203–233. doi:10.1007/s10828-007-9014-9

The influence of phonological factors on the expression of finiteness by children learning Dutch as their first and second language

Elma Blom & Nada Vasić
Utrecht University / University of Amsterdam

Previous research has indicated that children learning a first language (L1) and children learning a second language (L2) make errors with finiteness marking, even when they master the syntactic and morphological properties of finiteness marking in the target language. This study investigates whether such residual errors with finiteness marking are caused by phonological properties of the verb form. Three groups participated in the study: a Turkish L1 – Dutch L2 group (mean age = 7), an age-matched Dutch L1 group, and a younger Dutch L1 group (mean age = 5) that matched the L2 group on Dutch proficiency. All children took part in an elicited production task and a non-word repetition task. The results confirm the role of phonological properties of verb forms, in particular composition of the coda cluster. Accuracy was high across all groups, but the L2 children and age-matched L1 children performed slightly better than the younger L1 children. This observation suggests that L2 children can make use of L1 experience in the domain of verb inflection.

Keywords: finiteness; Dutch; acquisition; phonology; child L1 and L2

1. Introduction

Across languages, children between the ages of two and three years drop finite verb inflection or use an infinitival verb in contexts that require finite verb forms. This pattern has been observed in children learning French, German, Russian, Dutch, English, Swedish, Danish, Norwegian, Faroese, Irish, Czech, Brazilian Portuguese or Icelandic as their first language (L1) (cf. Brun et al. 1999; Haegeman 1994; Pierce 1989; Wexler 1998), and probably holds for many other languages. Although the morpho-syntactic properties of finiteness are acquired by the age of three, Dutch five-year old children may still occasionally omit finiteness marking (Polišenská 2010). L2 children also show a steep learning curve with respect to the development of finiteness (Haznedar 2001; Blom, Paradis & Sorenson Duncan 2012). Even if they do acquire

DOI 10.1075/la.231.10blo

the morphosyntactic properties of finiteness in the L2, they too sometimes omit finite verb inflection, as do Dutch L1 children (English: Haznedar 2001; Haznedar & Schwartz 1997; Ionin & Wexler 2002; Paradis, Rice, Crago & Marquis 2008; German: Prévost 2003; Dutch: Blom, Polišenská & Weerman 2006; Blom 2008; Blom & Baayen 2013).

Previous accounts of L1 and L2 children's errors with finiteness marking focus on morphosyntactic explanations. However, these explanations are relevant to earlier developmental stages and do not pertain to *residual* errors made by children who have acquired the morphosyntax of finiteness. The goal of the present study is to investigate the hypothesis that *phonological* factors may explain children's residual errors with finiteness marking. In order to test this hypothesis, we have conducted a speech production experiment that elicited inflected verbs with different phonological properties. This experiment was administered to Dutch L1 children and Dutch L2 children with Turkish L1. The same children also participated in a non-word repetition task where they had to produce words that phonologically overlapped with the verbs in the inflection task. In the Introduction (Section 1), we provide the theoretical and empirical background of the study. Section 2 describes the participants of our study and experimental method used. Section 3 presents the results. Section 4 is the discussion. Section 5 contains the conclusions.

1.1 Finiteness in Dutch

Dutch finiteness is expressed through position and form of the verb. Dutch is considered to be an Object-Verb language with verb second in main clauses. The verb second rule holds that in main clauses the finite verb moves from sentence-final position to a left-peripheral position adjacent to the sentence subject (den Besten 1989; Koster, 1975). The resulting, unmarked, word order in main clauses is Subject-Verb-Object; see (1a). In sentences where a non-subject is placed in first position due to topicalization or movement of the wh-word, subject and verb are reversed (i.e., subject-verb inversion) in order to maintain verb second. An example is given in (1b), in which an adverb is placed in first position. Non-finite verb forms, such as infinitives, are located in the verb's final base position, cf. (1c). Verb second only applies to Dutch main clauses, and hence, the finite verb in embedded clauses occupies the sentence-final base position (1d).

(1) a. Ik schrijf een boek
I write.FIN a book
'I am writing a book.'

b. Nu schrijf ik een boek
Now write.FIN I a book
'I am now writing a book.'

c. Ik wil een boek schrijven
I want a book write.INF
'I want to write a book.'

d. Ik zeg dat ik een boek schrijf
I say that I a book write.FIN
'I say that I am writing a book.'

Finiteness is also expressed through the form of the verb. In 1SG present tense contexts, the bare verb stem is used, as in (2a). (2b) shows that the bare verb stem also appears in 2SG contexts in sentences with subject-verb inversion. In main clauses without inversion, 2SG and 3SG present tense verbs are suffixed with *-t*; see (2c). The present plural is expressed via suffixation of *-en*; see (2d). The plural form is similar to the infinitival verb form (cf. (1c)), but whereas the Dutch infinitive is in sentence-final position following the object, the finite plural form is in verb second position, where it precedes the object.

(2) a. Ik schrijf een boek.
I write.1SG a book
'I am writing a book.'

b. Wat schrijf jij?
What write.2SG you
'What do you write?'

c. Jij/hij schrijft een boek
You/he write.2SG/3SG a book
'You/he are/is writing a book.'

d. Wij/jullie/zij schrijven een boek
We/you/they write.1PL/2PL/3PL a book
'We/you/they are writing a book.'

1.2 Finiteness in child L1 and child L2 Dutch

The development of finiteness in Dutch L1 children begins when children start to use root infinitives, i.e., main clauses with an infinitival verb instead of a finite verb form (de Haan 1987; Haegeman 1994; Jordens 1990, 2002; Wijnen 1998, 2000; Blom 2003, 2004, 2008; Blom & van Geert 2004). In adult Dutch root infinitives are marginally allowed in, for instance, exclamatives or narratives, as illustrated in (3) (examples are from Baauw, De Roo & Avrutin 2002). The sentences in (3) do not contain a finite verb; the verb is an infinitive as indicated by the combination of the *-en* suffix and sentence-final placement of the verb.

(3) a. Ik een huis kopen? Nooit!
me a house buy.INF never
'Me buy a house? Never!'

b. Maria vertelde Peter een mop. Hij lachen
Mary told Peter a joke he laugh.INF
'Mary told Peter a joke. He laugh!'

However, unlike adult speakers of Dutch, young children acquiring Dutch use root infinitives in a wide range of contexts. The child examples in (4) are selected from the CHILDES Groningen Corpus (MacWhinney, 2010; ⟨http://childes.psy.cmu.edu/⟩), and illustrate declarative root infinitives. In adult Dutch, declarative root infinitives are infelicitous.

(4) a. Vrachtwagen emmer doen — Matthijs 2;04.24
Truck bucket do.INF
'Truck bucket do.'

b. Op kist zitten — Josse 2;08.04
On box sit.INF
'On box sit.'

When children acquire finiteness, they acquire which verb forms to use in a certain context, taking into account properties of the sentence subject, the temporal properties of the sentence, and the position of the verb. This development takes place at the expense of root infinitives and around age three, Dutch L1 children's use of root infinitives has usually dropped to a target-like rate (Haegeman 1994; Wijnen 2000; Blom 2003; Gillis 2003).

The morphological and syntactic development of finiteness go largely hand-in-hand, but some asymmetries are found, showing that Dutch L1 children place the verb in the correct (second) position, but fail to express finiteness morphologically and omit the 3SG *-t* suffix (Blom 2007). An example is given in (5). (Examples are from the CHILDES Groningen Corpus).

(5) a. die heef-ø snor — Daan 2;04
that has.3SG mustache
'He has moustache.'

b. Audrey slaap-ø nog een tijdje. — Josse 2;07.20
Audrey sleep.3SG still for awhile
'Audrey will sleep for a while.'

Polišenská's (2010) experimental data show that up until they reach the age of five, L1 children continue to occasionally drop the suffix *-t* in both 2SG and 3SG contexts. Substitution errors are very rare. In addition, hardly any errors with finite plural *-en* are made. Table 1 summarizes Polišenská's findings. In this study, the verb forms were collected in main clauses and denoted present tense events.

In child L2 learners of Dutch, the morphological and the syntactic expression of finiteness are also acquired quite rapidly. Pooled data from Dutch L2 children

Table 1. Accuracy of finiteness marking in Dutch L1 children across age groups, based on Polišenská (2010, p. 93)

	1SG	2SG	3SG	3PL
3-year-olds (n = 12)	94% (15/16)	95% (19/20)	88% (15/17)	100% (14/14)
4-year-olds (n = 12)	100% (19/19)	81% (17/21)	89% (17/19)	100% (23/23)
5-year-olds (n = 12)	100% (25/25)	92% (23/25)	95% (21/22)	100% (22/22)
6-year-olds (n = 10)	100% (30/30)	100% (30/30)	100% (29/29)	100% (28/28)

between ages of five and eight indicate an overall level of 92% correct use of finite verbs (Blom et al. 2006). Interestingly, Dutch L2 children show a pattern similar to older L1 children, as their residual errors with finiteness are often omissions of the *-t* suffix in 2SG and 3SG contexts (Blom & Baayen 2013).

In sum, both Dutch L1 and L2 children acquire the morphosyntactic marking of finiteness without much effort. Nevertheless, despite their overall high accuracy rates, children in both groups make residual finiteness errors. The finite suffix *-t*, which is used in (non-inversion) 2SG and 3SG contexts, is the most vulnerable inflectional ending. The question that arises is, why does the finite suffix *-t* cause difficulties?

1.3 Approaches to the development of finiteness

Theories on the development of finiteness have emphasized children's morphosyntactic development. Most research in this area has revolved around the issue of whether learners (either L1 or L2) lack syntactic knowledge or have problems with morphology. Below we briefly summarize three approaches: maturational accounts, morphology-before-syntax accounts and syntax-before-morphology accounts.[1] We will argue that none of these three approaches can fully account for children's residual finiteness errors.

One view in the field of L1 acquisition holds that young children omit finiteness marking due to the immaturity of syntactic knowledge. Once the required syntactic principle (Rizzi 1993/4; Wexler 1998) has matured, children will use the appropriate verb form. This theory explains children's early use of root infinitives, but it does not account for the omission of the finite *-t* suffix. Moreover, this explanation applies to young children only. Therefore, other L1 researchers proposed that the projection

1. This distinction is based on White (2003).

of functional structure is triggered by morphological development (Clahsen, Eisenbeiss & Penke 1996; Eisenbeiss 2009). Thus, in order to create a verb second position, finite verb forms need to be learned. An equivalent approach in the field of L2 acquisition holds that L2 children omit finiteness marking because they start out with a bare Verb Phrase (VP) and gradually expand their syntactic representation with functional structure when they learn the morphemes related to functional categories such as Tense and Agreement (Morabaki, Vainikka & Young-Scholten 2008; Vainikka & Young-Scholten 2010). However, the Dutch residual finiteness errors seem to suggest a pattern in the opposite direction, that is, complete syntax with some morphological errors.

The Missing Surface Inflection Hypothesis or MSIH (Haznedar & Schwartz 1997) represents a third approach. This view could be summarized as 'syntax-before-morphology' and has been applied to L2 children and adults (White 2003); here we focus on L2 children, but the explanation could also apply to L1 children. According to the MSIH, L2 children's errors with finiteness marking result from insertion of a morphological default form (e.g., a zero suffix) in a functional position that is fully specified for Tense and Agreement (Haznedar 2001; Ionin & Wexler 2002; Prévost 2003). This default form is less specified than other forms in the paradigm, and is inserted if lexical access to more specific verb forms is hindered or delayed.[2] Discussing English, Ionin and Wexler (2002: 118) state that zero-marked verb forms "are finite forms that have simply not received morphological agreement marking and that can be used across all tense/agreement contexts." Prévost (2003: 88) assumes that in child L2 German such verb forms "are unspecified for person features but specified as [+finite]". In normal conditions, access to the bare verb form is blocked by inflected forms that are associated with person and number features, but if retrieval of the correct inflected form fails, the default rule applies, resulting in omission of finiteness marking on verbs that are syntactically finite.

The MSIH is interesting for our purposes because this hypothesis correctly predicts syntax-morphology asymmetries, and the occasional omission of finite inflection. However, this hypothesis does not provide further insight into the specific conditions under which residual errors with finiteness are made, other than that processing-related factors may be relevant. The goal of this study is to explore if *phonological* factors cause Dutch L1 and L2 children's residual errors, and in particular their failure to use the *-t* suffix. This hypothesis builds on earlier research that provides evidence for the role of phonological factors on supplying verbal inflection, in particular previous studies of English L1 children (Song, Sundara & Demuth 2009; Oetting & Horohov 1997;

2. The Distributed Morphology framework (Halle & Marantz 1993; Halle 1997) is assumed for this approach.

Marshall & van der Lely 2006; Johnson & Morris 2007; Leonard et al. 2007; Marinis & Chondrogianni 2010), English L2 children (Blom et al. 2012; Blom & Paradis 2013) and Dutch L2 children (Blom & Baayen 2013). In the next section we expand on this idea.

1.4 The impact of phonological factors on finiteness marking

Song et al. (2009) report naturalistic and experimental data showing that English L1 children drop the present tense habitual 3SG marker *-s* more frequently if the final coda cluster is complex. Thus, the final *-s* in *sees* is dropped less often than the final *-s* in a verb like *walks*. In their study, Song et al. made a binary distinction between singleton (C) codas and complex (CC or CCC) codas. Other evidence for such phonological effects comes from studies on past tense *-ed*. For instance, past tense marking is more often used with verbs ending a non-obstruent liquid or vowel (e.g., *show, try*) than with verbs that end in an obstruent (Eyer & Leonard 1994; Oetting & Horohov 1997; Marshall & van der Lely 2007; Johnson & Morris 2007). If a verb ends in an obstruent, suffixation of the regular past tense suffix will most often lead to a complex cluster. Likewise, suffixation of 2SG and 3SG *-t* in Dutch creates complex coda clusters. Coda cluster complexity may thus explain why Dutch L1 and L2 children tend to omit finiteness marking in contexts that require *-t* suffixation.

Interestingly, Song et al. found that children dropped 3SG *-s* less often in final position compared to medial position. This effect was amplified by sentence length: The longer a sentence, the more likely it was that *-s* was dropped in medial position. Similarly, Dutch L2 children use finite verb inflection more often when the finite verb was in final position (87%) compared to verb second position (74%) (Blom & Baayen 2013). Differences in time to (prepare to) produce the inflectional suffix in medial and in final position could have led to relatively more drop in medial position in both the English and Dutch study. This effect may have become more pronounced through phonological complexity and articulatory challenges that result from suffixation, in particular suffixation of *-t* in the Dutch study. As noted by Blom and Baayen (2013): None of the verbs in this study ended in a non-obstruent, and, therefore, suffixation of *-t* created complex coda clusters (CC or CCC). As suggested by Song et al. (2009), such clusters may be prone to errors, in particular under time restrictions, as is the case in medial position. In addition to coda complexity, difficulties with articulatory planning may have contributed to the dropping of *-t* when other words followed the verb.

Probably, children's accurate use of verb inflection is not only influenced by complexity of the coda but also phonotactic constraints, in particular sonority of the consonants in coda cluster. According to the Sonority Sequencing Principle, sonority in the coda must decrease from peak to margin (Clements 1990). In the case of (plosive) *-t* following a plosive stem-final sound a "sonority plateau" is created, which yields a marked coda (Selkirk 1984; Morelli 1999). This would predict that children may experience particular difficulties with using the *-t* suffix after a plosive sound. It is important to mention that such sonority effects will overlap to a large degree with phonotactic probability, i.e., the likelihood of x given y, because clusters that do not follow the Sonority Sequencing Principle will also consist of phoneme sequences with low phonotactic probability. Phonotactic probability of the coda has been found to influence children's use of finite verb inflection in studies on English L1 children (Marshall & van der Lely 2006; Leonard, David & Deevy 2007).

In sum, previous research indicates that complexity of the coda cluster and sonority of the consonants in the cluster are a source of children's errors with verb inflection. However, it is currently unclear if such factors also explain why Dutch L1 and L2 children sometimes fail to use finite *-t* suffix.

1.5 Comparing L1 and L2 groups

For the present study we analyzed data from Dutch L1 and L2 children. The inclusion of these two different types of learners raises the question whether group differences are expected. Compared to same-age monolingual peers, L2 children have a delayed development because of their later age of onset. Furthermore, L2 children's L1 may delay or accelerate their L1 development. Previous research has pointed to positive transfer in the child L2 acquisition of verb inflection, because children with an inflecting L1 are more accurate and develop L2 inflection more rapidly compared to children with an isolating L1 (Blom et al. 2012; Blom & Baayen 2013; Paradis 2011).

Turkish is an agglutinative, richly inflecting language with a present tense indicative paradigm with six different forms that distinguish between person (1, 2, 3) and number (SG, PL). Like Dutch, Turkish allows consonants as well as consonant clusters in word-final position (Lewis 1967). In addition, the Sonority Sequencing Principle holds across languages. So, experience with Turkish may provide the children in our study with experience that is relevant for finite inflection and for producing coda clusters, and thus for their ability to use 3SG *-t* inflection in Dutch.

1.6 Research questions for the study

The aim of this study is to systematically investigate the role of the composition of the coda cluster by comparing children's accuracies across different coda types based on sonority of the stem-final sound. In Dutch, consonant clusters generally follow the sonority scale, which means that these clusters are ordered from higher to lower sonority. Therefore, it would be expected that children will more often drop *-t* if the verb stem ends in a plosive. To investigate this issue, the following research question was formulated:

(6) Does sonority of the stem-final phoneme affect children's accuracy with the non-syllabic *-t* inflection?

The Turkish L1-Dutch L2 children in our study are expected to transfer knowledge and experience relevant for verb inflection from their L1 to their L2. Consequently, the L2 children in this study may show the same performance as Dutch L1 age-peers with respect to their use of *-t* inflection, despite lower Dutch proficiency due to a later age of onset. In contrast, they may be more accurate at using the finite *-t* suffix compared to younger Dutch L1 children with matching Dutch proficiency. These outcomes pertain to the second research question, given in (7).

(7) Do L2 children outperform younger Dutch L1 children with matching Dutch proficiency regarding verb inflection use, and is their performance similar to age-matched Dutch L1 peers?

In the following section, we describe the participant groups and provide details regarding the experimental method used and model of data-analysis applied.

2. Method

2.1 Participants

Three groups of children participated in the study: a bilingual Turkish L1-Dutch L2 group with children between ages six and eight (N = 21), a monolingual Dutch L1 group of the same age (N = 27), and a monolingual Dutch L1 group consisting of five-year olds (N = 21). None of the children had apparent speech or language problems. The children in the L2 group spoke Turkish at home and their age of onset of systematic and substantial exposure to Dutch was 2.5 years on average (SD = 0.5). Because the children learned Turkish from birth, and Dutch from age 2.5, we labeled the children "L2".[3] For all children parental consent was obtained.

Dutch language abilities were assessed with the *Taaltoets Alle Kinderen* (TAK) (Verhoeven & Vermeer 2001) subtests for receptive vocabulary and grammar. The TAK is a standardized test developed for native and non-native Dutch children. Details about the TAK procedures are in the *Procedures* section. A one-way ANOVA indicated a significant effect for TAK vocabulary ($F(2, 62) = 13.6$, $p < .001$) and TAK grammar ($F(2,62) = 3.8$, $p = .027$). The L2 group and the younger L1 group did not significantly differ on the two measures; henceforth we will refer to younger L1 group as the

3. Note that for researchers interested in pinpointing effects of age of onset in the domain of morphosyntax the children in our study may rather pattern like simultaneous bilinguals than L2 learners (Meisel 2004).

language-matched (L1-LM) group. The age-matched L1 group (L1-AM) outperformed the two other groups on vocabulary (L1-LM: $p = .009$; L2: $p < 001$). For grammar, no significant difference emerged between the two L1 groups, but the L1-AM group outperformed the L2 group ($p = .022$). The relevant group characteristics are in Table 2.

Table 2. Participants' age, TAK grammar and vocabulary scores

	L1-LM (N = 21)	L1-AM (N = 27)	L2 (N = 21)
Mean age in months (SD)	66 (4.2)	85 (6.9)	92 (9.1)
Mean TAK raw score Dutch grammar (SD)	33 (3.2)	35 (5.1)	31.5 (4.1)
Mean TAK raw score Dutch vocabulary (SD)	69 (9.4)	80 (5.6)	65 (9.2)

2.2 Materials

To test 3sg subject-verb agreement pictures were shown that depicted a male or a female agent who manipulated an object. The pictures were shown in pairs of two. Paired pictures depicted the same activity but a different agent manipulating a different object, e.g. a man cutting paper and a woman cutting hair, as shown in Figure 1.

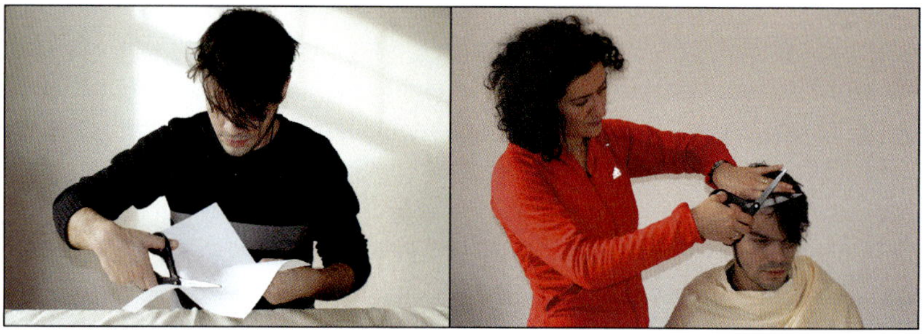

Figure 1. Example of experimental material 3sg production task: item *knippen* 'to cut'

The contrast between the pictures forced children to name the object, which was important for determining the error type in case a child produced the non-target form stem+en instead of the target form stem+t. In Dutch, the stem+en can either be a finite plural form or a non-finite infinitival verb form (Section 1.2). Placement of the verb relative to the object allowed disentangling whether a child used an incorrect plural form in 3sg contexts or used an infinitival verb form (see *Data-analysis*). The actions depicted nine different verbs, chosen based on transitivity, imageability, familiarity (based on the Lexilijst (Schlichting & Lutje Spelberg 2002)) and coda properties. The verb stems either had a sonorant coda, a fricative coda or a plosive coda. From these three coda's, sonorants are most sonorous and plosives are the least sonorous. All verb stems were monosyllabic. Table 3 lists the verbs in the test.

Table 3. Verbs in subject-verb agreement task and word frequencies in SUBTLEX-NL corpus

Sonorant	Frequency	Fricative	Frequency	Plosive	Frequency
/aai/ 'strike'	18	/was/ 'wash'	171	/knip/ 'cut'	77
/duw/ 'push'	178	/lees/ 'read'	1,112	/koop/ 'buy'	953
/sla/ 'hit'	2,763	/geef/ 'give'	14,471	/drink/ 'drink'	1,271

The frequency data in Table 5 are based on the SUBTLEX-NL corpus (Keuleers, Brysbaert & New 2010), a 44 million-word corpus from film and television subtitles. The verbs were not matched on frequency in advance and the average word frequencies for the fricatives (M = 5,251) was higher than plosives (M = 767) or sonorants (M = 986), with much variation between individual word frequencies. However, post-hoc statistical testing did not reveal an effect of frequency ($F(2) = 0.862, p = 0.468$), and hence, we can assume that there is no confounding effect of frequency and coda in our items. The experimental sentences are in Appendix 1.

In addition to the experimental production task, a non-word task was administered in order to evaluate whether errors with the targeted coda clusters also appeared in other contexts that did not involve suffixation, but memorization. The non-words are listed in Appendix 1.

2.3 Procedures

The data reported here were collected as part of a larger test battery comprising the production and processing of definite articles (Blom & Vasić 2011; Vasić & Blom 2011) and subject-verb agreement. Each child participated in three experimental sessions, which were not more than one week apart. The procedures described below were used in the first and second session. A native Dutch research assistant tested the children. Children's responses were scored afterwards based on audio recordings of the test sessions.

2.3.1 *TAK grammar comprehension and receptive vocabulary*

In the grammar comprehension task, children were read a sentence and asked to point to one of the three pictures that corresponded the best to the sentence they had heard. The sentences varied in syntactic complexity ranging from simple to demanding structures, examining the interpretation of moved/scrambled elements, pronouns, relative clauses, passive constructions etc. In the receptive vocabulary task, children were given a word and three pictures to choose from. The two distracter-pictures represented a semantically related item and an unrelated item that resembled the target item phonologically.

2.3.2 *Experimental task eliciting 3SG inflection*

In the experimental production task children had to describe pictures by completing a lead-in by the experimenter. The children's task was to describe the contrast between two pictures depicting the same action, but with different actors and objects. A question primed the use of the target verb by the children. The verb in the prime was in past participle form, as illustrated in (8).[4]

(8) EXP: Hier wordt gelezen.
'Here is reading being done.'
EXP: De man …
'The man'
CHI: leest een krant
'reads a newspaper'
EXP: en de vrouw
'and the woman'
CHI: leest een boek.
'reads a book.'

Each phonological condition (sonorant, fricative, stop) contained three verbs; the nine experimental items were mixed with 15 fillers on determiner-noun agreement. For each verb two responses were collected, as illustrated in (8). So, for each child a maximum of 18 responses could be collected.

2.3.3 *Non-word repetition task*

As part of our test battery, the children participated in a non-word repetition task in which they repeated words with the same sequence of sounds as in the coda of the 3SG verbs in the verb inflection test. This task was administered to assess whether the children were able to produce the required clusters. A non-word task was used because existing words with the relevant coda clusters (in particular plosives followed by *-t*) that are known by the children in our age group are rare. Comparing children's

4. For strong verbs, such as *lezen* 'read', the past participle ends in *-en*, while for weak verbs the past participle either ends in *-d* (*aaien* 'stroke' with past participle *geaaid*) or *-t* (*knippen* 'cut' with past participle *geknipt*); the *-d* and *-t* allomorphs are pronounced similarly in Dutch because of final devoicing in Dutch. Out of the nine verbs, four were weak verbs. There were no indications that children more often used 3SG *-t* with strong verbs due to phonological overlap with the prime.

behavior in the inflection test versus the non-word test can be informative for morphological reasons as well, and tell us more about the morphophonological interface. The inflected verbs are multimorphemic (stem+suffix) and retrieved from long-term memory. The non-words, in contrast, are monomorphemic and retrieved from verbal short-term memory. So although the phonological and articulatory processes required for using the inflected verbs and the non-words are similar, there are also morphological differences. We turn to this issue in the Discussion. In the non-word repetition task, the children had to repeat 14 non-existing Dutch nouns. Seven monosyllabic nouns had a final cluster that resembled the 3SG verb forms tested in the experimental task. An additional seven nouns were used as fillers and were disyllabic 'derived nouns' resembling past tense forms and adjectives with word-internal clusters. The 14 non-words were presented in random order, with two versions. The nouns were recorded as segments and played to the child through headphones. The child was asked to repeat the items and the responses were recorded.

3. Results

Table 4 gives an overview of the raw data, divided over the three groups. Accuracy was calculated based on a child's success or failure to produce correct subject-verb agreement with the target verb. Correct responses comprised the use of the target verb inflected with a *-t* suffix. Incorrect responses were responses in which a child used the target verb but either with zero-marking or incorrect inflection (i.e., the suffix *-en*).[5] All other responses (auxiliary constructions, different verbs, omission of the verb, past tense, verb said by experimenter) were excluded from the analysis (L1-LM: 58, L1-AM: 12, L2: 62). In one case a response was included that was not the targeted verb. This verb had the same stem-final phoneme, and hence, fell in the same phonological class as the verb that was targeted.

The results in Table 4 show that overall performance was highly accurate and errors were indeed residual errors. The raw numbers suggest that errors were more frequent when the stem ended in a plosive compared to a fricative or a sonorant: 1% (5/342) of the verbs in the sonorant class were produced with incorrect inflection, 2% (9/374) in the fricatives class were produced incorrectly, and 9% (31/331) in the plosives class. The L1-LM had a slightly lower accuracy score (93% correct) compared to the L1-AM group (97% correct) and the L2 group (96.5% correct).

The 22 errors in the L1-LM group came from 13 different children who all occasionally made an error. The 12 errors in the L1-AM group came from eight children.

5. Incorrect responses also included root infinitives.

Table 4. Numbers of correct and incorrect responses per class and group

	L1-LM (N = 21)		L1-AM (N = 27)		L2 (N = 21)	
	Correct	Incorrect	Correct	Incorrect	Correct	Incorrect
Sonorant	98	2	149	1	95	2
Fricative	107	6	153	0	114	3
Plosive	93	14	142	11	96	6
Total – raw numbers	298	22	444	12	305	11

The 11 errors in the L2 group came from five different children; six errors could be attributed to one single child (E005).

To evaluate whether the above differences between the three verb classes and between the three groups translated into statistically significant results, mixed logistic linear regression (Chatterjee & Hadi 2006) was used. Accuracy was the dependent variable, CHILD and VERB were included as random-effect predictor variables and GROUP (L1-LM, L1-AM, L2) and CODA (plosives, fricatives, sonorants) as fixed-effect predictor variables. Mixed logistic regression was used because the dependent variable is binary, and the groups are unequal. Furthermore, this method allows assessing the simultaneous effect of different predictor variables. The regression model revealed lower accuracy of the L1-LM group compared to the L1-AM group ($\beta = -1.24$, $SE = .55$, $Z = -2.26$, $p = .024$) and a trend toward a significant difference between the L1-LM group and the L2 group, with lower accuracy for the first compared to the second group ($\beta = -1.19$, $SE = .67$, $Z = -1.77$, $p = .077$). The children made more errors when the verb stem ended in a plosive compared to a fricative ($\beta = -1.56$, $SE = .63$, $Z = -2.45$, $p = .014$) and compared to a sonorant ($\beta = -2.00$, $SE = .72$, $Z = -2.77$, $p = .005$). No difference between fricatives and sonorants emerged.

An item analysis indicated that within the plosive condition, some differences were found between verb forms. In the full dataset, *knipt* 'cuts' yielded seven incorrect responses (5%; N = 128), *koopt* 'buys' yielded five incorrect responses (4.5%; N = 111), and *drinkt* 'drinks' yielded 19 incorrect responses (15%; N = 123). This unequal distribution, with a disproportionally high number of errors for *drinkt*, was rather consistent with how the children performed on the non-word repetition task. In this task, it was found that the pronunciation of *-t* when preceded by *-nk* caused difficulties: The non-word *binkt* led to cluster reduction in five L1-LM, two L1-AM, and three L2 children, who pronounced this word as *bint*. One of those children from the L1-LM group, and one from the L2 group, also pronounced *rikte* as *ritte*. In other phonological contexts, the pronunciation of *-t* was unproblematic for most of the children (but see comment below). However, although there was overlap between the children who failed to produce *drinkt* and *binkt*, it was not the case that all children who failed to produce *drinkt* also failed to produce *binkt*, and vice versa.

Recall that one L2 child made relatively many errors (E005). This child failed to produce the suffix *-t* in the plosive condition four times (once with *knipt*, once with *koopt* and twice with *drinkt*), but he did show the capability to produce the complex and marked coda clusters *-kt* and *-pt* in the non-word task. This child failed to produce *-t* in the non-word *dast*, and showed inconsistent behavior with respect to the verb forms *leest* and *wast* in the inflection task: for both items one incorrect and one correct response was obtained.

4. Discussion

4.1 The role of sonority in children's use of 3SG -t

The first question that guided our study was, does sonority of the stem-final phoneme affect children's accuracy with the non-syllabic *-t* inflection? In the inflection experiment, children had to produce 3SG *-t* inflection with verbs ending with a sonorant, a fricative or a plosive. The combination of a plosive and 3SG *-t* yields the most marked cluster (plosive-plosive), given the Sonority Sequencing Principle. The results of our study confirmed the effect of sonority because the children used 3SG *-t* inflection more often when the verb ended with a sonorant or fricative compared to a plosive. This outcome supports findings in other studies that indicated phonological effects on the use of English verb inflection (Blom et al. 2012; Blom & Paradis 2013; Song, Sundara & Demuth 2009; Oetting & Horohov 1997; Marshall & van der Lely 2006; Johnson & Morris 2007; Leonard et al. 2007; Marinis & Chondrogianni 2010).

Introducing the first research question, we mentioned the MSIH (Haznedar & Schwartz 1997; Haznedar 2001; Ionin & Wexler 2002; Prévost 2003) as a potentially promising account of children's residual errors with finiteness marking. According to the MSIH, processing-related factors (for instance, communication demands and time-pressure) lead to the use of the default form. Effects of phonological complexity and sonority[6] could be compatible with the MSIH, since these phonological factors impact on articulatory planning, which, in turn, affects processing costs.[7]

6. As explained in the Introduction, effects of sonority will overlap to a large degree with phonotactic probability.

7. In our study, correct versus incorrect verb form was used as an outcome variable. By implication, errors included bare form use, but also substituted verb forms (use of *-en* inflection) and root infinitives (with an omitted finite verb and an infinitival verb in sentence-final

4.2 Comparing L1 and L2 groups

The second research question formulated for this study was, do L2 children outperform younger Dutch L1 children with matching Dutch proficiency regarding verb inflection use, and is their performance similar to age-matched Dutch L1 peers? Accuracy in all groups was high, but the L1-AM and L2 children performed better than the younger L1-LM children. The L2 children were older (7;7 on average) than the L1-LM children (5;5 on average) but at time of testing the two groups had had a comparable length of exposure to Dutch, because the age of onset in the L2 group was 2.5, on average. Exposure measured in years is a very coarse measure of amount of input, but the two groups also had equal Dutch proficiency as measured by the TAK, and lower proficiency compared to the L1-AM group. However, with respect to use of 3SG *-t* inflection, the L2 and L1-AM group were equally accurate – despite shorter exposure of the L2 group – and more accurate than the L1-LM group. This outcome suggests that L2 children can benefit from their L1 in the domain of verb inflection, which parallels findings in other studies on child L2 Dutch (Blom & Baayen 2013) as well as child L2 English (Paradis 2011; Blom et al. 2012).

4.3 Sonority and complexity

With respect to the 'plosive verbs', it was observed that *drinkt* ('drinks') caused more errors than the other two verb forms where the verb stem ended in a plosive (*koopt* 'buys', *knipt* 'cuts'). Children's difficulties with *drinkt* cannot be attributed to frequency: out of the three verbs with a plosive coda, *drinkt* is the most frequent one. In the verb form *drinkt* two phonological factors are combined: sonority and complexity. It is thus possible that the greater complexity of *-nkt* (in *drinkt*) versus *-pt* (in *koopt* and *knipt*) may have caused more errors. Cluster complexity seems relevant because there was overlap between the (L1) children who failed to produce *drinkt* in the inflection task and *binkt* in the non-word task. Note also that some children may have pronounced *-nkt* using a velar nasal (/ŋt/). In order to assess this, additional acoustic analyses are required. This is beyond the scope of the present study, but it is important for future research.

Recall that one child in the L2 group made a relatively large amount of errors. Child E005 experienced relatively many difficulties with inflection and failed to supply

---

position). For our purposes, which is to investigate the effect of properties of the consonant cluster (and not to test the MSIH), such an analysis was relevant because all these errors imply 'avoidance' to produce the consonant cluster. However, the MSIH would predict consistency in errors, i.e., the occurrence of one particular error, which would be indicative of a default strategy.

3sg *-t* after both plosive and fricative stem-final sounds. His errors in the experimental task with fricatives were reflected in the non-word task. However, although E005 showed difficulties using *-t* after plosive stem-final sounds in the experimental task, no difficulties emerged in the same phonological condition in the non-word task. E005's difficulty with using *-t* after fricatives in both tasks, combined with the absence of problems using *-t* after sonorants, may point to the influence of cluster complexity, i.e., a complex (CC) coda versus a singleton (C) coda in line with the study conducted by Song et al. (2009).

4.4 The interplay between morphology and phonology

Interestingly, the children also showed asymmetries between the inflection task and the non-word repetition task. First, not all children who failed to produce *drinkt* in the inflection task also failed to produce *binkt* in the non-word repetition task, and vice versa. Second, when children were faced with the task to produce *-nkt* in the inflection task they left out *-t* (*drink*), while in the non-word repetition task they left out *-k* (*bint*).

One question that arises is whether phonological effects of the phoneme *following* the inflectional ending in the inflection task (but not in the non-word repetition task, where children produced words in isolation) could be relevant in explaining some of the asymmetries. In another study with the same materials and design but different groups, we found no effect of sonority of the sound following the finite verb on accuracy with 3sg *-t* inflection (Blom, Vasić & de Jong 2014).[8] This suggests that differences are related to retrieving and producing an inflected verb versus repeating and producing a non-word. Asymmetries in types of errors support this conclusion. Below, we discuss the observed asymmetries in view of current ideas about morphological processing.

A dual mechanism approach (cf. Pinker & Ullman 2002) holds that regularly inflected forms are generated by combining stem and suffix; both are stored in long-term memory. This contrasts with irregular forms, which are stored as a whole. Producing inflected forms thus requires an additional process (i.e., the application of a rule) and the consequence could be that children who show the ability to use certain coda clusters in the non-word task, may fail to produce them in the inflection task due to processing demands related to the process of suffixation. Also, different errors could be expected in the two tasks. In the inflection task the verb stem is preserved, while in the non-word task part of the "stem" may be omitted because the form is unanalyzed and does not consist of stem and suffix. This could result in two different types of coda

8. This could be due to the task where children may tend to pause after producing the 3sg verb in order to describe the contrast between the two adjacent photographs: the contrast was expressed through the direct object, which follows the finite verb in Dutch.

cluster reduction: omission of the *-t* in the inflection task (*drink* instead of *drinkt*) versus omission of the *-k* in the non-word repetition task (*bint* instead of *binkt*).

A single mechanism approach (cf. Bybee 2001) assumes that both regularly inflected forms and irregular forms are stored in long-term memory. By implication, both forms are part of an associative frequency-based network between words, based on phonological and semantic overlap between these words. In this view, children's (accurate) use of 3SG *-t* is influenced by the frequencies of other forms in the paradigm: the retrieval of *drinkt* (3SG) is impacted by associations with the verb forms *drink* (1SG) or *drinken* (PL), and so on. Also, from a single mechanism point of view, differences are to be expected between inflected verbs and non-words, because unlike inflected words, non-words are not stored in long-term memory[9] and they are not part of an inflectional paradigm.

All in all, both Dutch L1 and L2 children make errors with verb inflection due to phonological properties of the verbs, which may impact articulatory planning. However, analyses of types of errors indicate that phonological factors interact with morphological factors.

5. Concluding remarks

In this chapter we have presented experimental evidence for the hypothesis that phonological factors impact on Dutch L1 and L2 children's residual errors with finiteness. Overlap between children's performance in the inflection task and non-word repetition task indicates that coda cluster complexity and sonority characteristics of the consonants in the cluster influence children's use of 3SG *-t* inflection, while asymmetries between the two tasks point to the interplay between phonological and morphological factors. Furthermore, our results indicate that L2 children can make use of prior L1 experience for learning L2 verb inflection.

Acknowledgments

We thank Anne Baker, Vasiliki Chondrogianni, Jan de Jong, Theodoros Marinis and Fred Weerman for their advice, Petra van Alphen and Thomas Schlijper for helping prepare the materials, Anne-Marie Roorda, Iske Bakker, Marleen Dorlandt, Elianne de Ruiter, Nienke Verhoog and Janneke Verschoor for collecting the data, and the children and schools (Anne

9. Note that short-term memory and long-term memory do not operate entirely independently, so some influence of existing words in long-term memory that resemble the non-words could be expected.

Frank school Bunnik, Johannesschool Utrecht, De Wiekslag Amersfoort) for their cooperation. We are grateful to two reviewers for their helpful comments. This research was supported by the Netherlands Organisation for Scientific Research (NWO grant no. 254-70-121).

References

Baauw, Sergio, de Roo, Esteralla & Avrutin, Sergey. 2002. Determiner omission in language acquisition and language impairment: Syntactic and discourse factors. In *BUCLD 26: Proceedings of the* 26th *annual Conference on Language Acquisition and Development*, Barbora Skarabela, Sarah Fish & Anna H.-J. Do (eds.), 24–35. Somerville MA: Cascadilla Press.

Blom, Elma. 2003. From Root Infinitive to Finite Sentence. The Acquisition of Verbal Inflections and Auxiliaries. Ph.D. dissertation, Utrecht University.

Blom, Elma. 2007. Modality, infinitives and finite bare verbs in Dutch and English child language. *Language Acquisition* 14(1): 75–113. doi:10.1080/10489220701331821

Blom, Elma. 2008. Testing the domain-by-age model: Inflection and placement of Dutch verbs. In *Current Trends in Child Second Language Acquisition: A Generative Perspective* [Language Acquisition and Language Disorders 46], Belma Haznedar & Elena Gavruseva (eds.), 271–300. Amsterdam: John Benjamins. doi:10.1075/lald.46.14blo

Blom, Elma & van Geert, Paul. 2004. Signs of a developing grammar: Subject drop and inflection in early child Dutch. *Linguistics* 42(1): 195–234. doi:10.1515/ling.2004.003

Blom, Elma, Polišenská, Daniela & Weerman, Fred. 2006. Effects of age on the acquisition of agreement inflection. *Morphology* 16: 313–336. doi:10.1007/s11525-007-9110-1

Blom, Elma & Baayen, Harald. 2013. The impact of verb form, sentence position, home language and L2 proficiency on subject-verb agreement in child L2 Dutch. *Applied Psycholinguistics* 34(4): 777–811. doi:10.1017/S0142716412000021

Blom, Elma, Paradis, Johanne & Sorenson-Duncan, Tamara. 2012. Effects of input properties, vocabulary size and L1 on the development of third person singular -s in child L2 English. *Language Learning* 62(3): 965–994. doi:10.1111/j.1467-9922.2012.00715.x

Blom, Elma & Paradis, Johanne. 2013. Past tense production by English second language learners with and without language impairment. *Journal of Speech, Language and Hearing Research 56*: 281–294. doi:10.1044/1092-4388(2012/11-0112)

Blom, Elma & Vasić, Nada. 2011. The production and processing of determiner-noun agreement in child L2 Dutch. *Linguistic Approaches to Bilingualism* 1(3): 265–290. doi:10.1075/lab.1.3.03blo

Blom, Elma, Vasić, Nada & de Jong, Jan. 2014. Production and processing of subject-verb agreement in monolingual Dutch children with specific language impairment. *Journal of Speech, Language and Hearing Research* 57: 952–965. doi:10.1044/2014-JSLHR-L-13-0104

Brun, Dina, Avrutin, Sergey & Babyonyshev, Maria. 1999. Aspect and its temporal interpretation during the optional infinitive stage in Russian. In *BUCLD 23: Proceedings of the Annual Boston University Conference on Language Development 23,* Annabel Greenhill, Heather Littlefield & Cheryl Tano (eds.), 120–131. Somerville MA: Cascadilla Press.

Bybee, Joan. 2001. *Phonology and Language Use*. Cambridge: CUP. doi:10.1017/CBO9780511612886

Chatterjee, Samprit & Hadi, Ali. 2006. *Regression Analysis by Example*, 4th edn. New York NY: Wiley. doi:10.1002/0470055464

Clahsen, Harald, Eisenbeiss, Sonja & Penke, Martina. 1996. Underspecification and lexical learning in early child grammars. In *Generative Approaches to First and Second Language Acquisition. Empirical Findings, Theorectical Consideration and Crosslinguistic Comparisons* [Language Acquisition and Language Disorders 14], Harald Clahsen (ed.), 129–159. Amsterdam: John Benjamins. doi:10.1075/lald.14.08cla

Clements, Nick. 1990. The role of the sonority cycle in core syllabification. In *Papers in Laboratory Phonology* I, John Kingston & Mary Beckman (eds.), 283–333. Cambridge: CUP. doi:10.1017/CBO9780511627736.017

de Haan, Ger. 1987. A theory-bound approach to the acquisition of verb placement in Dutch. In *Formal Parameters of Generative Grammar: OTS Yearbook 1987*, Ger de Haan & Wim Zonneveld (eds.). Dordrecht: ICG.

den Besten, Hans. 1989. Studies in West Germanic Syntax. Ph.D. dissertation, KUB Tilburg.

Eisenbeiss, Sonja. 2009. Generative approaches to language learning. *Linguistics* 47(2): 273–310. doi:10.1515/LING.2009.011

Eyer, Julia & Leonard, Laurence. 1994. Learning past tense morphology with specific language impairment: A case study. *Child Language Teaching and Therapy* 10: 127–138. doi:10.1177/026565909401000201

Gillis, Steven. 2003. A case study of the early acquisition of verbs in Dutch. In *Development of Verb Inflection in First Language Acquisition: A Cross-linguistic Perspective*, Dagmar Bittner, Wolfgang Dressler & Marianne Kilani-Schoch (eds.), 171–203. Berlin: Mouton de Gruyter.

Haegeman, Liliane. 1994. Root infinitives, tense and truncated structures. *Language Acquisition* 4(3): 205–255. doi:10.1207/s15327817la0403_2

Halle, Morris. 1997. Distributed morphology: Impoverishment and fission. *MIT Working Papers in Linguistics* 30: 425–449.

Halle, Morris & Marantz, Alec. 1993. Distributed morphology and the pieces of inflection. In *The View from Building 20. Essays in Linguistics in Honor of Sylvain Bromberger*, Kenneth Hale & Samuel Jay Keyser (eds.), 111–176. Cambridge MA: The MIT Press.

Haznedar, Belma. 2001. The acquisition of the IP system in child L2 English. *Studies in Second Language Acquisition* 23: 1–39. doi:10.1017/S0272263101001012

Haznedar, Belma & Schwartz, Bonnie. 1997. Are there optional infinitives in child L2 acquisition? In *BUCLD 21: Proceedings of the* 21st *Annual Boston University Conference on Language Development*, Elizabeth Hughes, Mary Hughes & Annabel Greenhill (eds.), 257–268. Somerville MA: Cascadilla Press.

Ionin, Tania & Wexler, Kenneth. 2002. Why is 'is' easier than 's'? Acquisition of tense/agreement morphology by child L2-English learners. *Second Language Research* 18(2): 95–136. doi:10.1191/0267658302sr195oa

Johnson, Bonnie & Morris, Sherril. 2007. Clinical implications of the effects of lexical aspect and phonology on children's production of the regular past tense. *Child Language Teaching and Therapy* 23: 287–306. doi:10.1177/0265659007080682

Jordens, Peter. 1990. The acquisition of verb placement. *Linguistics* 28: 1407–1448. doi:10.1515/ling.1990.28.6.1407

Jordens, Peter. 2002. Finiteness in early child Dutch. *Linguistics* 40: 687–765. doi:10.1515/ling.2002.029

Keuleers, Emmanuel, Brysbaert, Marc & New, Boris. 2010. SUBTLEX-NL: A new frequency measure for Dutch words based on film subtitles. *Behavior Research Methods* 42(3): 643–650. doi:10.3758/BRM.42.3.643

Koster, Jan. 1975. Dutch as an SOV Language. *Linguistic Analysis* 1: 111–136.

Leonard, Laurence, Davy, Jennifer & Deevy, Patricia. 2007. Phonotactic probability and past tense use by children with specific language impairment and their typically developing peers. *Clinical Linguistics & Phonetics* 21(10): 747–758. doi:10.1080/02699200701495473

Lewis, Geoffrey. 1967. Turkish grammar. Oxford: Oxford University Press.

MacWhinney, Brian. 2010. *The CHILDES Project: Tools for Analyzing Talk*, WEB manual. Mahwah NJ: Lawrence Erlbaum Associates.

Marinis, Theodoros & Chondrogianni, Vasiliki. 2010. Production of tense marking in successive bilingual children: When do they converge with their monolingual peers? *International Journal of Speech-Language Pathology* 12(1): 19–28. doi:10.3109/17549500903434125

Marshall, Chloe & van der Lely, Heather. 2007. The impact of phonological complexity on past tense inflection in children with Grammatical-SLI. *Advances in Speech-Language Pathology* 9: 191–203. doi:10.1080/14417040701261509

Meisel, Jürgen. 2004. The bilingual child. In *The Handbook of Bilingualism*, Tej Bathia & William Ritchie (eds.), 91–113. Oxford: Blackwell.

Mobaraki, Mohsen, Vainikka, Anne & Young-Scholten, Martha. 2008. The status of subjects in early child L2 English. In *Current trends in Child Second Language Acquisition*, Belma Haznedar & Elena Gavruseva (eds.), 209–236. Amsterdam: John Benjamins. doi:10.1075/lald.46.11mob

Morelli, Frida. 1999. The Phonotactics and Phonology of Obstruent Clusters in Optimality Theory. Doctoral Dissertation University of Maryland.

Oetting, Janna & Horohov, Janice. 1997. Past tense marking by children with and without specific language impairment. *Journal of Speech, Language, and Hearing Research* 40: 62–74. doi:10.1044/jslhr.4001.62

Paradis, Johanne. (2011). Individual differences in child English second language acquisition: Comparing child-Internal and child-external factors. *Linguistic Approaches to Bilingualism.* 1:3, 213–237.

Paradis, Johanne, Rice, Mabel, Crago, Martha & Marquis, Janet. 2008. The acquisition of tense in English: Distinguishing child second language from first language and specific language impairment. *Applied Psycholinguistics* 29: 689–722. doi:10.1017/S0142716408080296

Pierce, Amy. 1989. On the Emergence of Syntax: A Cross-linguistic Study. Ph.D. dissertation, MIT.

Pinker, Steven & Ullman, Michael. 2002. The past and future of the past tense. *Trends in Cognitive Science* 6: 456–463. doi:10.1016/S1364-6613(02)01990-3

Polišenská, Daniela. 2010. Dutch Children's Acquisition of Verbal and Adjectival Inflection. Ph.D. dissertation, University of Amsterdam ⟨http://www.lotpublications.nl/publish/issues/Polisenska/index.html⟩.

Prévost, Philippe. 2003. Truncation and missing surface inflection in initial L2 German. *Studies in Second Language Acquisition* 25, 65–97. doi:10.1017/S0272263103000032

Rizzi, Luigi. 1993–1994. Some notes on linguistic theory and language development: The case of root infinitives. *Language Acquisition* 3: 371–393. doi:10.1207/s15327817la0304_2

Schlichting, Liesbeth & Lutje Spelberg, Henk. 2002. *Lexilijst NL*. Amsterdam: Pearson Assessment and Information.

Selkirk, Elisabeth. 1984. On the major class features and syllable theory. In Mark Aronoff & Richard Oehrle (eds.), *Language Sound Structures*, 107–136. Cambridge, MA: MIT Press.

Song, Jae Yung, Sundara, Megha & Demuth, Katherine. 2009. Phonological constraints on children's production of English third person singular -s. *Journal of Speech, Language and Hearing Research* 52, 623–642. doi:10.1044/1092-4388(2008/07-0258)

Vainikka, Anne & Young-Scholten, Martha. 2010. All acquisition begins with the projection of a bare verb phrase. *Applied Psycholinguistics* 31(2): 332–339. doi:10.1017/S0142716409990518

Vasić, Nada & Blom, Elma. 2011. Production and processing of determiners in Turkish-Dutch L2 children. In *BUCLD 35: Proceedings of the 35th annual Conference on Language Acquisition and Development*, Nick Danis, Kate Mesh & Hyunsuk Sung (eds.), 616–627. Somerville MA: Cascadilla Press.

Verhoeven, Ludo & Vermeer, Anne. 2001. *Taaltest Alle Kinderen (TAK)* (Language Assessment all Children). Arnhem: CITO.

Wexler, Kenneth. 1998. Very early parameter setting and the unique checking constraint: A new explanation of the optional infinitive stage. *Lingua* 106: 23–79. doi:10.1016/S0024-3841(98)00029-1

White, Lydia. 2003. *Second language acquisition and Universal Grammar*. Cambridge University Press.

Wijnen, Frank. 1998. The temporal interpretation of Dutch children's root infinitives: The effect of eventivity. *First Language* 18(3): 379–402. doi:10.1177/014272379801805406

Wijnen, Frank. 2000. Input, intake and sequence of syntactic development. In *From Sound to Sentence*, Mieke Beers, Beppie van den Bogaerde, Gerard Bol, Jan de Jong & Carola Rooijmans (eds.). Groningen: Center for Language and Cognition Groningen.

Appendix

A.1. Experimental sentences
Practice: De man tekent een boom en de vrouw tekent een huis

1. De jongen aait de hond en de vrouw aait de kat.
2. De jongen duwt de bank en de man duwt de auto
3. De man slaat een bal en de vrouw slaat een ballon.
4. De man wast een pan en de vrouw wast een kind.
5. De man leest een krant en de vrouw leest een boek.
6. De man geeft een roos en de vrouw geeft een appel
7. De man knipt papier en de vrouw knipt haar.
8. De man koopt een cadeau en de vrouw koopt een emmer.
9. De man drinkt sap en de brouw drinkt thee.

A.2. Non-words

Word-final	Word-medial between two syllables	Corresponding verb form
vaait	vermaaite	aait
puwt	veruwte	duwt
klaat	verblaate	slaat
dast	verpaste	wast/leest
peeft	keefte	geeft
moopt	versopte	koopt/knipt
blinkt	rikte	drinkt

Contradictory parameter settings in one mind

A case study of a Mandarin-Norwegian bilingual's acquisition of finiteness and V2 in Norwegian

Fufen Jin & Kristin Melum Eide
Norwegian University of Science and Technology

This paper reports a case study of Mandarin-Norwegian bilingual boy born into a Mandarin-speaking immigrant family in Norway. Mandarin and Norwegian are typologically distinct languages and presumably have contradictory parameters in the domains of finiteness and word order, the focal areas of the present study. The study explores whether there is cross-linguistic influence in the domains of finiteness and word order, leading the Mandarin-Norwegian bilingual child to lengthy periods of ungrammatical outcomes in Norwegian or a path of acquisition distinguishable from that of monolingual Norwegian children in relevant respects. The data are drawn from 5 files of a longitudinal corpus, when the boy was aged between 5;11 and 6;11. The production data indicate that the informant has essentially the same type of abstract linguistic system as Norwegian monolinguals, though limited cross-linguistic influence can be observed in word order and in markings of M-finiteness (i.e. morphological finiteness expressed as verbal inflection; term due to Lasser, 1997:77).

Keywords: bilingual acquisition; Norwegian; Mandarin; M-finiteness; word order; cross-linguistic influence; micro-cues

1. Introduction

A central theme of research in bilingual acquisition has been the question of monolingual-bilingual difference. That is, is bilingual acquisition the same as monolingual acquisition? It has been general consensus that the human language faculty has an endowment for bilingualism,[1] thus we expect the endpoint of bilingual acquisition to

---

1. Cf. e.g. Cook & Newson (2007:222): [T]here is […] a recognition that many, or indeed all, minds contain more than one grammar: "whatever the language faculty is it can assume many different states in parallel" (Chomsky 2000:59).

DOI 10.1075/la.231.11jin

be essentially the same as that of monolingual acquisition, given continuous exposure to dual speech input. What has been a topic of great controversy is whether the course and developmental patterns would turn out the same too. This is the question concerning the nature of bilingual development. In regard to this question, researchers are divided into two camps: autonomous vs. interdependent. Researchers in the autonomous camp (e.g. De Houwer 1990; Meisel 2001; Hinzelin 2003) claim that the two grammatical systems develop independently of each other, and that both languages in bilingual acquisition develop in the same fashion as for monolingual acquisition. Proponents of the interdependent development hypothesis (e.g. Hulk & Müller 2000; Yip and Matthews 2007), on the other hand, claim that there is a systematic influence of the grammar of one language on the grammar of the other language during acquisition. Accordingly, they argue that the course and developmental patterns of bilingual acquisition can be different from those of monolingual acquisition.

In this paper, the nature of bilingual acquisition will be investigated with respect to a Mandarin-Norwegian bilingual child born into a Chinese immigrant family in Trondheim, Norway. We look at the bilingual child at a later developmental stage, the age between 5;11 and 6;11. We believe this age period poses a particularly interesting research question, because it is our concern, as well as a concern to many others, whether a bilingual child at his preschool to school age[2] has the same linguistic competence as his monolingual peers. The grammatical domains we examine are Norwegian morphological marking of finiteness and verb second (V2). As we discuss in some detail in Section 2, Mandarin and Norwegian differ parametrically with respect to finiteness distinctions and V2. Thus, investigating bilingual acquisition with the pairing of Mandarin and Norwegian can be revealing of cross-linguistic influence and of the nature of bilingual acquisition.

A major reason for investigating word order phenomena like V2 in tandem with morphological, i.e. inflectional markings, is that there is a largely well documented relation in first language acquisition between the acquisition of finiteness and the acquisition of verb placement, here understood as verb raising past sentence negation and other sentence adverbs (but cf. Westergaard, this volume, for a different view). E.g. Meisel (1997:239) states that "The acquisition of sentence negation happens fast and virtually without errors in L1 acquisition. As soon as one finds evidence for the *productive use of finite forms* [our emphasis], NEG is placed clause-internally." This is illustrated for Swedish child data (from Platzack 1996, originally from Söderbergh 1973)

2. Note that children in Norway attend school from the age of 6. Most children attend kindergarten for at least a couple of years before this age, but this, unlike school, is not mandatory. There has been some concern about the fact that those children who do not attend kindergarten at all, are mostly children of immigrants.

in (1ab), for Dutch child data (from Blom 2003) in (1cd), and French child data (from Pierce 1989) in (1ef).

(1) a. Embla inte ha täcket
Embla not have blanket-DEF
'Embla not have the blanket'

b. älg säger inte mu
moose says not mu
'Moose doesn't say moo'

c. even buiten kijken
just outside look
'just outside look'

d. gaat niet
works not
'doesn't work'

e. pas casser
not break
'not break'

f. marche pas
works not
'doesn't work'

What makes the study even more intriguing is that the informant also simultaneously receives input from two varieties of spoken Norwegian: a standard Norwegian variety and the local *Trønder* dialect, which have micro-parametric differences with respect to finiteness morphology and V2.[3] So the bilingual child faces the challenges of the macro-parametric differences between Mandarin and Norwegian on the one hand, and the micro-parametric differences between the standard Norwegian and the

3. The so-called standard Norwegian in question is the Oslo-based, eastern Norwegian dialect, which is closest to the written standard called *Bokmål* 'book language'. In addition to this standard, there is another written standard called *Nynorsk* ('new Norwegian'), differing from the first mainly in the sets of inflectional paradigms, and to some extent the lexical inventory. The names Bokmål and Nynorsk are "misnomers resulting from political conflict and compromise" (Haugen 1987: 147) since both standards are written and Bokmål (BM) is in fact historically more recent than Nynorsk (NN). Nynorsk is currently the preferred written standard for approximately 17% of Norwegians, and official media are supposed to broadcast at least 25% of their programs in Nynorsk. All official documents are supposed to exist in both written standards. The *Trønder* dialect is spoken in the middle part of Norway, in the area where the city of Trondheim is the administrative and urban center.

local dialect.[4] Against this context, the study explores whether there is cross-linguistic influence in the domains of morphological finiteness marking and word order, leading Mandarin-Norwegian bilinguals to lengthy period of ungrammatical outcomes or an acquisition pattern differing from that of monolinguals.

The remaining sections are structured as follows. In Section 2, we present the relevant aspects of the Norwegian and the Mandarin grammar. Parametric differences between the two languages, which are likely to be susceptible to cross-linguistic influence, are discussed at some length. Specifically, we present the relevant data regarding verb placement and finiteness marking in Norwegian (Sections 2.1., 2.2. respectively) and finiteness marking and verb placement in Mandarin (Section 2.3.). In addition, the micro-parametric differences between the standard Norwegian and the local dialect are outlined here as well. In Section 3, we present the methodology of the case study. In Section 4, we present our findings and conclusions.

2. Parametric differences between Norwegian and Mandarin: Finiteness and V2

2.1 The verb second ("V2") feature of Norwegian

Like many other Germanic languages, Norwegian is known as an asymmetric V2 language. This means that the finite verb must occur in second position in declarative main clauses, whereas this requirement does not hold in embedded clauses. We can see the V2 requirement at work most clearly when the clause initial phrase is a topicalized non-subject (cf. (2a)), since in this case, the verb occurs to the left of the subject. However, even if the declarative main clause is subject initial (SVO), as are about 60% of declarative main clauses in Norwegian spoken and written corpora (cf. Eide and Sollid 2011, Eide 2011) we can still observe the V2 rule if the declarative main clause contains a sentence adverb, e.g. the negation adverb *ikke* 'not' or the sentence adverb *aldri* 'never' (cf. (2b)). When we compare the main clauses in (2ab) to the corresponding embedded clause in (2c), we find that the verb occurs to the left of the adverb in declarative main clauses (i.e. in the verb second, "V2" position), but not in the corresponding embedded clause. This difference is accounted

4. Note that these micro-parametric differences must be dealt with also by the "monolingual" children growing up in the Trondheim area. In fact, we need to emphasize that most children growing up in Norway face the same type of bi-dialectal situation unless they are raised in the Oslo area by two parents speaking the Oslo or eastern Norwegian variety, since their care-givers will usually be speaking one dialect and cartoons and children's books always will provide abound PLD (Primary Linguistic Data) input in the standard variety.

for by assuming that some property of declarative main clauses triggers verb movement, raising the finite verb from the VP to a head position in the C-domain, whereas in the embedded clause structure verb movement to C is prevented. Traditionally (cf. e.g. den Besten 1983), this difference was assumed to be connected to complementizer insertion into C in embedded clauses, preventing verb raising of the finite verb into the (same) C-position.

(2) a. Pannekaker spiser Jonas aldri.
pancakes eatPRES Jonas never
'Pancakes Jonas never eats.'

b. Jonas spiser aldri pannekaker.
Jonas eatPRES never pancakes
'Jonas never eats pancakes.'

c. Ettersom Jonas aldri spiser pannekaker,...
since Jonas never eatPRES pancakes
'Since Jonas never eats pancakes,...'

Main clause *wh*-questions are also subject to the V2 rule in standard Norwegian. The fronted *wh*-phrase is the first constituent and the verb is obligatorily the second constituent. Again we observe that the finite verb moves across the subject (and adverb) in (3a) or only across the adverb as in (3b), since here the subject happens to be the fronted *wh*-phrase.

(3) a. Hva spiser Jonas aldri?
what eatPRES Jonas never
'What does Jonas never eat?'

b. Hvem spiser aldri pannekaker?
who eatPRES never pancakes
'Who never eats pancakes?'

Closely related to the V2 feature is the V1 feature of certain other types of main clauses. Polarity questions and imperatives are among the clause types displaying the finite verb as the first element of the clausal string in V2 languages. Again we see that the verb moves to the left, across the subject and adverb, cf. (4a) or across an adverb (4b) (in imperatives the subject is usually not overtly realized); compare again to the word order of the embedded clause in (2c).

(4) a. Spiser Jonas aldri pannekaker?
eatPRES Jonas never pancakes
'Does Jonas never eat pancakes?'

b. Spis aldri pannekaker!
eatIMP never pancakes
'Never eat pancakes!'

As suggested above, Norwegian is assumed to display a strict V2 adherence in declarative main clauses and main clause *wh*-questions. However, there are recognized exceptions to the V2 rule in both types of clauses, albeit in somewhat different ways. One type of exception in main clause declaratives regards certain adverbs which trigger exceptional placement of the finite verb, especially *kanskje* 'maybe' and *bare* 'just, only'. Both of these adverbs seem to be quite frequent in spoken Norwegian (*kanskje* seemingly triggers non-V2 more often than *bare;* cf. Section 4.6). Observe in (5a) that the finite verb has moved neither to the left of the subject nor to the left of the adverb *aldri.* In (5b) the finite verb moves past the sentence adverb (in this case the negation adverb *ikke*), but this finite verb is still not the second constituent, since the adverb *bare* occurs between the topic (in this case the subject) and the finite verb.

(5) a. Kanskje Jonas aldri spiser pannekaker.
Maybe Jonas never eatPRES pancakes
'Maybe Jonas never eats pancakes.'

b. Jonas bare spiser ikke pannekaker.
Jonas just eatPRES not pancakes
'Jonas simply does not eat pancakes.'

To fully master the V2 rule, the acquirer of Norwegian also has to internalize a set of exception rules for left dislocation structures of the type exemplified in (6a) and (6b). The first illustrates what is known as the SÅ-construction (where the particle SÅ seems to act as a topic marker immediately following a shifted or contrastive topic), but this particle can also be replaced by a proadverb *da* 'then' (cf. Østbø 2006; Sollid & Eide 2007a, b; Nordström 2010; Eide & Sollid 2011; Eide 2011), in which case it behaves more like a typical left dislocation. Left dislocations can also target arguments, e.g. the subject, as in (6b), in which case the topic is repeated by a light (unstressed) pronoun between the topic and the verb.

(6) a. På fredager så/da spiser Jonas pannekaker.
On Fridays SÅ/then eatPRES Jonas pancakes
'On Fridays Jonas eats pancakes.'

b. Jonas han spiser ikke pannekaker.
Jonas he eatPRES not pancakes
'Jonas, he does not eat pancakes.'

Coordinators and connectives are smallish elements that sometimes cause trouble for (especially L2) acquirers of the V2 rule in Norwegian (cf. Hagen 1992: 30–31). Somehow, the acquirer has to learn that coordinators and certain connectives do not count as first constituents of sentences, when placement of the finite verb is calculated. The coordinators are *og* 'and', *men* 'but', *for* 'because', *eller* 'or', and a particularly frequent connective is *så* 'so' (note that this is a different *så* than the one occurring in the SÅ-construction).

(7) a. ...for pannekaker spiser Jonas aldri.
for pancakes eatPRES Jonas never
'...because Jonas never eats pancakes.'

b. ...så pannekaker spiser Jonas aldri.
so pancakes eatPRES Jonas never
'...so Jonas never eats pancakes.'

The connective *så,* and especially the word order that goes with it, is particularly hard to grasp for many acquirers[5] of Norwegian, since this particle has so many different meanings and functions. As a connective, as in (7b), it is followed by main clause word order, but in the SÅ-construction (cf. 6a) and in the *hvis – så* 'if-then' construction (8), the particle occurs after a fronted element (a topic or an *if*-clause) and is followed directly by the finite verb.

(8) Hvis du spør meg, så spiser Jonas aldri pannekaker.
If you ask me, then Jonas never eatPRES pancakes
'If you ask me, Jonas never eats pancakes.'

As discussed above, imperatives feature the finite verb in first position in Norwegian. However, even here the adverb *bare* 'just' shows a special behavior, together with the negation adverb *ikke* 'not'. These two adverbs, and only these,[6] regularly occur to the left of the verb in imperatives.

(9) a. Bare spis pannekaker!
just eat pancakes
'Go ahead and eat pancakes!'

b. Ikke spis pannekaker!
not eat pancakes
'Do not eat pancakes!'

Finally, we will mention a rather well-studied phenomenon (e.g. Åfarli 1986a, b; Fiva 1996; Lie 1992; Nilsen 1996; Nordgård 1985; Westergaard 2003; to mention but a few) from Norwegian non-standard dialects constituting another exception to otherwise well-behaved V2 (and V1) rules. This regards main clause *wh*-questions. Many Norwegian dialects allow for what looks like the word order of the corresponding

5. This is particularly evident with second language learners of Norwegian and in contact situations. Cf Sollid & Eide (2007a, b) for more on this particle in contact situations and in second language acquisition.

6. Certain speakers allow even the adverb *aldri* 'never' in this position.

embedded *wh*-clause instead of a V2 clause in main clause *wh*-questions. Certain dialects allow for the embedded word order when the *wh*-phrase is a complex *wh*-phrase (like *katti* 'what time', *koffor* 'what for', *kelles* 'what way'), but a non-V2 word order with a simplex, monosyllabic *wh*-phrase is much more widespread. Two important wh-phrases in this regard are *hva/ka* 'what' and *hvem/kæm* 'who'. Compare the V2 structures of standard Norwegian in (3a) and (3b) above to the non-V2 structures in (10a) and (10b), from the *Trønder* dialect constituting a considerable input in the primary linguistic data of our informant. Note that if the *wh*-phrase is the subject, this triggers the occurrence of the complementizer *som* (this is the case for the corresponding embedded *wh*-questions even in the standard varieties of Norwegian).

(10) a. Ka han spise?
what he eatPRES
'What does he eat?'

b. Kæm som spise pannjkake?
who compl eatPRES pancake
'Who is eating pancakes?'

The placement of the verb in dialectal *wh*-questions has been shown (Westergaard 2003, 2006, 2009) to be determined in part by the information structure of the clause, in part by the type of subject (whether it is a lexical noun phrase or a pronoun) and by the type of verb (lexical verb or a light verb like the copula). Lightfoot (2006) suggests that exposure to V2 structures e.g. like those illustrated in (2)–(3) above suffices to set the parameter for V2 at the right value, since exposure to V2 structures functions as parameter setting cues for the child. Building on Lightfoot's (2006) cue-based approach to language acquisition, Westergaard (2006) argues that the cue for V2, formulated by Lightfoot as in (11), would be much too coarse grained and would cause confusion to a child learning "a mixed V2 grammar" like the grammar of many Norwegian dialects.

(11) $_{CP}$[XP $_{C}$V...]

Instead, children must be sensitive to the specific type of element occurring as the XP in a structure like (11), and also many other aspects of the structure, like verb type, subject type, and the presence of adverbs giving rise to exceptional word orders (like *kanskje* 'maybe' and *bare* 'just'). Westergaard keeps the notion of cues, but suggests instead that children scan their linguistic environment for *micro-cues*:

> There is no global cue for V2 syntax, but separate cues for each clause type. When children scan the primary linguistic data for word order cues, this is presumably a selective process where only a particular clause type is relevant. [...] This means that no transfer of feature values [e.g. overgeneralization] is predicted from one clause type to another.

Hence, to master the rules of verb placement in Norwegian, the child must know whether the clause is a main clause or an embedded clause, whether it is a declarative, a polarity question, a *wh*-question or an imperative, (s)he must note the presence of coordinators and connectives that do not count to calculate the V2 position, and simultaneously note the presence of connectives and adverbs that do trigger particular instantiations of or exceptions to the V2 rule. All this while managing the micro-parametric differences between different varieties of Norwegian; e.g. standard Norwegian versus *Trønder*, where the rules of verb placement may differ considerably, in particular in *wh*-questions, as shown above.

2.2 Finiteness and the productive verbal paradigm in Norwegian

Norwegian verbs are productively inflected for tense and finiteness (cf. also Eide, this volume). There are two major classes, strong (irregular) verbs and weak (regular) verbs, characterized as follows in Simonsen and Bjerkan (1998: 253):

> The formal distinction between strong and weak verbs in Norwegian is based on whether they carry a syllabic suffix in the past tense or not; the verbs carrying a syllabic past tense suffix are weak (e.g. *kaste* 'throw' /kâst-e/-/ kâst-et/; *rope* 'call' /rûp-e/-/ rûp-te/,[7] and those without a syllabic suffix in the past tense are strong (e.g. *fryse* 'freeze' /fr^y:s-e/-/fr`ø:s/: *brenne* 'burn' /brên-e/-/brànt/- note that this last verb has a suffix in the past tense, but it is non-syllabic, and thus the verb is counted as strong). This entails that weak verbs end in an unstressed syllable in the past tense, while the past tense forms of strong verbs end in a stressed syllable.

However, according to these authors there is also an important subdivision within the class of weak verbs, distinguished through the specific different past suffixes they take. "The largest and generally productive class, the larger weak class, which we call the larger weak class (WL), takes a suffix beginning with a vowel (-/et/ or -/a/). The use of either -/et/ or -/a/ is sociolinguistically and stylistically determined. The smaller and less productive class, which we call the smaller weak class (WS), takes two suffixes beginning with a dental consonant (/te/ and -/de/)" (ibid). Based on the Norwegian *bokmål* dictionary, the authors show that from approximately 4800 verbs listed here, about 56% of the verbs belong to the WL class, 40% belong to the WS class, and 4% belong to the class of strong verbs (arguably the latter are quite frequent verbs).

Unlike English, where the productive paradigm of verbal inflection dictates that the infinitive equals the present tense (except for 3.P.SG) and the preterit equals the

7. "Norwegian has two word tones or tonemes, associated with the accented syllable of the word: Toneme 1 is a low tone, transcribed as /`/above the accented vowel, while toneme 2 is a falling tone, transcribed as /^/. In the transcription, suffixes are separated with a hyphen for ease of identification." Simonsen & Bjerkan (1998).

past participle form, the productive verbal paradigms in Norwegian clearly distinguish between finite and non-finite forms. This is true for standard Norwegian as well as the local dialect in question, i.e. the *Trønder* dialect. Thus we have the paradigms shown in Table 1 for class 1 weak verbs; dubbed WL by the authors Simonsen and Bjerkan (1998) in the quote above. Recall that this is the productive class; almost all new verbs are inflected according to this paradigm. Preferably, in illustrating the different verb paradigms, we use example verbs also attested in the informant's speech.

Table 1. Weak verb class 1, large class (WL)

	+finite	−finite		+finite	−finite
+past	kasta	kasta	+past	kasta	kasta
−past	kaster	kaste	−past	kaste	kast
Standard Norw.: *kaste* 'throw'			Trønder dialect: *kaste* 'throw'		

The paradigm of the WS class (referred to as class 2 of weak verbs in Faarlund, Lie and Vannebo (1997)) is shown in table (2) below. This class is less productive, but still many verbs in contemporary Norwegian belong to this class (about 40%, according to Simonsen and Bjerkan 1998).

Table 2. Weak verb class 2, small class (WS)

	+finite	−finite		+finite	−finite
+past	bygde	bygd	+past	bygd	bygd
−past	bygger	bygge	−past	bygge	bygg
Standard Norw.: *bygge* 'build'			Trønder dialect: *bygge* 'build'		

The inflectional paradigms of strong verbs are no longer productive, and only 4% of contemporary Norwegian verbs belong to this class. However, strong verbs are highly frequent; indeed, irregular verbs like these strong verbs are the most frequent verbs "in English and most other languages", according to Pinker (2000: 138).[8] There are six subclasses of strong verbs in *bokmål* (the relevant standard variety), separated by the specific vowel change ("*Ablaut*") at work (cf. Faarlund, Lie & Vannebo 1997: 487). For illustration we pick a verb from class 2 attested in the informant's speech, *skyte*.

8. Pinker in turn refers to Bybee (1985) for this observation. Pinker (2000: 137) gives a list of the ten most common verbs in English. They are all irregular verbs, and almost exclusively strong verbs.

Table 3. Strong verb class 2

	+finite	−finite		+finite	−finite
+past	skjøt	skutt	+past	skaut/skøyt	skotte/skutt
−past	skyter	skyte	−past	skyt	skyt
Standard Norw.: *skyte* 'shoot'			Trønder dialect: *skyte* 'shoot'		

Note that the infinitive of the standard Norwegian variety is often homophonous to the present tense of the local dialect; the infinitive of the local dialect regularly has a shorter form, and the preterit form [+past, +finite] is often different in the two varieties. Finally, we show the paradigm of the verb *komme* 'come, arrive' to illustrate that the inflections may differ quite substantially between the two relevant varieties of Norwegian. This verb belongs to strong verb class 6 in *bokmål* and class 5 in the local dialect (and *nynorsk*). This verb is a very frequent one in Norwegian, and is correspondingly frequently attested in the informant's speech, in various versions.

Table 4. Strong verb *komme* (class 6/5)

	+finite	−finite		+finite	−finite
+past	kom	kommet	+past	kum	komme
−past	kommer	komme	−past	kjæm	kom
Standard Norw.: *komme* 'come'			Trønder dialect: *komme* 'come'		

2.3 Finiteness and word order in Mandarin as compared with Norwegian

In contrast to verbs in Norwegian, verbs in Mandarin lack any finiteness or past/non-past distinction. Verbs in Mandarin are only inflected for aspects; and this via specific free-standing particles. There are basically three aspect markers, namely, *-le*, the marker of perfective aspect (cf. 12a), *-zhe*, the marker of durative aspect (cf. 12b), and *-guo*, the marker of experiential aspect (cf. 12c).

(12) a. Ta chi-*le* pingguo.
he eat-Asp apple
'He ate an apple.'

b. Ta chi-*zhe* pingguo.
he eat-Asp apple
'He's eating an apple.'

c. Ta chi-*guo* pingguo.
he eat-Asp apple
'He ate apples before.'

An obvious property of verbs in Mandarin, by assumption related to the lack of finiteness or tense distinctions (cf. Eide 2008; Eide 2009a, b; Eide & Hjelde 2015), is that they do not instantiate movement. We observe that in declaratives as in (13a), the verb does not move across negation/adverb, unlike in Norwegian, cf. (2ab) above. In yes/no questions as in (13b), the verb is not fronted (unlike the corresponding V1 structures in Norwegian; cf. (4) above). In *wh*-questions as in (13c), the *wh*-word as well as the verb stays in-situ, compare again to the corresponding structures in standard Norwegian (cf. 3) and the *Trønder* dialect (cf. 10) above.

(13) a. Ta *bu/keneng* chi pingguo.
he not/maybe eat apples
'He does not eat apples./He maybe eats apples.'

b. Ta *chi pinguo* ma?
He eat apple SFP
'Does he eat apples?'

c. Ta chi *shenme*?
he eat-Asp what
'What did he eat?'

From the above examples, it is clear that Mandarin word order is not featured with V2. In the literature (e.g. Li & Thompson 1981; Huang et al. 2009), Chinese is often referred to as a discourse oriented language with a topic-comment structure. A topic is loosely defined as 'what the sentence is about' (Li & Thompson 1981), whereas a comment 'says something about the topic' (Li & Thompson 1981). Example (14) illustrates a typical topic-comment structure in Mandarin:

(14) Zhe ge pingguo, ta hai meiyou chi.
This CL apple he yet not eat
'He has not eaten the apple yet.'

In (14), '*zhe ge pingguo*' is the topic of the sentence. The remaining sentence is a comment. Syntactically, '*zhe ge pingguo*', which is the object of the sentence, has been topicalized and moved to the front position, and the object position is null. This structure can be illustrated as in (15):

(15) [TOP zhe ge pingguo]$_i$ ta hai meiyou chi [e]$_i$

It should be noted that it is quite common even in Norwegian to topicalize the given information in the previous discourse. However, Norwegian differs from Mandarin in that it follows the V2 rule. So unlike Mandarin topic-comment structure where the verb follows the subject, in Norwegian once a constituent is topicalized, the sentence then has to instantiate subject-verb inversion in order to conform to the V2 rule. Some examples have appeared in Section (2.1). Here is one more relevant example:

(16) Denne filmen så jeg i går.
This film saw I yesterday
'I saw this film yesterday.'

As we can see, the Mandarin topic-comment structure and the Norwegian topicalized construction as illustrated above have both structural similarities and differences. The similarity lies in that the object moves from the object position to the topic position, leaving the object position null. They differ in that verbs in Norwegian must move to the second position in this process, whereas verbs in Mandarin stay in-situ. Table 5 recapitulates some relevant parametric differences between Mandarin, standard Norwegian and the *Trønder* dialect with regard to finiteness and V2.

Table 5. Some parametric differences between Mandarin, standard Norwegian and the *Trønder* dialect

	M-finiteness	V2	V1	*Wh*-mvm	V2 in root *wh*-clauses
Mandarin	–	–	–	–	–
Standard Norwegian	+	+	+	+	+
Trønder dialect	+	+	+	+	+ long *wh*-words; – short *wh*-words

Not surprisingly, standard Norwegian and the local *Trønder* dialect mostly group together against Mandarin. However, note again the feature V2 in root *wh*-clauses in standard Norwegian, versus non-V2 with simplex *wh*-words in the corresponding structures of the local dialect. Recall also from Section 2.2 that although standard Norwegian and the *Trønder* dialect both display productive tense and finiteness markings, the particular instantiations of these markings may differ, in some cases quite substantially between the two varieties of Norwegian, cf. e.g. the paradigm for the verb *komme* 'come, arrive' in Table 4 of Section 2.2 above. In general, the inflectional endings differ for at least some of the verb forms for each and every verb, e.g. the infinitive in Standard Norwegian is in general homophonous to the present tense of the *Trønder* dialect.

2.4 Hypotheses and predictions for the study

From the linguistic features outlined above, it becomes very clear that the bilingual child is faced with a number of challenges. The first challenge is the contradictory macro-parameter settings in Norwegian and Mandarin. The second challenge is the contradictory micro-parameter settings in standard Norwegian and the *Trønder* dialect. The third challenge comes from the contrast between the zero finiteness morphology in Mandarin versus complex finiteness morphology in Norwegian. And what makes the challenge even bigger is that the bilingual child has input from both the standard Norwegian and the local dialect, the two of which have different inflectional patterns in terms of finiteness.

Given these challenges faced by the bilingual child, the autonomous vs. interdependence hypothesis will make different predictions. The autonomous hypothesis predicts that the informant can set the proper parameter settings to proper language *and* dialect. In particular, it will predict that: (1) He has internalized the general rules regarding V2 and V1 syntax as well as the exceptional patterns involving particular adverbs, connectives and various left dislocation constructions, making no errors regarding word order, (2) he displays the same or a similar sensitivity to the relevant micro-cues of the V2 versus non-V2 features in root *wh*-clauses distinguishing the Standard Norwegian from the local dialect as has been attested for monolingual Norwegian children in earlier studies, cf. in particular Westergaard (2003, 2006, 2009), and (3) he has internalized the M-finiteness rules and will not differ from his monolingual peers in his performance in this respect.

The interdependence hypothesis assumes that there is cross-linguistic influence in these grammatical domains, leading our bilingual informant to lengthy periods of ungrammatical outcomes or a path of acquisition distinguishable from that of his monolingual Norwegian peers in relevant respects. According to the interdependence hypothesis, the bilingual informant is expected to experience difficulty in setting contradictory parameters to correct values, and make frequent errors with Norwegian word order. The micro-cues and exceptional patterns are considered as ambiguous data, which will make the V2 rule even more unlearnable. Similarly, the child is expected to make frequent errors in finiteness marking, using non-finite forms where finite forms are compulsory.

3. Methodology of the case study

The Mandarin-Norwegian bilingual child under study, a boy named Lele, was born into a Chinese immigrant family in Trondheim, Norway. He was first-born, and until he was at the age 5;11, he was the only child in the family. Both parents are native speakers of Mandarin, who immigrated to Norway in their late twenties. They were well-educated and had good knowledge of English and Norwegian, but the language of communication in Lele's home was definitely Mandarin.

Lele is thus a so-called second generation immigrant, and like many other second generation immigrants, his input conditions are situation-bound: Mandarin at home, Norwegian in the local community and the surrounding society. His Mandarin input comes mainly from his parents, who were committed to speaking Mandarin with their children. However, the parents played little or no role in his Norwegian development. His Norwegian input came mainly from the daycare center and subsequently from the pupils and teachers at school. Lele started to attend the daycare center on a full-day basis (e.g. 8 hours a day, five days a week) when he was 15 months old.[9] Before that age, his Mandarin input was clearly dominant. After he attended the day care center, his Norwegian input increased and soon became the dominant one. The adults who supposedly contributed most to Lele's Norwegian language development were the three caregivers in his daycare center. All three of them spoke the local dialect *Trønder*, resulting in the fact that the *Trønder* dialect also became the major form of Lele's spoken Norwegian.

In addition to input in *Trønder*, Lele simultaneously had input in the standard Norwegian variety *bokmål*. One main source of Lele's input in this standard Norwegian variety was from the daycare center. As a routine, the children had about one-hour story reading time, and the stories were read in *bokmål*. The other important source came from TV cartoon programs, which Lele watched regularly for about an hour daily. The language the cartoon figures speak is usually a spoken variant of this standard Norwegian variety.

Both *Trønder* and the standard Norwegian variety are reflected in Lele's Norwegian speech. The native Norwegian speakers (e.g. his caretakers in the daycare center, neighbors, and the parents of his Norwegian friends) attested to perceiving Lele as a quite competent speaker of Norwegian, little or no different from his monolingual Norwegian peers.

The data were collected at Lele's home.[10] Lele's Norwegian friends, who were his peers, served as the Norwegian speaking interlocutors. They were recorded with audio equipment in spontaneous interaction, mostly in free play. As the recordings hinged on how frequent his friends came to visit, and on how long they would play, the length of the recordings and the interval between recordings were dictated by availability. The recordings were transcribed by a research assistant, who was a native Norwegian speaker and master student of linguistics.[11] The transcriptions were then independently

9. One of the reviewers asks whether Lele should be considered as a simultaneous bilingual child or a successive bilingual child. In Lele's situation, in which he had regular exposure to both Norwegian and Mandarin starting from age 1;3, it is not justified to classify him as a successive bilingual child. We would rather consider him as a simultaneous bilingual child, though we note that before age 1;3 his input had been predominantly in Mandarin and that his Norwegian input had been sparse and irregular.

10. The data were collected both in a Mandarin language context and in a Norwegian language context. The interactions in Mandarin consisted of conversation between Lele and his parents. The Mandarin data are analyzed and discussed in another paper, cf. (Jin & Åfarli 2010).

11. This student was not a native speaker of the local dialect, but of a neighboring dialect still rather similar to the *Trønder* dialect in relevant respects. The transcriptions were taken down in a standard-like notation, which makes them more readily accessible to Norwegian

checked by both authors for accuracy. As the recordings were made in free play situations, unfortunately it happened quite often that the background noise marred the voice quality substantially. In case of discrepancies the two authors would listen to the recordings several times, and discuss the decisions until reaching an agreement. When there was doubt, the data were discarded and not considered for analysis.[12]

The corpus contains five audio recordings from when Lele was 5; 11 years old until 6; 11 years old. Table 6 gives the information of the five files, including Lele's age at the time of the recording, length of recording, and the Norwegian interlocutors' IDs. We did not calculate mean length of utterance, as it is not considered a reliable indicator for later bilingual development, i.e. after the age of 48 months (cf. Klee & Fitzgerald, 1985).

Table 6. Information of the recordings

No.	Lele's age	Length of recording	Interlocutors' ID
1	5; 11	0:34:13	HL
2	6; 03	0:14:08	SY
3	6; 06	0:52:08	SY
4	6; 10	0:58:00	HN
5	6; 11	0:44:18	AD

We readily acknowledge that our data are fairly limited, and the investigation period likewise covers only a limited time span. Our results are thus, quite clearly, highly tentative in nature. Further bilingual data with a larger time span is obviously needed in order to consolidate the results. We will still maintain that our investigation and our tentative results might have some merit, given that this type of study is very rare in a Norwegian context.

---

readers generally, but glosses over some potentially relevant lexical and phonological differences between the local dialect and *bokmål.* As a relevant example, the *wh*-words in the local dialect are *ka* 'what', *kæm* 'who', kor 'where', and *koffer* 'what for, why', but were written in the transcripts in their standard Norwegian version, as *hvem, hva, hvor, hvorfor,* respectively. This might not have been the best solution, since e.g. the non-V2 feature of root *wh*-clauses in Norwegian dialects occur only with the dialectal *wh*-words. This is at display e.g. in dialects where standard-like *wh*-words and dialectal *wh*-words co-exist in one and the same dialect; e.g. the dialect study of the *Skedsmokorset* dialect reported in Reite (2011). In this study, Reite shows that only the dialectal *wh*-words trigger non-V2 word order in root *wh*-clauses.

12. The recordings were interspersed with a few interactions between Lele and mother/father. In these situations, Lele always switched to Mandarin. Such Mandarin utterances produced by Lele were excluded for data analysis, as they were irrelevant for the present study.

4. Results

We first singled out the complete utterances produced by Lele in each recording.[13] The complete utterances were then divided into five groups according to sentence type: declarative, imperative, yes/no questions, *wh*-questions and embedded sentences. The distribution of each sentence type throughout the files is shown in Table 7.

Table 7. The distribution of the sentence types throughout Lele's files

File no.	Declarative sentence	Imperative sentence	*Wh*-questions	Yes/no questions	Embedded sentence	Total
1	170	19	8	9	21	227
2	15	2	0	0	1	18
3	244	21	19	36	25	345
4	157	16	9	37	30	249
5	165	12	10	22	24	233
Total	751	70	46	104	101	1072

As indicated in Table 7, Lele produced 751 declarative sentences, 70 imperatives, 46 *wh*-questions, 104 yes/no questions, and 101 embedded sentences throughout the files (not counting the discarded sentences; cf. the discussion of the transcription and selection process in section 3 above). We will take a close look at each sentence type in turn.

4.1 Declarative main clauses

The production data indicate that Lele's declarative sentences are overwhelmingly target-consistent V2, that is, the verb occurs in the second place of the relevant clauses. Among the 751 declarative main clauses, there are 102 utterances which contain negation or adverbs.[14] In such cases, the finite verbs moved across adverbs or negation. Some of the examples are given in (17).

(17) a. Vi trenger ikke mer. (5;11)
we need not more
'We do not need more.'

---

13. A complete utterance is defined as an utterance containing at least a verb, and that the subject and potentially the object are uttered, if they are not deliberately deleted.

14. Two adverbs, *bare* 'only' and *kanskje* 'perhaps', were excluded from this count, because they can trigger exceptions to the V2 rule. They are subject to independent analysis, cf. below.

b. Jeg har aldri levd langt. (6;06)
I have never lived long
'I have never lived long.'

c. Jeg har faktisk en av den her. (6;10)
I have actually one of that here
'I have actually one of that here.'

The declarative main clauses Lele produced are also featured with their fair share of fronted non-subject constituents. A total of 151 out of the 751 declaratives, up to 20.1%, have a fronted constituent other than the subject.[15] In such cases, all but one sentence displays subject-verb inversion. The fronted constituents in Lele's speech showed a great diversity in parts of speech, which is consistent with native Norwegian grammar. Here are some examples:

(18) a. Da mister vi raketten. (6;06)
Then lose we rocket-the
'Then we lose the rocket.'

b. Og så kan du få mine bakterier. (6;10)
Also can you get my bacteria
'You can also catch my bacteria.'

c. Huset har vi lagd. (5;11)
House-the have we built
'We have built the house.'

d. Bytte hodehjernen kan det. (5;11)
change headbrain-the kan it.
'It can change its headbrain.'

In (18a) and (18b), the fronted constituent is an adverbial. In (18c), the object is topicalized; in (18d) the fronted constituent is a verb phrase. We see that in all these examples, the finite verb occurs in the second place immediately following the fronted constituents, and the subject in turn follows the finite verb.

The only target divergent main clause Lele produced is found in file one, when Lele was at the age of 5;11.

(19) Den mammaen min bruker å ha å jobbe!
it mum-the my use to have to work
'My mum uses it for work!'

15. Cf. Eide & Sollid (2011), Eide (2011): In Norwegian written and spoken corpora containing the production of adult Norwegians the percentage of fronted non-subjects is about 24%. We have no figures from monolingual children at corresponding stages regarding this question.

In this utterance, we find that *den* 'it', which is the object of the sentence, is fronted, but the sentence does not display the target consistent subject-verb inversion, which amounts to a violation of the V2 rule. To better understand the context in which the utterance occurs, we give a larger chunk of the conversation, in which Lele's interlocutor is a monolingual Norwegian girl named HL.

(20) Lele: (pointing to the recorder, shouting):
Ikke ta det her ned der! Det er viktig!
not take this here down there! It is important
'Don't take that down! It is important!'

HL: Hm? Den der?
hm that there
'Hm? That one?'

Lele: Det er viktig! Den her er skikkelig viktig
it is important that here is really important
for mamma!
for mum
'It 'is important! This one is really important for mum!'

HL: Hvorfor det?
why it
'How come?'

Lele: Jo fordi da…
yes because then
'Just because…'

… …

HL: Hvorfor e den viktig da?
why is it important then
'So why is it important?'

Lele: Jasså det (…). Den mamman min bruker å ha å jobbe!
indeed it it mum-the my use to have to work
'Indeed… My mum uses it for work!'

When Lele discovered that HL obviously was intending to take down the recorder, he immediately warned HL not to do it. Lele's emotional reaction apparently startled HL, who in turn demanded an explanation for why the recorder was so important. It is in this communicatively (and evidently also emotionally) demanding situation that Lele produced this target divergent utterance.

What is the nature of this 'error' then? We suggest that this utterance is actually a topic comment structure that has been transferred from Mandarin Chinese. It is apparent from the context that the recorder is the topic of the conversation. Here *den* 'it (referring to the recorder)' moved from the object position to the topic position and the rest part of the sentence remain in-situ. As can be observed, this structure resembles the topic comment structure we have presented in Section 2 (Section 2.3). This remnant topic-comment structure, however, was only found in the very first file of Lele's recordings. In later files, Lele's main clauses are all target consistent.

4.2 Imperatives

Lele produced altogether 70 imperative sentences throughout the files. In all cases the verbs are in bare form, i.e. the infinitive form without *-e*, which is the targetlike form. Recall that imperatives in Norwegian are V1 structures, except in the presence of two adverbs which are allowed to occur in front of the bare verb in imperatives. One of the relevant adverbs is the negation word *ikke* 'not', the other is *bare* 'only'. Lele showed sensitivity to this exceptional rule. The imperatives he produced either have a bare verb in the very front (cf. 21 a), or are headed by *ikke/bare*, when these adverbs are needed (cf. 21bc).

(21) a. Trykk på den! (6;06)
Press on it
'Press it.'

b. Bare sett den på den fjøla. (6;10)
Just put it on that board-the
'Just put it on the board.'

c. Ikke les den! (6;11)
Not read it
'Don't read it.'

We conclude that Lele's imperatives are target consistent with respect to the relevant inflectional marking, the general V1 rule, as well as with the prominent exceptions to this rule (with adverbs *ikke* 'not' and *bare* 'just').

4.3 Yes/no questions (polarity questions)

All of the yes/no questions that Lele produced, 104 in number, are target consistent. The questions were all formed by moving the finite verb or auxiliary to the front, indicating that Lele had acquired the verb-movement rule in Norwegian at the period of recording. Some relevant examples are given in (22) below:

(22) a. Vet du hvorfor? (5;11)
know you why
'Do you know why?'

b. Skal vi leke med det? (6;06)
shall we play with it
'Shall we play with it?'

c. Så du det? (6;11)
saw you it
'Did you see it?'

4.4 *Wh*-questions

Wh-questions were relatively few in Lele's speech, only 46 throughout the files. However, they cover all the *wh*-words, including *hva* 'what' (cf. 23a), *hvem* 'who' (cf.23b), *hvor* 'where' (cf. 23c), *når* 'when' (cf. 23d), *hvordan* 'how' (cf. 23e), *hvorfor* 'why' (cf. 23f), *hvilken* 'which' (cf. 23g). In all of the *wh*-questions, we find that Lele fronted the relevant *wh*-word, indicating that he had acquired *wh*-movement in Norwegian at the time of recording. Hence, in this respect we find no cross-linguistic interference from Mandarin, where *wh*-phrases do not move from their in-situ position.

(23) a. Hva skal jeg bygge? (6;10)
what shall I build
'What shall I build?'

b. Hvem skal kjøre den her? (5;11)
who shall drive it here
'Who will drive it?'

c. Hvor er pengene våre? (6;11)
where is money-the our
'Where is our money?'

d. Når går den? (6;10)
when goes it?
'When does it go?'

e. Hvordan gikk det på da? (6;11)
how went it on then
'How did it get on?'

f. Hvorfor spiser du så mange på en gang? (6;10)
why eat you so many at one time
'Why do you eat so many at once?'

g. Hvilken er best? (6;06)
which is best
'Which one is the best one?'

Recall that the standard Norwegian and the local dialect, both spoken forms in which Lele received input, differ in terms of verb placement in root *wh*-clauses. In standard Norwegian, the V2 rule applies for all *wh*-words, whereas in the local dialect *wh*-questions can have non-V2 with simplex *wh*-words. We find that this difference is reflected in Lele's speech. Compare the examples in (23), where the verb or auxiliary is verb second, to the examples listed in (24) below. These examples constitute the total of 6 non-V2 *wh*-questions attested in the files (recall that the total of root *wh*-clauses was 46).

(24) a. Hva du bygger? (5;11)
what you build
'What are you building?'

b. Hva vi skal spille? (6;06)
what we shall play
'What shall we play?'

c. Hva du kjører nå? (6;06)
what you drive now?
'What are you driving now?'

d. Hvem det er? (6;06)
who it is
'Who is it?'

e. Hva du liker best? (6;10)
what you like best
'What do you like best?'

f. Hva det er? (6;11)
what it is
'What is it?'

We can see that only two *wh*-words are represented: one is *hva* 'what', the other is *hvem* 'who', with a proportion of 5:1. Another simplex *wh*-word which is relatively frequent (10 cases) is *hvor* 'where' (cf. 23c). However, we did not find a single case of non-V2 in *wh*-questions beginning with *hvor*. This seems to suggest that although Lele was sensitive to non-V2 rule, he only applied to the rule in connection with *hva/hvem*, rather than with other simplex *wh*-words. We should note, however, that this conclusion is rather tentative, because our data are rather limited in this regard. After all, we only have a total of 46 *wh*-questions in our database. It is obvious that more data points in this regard are needed in order to justify the conclusion. Another important point is that although adults in this dialect may produce non-V2 structures with *hvor*, we do not know at what rate, and we also do not know whether monolingual children who are speakers of this dialect use the non-V2 structure with this particular *wh*-word. The evidence from Lele's interlocutors in this respect is scarce, and if Lele's monolingual peers also do not use this construction, it would seem unjust to subject Lele's grammar to an even stricter judgment.

4.5 Embedded sentences

Given his age, Lele produced a rather impressive number of embedded sentences throughout the files, 101 in all. This attests to the fact that he, at the age period 5;11–6;11, was in the position to express his ideas with rather complex grammatical strategies. We found that his embedded sentences were overwhelmingly target consistent. First, in embedded questions, the subject and the verb are not inverted; second, in subordinate clauses the complimentizers, when present, are targetlike (cf. 25ab).

(25) a. Jeg vet [hvordan det skal være]. (5;11)
I know how it shall be
'I know how it is supposed to be.'

b. Jeg vil [at det er han som skal dø]. (6;03)
I will that it is he who shall die
'I wish that it is he who shall die.'

Although (25a) suggests that Lele has acquired at least one aspect of the non-V2 rule connected with subordinate clauses (since the verb is not V2 in the subordinate clause), we know that there are two types of non-V2. One type has some element occurring between the topic and the finite verb, but the verb has still moved across a sentence adverb or negation; (cf. (5b) above). In the other type of non-V2, the verb does not even move across the adverb (cf. e.g. (5a) above), and it is this latter type we find at display in Norwegian subordinate clauses. In order to see if Lele has acquired even this latter type of V2 and uses it correctly in embedded clauses, we need to single out the subordinate sentences containing negation or adverbs, because obviously these are the only sentences where we can observe whether or not Lele leaves the finite verb to the right of negation/adverbs. Our search resulted in 6 cases that met the requirements. We list them below:

(26) a. [Hvis de ikke jobber], da får du ikke penger. (5;11)
if they not work, than get you not money
'If they don't work, you don't get any money.'

b. [Hvis du har ikke det her], så får ikke (5;11)
if you have not this here, then get not
mammaen min penger.
mum-the my money
'If you don't have this, my mum won't get any money.'

c. Bare én som vi har ikke lagd. (5;11)
only one that we have not made
'Only one which we haven't made.'

d. …at du ikke skal dø. (6;06)
that you not shall die
'…that you won't die.'

e. [Men hvis du ikke har spist på dette her], (6;10)
but if you not have eaten on this here,
så går det helt greit.
then goes it just fine
'But if you haven't nibbled on this one, that's just fine.'

f. Jeg kunne ønsket [ikke jeg har vært syk så mange (6;10)
I could wished not I have been sick so many
ganger i England].
times in England
'I wish I hadn't been sick so many times in England.'

We found that in file one Lele showed some variability with regard to the placement of negation in subordinate clauses. In utterance (26a), the position of negation is target consistent, that is, the finite verb did not move across negation, whereas in utterances (26bc), the placement of negation was target divergent – the finite verbs moved across the negation as they do in root clauses. It so happened that the two utterances both involve the combination of *har* and *ikke*. So this ungrammaticality could well be due to overgeneralization of the chunk from root clauses. Monolingual Norwegian children at the same age period also have difficulty with the placement of negation/adverbs in subordinate clauses (Westergaard 2009). Thus we cannot conclude that Lele's development is delayed in this regard. Moreover, we found that in later files, the placement of negation in subordinate clauses was target consistent, suggesting that Lele had acquired the non-V2 rule in subordinate clauses in a later age period. A final note on the example in (26f): Here Lele places the negation at the very beginning of the embedded clause. Firstly, this would be target consistent had the negation in question been a constituent negation, negating only the subject *jeg* 'I', giving a contrastive reading of this subject. However, the context does not favor this reading. Secondly, the negation in the local dialect *Trønder* is a very light element in most cases taking the form of a clitic, and it may cliticize to an element in C^0, for instance a verb or a complementizer. Here there is no such overt complementizer, but it is also not uncommon that this clitic negation floats past a non-lexicalized C^0 and cliticizes to the verb in the upstairs clause, e.g. as in (27):

(27) Æ håpe-ikke du tenkte å ta den der.
I hope-not you thought to take that there
'I hope you didn't plan to take that one.'

Thus placement of the verb relative to negation varies in Lele's speech, but this placement may vary considerably in the target language too, and especially in the dialect *Trønder* which makes up the major part of Lele's Norwegian input and primary linguistic data.

4.6 Micro non-V2 cues

Finally, we will examine whether Lele showed sensitivity to micro-cues with respect to some other non-V2 rules in Norwegian, just as monolingual Norwegian children do. In Section 2, in particular in Section 2.1, we discussed several types of micro-cues connected with V2/non-V2 rules in Norwegian. In addition to root *wh*-questions, where the *Trønder* dialect differs from standard Norwegian variety, discussed in Section 4.4 above, and the assumed micro-cue regarding the difference between root and embedded sentences discussed in Section 4.5, there are numerous other potential micro-cues to consider. We list some relevant contexts in roman numerals below:

i. Recognized exceptions to V2 in declaratives with *bare* 'only' and *kanskje* 'maybe'
ii. The coordinators (*og*, 'and'; *men* 'but', *for* 'for', *eller* 'or',) and certain connectives, like *så* 'thus' do not count as "first elements" for calculating the V2 position
iii. The *Hvis…så/da* (if…then) construction
iv. Left dislocations

We observe all these non-V2 micro-cues reflected in Lele's speech. We first give examples of non-V2 word order in root declaratives featuring the adverbs *bare/kanskje*, two examples for *bare* (28ab) and two for *kanskje* (28cd).

(28) a. Jeg bare spoler over den her jeg. (6;06)
I just fast-forward over this one I
'I'll just fast-forward over this one.'

b. Vi bare leker. (6;10)
we just play
'We are just playing.'

c. Kanskje de vasker bilen. (5;11)
maybe they wash car-the
'Maybe they are washing the car.'

d. Kanskje jeg kunne få en. (6;10)
maybe I could get one
'Maybe I could have one?'

We note, however, that the frequency of non-V2 sentences with *kanskje* is much higher than those with *bare* in Lele's files. For *bare*, the frequency is 6.1%. That is, of 33 occurrences of *bare*, only 2 triggered non-V2. For *kanskje* the frequency is 55.6%, i.e. 5 out of 9 occurrences of *kanskje* triggered non-V2 word order. Thus it seems that *kanskje* is a stronger micro-cue for non-V2 than *bare*, if strength of a cue is in any way related to the input frequency of its trigger (cf. e.g. Westergaard 2010: 109 for a discussion on children's acquisition of micro-cues related to frequency).[16]

16. Cf. for instance Westergaard (2010: 109 ff): "[E]ven though children are sensitive to very minor distinctions in language, a low frequency of the triggers for a particular cue in the P(rimary) L(inguistic) D(ata), and a corresponding high frequency of a conflicting trigger, will make a micro-cue vulnerable to change. That is, structures with an extremely low input

Meanwhile, Lele demonstrates good knowledge of what coordinators are; that they do not count as "first position" elements, and that they take complements with the main clause word order in Norwegian. Examples follow in (29).

(29) a. ...for vi trenger tre. (5;11)
for we need three
'...because we need three.'

b. Men jeg tror ikke det er det. (6;06)
but I think not it is it.
'But I don't think that's what it is.'

c. Nei det har vi jo bygga før da, så det slipper vi. (6;10)
No that have we built before then, thus it let-go we
'No. We have built that before, so we don't need to do that.'

Searching for *hvis...så/da* constructions in Lele's files, we find many attested examples. We list two such constructions in (30ab), and note that the word order is target consistent, the pro-adverb *da/så* are both immediately followed by the finite verb.

(30) a. Hvis det ha vært sykefly, da hadde det (5:11)
If it had been emergency plane, then had there
vært rødt kryss.
been red cross
'If this had been an emergency plane, it should have had a red cross.'

b. Hvis du ikke har spist på dette her, så går det (6;10)
If you not have eaten on this, then goes it
helt greit.
just fine.
'If you have not nibbled on this, that's just fine.'

Left dislocations targeting arguments are not frequent in our material. We only find the following two examples throughout Lele's files:

(31) a. Sikkerhetsvakta, han kjører til det her også. (5;11)
security guard-the he drives to it here also
'The security guard, he also drives to this one.'

b. Babyen, han er opp-ned (6;10)
Baby-the he is up-down
'The baby, he is upside down.'

frequency may be ignored by children in the acquisition process and disappear from the I-language grammar of the next generation."

To sum up, the production data indicated that Lele showed sensitivity to every type of relevant micro-cue restricting the V2/non-V2 rule in Norwegian that we discussed in 2.1.

4.7 M-finiteness

As discussed in the introduction and also in Section 2.2 above, a bilingual child like Lele not only faces the challenges of setting the right macro-parameters for Norwegian versus Mandarin and the micro-parameters governed by micro-cues regulating the general rules and exceptions of V2 and non-V2 placement of the finite verb, within the variants *bokmål* and *Trønder* and also across the variants he is exposed to through his primary linguistic data (e.g. V2 and non-V2 in root *wh*-questions). In addition to these challenges, Lele also has to face the task of assigning no tense and finiteness morphology to the verb in Mandarin, and productive tense and finiteness inflections in Norwegian, but where the specific inflectional systems and instantiations once again vary sometimes quite substantially across the two relevant varieties.

Simonsen and Bjerkan (1998) investigated the acquisition of finite past tense inflections by Norwegian normally developing monolingual children and children diagnosed with specific language impairment (SLI) via an elicitation task requiring the informants to equip a list of given verbs with the correct finite past marker. They compared these results with the performance of an adult control group, and found that there is a clear developmental effect in normally developing children in that that the percent of correct answers increases substantially with age. The mean percent of correct answers for the group of 4-year-olds was 51%, for the 6-year-olds 72%, for the 8-year-olds 90% and for the adults 94%. However, performance varies across verb types (large weak class WL; small weak class WS, and strong verbs), as shown in Table 8 adapted from Simonsen and Bjerkan (1998: Table 5).

Table 8. Acquisition of finite past tense inflection

	WL class	WS class	Strong verbs
Age 4	85%	47%	33%
Age 6	94%	71%	60%
Age 8	96%	91%	86%
Adults	91%	97%	94%

In normally developing monolingual Norwegian children as in Simonsen and Bjerkan (1998), we see that although the most productive class falls into place quite early, there is still quite a development taking place from age 6 to age 8 (and even between age 8 and adult age). Our bilingual informant in this study was between the age of 5; 11 years old and 6; 11 years old at the time of the recording, thus mostly at an age between the 6-year-olds and the 8-year-olds. For Lele's monolingual peers we see that there is still quite a development taking place in the domain of M-finiteness markings at this stage. Moreover, the incorrect inflection marking consists in overgeneralizing the inflectional paradigm of the most productive class WL to other verb types; this is the case for both 4-year-olds and 6-year-olds (though the 8-year-olds overgeneralize both weak paradigms, i.e. both WL and WS). Thus the typical mainstream 6-year-old in this study will master the inflections of the WL class almost perfectly, but will perform quite a few errors with the WS class and the strong verbs, and the typical error will consist in overgeneralizing the WL class so as to inflect WS verbs and strong verbs according to the WL paradigm.

These are exactly the types of errors we find in Lele's production. Although we have not calculated the percentages of error types attested in Lele's files, we clearly recognize the pattern described for Norwegian monolingual children. Thus, we find examples of Lele overgeneralizing the WL class to both strong verbs and the WS class; cf Table 9, where we show examples of overgeneralization of this paradigm to strong verb class 2 *skyte*. Lele uses this inflection even for the very frequent verb *komme* 'come', which is a strong verb of class 6 in *bokmål* and strong verb class 5 in the local *Trønder* dialect. The table also shows an example of overgeneralization of WL into the WS class, preterit of the verb *bygge*. Note that in these cases, Lele uses neither of the two (different) forms available to him via *bokmål* and *Trønder*, but chooses instead to use the inflection belonging to the WL class.

Table 9. Overgeneralization of the WL paradigm

Bokmål preterit	Trønder preterit	Lele's preterit	Gloss
skjøt	*skaut/skøyt*	*skyta*	'shot'
kom	*kum*	*komma*	'came'
bygde	*bygd*	*bygga*	'built'

We also find some instances where our little informant seems to be negotiating between forms; in some utterances, after overgeneralizing the WL class, Lele finds the right form; as in (32), where he after trying out the WL form settles for the correct WS inflection:

(32) a. Der gjømma han sæ, gjømt sæ i flystasjona
there hid he himself, hid himself in plane station-the
'The he hid himself, hid himself in the plane station.'

We find certain examples of cross-linguistic influence. Firstly, we find that Lele sometimes mixes the M-finiteness markings, and sometimes uses the standard Norwegian form, and sometimes the *Trønder* dialectal form. Thus in (33a), he uses the dialectal form *kjæm* 'comes' and in (33b) the standard Norwegian *kommer* 'comes' in his speech. (cf. full paradigm for this verb in Table 4, Section 2.2 above). Moreover, we even find a few examples where he mixes these variants in one and the same sentence, e.g. (33c), where he uses both the dialectal preterit *ha* and the standard Norwegian preterit *hadde* of the verb *ha* 'have'. Cf. the paradigm for this verb given in table (10) below.

(33) a. Når dem lander, da kjæm dem bare langt.
when they land, then comePRES they only far
'When they land, they only get far.'

b. OK, nå! Æ skal vise deg hvordan dem kommer dit.
OK, now! I shall show you how they comePRES there
'Ok, now! I'll show you how they get there.'

c. Hvis det ha vært sykefly, da hadde det
If it hadPRET been ambulance-plane, then hadPRET it
vært rødt kryss.
been red cross
'If it had been an ambulance plane, it would have had a red cross.'

Table 10. Weak verb *ha* (WS class)

	+finite	–finite
+past	hadde	hatt
–past	har	ha
Standard Norw.: *ha* 'have'		

	+finite	–finite
+past	ha	hatt
–past	ha(r)	ha
Trønder dialect: *ha* 'have'		

Finally, we note that there are certain examples of cross-linguistic influence even at the macro-parameter level, although they are few. In the overwhelming majority of utterances, Lele uses finite forms where this is appropriate, and non-finite forms where this is required according to the target grammar. However, we do find examples where he seems to have transferred the quite useful construction *Topic chain* from his Mandarin L1 into his spoken Norwegian. In this case, the chain consists of three verbs describing a sequence of events. All three verbs ought to have the finite, preterit form. Instead, we find one preterit verb, one infinitive, and one past participle in this chain. Also, we note that the construction features topic drop in all three clauses of the chain, where we would expect to find the topic overtly realized in the first clause in Norwegian.

Compare this structure to the Mandarin topic chain in (34 b), and we can clearly see the similarities.

(34) a. ...men tok nøkkelen, og [e] låse opp døra og [e] gått
but took key-the, and lock up door-the and gone
inn det her.[17]
in this here
'...but he took the key, opened the door, and went inside this one.'

b. Na-liang che$_i$ jiaqian tai gui, [e$_i$] yanse ye bu hao,
that-CL car, price too high, color also not good,
wo$_j$ bu xiang mai [e$_i$].
I not want buy.
'That car costs too much, has the wrong color, so I don't want to buy it.'

In this connection, let us note that when monolingual Norwegian children give a non-preterit form in the elicitation experiment reported in Simonsen and Bjerkan (1998:260), they provide an infinitive or a present tense where a preterit would be appropriate. Adults, when they provide a non-past form in a preterit context, this form is always the past participle. Here we see that Lele provides one infinitive and one past participle where a preterit would be appropriate. Thus, his behavior resembles his six-year-old peers in some respects, but in this respect he also features traits similar to adult monolingual Norwegians.[18]

4.8 Conclusion

Our bilingual informant Lele performs at an attainment level at least comparable to his monolingual Norwegian peers regarding finiteness-related phenomena, i.e. verb placement in root clause declaratives, embedded declaratives, root *wh*-questions, polarity questions, and imperatives. His production data in Norwegian indicates that he does not exhibit much difficulty in setting the contradictory parameters to their

17. It is a general feature of Norwegian children's narrative plays that the narrative itself is given in the preterit, whereas when the interlocutors negotiate the rules of the narrative or game, distribute the characters, the setting and frame of the narrative, they use the present tense. This seems to be a modal function of the preterit, and can be found among very young children; cf. e.g. Dannemark (1985), Åm (1989) and Eliassen (1998).

18. Of course we have to note that Lele's data are not the result of elicitation tasks, but production data given in a naturalistic context. Thus, there may very well be a number of differences resulting from the two different modes of acquiring data. We still wanted to point to the fact that, according to Simonsen and Bjerkan (1998), monolingual Norwegian children do not mix up preterits and past participles, unlike adults, and unlike Lele.

proper values. He is also sensitive to micro-cues e.g. placement of verbs occurring with simplex *wh*-words, presence and absence of adverbs that trigger non-V2 word order in root declaratives, as well as the presence of connectives, coordinators, and left dislocation constructions.

On the morphological level, we find that Lele again performs at the level of his peers. We compared his results to the results of acquisition of tense inflection reported for monolingual Norwegian children at ages 4, 6 and 8 (Simonsen & Bjerkan 1998), whereas Lele was roughly between 6 and 7 when our recordings were made. There is a tendency among his monolingual peers to overgeneralize the paradigm of the large weak class WL into the small weak class WS and the strong verb class, and we find just the same tendency for Lele. In addition, we find a tendency to negotiate between forms, trying out several forms for one and the same verb. Sometimes he decides on a different verb class, and sometimes he uses the dialectal form and the standard Norwegian form side by side, even in one and the same sentence. In this respect there is some cross-linguistic influence from one Norwegian variety to another, that is, on the micro-level.

On the macro-level, we find little evidence of cross-linguistic influence from Mandarin into Lele's spoken Norwegian. The only clear verb placement errors we find possibly resulting from transfer of Mandarin features are uttered under circumstances quite challenging communicatively and emotionally (cf. discussion of example (20)). We do find certain utterances where the finiteness distinction is not observed as required, cf. example (34) where Lele seems to be transferring the construction Topic chain from his Mandarin first language. However, the rate at which errors are made regarding both verb placement and inflectional paradigms is no higher than monolingual Norwegian children at a comparable age. Thus our tentative results indicate that at least for our bilingual informant at this age, no developmental delay or differing developmental path can be observed as compared to that of monolingual Norwegian-speaking children.[19] We thus conclude that our findings are more consistent with the autonomous hypothesis.

References

Åarli, Tor, A. 1986a. Some syntactic structures in a dialect of Norwegian. *University of Trondheim Working Papers in Linguistics* 3: 93–111.

19. Recent research points instead to great cognitive advantages of bilingualism, e.g. Lauchlan, Farisi & Fadda (2012), Bialystok (2001), Bialystok and Martin (2004) and many others.

Åfarli, Tor, A. 1986b. Absence of V2 effects in a dialect of Norwegian. In *Scandinavian Syntax: Workshop at the Ninth Scandinavian Conference of Linguistics*, Östen Dahl & Anders Holmberg (eds.), 8–20. Stockhom: Stockholms universitet, Institut för lingvistik.

Åm, Eli. 1989. *På Jakt etter barneperspektivet*. Oslo: Universitetsforlaget.

Bialystok, Ellen. 2001. *Bilingualism in Development: Language, Literacy and Cognition*. Cambridge: CUP. doi:10.1017/CBO9780511605963

Bialystok, Ellen & Martin, Michelle M. 2004. Attention and inhibition in bilingual children: Evidence from the dimensional change card sort task. *Developmental Science* 7: 325–339. doi:10.1111/j.1467-7687.2004.00351.x

Blom, Elma. 2003. From Root Infinitive to Finite Sentence. Ph.D. dissertation, Utrecht University.

Bybee, Joan L. 1985. *Morphology: A Study of the Relation between Meaning and Form* [Typological Studies in Language 9]. Amsterdam: John Benjamins. doi:10.1075/tsl.9

Chomsky, Noam. 2000. *The Architecture of Language*. Oxford: OUP.

Cook, Vivian & Newson, Mark. 2007. *Chomsky's Universal Grammar: An Introduction*. Malden MA: Blackwell.

Dannemark, Nils I.S. 1985. Om pretetitum hos nokre fem-sjuåringar (On the preterit in some five-to-seven-year-olds). *NAVFs Skriftserie* 8: 250–263. Norsk senter for barneforskning.

De Houwer, Annick. 1990. *The Acquisition of Two Languages from Birth: A Case Study*. Cambridge: CUP. doi:10.1017/CBO9780511519789

den Besten, Hans. 1983. On the interaction of root transformations and lexical deletive rules. Ms, University of Amsterdam & MIT, later published in Abraham, Werner (ed.). 1983. *On the Formal Syntax of the Westgermania* [Linguistik Aktuell/Linguistics Today 3], 47–132. Amsterdam: John Benjamins, and den Besten, Hans. 1990. Studies in Westgermanic Syntax, Ph.D. dissertation, University of Tilburg. doi:10.1075/la.3.03bes

Eide, Kristin Melum. 2008. Finiteness in Norwegian, English, …and Chinese? In *Comparative Grammar and Language Acquisition in the Age of Globalization: Norwegian and Chinese,* Tor A. Åfarli & Fufen Jin (eds.), 39–64. Trondheim: Tapir.

Eide, Kristin Melum. 2009a. Tense, finiteness and the survive principle: Temporal chains in a crash-proof grammar. In *Towards a Derivational Syntax: Survive-minimalism* [Linguistik Aktuell/Linguistics Today 144] Michael Putnam (ed.), 91–132. Amsterdam: John Benjamins. doi:10.1075/la.144.05eid

Eide, Kristin Melum. 2009b. Finiteness: The haves and the have-nots. In *Advances in Comparative Germanic Syntax* [Linguistik Aktuell/Linguistics Today 141], Artemis Alexiadou, Jorge Hankamer, Thomas McFadden, Justin Nuger & Florian Schäfer (eds.), 357–390. Amsterdam: John Benjamins. doi:10.1075/la.141.15fin

Eide, Kristin Melum. 2011. Norwegian (non-V2) declaratives, resumptive elements, and the Wackernagel position. *Nordic Journal of Linguistics* 34 (2):179–213. doi:10.1017/S0332586511000163

Eide, Kristin Melum & Hjelde, Arnstein. 2015. Verb second and finiteness morphology in Norwegian heritage language of the American Midwest. In *Moribund Germanic Heritage Languages in North America: Theoretical Perspectives and Empirical Findings,* Michael T. Putnam & Richard Page (eds.), 64–101. Leiden: Brill. doi:10.1163/9789004290211_005

Eide, Kristin Melum & Sollid, Hilde. 2011. Norwegian Main Clause Declaratives: Variation within and across Grammars. In *Linguistic Universals and Language Variation*, Peter Siemund (ed.), 327–360. Berlin: Mouton de Gruyter. doi:10.1515/9783110238068.327

Eliassen, Camilla. 1998. Rollelekspråk (Role Play Language). MA thesis, Norwegian Univeristy of Science and Technology.

Faarlund, Jan Terje, Lie, Svein & Vannebo, Kjell Ivar. 1997. *Norsk Referansegrammatikk*. Oslo: Universitetsforlaget.

Fiva, Toril. 1996. 'Spørresetninger i Tromsø-dialekten' (Interrogative clauses in the Tromsødialect). *Nordica Bergensia* 9: 139–155.

Hagen, Jon Erik. 1992. Feilinvertering, overinvertering og underinvertering (Faulty inversion, overinversion and underinversion). *NOA* 15: 27–38.

Haugen, Einar. 1987. Danish, Norwegian and Swedish. In *The Major Languages of Western Europe*, Bernard Comrie (ed.), 147–169. London: Routledge.

Hinzelin, Marc-Oliver. 2003. The acquisition of subjects in bilingual children: Pronoun use in Portuguese-German children. In *(In)Vulnerable Domains in Multilingualism* [Hamburg Studies on Multilingualism 1], Natascha Müller (ed.), 107–137. Amsterdam: John Benjamins. doi:10.1075/hsm.1.05hin

Huang, James C.-T., Li, Audrey Y.-H., & Li, Yafei. 2009. *The Syntax of Chinese*. Cambridge: CUP. doi:10.1017/CBO9781139166935

Hulk, Aafke & Müller, Natascha. 2000. Bilingual first language acquisition at the interface between syntax and pragmatics. *Bilingualism: Language and Cognition* 3: 227–244. doi:10.1017/S1366728900000353

Jin, Fufen & Åfarli, Tor A. 2010. Linguistic competence in the minority language. Paper presented at GSFL conference. Trondheim: NTNU.

Klee, Thomas & Fitzgerald, Martha D. 1985. The relation between grammatical development and mean length of utterance in morphemes. *Journal of Child Language* 12: 251–269. doi:10.1017/S0305000900006437

Lasser, Ingeborg. 1997. *Finiteness in Adult and Child German*. [MPI Series in Psycholinguistics 8]. Wageningen: Ponsen and Looijen.

Lauchlan, Fraser, Parisi, Marinella & Fadda, Roberta. 2012. Bilingualism in Sardinia and Scotland: Exploring the cognitive benefits of speaking a 'minority' language. *International Journal of Bilingualism*, Published online before print April 16, 2012.

Li, Charles N. & Thompson, Sandra. 1981. *Mandarin Chinese: A Functional Reference Grammar*. Berkeley CA: University of California Press.

Lie, Svein. 1992. 'Ka du sei?' (What you say?). *Maal og Minne*, 62–77.

Lightfoot, David. 2006. *How New Languages Emerge*. Cambridge: CUP. doi:10.1017/CBO9780511616204

Meisel, Jürgen M. 1997. The acquisition of the syntax of negation in French and German: contrasting first and second language development. *Second Language Research* 13: 374–85. doi:10.1191/026765897675365945

Meisel, Jürgen M. 2001. The simultaneous acquisition of two first languages: Early differentiation and subsequent development of grammars. In *Trends in Bilingual Acquisition* [Trends in Language Acquisition Research 1], Jasone Cenoz & Fred Genesee (eds.), 11–41. Amsterdam: John Benjamins. doi:10.1075/tilar.1.03mei

Nilsen, Hilde. 1996. 'Kofføor dem sir det? Spørresetninger i nordreisadialekten' (Why they say that? Interrogative Sentences in the Nordreisa Dialect). Cand. Philol. dissertation, Universityof Tromsø.

Nordgård, Torbjørn. 1985. Word Order, Binding and the Empty Category Principle. Cand. Philol. dissertation, University of Trondheim.

Nordström, Jackie. 2010. The Swedish *så*-construction, a new point of departure. *Working Papers in Scandinavian Syntax* 85: 37–63.

Østbø Munch, Christine. B. 2006. The Norwegian function word *så* and Norwegian CP syntax. Paper presented at Workshop on inversion and verb movement. Trømsø, CASTL V2 workshop.

Pierce, Amy E. 1989. On the Emergence of Syntax: A Crosslinguistic Study. Ph.D. dissertation, MIT.

Pinker, Steven. 2000. *Words and Rules: The Ingredients of Language.* London: Phoenix.

Platzack, Christer. 1996. The initial hypothesis of syntax: A minimalist perspective on language acquisition and attrition. In *Generative Perspectives on language Acquisition. Emprical Findings, Theoretical Considerations and Crosslinguistic Comparisons* [Language Acquisition and Language Disorders 14], Harald Clahsen (ed.). Amsterdam: John Benjamins. doi: 10.1075/lald.14

Reite, André Midtskogseter. 2011. Spørjing i skedsmokorsmålet: Ein generativ analyse av leddstelling og spørjeord i interrogative hovudsetningar i talemålet på Skedsmokorset. MA thesis, Norwegian University of Science and Technology.

Simonsen, Hanne G.& Bjerkan, Kirsten M. 1998. Testing past tense inflection in Norwegian: A diagnostic tool for identifying SLI children? *International Journal of Applied Linguistics* 8(2): 251–270. doi:10.1111/j.1473-4192.1998.tb00132.x

Sollid, Hilde & Eide, Kristin M. 2007a. Om verbplassering og *så*-konstruksjonen i to språkmøter. *NOA (norsk som andrespråk)* 2: 5–32.

Sollid, Hilde & Eide, Kristin M. 2007b. On verb second and the *så*-construction in Mainland Scandinavian L2. In *Proceedings from Workshop on Language Acquisition, 22nd Scandinavian Conference of Linguistics,* Marit Westergaard & Merete Andersen (eds.).

Söderbergh, Ranghild. 1973. Project Child Language Syntax and Project Early Reading: A theoretical investigation and its practical application. Report 2. Stockholm: Stockholms Universitet.

Westergaard, Marit. 2003. Word order in wh-questions in a North Norwegian dialect: Some evidence from an acquisition study. *Nordic Journal of Linguistics* 26(1): 81–109. doi:10.1017/S0332586503001021

Westergaard, Marit. 2006. *Triggering V2: The Amount of Input Needed for Parameter Setting in a Split-CP Model of Word Order.* Newcastle upon Tyne: Cambridge Scholars.

Westergaard, Marit. 2009. Microvariation as diachrony: A view from acquisition. *Journal of Comparative Germanic Linguistics* 12(1): 49–79. doi:10.1007/s10828-009-9025-9

Westergaard, Marit. 2010. Cue-based acquisition and information structure drift in diachronic language development. In *Diachronic Studies on Information Structure. Language Acquisition and Change,* Vol. 10, Gisella Ferraresia & Rosemarie Lühr (eds.), 87–116.

Yip, Virginia & Matthews, Stephen. 2007. *The Bilingual Child: Early Development and Language Contact.* Cambridge: CUP. doi:10.1017/CBO9780511620744

Index